Authoritarianism and Underdevelopment in Pakistan 1947–1958

The Role of the Punjab

Lubna Saif

OXFORD
UNIVERSITY PRESS

OXFORD
UNIVERSITY PRESS

Great Clarendon Street, Oxford ox2 6DP

Oxford University Press is a department of the University of Oxford.
It furthers the University's objective of excellence in research, scholarship,
and education by publishing worldwide in

Oxford New York

Auckland Cape Town Dar es Salaam Hong Kong Karachi
Kuala Lumpur Madrid Melbourne Mexico City Nairobi
New Delhi Shanghai Taipei Toronto

with offices in

Argentina Austria Brazil Chile Czech Republic France Greece
Guatemala Hungary Italy Japan Poland Portugal Singapore
South Korea Switzerland Turkey Ukraine Vietnam

Oxford is a registered trade mark of Oxford University Press
in the UK and in certain other countries

© Oxford University Press 2010

The moral rights of the author have been asserted

First published 2010

All rights reserved. No part of this publication may be reproduced, translated,
stored in a retrieval system, or transmitted, in any form or by any means,
without the prior permission in writing of Oxford University Press.
Enquiries concerning reproduction should be sent to
Oxford University Press at the address below.

This book is sold subject to the condition that it shall not, by way
of trade or otherwise, be lent, re-sold, hired out or otherwise circulated
without the publisher's prior consent in any form of binding or cover
other than that in which it is published and without a similar condition
including this condition being imposed on the subsequent purchaser.

ISBN 978-0-19-547703-0

Typeset in Minion Pro
Printed in Pakistan by
Kagzi Printers, Karachi.
Published by
Ameena Saiyid, Oxford University Press
No. 38, Sector 15, Korangi Industrial Area, PO Box 8214
Karachi-74900, Pakistan.

Authoritarianism and Underdevelopment in Pakistan 1947–1958
The Role of the Punjab

To
my parents
Ikhtisar Sultana, Rashid Akhtar Nadvi
and
Amatun-Nabi, Noor Ahmad Noorie

Contents

List of Tables	ix
Abbreviations	xi
Acknowledgements	xiii
Introduction	xv

1. COLONIAL CAPITALISM AND THE PUNJAB — 1
- Colonial Capitalism — 1
- Pre-colonial Structures — 5
- Pre-colonial Structures of the Punjab — 10
- Establishment of Colonial Capitalism in the Punjab — 14
- Emergence of the Punjab as the Sword Arm of the Raj and Creation of its Landed Elite — 16
- The Colonial Administrative Structure and its Land Settlement Policy — 26

2. CONSTRUCTING THE POST-COLONIAL STATE — 43
- Construction of a Post-colonial State in the Context of the American Power System: A Neo-colonial Model — 43
- The Background of the Cold War Era and the Resulting American System of Power — 45
- Continuation of the Colonial Legacy of a Security State — 49
- Building of the Defence Establishment at the Cost of Economic Development — 57
- Subverting Stalin's Initiative—First Major Success of the American Power System — 69
- Liaquat's Visit to the United States—A Quest for Territorial Guarantees — 74

3. EMERGENCE OF THE INSTITUTIONAL IMBALANCE — 85
- Bureaucracy, Army, the Feudal Nexus, and Pursuance of a Neo-colonial Model — 85
- Role of the Civil Bureaucracy — 88
- Role of the Army — 93

- Punjab's Role in Creating the Institutional Imbalance 104
- Islamic Ideology—A Shield against Communist Ideology and a Guardian of Neo-colonial Economic Policies 116

4. The Destruction of Democracy and Consolidation of an Authoritarian State — 138
- Emergence of a 'Client State' 138
- Defence Pacts and Authoritarianism in Pakistan 154
- Pakistan and SEATO 156
- Pakistan and the Baghdad Pact 166

5. Authoritarianism and Underdevelopment — 181
- Forms of Authoritarianism and Theories of Development 181
- Modernization Theories and Neo-modernization 182
- The Dependency Theory and Neo-colonialism 189
- A Neo-colonial Capitalist Model and Pakistan 194
- Centre vs. the Provinces—Unequal Distribution of Resources and Unequal Development 202
- Neo-colonial States and Economic Development— A Comparative Analysis of Underdevelopment in Pakistan and India 206

Conclusion 222
Select Bibliography 235
Index 247

List of Tables

Table 1	Showing Natural Divisions of the Punjab	15
Table 2	Showing the Communal Ratio of Population of the Punjab in 1921	15
Table 3	Defence Expenditures 1947-59	65
Table 4	Population of Pakistan in 1951	106
Table 5	Indicators of Political Freedom and Economic Growth (Un-free countries: Rating 5.5-7)	187
Table 6	Indicators of Political Freedom and Economic Growth (Partly-free countries: Rating 3-5.5)	187
Table 7	Indicators of Political Freedom and Economic Growth (Free countries: Rating 1-2.5)	187
Table 8	Export, Imports, and Foreign Assistance in the 1950s and 1960s	197
Table 9	Budgetary Allocations between the Centre and the Provinces in the First Five-Year Plan	204
Table 10	Status of Underdevelopment in India and Pakistan in the First Decade	207
Table 11	Profile of Spending in India and Pakistan	210

Abbreviations

IOR	India Office Record, London
NA	The US National Archives and Record Administration, College Park, MD
PA	Punjab Archives, Lahore
TNA: PRO	The National Archives, London and the Public Record Office, London
UNDP	United Nations Development Program
UNICEF	United Nations International Children's Emergency Fund

Acknowledgements

I am deeply grateful to all the people who generously helped me during the long years of research. First of all I admire the guidance and unlimited patience of my PhD supervisor, Professor Lutfullah Mangi. This work would not have been possible without his inspiration and continuous assistance. I am equally indebted to Dr Dorothy K. Billings of the Wichita State University, USA, for nurturing my interest in Development Studies and International Relations. I owe a special debt of gratitude to Professor David N. Farnsworth, for sharing with me his views and experiences about 'underdevelopment' and the Third World. I would like to express my thanks to the faculty and students of the Sindh University, especially Professor Rafia Ahmed Sheikh, Dean, Faculty of the Arts, for their suggestions. I am particularly grateful to Mazhar-ul-Haq Siddiqui, Vice Chancellor of the Sindh University, for his appreciation of this work. Special thanks are also due to my colleague Dr Aman Memon for his support and assistance.

I wish to acknowledge the cooperation and assistance provided by the staff of the National Archives, Islamabad; Punjab Archives, Lahore; National Archives—Public Record Office, London; British Library—India Office Record, London; and the National Archives, Washington, D.C. Finally, I am greatly indebted to my husband, Saif, and daughter, Wajeeha, for their love and understanding.

Introduction

Sixty years after its creation, Pakistan is still in 'transition'. A federation which was created by the voting power of the masses has been repeatedly challenged to prove that the very same people are capable of enjoying the fruits of a fully-grown democracy. The 'mandate' of the people has so often been crushed under the heavy boot of the army, that today, Pakistan is faced with a serious threat of disintegration if this trend remains unaltered. After every spell of a long rule by the army, the people of Pakistan rekindle their faith in democracy by rejecting any other system of government. The elections held on 18 February 2008 are a loud reminder of this fact. However, the army has penetrated so deeply into the civilian economy, it is improbable that the army will 'withdraw from power because of its institutional involvement in the economy and Pakistani society.'[1] With the military in control of the state's resources, and in alliance with the bureaucracy and the landed class, steering the national, political, and economic processes according to its needs, there will be little chance for democracy to grow and tackle underdevelopment. The culture of authoritarianism cultivated in the nation's formative years is so deeply-rooted that it is feared that 'a full-blown democracy, in which the armed forces come under firm civilian control, will be impossible until Pakistan's strategic environment alters in such a way that the army retreats from its role as guardian of the state.'[2]

This book, based on my PhD research, will focus on the dialectic between state-construction and the political process in Pakistan in the first decade of its independence. Using the Dependency Paradigm as an evaluation tool, this book examines the international, political, and economic forces which, in alliance with the domestic and regional forces, shaped the structure of the Pakistani state according to the interests of the major players of the neo-colonial world in the Cold War era. The first decade of Pakistan's history (1947-1958) produced developments of great significance for the construction of the post-colonial state that need to be examined in the context of the Cold War era. It was during this period that democratic institutions were destroyed and authoritarianism was consolidated, which generated underdevelopment, and Pakistan took the shape of a 'client' state of the United States. These anti-democratic developments concluded in the first direct military rule in 1958, and since then, military intervention in the political domain has become a permanent feature of Pakistan's political life, at the cost of evolution of civil society, and other participatory institutions. An analytical study of the formative years of Pakistan in the context of the 'dependency paradigm' may provide new insights for understanding the broader issues regarding military's intervention in politics and the authoritarian nature of the state, and its links with underdevelopment in the Third World, particularly in South Asia.

This book is an attempt to investigate how the civil bureaucracy and the military rose to prominence in Pakistan and how their alliance succeeded in turning the institutional balance against the political parties and the politicians, thus, resulting in the centralization of authority and power in the State. In the process, institutions considered essential for the construction of a nation-state, namely, political parties and the legislatures, were replaced with elite, non representative groups, including the civil and military bureaucracies and the landed class. These elite groups were a product of British colonialism and mainly belonged to the province of Punjab, which was not only instrumental in determining the fate of the Pakistan Movement, but has also been the most influential force in constructing the structures of the new nation-state. Punjab's hegemonic role in the formative years of Pakistan's life created an imbalance of power which threatened the process of nation-building. The premise of the inquiry is the analysis of the structural composition of these three institutions with the primary aim to understand how these representative institutions of a colonial state continued to dominate the formation of a post-colonial state, and jeopardized its evolution.

At the time of its birth, Pakistan had the fifth-largest population in the world and was the world's largest Muslim state. Each of those areas of British India, which constituted the state of Pakistan, had a different colonial heritage, and therefore, viewed the emergence of Pakistan with varied eyes. The provinces of north-west India including West Punjab, Sindh, British Balochistan, NWFP, along with the tribal agencies, and ten princely states, including Bahawalpur—in the Punjab, Khairpur—in Sindh, Swat, Chitral, Dir and Amb—in the NWFP, and Kalat, Kharan, Mekran, and Las Bela, in Balochistan, constituted the western wing of Pakistan, while East Bengal, and the district of Sylhet, constituted its eastern wing. The distance was not the only dividing factor between the two wings of Pakistan, the geography and the colonial inheritance were two other major factors which contributed to producing a different political culture in the two wings. Bengal, which was the first Mughal province to be annexed by the East India Company, had a very strong tradition of independent rule and a long history of struggle by the freedom movements.

> By the victories of Plassey and Buxar (1757 and 1764), the East India Company became heir to the Mughal Empire, and in the following half century extended its control over the greater part of the subcontinent.[3]

The company annexed Bengal to monopolize trade and to control the resources of the richest province of India. On the contrary, in north-west India, colonial rule was 'prompted by strategic rather than commercial considerations', on a piecemeal basis.[4] When Bengal became the Crown's province after the 1857 Revolt, it became the first province to taste British democracy. Under the Indian Councils Act of 1861, a legislative council was set up in the province, and Bengal became the first 'regulation province' of India, working under the jurisdiction of a High Court. As a result of the introduction of the political reforms and the higher educational attainment of its population, political consciousness developed much earlier in Bengal than in the other provinces of India, placing it at the forefront of Indian politics from 1905 onwards.[5] The Muslim League was formed in Dhaka in 1906 and Bengali Muslims played a leading role in Muslim politics.

Since Bengal was not a part of the British security state as the north-west of India, it did not go through the same experience of colonial capitalism. As a consequence, the three representative institutions of British Colonialism: army, civil bureaucracy, and the landed class, which were created in the north-western provinces of British India 'to establish a security state', were absent in Bengal. Bengal was the first 'regulation province' where democratic institutions were more developed in comparison to 'non-regulation' provinces of the north-west 'security zone', including the NWFP, Sindh, and the Punjab.

The provinces forming the west wing of Pakistan inherited a tradition of bureaucratic authoritarianism. The hallmarks of this tradition were paternalism, wide discretionary powers, personalization of authority, and the supremacy of executive over representative institutions. Political institutions were deliberately kept weak to patronize the local rural elite in the north-west security state area. This not only retarded political institutionalization, but also placed insurmountable deterrents in the way of future socio-economic reforms, by creating a structure for dominant, feudal and political interests. 'The autocratic traditions attendant on the early period of British rule thus persisted within them well beyond the high noon of Empire.'[6] In colonial Punjab, often considered as the future heartland of Pakistan, a special bond was established between the peasantry and the army, which proved to be a vital factor in the latter's dominance in independent Pakistan.[7]

In the post-colonial state-formation process, Punjab, the largest province of West Pakistan, which enjoyed the reputation as the 'loyal' province of the Raj, and was represented by three bases of colonial power—army, civil bureaucracy, and the landed class—emerged as the most powerful negotiator, 'the arbiter of national authority.'[8] 'It was difficult for a national government to remain in office without keeping its bridges with the Punjab in good repair.'[9]

Definitions of Authoritarianism

The term authoritarianism is used to describe an organization or a state which enforces strong and sometimes oppressive measures against the population. Linz described authoritarianism as a political system that focuses on constraining political participation, while simultaneously ensuring mass subservience to the regime. It is characterized by four components: (1) constraints on political institutions'; (2) a basis for the regime's legitimacy; (3) constraints on the mass public; and (4) ill-defined executive power.[10] In an authoritarian state, citizens are subject to state authority in many aspects of their lives, including some that other political philosophies would see as matters of personal choice. Jalal defines,

> Authoritarianism as organized power embedded in the institutional structure of the state. It is seen as distinguishable, though not insulated, from the myriad structures of dominance lining the larger body politics. So, while an element of covert authoritarianism inheres in any state structure, the degree of its overt manifestation is contingent upon the existence or the absence of formal, much less substantive, democracy.[11]

Authoritarianism is characterized by moral and philosophical certainty coupled with a taste for the use of force by the state. History teaches us that:

Authoritarian regimes leave an imprint on society long after their leaders have been overthrown because they systematically seek to alter the traditional roles of important social institutions such as the church and the military.[12]

For democracy, three inter-dependent elements are necessary. Firstly, there should be institutional procedures which enable citizens to be able to effectively express their preferences about alternative policies. Provision of institutionalized constraints on the exercise of power by the executive, is the second element. And 'third is the guarantee of civil rights to all citizens.'[13] It is argued that while competitive political participation is sharply restricted or suppressed by authoritarian regimes, 'their chief executives are chosen in a regularized process of selection within the political elite, and once in office they exercise their power without institutional constraints.'[14]

Barrington Moore and other social structural analysts advocate that 'democracy' requires a 'balance' between the state/ruler and independent classes, in which the state is neither wholly autonomous of dominant classes nor captured by them, allowing a space within which civil society can flourish. Democratization requires a 'democratic coalition' that historically has been variedly made up of the bourgeoisie, the middle classes, and the working class. Where the landed aristocracy subordinates the bourgeoisie and the peasants, and dominates the state, the outcome is *authoritarianism of the right*. Where peasants and workers are mobilized in the overthrow of the aristocracy, the result is *authoritarianism of the left*.[15] The distinction between authoritarianism and totalitarianism was a crucial part of the Kirkpatrick Doctrine, a political doctrine expounded by the United States ambassador to the United Nations, which attempted to justify US support for right-wing, anti-communist dictatorships in the Third World,[16] in the context of the Cold War. Kirkpatrick claimed that pro-Soviet communist states were totalitarian regimes while, pro-Western, anti-communist Third World dictatorships, were authoritarian ones.[17] It argued that totalitarian regimes were more stable than authoritarian regimes, and thus had more chances to influence neighbouring countries. The Kirkpatrick Doctrine asserted that the United States could work with authoritarian nations with a bad human rights record because they were more capable of fundamental reform and less dangerous than the totalitarian nations.[18]

Authoritarianism and Underdevelopment

For alleviation of poverty it is absolutely necessary to empower people to make collective choices and involve them in the decision-making process, which can only be done through a participatory form of government. Unfortunately, Pakistan has not yet evolved a system of participatory government which could guarantee the provision of fundamental human rights for every citizen of its federating units. The institutional imbalance in favour of non-democratic institutions, which were created in the early years of the country's life, has become a permanent feature, depriving a majority of its people from their rightful share of the development, thus, causing underdevelopment in Pakistan. The widespread myth that the poor are not concerned with political and civil rights is often challenged by the struggle for democratic freedoms in South Korea, Thailand, Bangladesh, Myanmar, Indonesia, Pakistan, and many other countries of Asia and Africa.[19] The claim that non-democratic systems are better at bringing about economic development is not true. 'There is in fact, no convincing general evidence that authoritarian governance and the suppression of political and civil rights are really beneficial to economic development.'[20] Discussing the role of democracy and economic development, Sen argues that the protective role of democracy is essential for prevention of economic disaster and there is a need to go beyond the 'narrow confines of economic growth and scrutinize the broader demands of economic growth'.[21] He invites us to see the connection between civil and political rights and economic development, and argues that the poorest nations need democracy the most. Emphasizing the protective role of democracy for the poor, Sen observes that 'People in economic need also need a political voice. Democracy is not a luxury that can await the arrival of general prosperity.'[22]

Analyzing the development policies of Pakistan, Mahbub ul Haq observes that if the poor are socially excluded and politically marginalized, no development model will work. He suggests that the:

> real answer lies in changing the very model of development, from traditional economic growth to human development, where people become the real agents and beneficiaries of economic growth rather than remain an abstract residual of inhuman development process.[23]

This development model can only be achieved through participatory institutions. Unfortunately, in the formative years of Pakistan's life, non-representative 'elite groups' consisting of the army, bureaucracy, and the landed class, overshadowed the democratic institutions and pursued a neo-colonial capitalist model, which favoured growth over distribution, and social justice.

All authoritarian governments are dependent or linked to industrial world order. Many writers concerned with the issue of development view this industrial world order as a new form of colonialism, which ensures the political and economic control over previous 'colonies'.[24] Dependence on an international economy, over which these elite governments of post-colonial states have very little influence, makes them vulnerable, especially to recessions in the Western industrial economies. The World Bank (WB) and the International Monetary Fund (IMF) can negotiate with unstable governments/non-representative/authoritarian rulers, to dictate their policies. The neo-colonial capitalist model pursued by authoritarian regimes, which favours economic growth over distribution and social justice, has drowned the majority of people of these nation-states in an ocean of absolute poverty.

This book is divided into five chapters. Chapter 1 traces the historical development of colonial capitalism, focusing on the province of Punjab, and suggests that the underdevelopment found in the Pakistani society owes its origin to the British colonial capitalist system in India. The continuation of those developmental policies in the post-colonial state is the main focus of this chapter. This chapter explores the process through which the colonial power established local economic and political elite in the colony, especially in the frontier provinces of north-west India, which was of strategic importance for the defence of British India. The focus of inquiry is the province of Punjab, which became the stronghold of British colonialism and earned a reputation as the 'Sword Arm of the Raj'. An analysis of the process of establishing the colonial capitalism and its impact on the social, political, and economic structures of Punjabi society is presented. An analysis of 'colonial capitalism' in Punjab, and the kind of elite groups which emerged during the colonial period, will reveal the real causes of underdevelopment prevailing in today's Pakistan, since these elite groups have continued to shape the contours of the post-colonial state as well.

Chapter 2 discusses the construction of a post-colonial state in the context of the American Power System. It argues that although the country attained freedom from British colonialism in 1947, its representatives—the civil bureaucracy, army, and the landed class—, however, operating within the imperatives of neo-colonial capitalism, continued to dominate the national scene and never allowed the representative institutions to flourish. Chapter 3 examines the emergence of institutional imbalance and the manipulating powers of international connections, and argues that the development of the institutional imbalances, which have plagued Pakistan's history, was due to the crafty approach of international managers of the Cold War, who allied with the domestic actors to continue the colonial legacy of 'controlling the democratic institutions' through an authoritarian administrative structure. Discussing the dominance of the civil bureaucracy and the army in the early years of Pakistan's growth as a nation-state, this chapter highlights the role of the Punjab in creating this institutional imbalance. This chapter also examines the role of religion in strengthening the military-bureaucracy nexus in the early years of the state formation process, when with the Chinese Revolution in 1949, the spread of communism in Asia became a nightmare for the planners of the neo-colonial world. In addition to building a large defence establishment, the powerful ruling clique, in alliance with the British and American intelligence networks, contrived the wall of religion as a shield in the form of 'Islamic Ideology' to promote the fear of communism. Chapter 4 evaluates the destruction of democracy and consolidation of an authoritarian state, in the context of the 'Patron-Client Model'. Pakistan's emergence as a 'Client State' of the United States in the period between April 1953 and October 1954, and consolidation of authoritarian structures are interrelated developments, which are examined in this chapter. Chapter 5 discusses various forms of authoritarianism and theories of development focusing on divergence in development. The chapter examines underdevelopment in Pakistan using the theoretical model of the dependency theory, and argues that the authoritarian model of development in South East Asia cannot be applied to the countries of the Third World, including Pakistan. A comparative analysis of underdevelopment in India in the context of neo-colonial states and economic development is presented to understand the nature and level of underdevelopment in the two inheritor states of British colonialism.

NOTES

1. Stephen P. Cohen, 2005, *The Idea of Pakistan*, Lahore: Vanguard Books, pp. 274-5.
2. Ibid., p. 278.
3. Hugh Tinker, 1967, *India and Pakistan: A Political Analysis*, London: Pall Mall Press, p. 9.
4. Ian Talbot, 1999, *Pakistan: A Modern History*, Lahore: Vanguard Books, p. 11.
5. J. Brown, 1995, *Modern India: The Origins of an Asian Democracy*, Oxford: Oxford University Press, pp. 123ff.
6. I. Talbot, *Pakistan: A Modern History*, op. cit., p. 55.
7. C. Dewy, 1991, 'The Rural Roots of Pakistan Militarism' in D.A. Low (ed.), *The Political Inheritance of Pakistan*, London: Macmillan, 1991, p. 261.
8. Ibid., p. 14.
9. Ayesha Jalal, 1990, *The State of Martial Rule: The Origins of Pakistan's Political Economy of Defense*, Cambridge: Cambridge University Press, pp. 144-5.
10. Quoted in Gretchen Casper, 1995, *Fragile Democracies: The Legacies of Authoritarian Rule*, Pittsburgh: University of Pittsburgh Press, p. 40.
11. Ayesha Jalal, 1995, *Democracy and Authoritarianism in South Asia: A Comparative and Historical Perspective*, New York: Cambridge University Press, p. 3.
12. Gretchen Casper, *Fragile Democracies: The Legacies of Authoritarian Rule*, op. cit., p. 3.
13. Ted Robert Gurr, Keith Jaggers, and Will Moore, Spring 1990, 'The Transformation of the Western State: The Growth of Democracy, Autocracy, and State Power Since 1800', *Studies in Comparative International Development*, 25(1), pp. 83-5.
14. Ibid.
15. Barrington Moore, 1966, *Social Origins of Dictatorship and Democracy: Lord and Peasants in the Making of the Modern World*, Boston: Beacon Press; D. Rueschemeyer, E. Stephans, and J. Stephans, 1992, *Capitalist Development and Democracy*, Cambridge: Polity Press.
16. In the post-Cold War period it is also known as the developing world. The term Third World is used to refer to the developing world.
17. 'Kirkpatrick Doctrine', Wikipedia—Free Encyclopaedia, retrieved 21 December 2002, http://en.wikipedia.org/wiki/Kirkpatrick_Doctrine
18. Ibid.
19. Amartya Sen, 2003, 'Democracy As a Universal Value', in Lubna Saif and Javed Iqbal Syed (ed.), *Pakistani Society and Culture*, Vol. II, Islamabad: National Book Foundation, pp. 160-70.
20. Ibid., p. 162.
21. Ibid., p. 163.
22. Ibid., pp. 166-67.
23. Mahbub ul Haq, 1976, *The Poverty Curtain: Choices for the Third World*, New York, p. 19.
24. Hassan Gardezi, 1973, 'Neo-Colonial Alliances and the Crisis of Pakistan', in Kathleen Gough and Hari P. Sharma (eds.), *Imperialism and Revolution in South Asia*, New York: Monthly Review Press, pp. 130-44.

1

Colonial Capitalism and the Punjab

COLONIAL CAPITALISM

Pakistan inherited a rigid social structure which promoted underdevelopment—a product of colonial capitalism. The underdevelopment, presently prevalent in Pakistani society, reflects the continuation of developmental policies introduced by the colonial system that the country inherited from British India at the time of its independence in 1947.[1] In a predominantly agrarian society such as Pakistan, the ownership of land is a key issue in development. Much of the country, and in particular its most productive areas, are still characterized by highly inequitable forms of land tenure. Despite three land reforms, a large number of cultivators are sharecroppers on land owned by few, in most cases, absentee, landowners. As Mahbub ul Haq notes, 'Pakistan's capitalistic system is still one of the most primitive in the world. It is a system in which economic feudalism prevails'.[2] This 'capitalistic system characterized by economic feudalism' is the product of colonialism. Colonialism introduced capitalism in agriculture with the recognition of the institution of private property, and initiation of commercial farming. This wrought major changes in the political economy of India, particularly in the Punjab province.[3] Examining colonial capitalism, described by him as 'peripheral capitalism', Alavi argues that the colonial impact introduced a 'specific bourgeois revolution in the colonies, establishing a structure of specifically colonial capitalism. Given that structure, various internal developments follow in the process of the creation of a colonial economy'.[4] He contends that in the post-colonial period, although there were some modifications, 'the structure was not fundamentally altered after independence'.[5] Alavi further argues that 'the post-colonial state...functions within the framework of peripheral capitalism and its imperatives and constraints'.[6] Similarly, Imran Ali argues that the British colonial strategy in Punjab retarded the 'national development' and 'capitalist revolution' in the region and resulted in the continued backwardness of the region even after the departure of the British. Many socio-economic and political problems in the post-colonial state owe their existence to colonial policies.[7]

Those regions that experienced an enormous volume of contact with developed countries in the past are today's most depressed regions. Frank observed that this contradicts the thesis that underdevelopment results from isolation and pre-capitalistic institutions.[8] The colonial experience had affected every aspect of a colonial society. Land distribution, land tenure, agricultural practices, social and legal traditions, political authority, the national economic structure, and regional and international economic relations, were so fundamentally distorted that the damage continues to affect the development of ex-colonies to this day.

The social and political consequences of this colonial economy were the creation of 'elite', or dominant local interests, given the nature of class arrangements emerging from the characteristics of 'peripheral economies'.[9]

The explanation for the continuation of underdevelopment in traditional societies, like Pakistan, is to be sought in the process through which the colonial power established the local economic and political elite in the colony,[10] especially in the frontier provinces of north-west India, which was of strategic importance for the defence of British India. The focus of inquiry is the province of Punjab, which became the stronghold of British colonialism by contributing the most loyal recruits for the Indian army, which earned it a reputation as the 'Sword Arm of the Raj'. This chapter explores how Punjab acquired the status of the 'Sword Arm of the Raj', and served the colonial interests as the most 'loyal province'.

With the advent of British colonial rule, Indian society experienced profound changes, especially in terms of 'the structure of relationship between the cultivator and the social relations of production'.[11] Three major colonial institutions can be identified, which transformed these social relations of production: the institution of property, civil bureaucracy, and the legal system. These three institutions were interrelated; the establishment of the colonial legal system was linked to the question of ownership of property, and the institution of civil bureaucracy was meant to translate these ideals into action. Historians argue that 'the British wanted to pull resources out of India, not to put their own into India'.[12] For them the obvious choice was to build their administrative and military systems with the Indian revenues. The main source of Indian revenue was rent from its land which had to be collected from millions of payers.

> It was in the administration of localities that the vital economies in ruling had to be made. There, governance had to be pursued by simpler arrangements.... By enlisting the co-operation of *zamindars, mirasidars, talukdars,* and urban *rais*.[13]

With the advent of the British, the pre-colonial economy underwent a transformation. Colonial rulers brought with them established eighteenth century ideas of absolute property and the prime value of a landowning gentry or aristocracy, as the backbone of the nation. It was natural for them to search, in India, for the 'rightful' proprietors of the land, and when they did not find any, they created them by changing the 'rights to rule' the land to 'rights to own' the land.[14] By doing this, the British legalized the private right to absolute land ownership. They repeated this practice in different ways in different parts of India with the same consequences: the cultivators had to give away their customary rights, while most of the land ownership was concentrated in a few hands belonging to the upper classes. The primary motive to create a landowning class was to provide 'leadership' with whom the British could bargain.[15]

'Close Border Policy', and then 'Forward Policy' in Balochistan and the North West Frontier Province (NWFP), and the Land Settlement and Land Alienation Act of 1900 in the provinces of Punjab and Sindh, created a reliable and loyal class of landowners whose interests were dependent upon allegiance to the colonial rulers. This landed class later attained the status of 'local political leadership', and dominated the political scene. In the period between the two World Wars, Punjab assumed the status of the 'Sword Arm of the British Raj', especially the '*barani areas*' of Punjab. Punjab's rise as the 'Sword Arm of the British Raj' and colonial capitalism are inseparable. The character of economic structure developed under colonial capitalism in India, including the Punjab, had three features. First, 'the institution of private property in land'; second, 'the growth of merchant capital in Punjab'; and third, 'the establishment of a cash nexus as the primary form of surplus extraction by the colonial state'.[16] This economic structure resulted in marginalization of the peasantry and concentration of land in a few hands, which ultimately pushed the peasants into the colonial army. Discussing the effects of British imperialism on the Punjabi society,

Imran Ali presents an excellent analysis of the efforts of the state to channel the land settlement policies, especially in canal colonies towards the fulfilment of military needs, and examines the rural bases of military recruitment patterns.[17] He examines the penetrating process of the military into the 'seminal source of societal authority, the control and possession of agricultural land', and argues that the participation of the military in Punjab cannot be seen in the 'context of modernization', and it 'would be more appropriate to draw parallel with feudalism'.[18] Gilmartin's study, *Empire and Islam: Punjab and the Making of Pakistan*, provides a remarkable understanding of the close link between the ideology of the British colonial empire and the Muslim politics in Punjab.[19] He examines the:

> structure and ideology of British rule in Punjab, showing how the British attempted to build an indigenous, hierarchical ideology of state authority by appealing directly to the political primacy of local Punjabi identities.

The theory of martial races was the official explanation for specialization of Punjab as the sword arm of the Raj. The chief architect of the theory of martial races in India was Lord Roberts, the commander-in-chief of the British Indian army from 1885 to 1893. Throughout the nineteenth and twentieth centuries, the British were preoccupied with the threat from the North. To defend India against the Russian threat and to prevent them from reaching the warm waters of the Indian Ocean, Roberts held the view that the Indian army required the finest material. According to his conviction, the finest fighting material was only available in the north-western areas of India, particularly in the Punjab. Roberts based his theory of martial races upon 'racial deterioration'.[20] His thesis of 'racial deterioration' was in line with the widespread use of racial theories in Europe, a product of European colonialism. The theory of martial races proceeded from an argument based on the innate superiority of the Europeans in comparison to non-Europeans, especially the colonized natives. Although the theory of martial races is full of inconsistencies, it is still being used to provide an explanation for the colonial recruitment policy. Surprisingly, in the post-colonial period, the military authorities find justification in propagating this theory for the over-representation of certain ethnic groups and the under-representation of others.[21]

In *Pakistan: A Modern History*, Talbot supports the observation made by Jalal and Alavi that Pakistan's 'overdeveloped' administrative and military institutions are linked to the colonial legacy, which established a 'security state in north-west India, where political participation was far less developed and its survival was dependent upon the support of certain tribal and landowning interests'.[22] In his major work, *Punjab and the Raj 1847-1947,* Talbot shows how the support of local allies, crucial to the colonial control, was sought; his focus of inquiry is the Punjab for its immense value to the British strategic interests, and its reputation for political loyalty to the Raj.[23] Talbot's interesting study, *Khizr Tiwana: The Punjab Unionist Party and the Partition of India* reveals that the cooperation between the large landlords and the British colonial state was primarily motivated by the Punjab's emergence as the sword arm of India and contends that this development was partly rooted in the rural elites' response to the '1857 Revolt'.[24] Similarly, Imran Ali displays how, by subordinating developmental goals to its political and military imperatives, the colonial state cooperated with the dominant social classes, whose members became the major beneficiaries of agricultural colonization.[25] To evaluate the impact of 'colonial capitalism', an understanding of pre-colonial structures is necessary.

Pre-colonial Structures

In northern India, the concept of absolute private ownership did not exist before the arrival of the British in the eighteenth century.[26] Rights to land, not the land itself, belonged to the group: the village, extended family, or the lineage group.[27] Occupancy rights for cultivation were in farmers' hands, which were not allowed to transfer, or alienate land to someone else, except hand down occupancy rights to their heirs.[28]

> However, it was possible to mortgage or sell the occupancy right to members of the community. Though, there was a custom of pre-emption, which required that the decision to transfer be not made individually.[29]

Habib writes:

> There was no question of free alienation—the right to abandon or dispose of land as its holder might choose which is an essential feature of modern proprietary right.... He could not leave it or refuse to cultivate it.[30]

To provide itself the base for colonial power in India, British colonial rulers exploited the Mughal mode of production. The Mughal mode of production was different from colonial capitalism because it had no concept of 'private ownership'. Habib notes, 'the ownership was by and large confined to particular rights over land and, not...as an alienable and unrestricted claim over land'.[31] Alavi argues that the '*zamindari* rights of Mughal period that could be bought and sold', cannot be considered as property rights.[32] Gardezi observes that, 'the Mughals, in particular, introduced measures to prevent their official aristocracy from developing strong property rights in land'.[33] He notes that strong property rights were the creation of British colonial policy.[34] Analyzing British colonial policies, Imran Ali writes, 'they encouraged individualization in property rights, which was a marked shift from the collective ownership by village communities...existed in the pre-British period'.[35] He observes that with the process of individualization, 'probably for the first time', the prospect of alienation of land rights was created.[36] The term *zamindar* is a Persian compound, which means keeper, or holder of land, 'the term began to be used more and more often from Akbar's time onward for any person with any hereditary claim to a direct share in the peasant's produce'.[37] During the seventeenth century, the term *zamindari* replaced all other local terms for agrarian rights of any kind.[38] In the larger parts of Mughal India, the *zamindar* was expected to collect tax from the primary assesses (cultivators), in return, simply, for an allowance of one-tenth, given either in cash or in allotments of revenue-free land. The important fact to note is that the 'Mughal land revenue', or *mal,* was not rent or even a land tax like in any feudal economy. It was sharing of a crop (*ghala batai*), or tax on the surplus, or 'a claim on behalf of the state to a share of a crop'.[39] *Mal* had nothing in common with the 'land revenue' of the British settlements, which was instituted as a standard burden fixed on a particular area of land, without taking into account the produce of the land.[40]

The Mughal administration was based on the *mansabdari* system, in which administrators were ranked into different *mansabs* in accordance with the services and duties assigned.[41] Though the *mansab* was not inheritable, however, in most of the cases, sons or relations of higher *mansab*-holders were given due consideration. It was a tenure job, an uncertain tenure, dependent upon the emperor's will.[42] In addition to paid salaries, these *mansabdars* were assigned *jagirs*, or estates; *jagirs* were transferred on a constant basis to weaken their ties with the land and its cultivators,[43] and by imparting the temporary character to the *jagir*, the control of the emperor was further strengthened.[44] Habib writes that 'the *mansab*-holder was entitled to a *jagir*, but not to a particular tract of land in *jagir*, and not the same land year after year'. These *mansab-holders* were subject to review from time to time and awarded 'promotion or demotion' on the basis of their performance. Similarly, there was a system of regular:

> transfers of officials from one province to another; in each such case, a block of territory had to be carved out for the official in the new province...the result was that no one could be sure of how long he would remain in possession of a particular area.[45]

The Mughals introduced an elaborate and complex system of revenue collection, in which 'alternative and overlapping institutions for revenue extraction—*khalisa*, *jagir*, *zamindari*, and *raiyati* villages...were not neatly segregated one from the other'.[46] This system, originally derived from outside the imperial system, rested profoundly on the *zamindars*, whose rights and powers were reinforced.[47] These *zamindari* rights, 'heritable, saleable and actually mortgaged' were not uniform, and created a heterogeneous body of *zamindars*. As noted by Habib, 'some *zamindars* paying tribute, others holding their land as *jagirs*, while still others acquired non-hereditary rights by royal order'.[48] With the development of revenue farming, 'powerful *zamindars*' were able to purchase *zamindari* rights of other *zamindars* and a new concept of *ta'luqqdari* came into vogue, defined 'as a newly purchased *zamindari* and a tenure which entitled its holder to engage on behalf of other *zamindars*'.[49] The *ta'luqqdari* was common in two of the Mughal provinces, Bengal and Awadh, but it did not exist in the Punjab. The sale price of *zamindari* rights was in relation to the annual land revenue, for instance, the sale price of *zamindari* in five villages in the 1670s and 1680s in the province of Awadh amounted to nearly double the annual land revenue.[50] Habib observes that 'the most important feature of the *zamindari* right was its uneven development'. Within the same district, some villages would fall into the category of *zamindari* villages and some villages would be (peasant-held) *raiyati* villages. For instance in Fathepur, a single *pargana* contained eight raiyati and nine zamindari villages.[51] The state did not favour any particular type of villages—there are numerous instances of establishing fresh villages without any intermediation, and at the same time supplementing *zamindari* villages by creating *zamindari* villages.[52]

Three basic institutions, the family, the caste, and the village community, regulated pre-colonial Indian society.[53] Customary laws and traditional rules governed these institutions outside the preview of the state. *Punchayat,* or the council of elders, was the arbitrary. The vastness of the area never allowed any central state to interfere in the social organization of people.[54] Because of their isolation, few villages were linked with the central power. The following description of the village community provided by Habib illustrates this point:

> The Indian village presented the appearance of a closed, custom-based social and economic unit. The close settlement of peasant households and the needs for peasant migrants to move in a body for better protection furnished the basis for a collective organization of peasants, within the framework of clan and caste, the Indian Village Community…to a certain degree an Indian village was a stable economic unit, self-sufficient in respect to its own consumption needs.[55]

During the sixteenth and seventeenth centuries, though the majority population lived in a predominantly agrarian environment, and only a small minority was acquainted with urban living, the urban population of Mughal India possessed an economic and cultural significance far exceeding its actual size.[56] Like the Indian villages, cities and towns of Mughal India were largely self-regulating, since the state was concerned with little beyond the levying of taxes, the maintenance of internal security, and a few additional functions, such as the regulation of the markets, and in some instances, the provision of water supply.[57] Habib writes, 'from the point of view of the government, cities and towns were no more than conglomerations of adjacent villages…They possessed no rights, exemptions or charters and had no distinct legal personality'.[58] The cities lacked any kind of corporate or municipal institutions through which the state dealt with the cities at a high level, except through the provincial officials (*subedars, faujdars,* etc.), who were responsible for the entire *suba* (province), or *sarkar* (government). Three other officials, Qazi, Kotwal, and Muhtasib need to be mentioned here; Qazi's job was to enforce the *Sharia* (Islamic Law); Muhtasib's main responsibility was to supervise the markets; and Kotwal was the chief of police, who maintained law and order with the assistance of *mahaladars,* and a body of armed staff, including a horseman and twenty to thirty foot soldiers. Every city or town was subdivided into wards (*mahalla, mahal*). Each *mahalla* had its own organic identity, 'which could be defined in terms of economic organization or occupation, a common caste or sectarian affiliation, a shared ancestral migration from a particular village or region, a client-patron relationship with a particular family under whose protection that *mahalla* lived'.[59] To some extent, many *mahallas* were self-sufficient, in the sense that they could provide some of the basic needs of their inhabitants. To reinforce group identity, each *mahalla* was walled off from its neighbours with gates, which could be closed at night, or during periods of disorder and insecurity. Like a village, each *mahalla* had its own *punchayat* to settle any common or individual concerns. Appeals beyond the bounds of the *mahalla* or village *punchayat* to a representative of the imperial government were very rare.[60] Habib writes that it can now be concluded with certainty that cities and towns had diverse and overlapping roles in Mughal India.

> The largest were thriving centres of manufacturing and marketing, banking and entrepreneurial activities, intersections in a network of communications by land and water which crossed and re-crossed the subcontinent and extend far beyond, to South-East Asia, to the Middle East, to Western Europe, and elsewhere.

Following this pattern, smaller urban centres functioned in 'a more modest role in relation to local commerce, local resources and local consumer needs' in a contracted network of regional or sub-regional markets.[61]

The activity and prosperity of the urban centres was recorded by many European travellers who visited India in times of Jahangir and Shahjahan, especially those engaged in weaving and textile manufacturing. Habib observes that great variety and vigour characterized the manufacturing sector of Mughal India. The manufacturing sector was not concentrated in one region or cities alone, rather it was predominantly a rural activity.[62] The large quantity of the rural manufacturers was produced by the hereditary artisan castes, linked to the agricultural castes by traditional ties of the client-patron relationship, and collectively sustained. Similarly, the peasants' involvement in a range of commodities was an essential part of the manufacturing economy. At the same time, rural artisans served the village community as hereditary servants and were 'very often enlisted by the peasant as auxiliary agricultural work'.[63] The interdependence of cities and the rural manufacturing sector knitted the Indian society into a single fabric. British colonialism distorted this relationship and created a rural-urban divide at the cost of rural manufacturers.

Habib notes that the importance of the cities in the economic and cultural life of Mughal India was not only dependent upon their commercial and manufacturing roles. The prosperity of a large number of metropolitan cities was dependant on their role as political centres and administrative headquarters. Three major cities of the empire, Lahore, Agra and Shahjahanabad (Delhi), owed their existence to the Mughals, besides the short-lived Fatehpur Sikri. Lahore and Agra were mere villages before they gained the status of Mughal administrative centres. The Mughals also built some of the provincial capitals including Aurangabad and Dacca (now Dhaka). There were other cities and towns, which had sacral, which supplemented and surmounted their economic or political significance. There were 3,200 *qasbas* (towns) recorded in Akbar's time, 'foci of exchange in the heart of the countryside', which served as storage places for collected revenue, markets for the sale of surplus crops and distribution and transportation points for grain.[64] Primarily, the cities and towns of the subcontinent served as a reservoir for higher culture and learning, which not only preserved the Sansikritic and Indo-Islamic 'Great Traditions', but also transmitted those traditions to the society as a whole. Habib has identified four distinct types of urban centres in Northern India; first, cities whose prime function was administrative while other roles had secondary importance. Second, cities with a predominantly commercial and manufacturing character; their administrative functions remained subordinate to their economic functions. Third, cities of sacral importance, or pilgrimage centres, enjoying trade and craft activities. And the fourth, were centres which grew because of some distinct manufacturing technique, craft or skill, or local commodity. Habib observes that the period of the Mughal Empire can be described as a 'veritable golden age of urbanization', at least for much of northern and central India.[65] However, in the second half of the eighteenth century, with the decline of Mughal authority, political instability and peasants' revolts hampered the urban prosperity over large areas of the Punjab, Rajasthan, and the Jumna-Ganges Doab.

Pre-colonial Structures of the Punjab

Punjab was a landlocked region in the north-west of India, situated at the traditional route of trading caravans and invading armies coming from Central Asia through the passes of Afghanistan. It was always the first province of subcontinent India to be annexed—a gateway to India—and had been part of many Central Asian empires in various historical periods; and was subject to numerous invasions. The Punjab has been described as a passage of human movement from Central Asia to northern India, a 'cultural and political route zone'.[66] The majority of the people of Punjab belonged to Central Asian nomadic tribes who had accompanied the invading armies, and eventually settled in its plains.

Its location and extensive riverine system, were the two main influencing factors in the making of Punjab's history. The province derived its name from its five major rivers—the 'Punjab' means the 'land of the five rivers'. It had been the cradle of many civilizations, such as the Harrapan and Gandharan, which adorn its past. The Punjab is home to many of India's major religions including, Hinduism, Buddhism, Islam, and Sikhism. In the eleventh century, the Punjab was included in the Ghaznavid Muslim Empire and continued to be a part of different Indo-Muslim empires till the decline of the last Muslim Empire—the Mughals—in the eighteenth century. Punjab was an important province of Mughal India. Besides Agra, Lahore was one of the capitals built by the Mughals, and two Mughal emperors, Jahangir and Shahjahan, were very fond of it.

Although, more than 80 per cent of the population of the Punjab was engaged in agriculture, there was a relatively high level of urbanization in Mughal India. Cities emerged as important trading and manufacturing centres, but suffered a major reverse in the Punjab, following the decline of Mughal rule, especially under its successor Sikh state.[67] This process was completed in the British period, when towns lost their status as commercial and cultural centres, and the focus of the state shifted to the rural Punjab, particularly the arid, western parts of the Punjab, which became the main recruiting region for the British Indian army. Agricultural colonization of western Punjab was linked to the recruitment of the Indian army in the aftermath of the 1857 Revolt.

In Mughal Punjab, two types of *zamindars* could be identified: (1) intermediary *zamindars*, and (2) primary *zamindars*.[68] Intermediary zamindars were responsible for revenue collection in *zamindari* villages and possessed a right to a certain share of the produce of land, which they did not cultivate themselves. Primary *zamindars* were peasants of *zamindari* and *raiyati* villages, who were given proprietary rights to cultivate the land themselves, or with the help of hired labour.[69] In Punjab, *zamindari* and *raiyati* villages were more familiar, and the class of autonomous chieftains found in other Mughal provinces was absent. In *zamindari* villages, *zamindars* were responsible for collection of revenue, while in *raiyati* villages, the peasant community enjoyed a relative degree of autonomy from the *zamindar*,[70] and the revenue was collected by *muqaddams* (the village headmen). Gardezi notes that *muqaddam* was a 'more permanent figure in the social structure of the village...he often cultivated his own land and was directly responsible for the collection of the revenue from the villagers'.[71] *Raiyati* villages were coparcenaries, the lands and wells being divided amongst cultivators on the basis of fixed, customary shares. Those tenant cultivators, who enjoyed hereditary occupancy rights and paid the revenue themselves, counted as primary *zamindars* too.[72] During the Sikh rule and its successor, the British Raj, the *muqaddam* was replaced by the *chaudary* and the *lambardar*; though the functionary remained the same, the new structural changes completely altered its function, particularly during the British Raj, when the *lambardar*—a paid local agent of the Raj—replaced the traditional institution of the 'headman'. The Land Administrative Manual prepared by the early British administrators stated:

> The affairs of the brotherhood were formally managed by an informal village council or *Punchayat*. But this body was too numerous and loosely constructed to fittingly represent the community in its dealings with the Government officials. A few of its leading members were, therefore, selected as headmen or *lambardars*, and the appointment of headmen naturally came to be confined to particular families. From a revenue point of view the most important function of the headmen is to collect the revenue from the coparceners and pay it into the treasury. The social position assigned to the *lambardars* and the action of our courts stripped the *Punchayat* of its influence, and practically it has ceased to exist.[73]

The social organization of both the rural and urban communities of North India has already been discussed. This description reflects the social organization of Mughal Punjab during the sixteenth and seventeenth centuries. In the eighteenth century, with the collapse of a central power in the Mughal Empire, the provinces became autonomous, and the Mughal viceroys established their independent rule. Although the decline of a central authority led the way for regional autonomy, the Mughal political and social structures continued, especially in the provinces of Awadh, Bengal and Hyderabad. In Punjab, this social and political continuity was interrupted for two reasons; first, there was no class of the local chiefs, such as the *Taluqdars* of Awadh, or the *Zamindars* of Bengal,[74] who could establish regional autonomy, and second, the province had become subject to various Afghan invasions. This caused complete social disorder and the Punjab became a hunting ground for all kinds of warlords, and its political economy was in a constant state of disintegration. By the second half of the eighteenth century, on the eve of the Sikh ascendancy, Punjab was in total disarray, which began with the Sikh peasantry's revolt against the Mughal intermediary *zamindars*' agrarian policies of extraction of the surplus, and concluded in the organization of *misls*, or armed bands. Sikhs had a history of conflict with the Mughals as their eighth Guru Tegh Bahadur, was executed on Aurangzeb's order in 1675. Aurangzeb's religious intolerance forced the last Sikh Guru, Gobind Singh, to transform the Sikhs from a passive sect into a militant brotherhood. With the collapse of the Mughal authority, the Sikhs started to gain control of the plains of Punjab, and 'their armed confederacies took advantage of the power vacuum to carve out petty states'.[75] The group most affected by this disorder, in the post-Mughal Punjab, was the urban hierarchy, concentrated in the Mughal capital cities of Lahore, Multan, and Sirhind. These cities were a special target of Sikh war-bands. By 1823, Ranjit Singh had completely established his sovereignty by replacing the Mughal aristocracy, and subjugating all other *misls*. A.J. Major writes:

> The Kingdom of Lahore, proclaimed by Maharaja Ranjit Singh in 1801, was a military patronage state, initially created by Ranjit Singh's subjugation of the powerful Sikh *misls* of central and eastern Punjab.[76]

The new Sikh state was a military state and all power belonged to Ranjit Singh. Although Sikh *misls* revolted against Mughal intermediary *zamindars,* Ranjit Singh continued the Mughal system of revenue collection and the practice of granting *jagirs* to the governors in lieu of services. However, the layer of intermediary *zamindars* was abolished, and the state extracted surplus from the peasantry in exorbitant proportions through a system of 'highest bidders'.[77] During Sikh rule, Punjab was divided into several provinces and districts. These provinces were assigned to the 'highest bidders' who squeezed the peasants at their own pleasure. A *'nazim'* supervised the administration of a given territory, using force to extract the surplus, which was absorbed either by the Sikh army, or the durbar.

After Ranjit Singh's death, the Sikh state collapsed,[78] and soon after his death, the British adopted an aggressive policy in an attempt to subjugate Sikh-ruled Punjab. Between 1839 and 1849, most of the territories of the province were integrated into the British Punjab.

Establishment of Colonial Capitalism in the Punjab

According to the census of 1868, the population of the Punjab region, excluding that of the princely states, was around 9.5 million, of which the Muslims constituted 63 per cent, Hindus, 22 per cent, and the Sikhs about 8 per cent.[79] Punjab was the second-last province of India to be annexed. At the time of its annexation, the territorial domains of the province included undivided Punjab in the west with present-day Haryana, Himachal Pradesh, Delhi and the north-west districts. On 25 October 1901, the five districts in the North-West Frontier were carved out to form the North West Frontier Province, comprising territories which lay west of river Indus. Though the British did not follow the traditional route, the Punjab's location—its proximity to the Czarist Russian Empire—and its extensive river line system, were the determining factors in shaping the colonial development policies.[80]

Ranging from Delhi to Attock, Punjab was characterized by religious and geographical diversity. The crucial factor of the geographical diversity was the varying levels of availability of water, across the region, for either cultivation or natural vegetation. Three hydraulic zones could be identified: (1) the moist zone; (2) the marginal zone; and (3) the arid zone. At the time of the 1911 census, the natural divisions, as shown in Table 1, were recognized:

Table 1: Showing Natural Divisions of the Punjab

Name	Total Area (in Sq. Miles)	Total Population	Density per Sq. Mile Total Area	Density per Sq. Mile Cultivated Area
Himalayas	22,050	1,724,480	78	965
Sub-Himalayan	19,045	5,805,081	305	612
Indo-Gangetic Plain	38,525	11,027,490	286	435
North Western Dry Area	56,710	5,630,699	99	432

Source: M.S. Leigh, *The Punjab and the War* (Lahore: Government Printing Punjab, 1922), p. 1, PA.

Table 2: Showing the Communal Ratio of Population of the Punjab in 1921 (%)

Muslims	Hindus	Sikhs
55.33	33.58	11

Source: Government of India, *Census of 1921* (Calcutta: Government Central Printing, 1923) PA.

The 1921 census shows that more than 55 per cent of the population was Muslim who were mainly concentrated in the north-western dry areas, consisting of the marginal and arid zones, while the Sikhs, an important minority, were housed in the central-moist zone of the province, in the predominantly Hindu districts. Western Punjab played the most vital role in strengthening colonial rule by attaining the status of the 'Sword Arm of the Raj'. Agricultural colonization of the western Punjab, which was considered by the British administrators as their proud achievement, aimed at the transformation of a backward economy into a more developed one, turned out to be a classic case of 'colonial development', rather underdevelopment.[81] The agricultural colonization, linked to the recruitment of the Indian army, brought rapid and extensive economic growth at the cost of underdevelopment of the province. Consequently, the Punjab underwent a dramatic change, and took a shape, which was essential for the promotion of colonial capitalism. Colonial capitalism completely distorted the pre-colonial structures and introduced the worst kind of feudalism in the disguise of agricultural reforms and economic development.

In the following discussion, an analysis of the process of establishing colonial capitalism and its impact on the social, political, and economic structures of Punjabi society is presented. An analysis of 'colonial capitalism' in Punjab, and the kinds of elite groups which emerged during the colonial period, will reveal the real causes of underdevelopment prevailing in today's Pakistan, since these elite groups continued to shape the contours of the post-colonial state.

Emergence of the Punjab as the Sword Arm of the Raj and Creation of its Landed Elite

Punjab's rise as the 'Sword Arm of the British Raj', and colonial capitalism, are inseparable. The character of economic structure developed under colonial capitalism in India, including in the Punjab, had three features. First, 'the institution of private property in land'; second, 'the growth of merchant capital in Punjab'; and third, 'the establishment of a cash nexus as the primary form of surplus extraction by the colonial state'.[82] This economic structure resulted in marginalization of the peasantry and concentration of land in a few hands, which ultimately pushed the peasants into the colonial army. British Imperial interests were dependent upon an Indian army, which not only stood in reserve to maintain law and order throughout the subcontinent itself, but also fortified British control of the Middle East and the Indian Ocean.[83] At the outbreak of the First World War, the Indian army was the largest volunteer army, to date, in the world's history, and 'consisted largely of officers and men drawn from one province—the Punjab'.[84] The period 1875-1914, witnessed a complete alteration in the composition of the Indian army. Talbot observes that:

> at the beginning of this period Punjabi troops accounted for just a third of its total strength and the army's main recruiting areas still lay in Bengal, Madras, and Bombay. By the end, however, three-fifths of the troops came from the Punjab and the Army had made its home there.[85]

The support of local allies was crucial to colonial control of the Punjab for its immense value to the British strategic interests and its reputation for political loyalty to the Raj.[86] The colonial state used 'the land settlement policies', especially in the canal colonies, for the fulfilment of military needs and provided the rural basis of military recruitment patterns.[87] The penetrating process of the military into the 'seminal source of societal authority, the control and possession of agricultural land', cannot be seen in the 'context of modernization', rather it 'would be more appropriate to draw parallel with feudalism'.[88] Subordinating development goals to its political and military imperatives, the colonial state promoted the social elite, members of which became the major beneficiaries of the agricultural colonization.[89]

Cooperation between the large landowners—a class of Punjab chieftains created by colonialism—and the British colonial state was primarily motivated by the Punjab's emergence as the sword arm of India in the aftermath of the 1857 Revolt. Colonial administrative policies in the 1860s and early 1870s generated this class of Punjabi chieftains, which not only dominated the political and economic life of the province in the years of the Raj, but also continued to play the most important role in the creation of the post-colonial state of Pakistan. For our purpose of inquiry, the focus is on the creation of the class of Muslim chieftains of western Punjab, a region which became the 'flower-bed' for the recruitment of Indian soldiers.[90] This development was rooted of the response of some of the rural families to the '1857 Revolt'.[91] David Page wrote that:

> the Muslims of West Punjab had played an important role in the annexation of the province, and both the Muslims and the Sikhs provided the forces, which enabled the government to put down the Mutiny of 1857.[92]

These rural Muslim families were the ones who provided military services to the Sikhs and served the Sikh durbar in various administrative capacities and had been given *jagirs*.[93] Most of these families were of peasant origin and attained a prominent status by supporting, and in some cases, joining the winning *misls*.[94] Their real moment of fortune came in 1857, when they joined and helped the British officers in the 'dark and thick clouds' of the 'Revolt of the Indian Army'. The British recognized the heads of these families as 'tribal leaders', their local allies, without whose support a strong, loyal, Punjab, geared to bear the burden of the Indian army, could not be built. These 'tribal leaders' were promoted as 'chieftains', representatives of the landed class, since 'the British found few established tribal leaders in Punjab as they began to construct their rural administration'.[95]

In the absence of any 'traces of former leadership', structuring a reliable rural administration was a great challenge for the early British administrators. They constructed this foundation by redesigning the Punjabi rural structures and creating a 'tribal social organization', in which 'tribes' became the basis of authority.[96] Establishing a landowning class based upon 'tribes' in Punjab is linked to the 'colonial recruitment policy of the Indian army'. The Punjab government 'very heavily relied on this landowning class in the recruitment of soldiers for the Army'.[97] The relationship between the Muslim landed leadership and the Raj was determined by two factors: 'the first administrative and the second military'.[98] In the following discussion, we will examine how this Muslim landed leadership was created and sustained through a special set of administrative arrangements for the province of Punjab.

An analysis of British colonial policies in north-west India reveals how the British, in their quest for military and strategic interests on the borderlands, were dependent upon the support of certain tribal and landowning interests. Highlighting the contrast between British policies in the north-west and other parts of India, Ian Talbot argues, that security, rather than commercial considerations, prompted the British administrative policies in predominantly Muslim north-west India. He writes that:

> The British interest in harnessing the waters of Punjab and Sindh notwithstanding, their advance in Muslim north-west India was prompted by military rather than commercial considerations.

Talbot has noted that the expanding Russian Empire in Central Asia posed a threat to British India through Afghanistan. 'Punjab was thus seen as a base for military operations, whilst the Frontier and Baluchistan regions were buffer zones against a possible attack'.[99] Similarly, David Page has observed that the 'fear of Russian expansion' and 'the location of the Punjab' created the dependence of Indian defence upon a strong Punjab.[100] Talbot argues that

> it is unlikely that the region would have assumed importance as a centre of colonial military recruitment, if it had not been near the Indian Army's main theatre of War in Afghanistan.[101]

However, most of the British administrators traced this development to the turbulent history of the Punjab, and claimed that the Indian army was built on the 'military prowess' and martial values of the people of the Punjab.[102] The theory of martial races was the official explanation for specialization of Punjab as the sword arm of the Raj. As discussed earlier, the chief architect of the theory of martial races in India, was Lord Roberts, commander-in-chief of the Indian army, from 1885 to 1893.

Though the theory of martial races is full of inconsistencies, it is still being used to provide an explanation for the colonial recruitment policy. Surprisingly, in the post-colonial period, the military authorities find justification in propagating this theory for the over-representation of certain ethnic groups, and the under-representation of others.[103] There is a strong argument that Pakistan's 'overdeveloped' administrative and military institutions have their roots in the colonial legacy. Colonial rulers' concerns forced them to establish a 'security state in the north-west India'. Such a state could not afford political participation of the people resulting in far less developed political institutions and its survival dependent upon the support of certain tribal and landowning interests.[104] This is evident in Sir Michael O' Dwyer's speech delivered to the Imperial Council in 1917, in which he explained that the Punjab government relied on two classes, the landed aristocracy and the mass of peasant proprietors, and according to him these two classes were not interested in political reforms.[105] Giving the details of the legislative and administrative measures to protect the landed interests, Sir Michael O' Dwyer very proudly declared that 'all these things…[were] done in the interests of our *zamindars* and especially of those tribes and classes which enlist[ed] so freely in the Indian Army'.[106] These 'tribes and classes' were classified by Sir Michael O' Dwyer as 'martial classes'.[107]

Examining the structures created by the Raj, Talbot writes, 'the strongest alliance between the colonial state and the leading landowners existed in its Punjab bastion'.[108] He pointed out that the 'long-term influence of the British reliance on the collaboration of local rural intermediaries' not only 'jeopardized the achievement of Pakistan, but also threatened its post-colonial democratic development'.[109] The collaboration resulted in the 'retarded political institutionalization' and introduced a culture of 'clientelism'.[110] These local rural intermediaries were created through a process which started with the 'land settlement' policy, which resulted in the creation of homogenous administrative units called *zails*, and took its final shape through the Land Alienation Act of 1900, in the form of a system of indirect rule resting on the dominance of feudal and semi-feudal landowners and *Pirs*, who were instrumental in the recruitment of Punjabi soldiers. During the First

World War, heads of some Muslim families of western Punjab showed their loyalty by enlisting recruits for the Indian army. Most notable amongst them were: Sardar Mohammad Nawaz Khan and Sikandar Hayat Khan in Shahpur and Jhelum districts, respectively, who were assisted by Pirs, such as Pir Ghulam Abbas of Makhad, Pir Fazal Shah of Jalalpur, Pir Badshah of Bhera, Pir Chan, and Pir Sultan Ali Shah of Jahanian Shah. All these Pirs directed their Muslim followers in the Shahpur and Jhelum districts to enlist. The involvement of Pirs in raising recruits was very important since the Indian army was fighting against the Ottoman armies in Mesopotamia.[111]

In backward districts of western Punjab like Muzzafargarh, Multan, Sahiwal, Shahpur and Jhang, many families of loyal Pirs were converted into major landowners under the Land Alienation Act of 1900, by obtaining the status of agricultural tribes whose land could not be alienated.[112] By declaring them agricultural tribes, the British, not only provided protection to these hereditary custodians, but also made them *zaildars*, honorary magistrates, and district board members.[113] These hereditary custodians of shrines were also given maintenance grants, subject to the good conduct of their wardens, in addition to 'landed gentry's grants', in the canal colonies. For instance, Pir Sultan Ali Shah, head of the Syeds of Jahanian Shah in Jhang, received five squares as a 'landed gentry' grant, a First Class *Khillat* in 1917, and a Sword of Honour in 1919, and Syed Ghulam Mohammad Shah was given a seat on the Bench of Honorary Magistrate at Sahiwal for his 'hard work to induce the people of their *zail* to enlist, and met with a very fair measure of success'.[114]

> The Punjab Government's recognition of the Pirs as part of the "landed gentry" had important political repercussions in establishing a unity of political interests between the landlords and the Pirs.[115]

The formation of the Unionist party in the early 1920s was based upon this close cooperation, which provided strong support for colonial rule that continued till the last days of the Raj.

Along with the Pirs, a class of big Muslim landowners emerged in west Punjab. As discussed earlier, these were families who had proved their loyalty to the East India Company during the 1857 Revolt. In Talbot's words, 'many rural Punjabi families embarked at this time on what were to prove lengthy and lucrative "loyalist" careers'.[116] Around forty-seven Sikh and Muslim families were rewarded for their collaboration in 1857 and they received titles like Khan Bahadur or Sardar Bahadur, military honours like the Order of British India, or the Order of Merit, cash, jagirs, and land grants—either a proprietary title or a landlord title—was conferred.[117] For example, Tiwana Maliks in the Shahpur district were rewarded for their past services and bound to the new colonial regime by the creation of new *jagirs*.[118] Those, who received land grants were also presented with *sanads* (deeds), in which it was specified that the continuation of the grant was conditional on the good conduct of the grantee and his family.[119] On 26 May 1860, the Punjab government announced the names of twenty-five 'loyal chieftains' who were to be given special powers of an assistant commissioner and were called Jagirdari Magistrates. These were limited administrative powers, which enabled them to only decide those revenue and criminal cases whose value did not exceed Rs 300. They were also made incharge of village constabulary within their estates, and for these police duties, they were to receive *inams*. By 1865, the number of Jagirdari Magistrates was increased to thirty-eight.[120] The principle of conferring limited judicial powers was extended to allow the appointment of other 'chieftains' and 'influential' Punjabis as honorary magistrates. They were given the judicial powers to investigate and render decisions on petty criminal cases that were in the jurisdiction of the regular courts located in cities.[121] Later on, their powers were expanded to include certain civil cases as well. Gradually, the system of honorary magistrates was extended to the smaller district courts.[122] The Court of Wards Administration was another important tool through which the colonial rulers reinforced the loyalty of the class of 'chieftains'. It was established to create and maintain estates for loyal families. For instance, the Tiwana family of Kalra estate in Shahpur proved to be the most loyal family of the Raj; Khizr Hayat Tiwana as a minor heir, was put under the supervision of the colonial state and his estate, Kalra, was developed as one of the largest and most influential estates under the control of the Court of Wards Administration.

The inheritance of these estates was dependent upon the evidence of loyalty to the colonial government. The law of primogeniture gave the British authorities the right to withhold recognition of certain politically undesirable inheritance arrangements. Through the Punjab Laws Act of 1872, the government was able to bring estates of the 'chieftains' within the jurisdiction of the Court of Wards, which gave deputy commissioners control over the affairs of these estates.[123] In 1895, there were sixty-five estates with an area of over 344,000 acres under the control of the Court of Wards Administration.[124] To strengthen the 'chieftain class' and attach it to the British rule, an education policy was designed. Aitchison College was established in Lahore in 1886, to provide education for the sons of leading landowners. Its admission was restricted only to sons of loyal chieftains. A large number of these Aitchisonian boys went on to have important political careers under the colonial patronage. The 'class of chieftains' or 'big landowners' created by the Act, and through systems of honours, nominations to local durbars, and district boards, and appointments as honorary magistrates and *zaildars,* became the guardian of the British rule, and with its alliance, Punjab became the major recruiting area of the Indian Army.[125]

During the First World War, rural Punjab proved to be the most loyal province of the British Raj by responding to the government's campaign for enlisting recruits to the Indian army to fight along with the allied forces. Giving details about India's contribution to the Great War, Michael O' Dwyer, very pompously declared that:

> At the beginning of World War I, Punjab had about one hundred thousand men of all ranks in the Army. At the close of the war, no less than half a million had served it. Roughly, 360,000 Punjabi recruits were enlisted in 4 years between 1914 and 1918, comprising one half of the total number raised in India.[126]

Three rural communities provided the lion's share of soldiers, the Muslims of west Punjab, the Jat Sikhs of central Punjab, and the Hindu Jats of the Ambala division. The five districts of Rawalpindi division (Rawalpindi, Jhelum, Attock, Gujrat, and Shahpur) were amongst the eight most heavily recruited districts in the entire Punjab, the others were Ludhiana and Amritsar, the two main Sikh recruiting areas. In Rawalpindi and Jhelum districts, over 33 per cent of the male population went to the War; in Attock district the figure was 16 per cent; in Gujrat 13 per cent; and in Shahpur, 10 per cent.[127]

> The north-western districts especially were areas of concentrated recruitment of soldiers, and much of the activity of elite formation was based around the organized delivery of these recruits to the army.[128]

Recruitment was not voluntary as under the oppressive government of O' Dwyer, war efforts included the collaboration of Pirs and big landowners for forced enlistment. This is evident in the speech of Sir Michael O' Dwyer, lieutenant governor of the Punjab, delivered at the

Special Durbar held at Dera Ghazi Khan on 18 February 1918, which stated:

> The Tumendars have recently received liberal grants of land from the Sarkar in the Lower Bari Doab Colony in recognition of their position and past services. These grants are conditioned on active loyalty, and I am confident that they will give proof of this by redoubling their efforts to raise recruits among their tribes.[129]

The other major reason for recruitment from the *barani* tracts of western Punjab was the underdevelopment and poverty created by colonial capitalism, which pushed the poor peasants into the army, since there was no other opportunity of employment in this arid land which had a very low level of productivity.

The rural elite of Punjab were rewarded, for its response to the 'government exhortations to enlist' for the War by the Punjab government, in its proposals to the Montagu-Chelmsford Report, in the form of the distribution of urban and rural seats, and its recommendations concerning the franchise. According to the Reform Report, the council was to contain a minimum of fifty members, and 30 per cent of the members were to be nominated. Thirty-four members were to be elected. The distribution of these elected seats displayed a 'strong bias' towards rural 'loyal' groups. Twenty-five seats out of thirty-five were to be given to the rural areas. Of the rural seats, ten were allocated to the Muslims, six to the Hindus, five to large landowners and four to the Sikhs. The government also proposed special treatment for the Punjabi electorate that had to be more restricted, which made it the smallest in India. Punjab was a 'security province' where large-scale political participation could not be allowed in the 'interest of the Raj'. Therefore, special qualifications were proposed for the franchise in the Punjab. The most striking example to control the franchise was the right to vote given to the officially appointed *lambardar* in each village, which made it impossible for any candidate to win without official patronage.[130]

The allocation of five seats to the big *zamindars* also indicated the government's desire to strengthen the influence of its 'proven loyal elite' in order to control the rural population and its presence in the council was meant to keep the liberal educated urban representatives in control.[131] In the urban areas, the number of seats was restricted to a bare minimum and very high voting qualifications were proposed. These qualifications restricted the vote to just 3 per cent of the urban population. Similarly, the government, in its desire to secure an adequate representation of the army's interests, proposed separate representation for the retired military men, not only by nomination, but also through the rural electorate.[132] In response to the Franchise Committee Report, the recommendations of the Government of India, and the decision of the Joint Select Committee, the Punjab government had to modify its few proposals and accept a larger council, and a larger electorate under the Montagu-Chelmsford constitution. However, the distribution of seats continued to favour the rural elite, and in addition, its proposal for enfranchising the Punjab soldier was accepted by the House of Commons, despite the opinion of the Joint Select Committee, that 'this might mean that the soldiers in the Punjab would have a preponderating voice in elections'.[133] In the final constitution, the right to vote was awarded to the ex-sepoy, making the military vote the most substantial element in the rural electorate.[134] As a result of the 1919 Reforms, men who returned to the council after 1920 were those who were committed to the 'maintenance of the Punjab military machine' and they were facilitated to form the government. Consequently, the classes recruited to the army were the most privileged under the new constitution, and were getting the maximum benefits.

As the chief representative of the military lobby, Sir Umar Hayat Khan, whose son became the last premier of colonial Punjab, had proposed to the Punjab government that military classes should be given their own representatives along with the landholders.[135] Sir Umar Hayat was speaking on behalf of the Punjab government. He was the representative of the landed class, which was created and sustained by colonial policies, to maintain Punjab's status as the 'Sword Arm of the Raj'. The Punjab government's reliance on this class was again displayed when the Punjab Council was formed under the Montagu-Chelmsford Reforms of 1919. The large majority of Muslims who dominated the council in the following years belonged to the Punjab Muslim Association and belonged to those 'families of note' who were involved in recruitment during the First World War. In Punjab, the Montagu-Chelmsford Reforms provided an excellent opportunity to all the partners of colonial control, which strengthened their bonds of alliance. The division of seats in the Legislative Council on the basis of urban and rural constituencies, provision of vote to officially appointed *lambardars*, and the ex-sepoy, consolidated the bargaining power of rural elite in favour of the Raj, and retarded the process of nationalism.

> When a degree of democracy was introduced into the province, the servicemen and their comrades exerted a powerful influence...being granted land or government office as a reward of their loyalty, they came to dominate the restricted electorate.[136]

The ratio of Muslim voters was the highest in rural areas, having set a record for recruiting servicemen, i.e. voters in Jhelum and Rawalpindi comprised 14 per cent of the total Muslim electorate in the Punjab.[137]

Emergence of the Punjab National Unionist Party in 1923, as representative of the military lobby, belonging to the three communities—Muslims, Sikhs and Hindus, though predominantly Muslim—should be seen in this perspective, which continued to rule Punjab till the last days of the Raj. Two leading personalities of the Unionist party, Sir Sikandar Hayat Khan, the first premier, and Sir Khizr Hayat Tiwana, the last premier, belonged to families who had a history of loyalty to the Raj, and were instrumental in making Punjab the 'flower bed of Indian Army'. The Punjab National Unionist Party was born as an alliance of the Punjab Muslim Association and the Punjab Zamindar Central Association, representing the landed and military interests in the aftermath of the Reforms, and continued to dominate Punjabi politics for almost a quarter of a century before the partition. The Unionist ideology was consistent with dependence on a rural hierarchy. The 1935 Act introduced a new element in Indian politics: provincial autonomy. It gave the Unionists a new weapon to consolidate their base in the Punjab and keep it isolated from all Indian politics. The politics of the Unionists did not allow the political participation of people and growth of democratic institutions, a legacy Punjab inherited, and continued after the independence.

The landed elite created by the Raj was quickly eliminated in eastern (Indian) Punjab soon after independence by the anti-*zamindari* legislation, the absorption of the princely states, and the rise to political dominance of the Jat peasantry. However, in western (Pakistani) Punjab it suffered no such loss as[138] till 1959, the *jagirs*, the system of *begar* (labour rent or corvee), and the princely states were not abolished. Despite the land reforms of Ayub Khan and Zulfikar Ali Bhutto, the landed elite managed to retain its former position of control over power structures and continued its colonial legacy of protecting military interests at the cost of democratic institutions. The 'Unionists' who joined the Muslim League in the 1946 elections in an urge to survive after independence, contrived to monopolize the political institutions, and the new post-colonial state was never allowed to develop as a democratic state. Policies were adopted which followed the colonial legacy of the obsession with the Russian invasion, and the new state was seen as a security state in the region by the minds trained by the British strategists, especially during the era of the Cold War.

The Colonial Administrative Structure and its Land Settlement Policy

The Administrative System

Until the 1919 Reforms, Punjab was deprived of a constitutional government, and was maintained as a non-regulation province. There was no Executive Council or High Court and it did not have any effective representation in the Imperial Council, either. Immediately after its annexation, the Province was placed under the authoritarian form of administration by Lord Dalhousie's hand-picked British officers, which came to be known as the Punjab School of Administration, having a paternalistic attitude towards the province.[139] Thorburn writes:

> When Lord Dalhousie rounded off the north-west boundary of our Indian domination by annexing the Punjab, he had by right of conquest a clean state to work upon and he then...introduced changes in the land revenue system which, however convenient for budgets and disbursements, was fraught with serious consequences for the rural communities of the province.[140]

The Punjab was a 'clean state' for Dalhousie for 'an imperial experiment, imperially conducted'.[141] The 'imperial experiment' that was conducted in the Punjab between 1849-1856, the period of Lord Dalhousie's governor-generalship, was essentially an experience in authoritarianism and political exclusiveness, which became a trademark of colonial policies in the Punjab. The province was put under the control of the bureaucracy as a non-regulation province, a unique system of government run by a Board of Administration comprising three members.[142] These three members were given extraordinary powers to settle the land revenue demands, regulate the excise, supervise the police, and impose the death penalty for serious crimes. In this form of government, day-to-day business was carried out in accordance with an extremely flexible interpretation of basic administrative instructions contained in printed codes and circulars, instead of observing legislative regulations, as was the case elsewhere in British India.[143] Dalhousie exercised personal control over the Punjab administration; it was a 'military way of government' carried out by executive orders.[144] Under the Board of Administration were seven commissioners, 'to exercise a stricter supervision and control over the Deputy Commissioners'.[145] The deputy commissioner was the head of the district, the collector of the land revenue and also the district magistrate, who exercised his authority and collected revenue largely with the assistance of officially appointed *zaildars* and *lambardars*. All authority, whether executive, revenue or judicial, was concentrated in the hands of the deputy commissioner, who was a 'Government' for the majority of his people.[146] Thorburn called him 'a little king within his own domain, subject to loosely defined limitations'.[147] The districts were the centrepieces of the British administration, with villages as the lowest rung and the province as the highest. In the Punjab, the district assumed added significance because the Punjab was a non-regulation province.[148] Sir Patrick Fagan described the defining element of the non-regulation provinces like Punjab in the following words: 'The union of all powers, executive, magisterial and judicial, in the hands of the district officer, here termed deputy commissioner in place of magistrate and collector'.[149]

Under the Indian Councils Act of 1861, legislative councils were set up in other provinces of India, except Punjab, where every effort was made to restrain the establishment of the Punjab Legislative Council. The first Punjab Legislative Council was established in 1897, after a long gap of three decades, and even then it was denied the powers of interpretation or the privilege of discussing the annual budget given to other legislative councils under the Indian Councils Act of 1892. The Punjab Legislative Council was meant to be a loyal body, all of its five Indian members were to be nominated by the governor, and the sole criterion of their nomination was 'their loyalty first and then their wealth and rank'.[150] For every legislation, the sanction of both the governor-general and the secretary of state was mandatory, and the council had very limited powers. The governor was the council's president and empowered to convene the council's meetings. Between 1897 and 1909, it met only twenty-six times, and the four British members transacted virtually all its business.[151] As a result of the Morley-Minto Reforms, the council was expanded. The 1909 Indian Councils Act extended the powers and membership of the council by introducing an element of indirect election into this. However, the majority of its Indian members came from the landed class, who rarely participated in any debate and left the committees' work to the British officials.[152] The record of the legislative council from the years 1910-12, reveals the lack of participation of the Indian members in the council's proceedings, questions were rarely asked about the financial statements presented in the council, and no resolution was passed during this period.[153] The tradition of non-participation by the Indian members in the legislative council continued till 1919, when more power was given to the councils, membership was enlarged, and the concept of a 'restricted franchise' was introduced. Punjab was not allowed to develop democratic institutions, like other Indian provinces, in the wake of the 1919 Reforms. In the earlier discussion, we have seen the political process developed in the Punjab under the tight grip of British control over democratic institutions after the 1919 Reforms.

Land Settlement Policy

Along with the administrative structure, the 'imperial experiment' of Dalhousie also introduced a 'land settlement policy', which became the major instrument of colonial capitalism in the Punjab. Through this policy the colonial rulers transformed the agrarian structure of the Punjabi society. As discussed earlier, in the absence of any 'traces of established leadership', structuring a reliable rural administration was a great challenge for the early British administrators of Punjab. This was achieved by redesigning the Punjabi rural structures and creating a 'tribal social organization' in which 'tribes' became the basis of the authority.[154] To safeguard their colonial interests, the British introduced a system, 'which generated the worst kind of feudal exploitation of the Muslim peasants'.[155] Alavi observed that 'the new concept of property in land that was introduced by the colonial regime was premised on dispossession of the peasants'.[156] The traditional self-sufficient village communities were replaced by *zails* headed by *zaildars* who were politically and economically dependent on the British authority.[157]

The 'settlement' was a set of arrangements with a two-fold purpose: first, the assessment of the land revenue; and second, the framing of a record of rights. Under this 'set of arrangements', districts in the Punjab were divided into administrative units called *zails* (circles), varying in size from ten to forty villages, with the intention of incorporating tribal organization into their administration by concentrating particular *biradries* in particular *zails* along the lines of tribal kinship residence rules. Each *zail* was headed by a *zaildar* appointed by the British administrators, and was 'the representative of Government in his circle'[158] and very often the existing traditions of lineage or *biradri* leadership were ignored to create a class of tribal leaders who represented British authority in *zails*. In 1872, the Punjab government established the *zaildari* system on a formal basis, laying down the duties and remuneration of the *zaildars*. The *zaildars* and their assistants, the *ala-lambardars*, were described by the colonial rulers as the 'channel of communication' or the 'missing link'.[159] Khalid Bin Sayeed observes, 'whatever authority the village community had exercised was disintegrating under the British and gravitating toward the *zaildar*'.[160] The *zaildari* system replaced the village communities as a self-sufficient political and economic unit with a political organization based upon extended kinship ties, or 'tribes'.[161] *Biradries* in rural Punjab were treated as tribes by the British administrators who emphasized the importance of 'tribes', and the importance of extensive supra-village, kinship ties, based on tribal affinity, in establishing the secular bonds holding the Punjabi village society together.[162]

In arranging the *zails*, in 1873, the government instructed that:

> care should be taken to include in one circle as far as possible the people of one tribe-or having some sort of affinity so that discordant elements... [could] be reduced to a minimum.[163]

Through the delineation of *zails*, in accordance with the patterns of tribal settlement, colonial rulers established a framework within which the problem of local leadership could be confronted. *Zaildari* became a vehicle by which the British could enoble a family, and give it a status of a local leader—a fact noted by many settlement officers.[164] Selection of *zaildars* produced families of considerable local influence, who used their position to claim the leadership of the *zails*' dominant 'tribes'. The granting of *zaildari* represented a means by which a class of rural leaders was created, tied closely to the colonial administration, practicing its authority largely in a 'tribal' idiom. In this colonial system of control, the influence of *zaildars* was linked to their relationship with the administration and their status depended on their claims to tribal leadership. The land control and 'tribal' leadership became the central element in establishing the legitimacy of a politically effective intermediary elite in rural Punjab. Special *zails* were created to accommodate the 'loyal' families of western Punjab through the granting of *inams,* or revenue-free land, in each district. The authority of these families was enforced by making their leading men *zaildars*. For instance in Shahpur district, the British administrators named the 'loyal' Tiwanas and Noons as honorary *zaildars* 'within the estates owned by themselves or their near relations'.[165] After 1890, like the 'loyal chieftains' of Punjab, the majority of *zaildars* were also converted into the landed class through the wide-scale use of grants of land in the newly-created canal colonies.

It has been discussed earlier how this class became so vital to the structure of colonial rule in Punjab. Another major instrument in the creation of this class was the Land Alienation Act of 1900, which declared certain 'tribes' as agricultural tribes whose land could not be alienated. The Act, which was based upon the 'tribal idiom', declared that an agriculturist was the one who was born in a particular caste, and was not necessarily the actual tiller of the soil. This definition of an agriculturist along with the land settlement policy defined landed patrons as legitimate links between the colonial state and the populace.[166] Analyzing the impact of the Act, K.B. Sayeed writes, 'the Land Alienation Act of 1900 turned out to be a license for land grabbing on the part of big landowners.[167] Sir Michael O' Dwyer the governor of Punjab, noted: 'It is now regarded by hereditary landowners of all religions and castes as their Magna Carta'.[168] Another aspect of land settlement policy was the colonization of the wasteland and creation of canal colonies. To meet the needs of the Indian army, it was necessary to bring into cultivation the vast arid areas of western Punjab. For this purpose, a huge network of irrigation canals was constructed which converted the wastelands of western *doabs* into 'canal colonies' and introduced commercial agriculture in Punjab. In their pursuit to consolidate their political position, the British used land distribution to fulfil military requirements, and maintain an extractive system which could finance their administrative system. Talbot writes that:

> the creation of the Canal Colonies was closely linked with the other major development of the late nineteenth century, the Punjab's emergence as the leading recruitment centre of the Indian Army.

He noted that the British policy of rewarding ex-servicemen with lucrative grants of land in the colonies became one of the important incentives for enlistment.[169]

Since these colonies were established on the Crown wasteland, the colonial state had the right not only over land distribution, but also over the distribution of water, a new phenomenon in the agricultural life of the province. The canal colonies became the most influential tool in the hands of the colonial administrators to protect the landed and military interests by giving grants of land for military purposes to the class of Muslim landowners, who were committed to the maintenance of the Punjab 'military machine'. Sir Michael O' Dwyer's scheme for grants to the 'landed gentry', which was first developed in 1914 in connection with the distribution of land in the Lower Bari Doab colony, helped to consolidate the landed elite in western Punjab.[170] Under this scheme of 'landed gentry', loyal families of western Punjab, including Tiwanas and Noons of Shahpur, and the Tumendars of Dera Ghazi Khan, received numerous grants in lieu of their 'loyal' services to the colonial rulers.[171] Commenting on the distribution of land in canal colonies, Imran Ali writes:

> The rural elite of this region was incorporated into the emergent landholding structures of these commercially valuable lands, through several different types of grants...'Yeoman' grants of 50-150 acres, 'Capitalist' grants of 150-600 acres...Yeoman Horse-breeding and 'stud farm' grants, the 'Landed Gentry' grants...Additional holdings came in the form of 'Reward' grants for administrative, political and military related services.[172]

Imran Ali observes that through these grants, 'concessionary leaseholds', and many other '*ad hoc* arrangements' to acquire land, new lands were monopolized by the agriculturist elite, and the landless rural population was denied a landholding status in the canal colonies.[173]

> The strengthening of the upper classes through this extensive process of land acquisition and economic growth provided the cement to bind the Punjabi political structure dominated as it was by the rural interests, with British rule.[174]

This process not only resulted in the underdevelopment of the region, it also hampered the growth of nationalism. Punjab was the only province of British India whose elite remained loyal to the colonial rulers till the last days of the empire, against the general wish of the people. The colonial state did not allow the establishment of democratic institutions in Punjab. As a result, no major national political party such as the Indian National Congress or the All-India Muslim League could play an effective role in its politics. Although the Muslim League emerged as the majority party in the elections of 1946, it was not because of the League's organizational skills, rather, it was the opportunity strategy of a large number of Unionists who joined the Muslim League when they realized that colonial rule was coming to its end. They were trained in picking the right allies at the right moment with the sole aim of getting the maximum benefits out of any situation. In the post-colonial state, they carried these traditions with them and thus plagued the process of nation-building. Their alliance with the military and bureaucracy continued in the post-colonial state, and very soon this alliance overshadowed the democratic institutions of the new state.

Within the background of weak democratic traditions, the 'undeniable eminence that the military attained in colonial Punjab, could well have facilitated its assumption of political power in the new nation'.[175] Similarly, the bureaucracy, which was trained in administrating the Punjab under its tight grip, and enjoyed extraordinary executive and judicial powers in the colonial state, continued its tradition of ruling unchallenged in the new state, since the political institutions were still in their formative stage. Soon after its creation, the newly independent state of Pakistan—a federation of five provinces—was subject to the domination of one province, the Punjab, and its two strong institutions, the army and bureaucracy, having their roots in rural Punjab, started assuming political power. In the next chapter we will explore how this happened, and which external and internal forces facilitated this process.

NOTES

1. See Khalid Bin Sayeed, 1980, *Politics in Pakistan: The Nature and Direction of Change*, New York: Preager Press, pp. 2-5; Hamza Alavi, 1973, 'The State in Post-Colonial Societies: Pakistan and Bangladesh', in Kathleen Gough and Hari P. Sharma (eds.), *Imperialism and Revolution in South Asia*, New York: Monthly Review Press, pp. 145-73; Hamza Alavi, 1983, 'Class and State in Pakistan', in Hassan Gardezi and Jamil Rashid (eds.), *Pakistan: The Unstable State*, Lahore: Vanguard Books, pp. 40-93; Hassan Gardezi, 'Neo-Colonial Alliances and the Crisis of Pakistan', in Kathleen Gough and Hari P. Sharma, pp. 130-44; Hassan Gardezi, 'Feudal and Capitalist Relations in Pakistan', in Hassan Gardezi and Jamil Rashid (eds.), op. cit., pp. 19-39.
2. Mahbub ul Haq, 22 March 1973, *The London Times*, quoted in Mahbub ul Haq, *The Poverty Curtain: Choices for the Third World*, op. cit., p. 7.

COLONIAL CAPITALISM AND THE PUNJAB 33

3. For a detailed discussion on colonial economic and political engineering in the Punjab, see Imran Ali, 1988, *The Punjab Under Imperialism, 1885-1947*, Princeton: Princeton University Press; Ian Talbot, 1996, *Khizr Hayat: The Punjab Unionist Party and the Partition of India*, Richmond, Surrey: Curzon Press.
4. Hamza Alavi, 1980, 'India: Transition from Feudalism to Colonial Capitalism', *Journal of Contemporary Asia*, 10 (397).
5. Ibid.
6. H. Alavi, 'Class and State in Pakistan', in Hassan Gardezi and Jamil Rashid (eds.), *Pakistan: The Unstable State*, op. cit., p. 43. Alavi defines the structure of peripheral capitalism as the colonial mode of production. For a discussion on peripheral capitalism, also see S. Amin, 1976, *Unequal Development: An Essay on the Social Formation of Peripheral Capitalism*, New York: Monthly Review Press.
7. Imran Ali, *The Punjab Under Imperialism, 1885-1947*, op. cit.
8. Andre G. Frank, September 1966, 'The Development of Underdevelopment', *Monthly Review*, 18: 17-19.
9. William W. Murdoch, 1980, *The Poverty of Nations*, Baltimore: Johns Hopkins University Press, 1980, p. 53.
10. See Hassan Gardezi, 'Feudal and Capitalist Relations in Pakistan', in Hassan Gardezi and Jamil Rashid (eds.), op. cit.; Khalid B. Sayeed, *Politics in Pakistan: The Nature and Directions of Change*, op. cit., pp. 2-7; Hamza Alavi, 'India; Transition from Feudalism to Colonial Capitalism', op. cit. In this regard also see Kathleen Gough and Hari P. Sharma (eds.), *Imperialism and Revolution in South Asia*, op. cit.
11. Hamza Alavi, 'India: Transition from Feudalism to Colonial Capitalism', op. cit., p. 370.
12. J. Gallagher, 1973, J. Gordon and A. Seal, *Locality, Province and Nation: Essays on Indian Politics 1879-1940*, Cambridge: Cambridge University Press, p. 8.
13. Ibid.
14. Tapan Raychaudhuri and Irfan Habib (eds.), 1984, *The Cambridge Economic History of India, Volume 1, c. 1200. 1750*, Hyderabad, pp. 172-90.
15. See Khalid Bin Sayeed, *Government and Politics: The Nature and Direction of Change*, op. cit.; Hamza Alavi, 'The State in Post-Colonial Societies: Pakistan and Bangladesh', in Kathleen Gough and Hari P. Sharma (eds.), op. cit.; H. Alavi, 'Class and State in Pakistan', in Hassan Gardezi and Jamil Rashid (eds.), 1983, *Pakistan: The Unstable State*, Lahore: Vanguard Books, pp. 40-93; Hassan Gardezi, 'Neo-Colonial Alliances and the Crisis of Pakistan', in Kathleen Gough and Hari P. Sharma (eds.), op. cit., pp. 130-44; and H. Gardezi, 'Feudal and Capitalist Relations in Pakistan', in Hassan Gardezi and Jamil Rashid (eds.), op. cit., pp. 19-39.
16. Mustafa Kamal Pasha, 1998, *Colonial Political Economy: Recruitment and Underdevelopment in the Punjab*, Karachi: Oxford University Press, p. 108.
17. Imran Ali, *The Punjab under Imperialism: 1885-1947*, op. cit.
18. Ibid., p. 109.
19. David Gilmartin, 1988, *Empire and Islam, Punjab and the Making of Pakistan*, London: I.B. Tauris Co. Ltd.
20. Lord Roberts, 1898, *Forty-one Years in India: From Subaltern to Commander-in-Chief*, London.
21. Stephen P. Cohen, 1984, *The Indian Army: Its Contribution to the Development of a Nation*, Berkeley: University of California Press (1971); S.P. Cohen, 1983, *The Pakistan Army*, Berkeley: University of California Press; and S.P. Cohen, September 1980, *Security Decision-Making in Pakistan*, a report prepared for the Office of

External Research, Department of State, Contract # 1722-020167, University of Illinois, Urbana, Unclassified monograph, Copy # 45.
22. Ian Talbot, 1990, *Pakistan: A Modern History*, Lahore.
23. Ian Talbot, 1988, *Punjab and the Raj: 1847-1947*, New Delhi.
24. Ian Talbot, *Khizr Tiwana: The Punjab Unionist Party and the Partition of India*, op. cit.
25. Imran Ali, *The Punjab under Imperialism: 1885-1947*, op. cit.
26. For a detailed discussion see Hassan Gardezi, 'Feudal and Capitalist Relations in Pakistan', in Hassan Gardezi and Jamil Rashid (eds.), op. cit.; Khalid B. Sayeed, *Politics in Pakistan: The Nature and Directions of Change*, op. cit.; Tapan Raychaudhuri and Irfan Habib (eds.), 1984, *The Cambridge Economic History of India, Volume 1, c. 1200. 1750*, Hyderabad: Orient Longman in association with Cambridge University Press, pp. 172-90; and Hamza Alavi, 'India: Transition from Feudalism to Colonial Capitalism', op. cit.
27. See Khalid B. Sayeed, *Politics in Pakistan: The Nature and Directions of Change*, op. cit., pp. 2-6; and S.M. Naseem, 1980, *Underdevelopment, Poverty and Inequality in Pakistan*, Lahore: Vanguard Books, p. 14.
28. S.M. Naseem, *Underdevelopment, Poverty and Inequality in Pakistan*, op. cit., p. 14.
29. Irfan Habib, 'The State and the Economy', in Tapan Raychaudhuri and Irfan Habib (eds.), op. cit., pp. 176-77.
30. Irfan Habib, 1963, *The Agrarian System of Mughal India (1556-1707)*, Bombay: Asia Publishing House, quoted in S.M. Naseem, *Underdevelopment, Poverty and Inequality in Pakistan*, op. cit., p. 14.
31. Irfan Habib, 'The State and the Economy—Mughal India', in Tapan Raychaudhuri and Irfan Habib (eds.), op. cit., p. 176.
32. Hamza Alavi, 'India: Transition from Feudalism to Colonial Capitalism', op. cit., p. 371.
33. Hassan Gardezi, 'Feudal and Capitalist Relations in Pakistan', in Hassan Gardezi and Jamil Rashid (eds.), op. cit., p. 24.
34. Ibid., p. 38, see notes.
35. Imran Ali, *The Punjab under Imperialism, 1885-1947*, op. cit., p. 4.
36. Ibid.
37. Irfan Habib, 'The State and the Economy—Mughal India', in Tapan Raychaudhuri and Irfan Habib (eds.), op. cit., p. 176.
38. Ibid.
39. Irfan Habib, 'Agrarian Relations and Land Revenue', in Tapan Raychaudhuri and Irfan Habib (eds.), op. cit., p. 235.
40. Ibid.
41. Giving the description of the Mughal ruling class, Habib writes that the Mughal ruling class consisted of about 8,000 *mansabdars*, who were responsible for maintaining military contingents available at the service of the state. Irfan Habib, 1965, *The Agrarian System of Mughal India (1556-1707)*, op. cit., p. 260; and Percival Spear, *A History of India, Vol. 2*, Harmondsworth, Middlesex: Penguin Books, p. 35.
42. Irfan Habib, 'Agrarian Relations and Land Revenue', in Tapan Raychaudhuri and Irfan Habib (eds.), p. 241.
43. Percival Spear, 1965, *A History of India, Vol. 2*, Harmondsworth, Middlesex: Penguin Books, p. 41.

44. Irfan Habib, 'Agrarian Relations and Land Revenue', in Tapan Raychaudhuri and Irfan Habib (eds.), op. cit., p. 241.
45. Ibid., p. 243.
46. Irfan Habib, 'The State and the Economy', in Tapan Raychaudhuri and Irfan Habib (eds.), op. cit., p. 176. Land which was not assigned but from which land revenue was extracted by the state was called the *khalisa*. Alavi notes that in *zamindari* villages, *zamindars* were responsible for collection of revenue, while in *raiyati* villages, the peasant community enjoyed a relative degree of autonomy from the *zamindar* or *taluqdar*, as in these villages revenue was collected by *muqaddams* (village headmen). Hamza Alavi, 'India: Transition from Feudalism to Colonial Capitalism', op. cit., pp. 367-8.
47. Irfan Habib, 'The State and the Economy', in Tapan Raychaudhuri and Irfan Habib (eds.), op. cit., p. 177.
48. Ibid.
49. N.A. Siddiqui, 1970, *Land Revenue Administration under the Mughals*, Bombay: Asia Publishing House, quoted in Tapan Raychaudhuri and Irfan Habib (eds.), op. cit., p. 177.
50. Irfan Habib, *Agrarian System of Mughal India*, op. cit., pp. 151-3. There are cases when *zamindari* was purchased at a low sale price. A case in point is of the English Company's purchase of the *zamindari* of the villages constituting the nucleus of the future city of Calcutta in 1703 at the sale price of Rs 1300, when the annual land revenue was Rs 1194. Cf., G. Blyn, 1964, 'Revenue Administration of Calcutta in the first half of the 18th century', *The Indian Economic and Social History Review*, New Delhi 1(4): 121-2.
51. Irfan Habib, *The Agrarian System of Mughal India (1556-1707)*, op. cit., p. 260.
52. Irfan Habib, 'Agrarian Relations and Land Revenue', in Tapan Raychaudhuri and Irfan Habib (eds.), op. cit., p. 247.
53. N.V. Sovani, April 1954, 'British Impact on India After 1850-57', *Journal of World History*, II: 78.
54. Ibn Hassan, 1967, *The Central Structure of the Mughal Empire*, London: Oxford University Press, p. 32.
55. Irfan Habib, 1969, 'Potentialities of Capitalistic Development in the Economy of Mughal India', *The Journal of Economic History*, XXIX: 37.
56. According to an estimate of the population in the sixteenth and seventeenth centuries provided by Habib, 85 per cent was rural, and 15 per cent urban. Tapan Raychaudhuri and Irfan Habib (eds.), op. cit., pp. 434-51.
57. Irfan Habib, 'Towns and Cities—Mughal India', in Tapan Raychaudhuri and Irfan Habib (eds.), op. cit., p. 448.
58. Ibid.
59. Ibid.
60. This account is based on the *Cambridge Economic History of India*, Tapan Raychaudhuri and Irfan Habib (eds.), op. cit., pp. 434-51.
61. Irfan Habib, 'Towns and Cities—Mughal India', in Tapan Raychaudhuri and Irfan Habib (eds.), op. cit., p. 434.
62. Ibid., pp. 278-86.
63. Ibid., p. 279.
64. Irfan Habib, 'Non-agrarian Production', in Tapan Raychaudhuri and Irfan Habib (eds.), op. cit., p. 262.
65. Irfan Habib, 'Towns and Cities—Mughal India', in Tapan Raychaudhuri and Irfan Habib (eds.), op. cit., p. 436.

66. Bernard S. Cohen, *India: The Social Organization of a Civilization*, op. cit., p. 25.
67. Irfan Habib, 'Towns and Cities—Mughal India', in Tapan Raychaudhuri and Irfan Habib (eds.), op. cit., pp. 434-51.
68. Nurul Hassan, 1969, 'Zamindars under the Mughals', in Richard E. Frykenberg (ed.), *Land Control and Social Structure in Indian History*, Madison: University of Wisconsin, pp. 17-31.
69. Discussing the main features of proprietary rights in Punjab, *the Manual of Land Settlement* produced by early British administrators, states, '(a) that the right-holder is entitled to the use and occupation of the land during his lifetime; (b) that on his death this title passes to his descendants, subject to customary rules of inheritance, which usually exclude females; (c) that the right-holder is entitled to let the land to tenants on such terms as he thinks fit; (d) that the right-holder can sell or mortgage the land subject to customary and legal restrictions which give to members of the same family or village community a right to interfere under certain circumstances. This right is based originally on kinship, real or assumed, and not on any claim on the part of the objector to a superior title. Mr Thomason regarded freedom of transfer as a necessary feature of proprietary right. But the Indian idea of property in land is that it is vested in a family, and not in an individual. In many parts of the country the possession of unlimited powers of alienation by the recorded right-holder was entirely opposed to native sentiment, and restrictions on the power of alienation have never been wholly wanting in the Punjab, and have been greatly extended by the Alienation of Land Act, XIII of 1900; (e) that the right-holder is entitled to engage for the payment of the land-revenue. This last feature of proprietary right is mainly the creation of our rule'. J.M. Moudie, 1908, *The Punjab Administrative Manual*, Government of India, p. 58, Punjab Archives, Lahore [henceforth PA].
70. Hamza Alavi, 'India: Transition from Feudalism to Colonial Capitalism', op. cit., pp. 367-8.
71. Hassan Gardezi, 'Feudal and Capitalist Relations in Pakistan', in Hassan Gardezi and Jamil Rashid (eds.), op. cit., p. 24.
72. 'A village community is a body of proprietors who now or formerly owned part of the village lands in common, and who are jointly responsible for payment of the revenue. As time goes on the tendency is for the area held in severalty to increase, but it is rare indeed to find a village, which was one of the communal types, in which there is no common property remaining. Joint responsibility has been made a prominent feature of village tenure by the British Government. Under native rule it did not exist when the State realized its dues by division of crop or by appraisement. Even when a cash assessment was made only a few leading members of the community became responsible and they generally occupied the position of revenue farmers in their dealings with the rest of the brotherhood'. J.M. Moudie, *The Punjab Land Administrative Manual*, op. cit., p. 61.
73. Ibid., p. 62.
74. See B.H. Baden-Powell, 1982, *Land Systems of British India*, Oxford: Clarendon Press.
75. Ian Talbot, *Punjab and the Raj*, op. cit., p. 32.
76. Andrew J. Major, 1991, 'The Punjab Chieftains and the Transition from Sikh to British Rule', in D.A. Low (ed.), *The Political Inheritance of Pakistan*, London: Macmillan, p. 54.
77. Under Sikh rule, the Punjab was divided into several provinces and districts. These provinces were assigned to the 'highest bidders' who squeezed the peasant at their

own pleasure. A '*nazim*' supervised the administration of a given territory, using force to extract the surplus, which was absorbed either by the Sikh army or the durbar.
78. Without established institutions, the Sikh state, which was centred around a Sikh oligarchy, had to disintegrate due to internal decay and external pressures.
79. Punjab Census 1868, 1970, General Statements nos. 2 and 7, Lahore: Government of Punjab, PA.
80. Ian Talbot, *Punjab and the Raj*, op. cit., p. 11.
81. Imran Ali, *The Punjab under Imperialism, 1885-1947*, op. cit., pp. 237-44.
82. Mustafa Kamal Pasha, 1998, *Colonial Political Economy: Recruitment and Underdevelopment in the Punjab*, Karachi: Oxford University Press, p. 108.
83. Ian Talbot, *Punjab and the Raj*, op. cit., p. 41.
84. Ibid.
85. Ibid.
86. Ibid., p. 48.
87. Imran Ali, *The Punjab Under Imperialism, 1885-1947*, op. cit., pp. 109-11; M.S. Leigh, 1922, *The Punjab and the War*, Lahore, Government Printing Punjab, p. 8.
88. Imran Ali, *The Punjab under Imperialism, 1885-1947*, op. cit., pp. 109-11.
89. Ibid., pp. 237-39.
90. 'A year ago I told you with pride that since the War began the Punjab had furnished 124,000 men. That was soared over 2 & ½ years. What have we done within the last year? We have furnished 127,095 combatants or more than in the previous 2 & ½ years. All the rest of India including the Native States with more than 12 times our population has raised in the last 2 & ½ years 137,000 or slightly more than one single province. Since the war began, we have raised 250,000 men to fight the battles of Empire, besides some 60,000 or 70,000 men serving as non-combatants...It is a truly remarkable one for a single Indian province'. Speech of Sir Michael O' Dwyer on 26 April 1918 in the Punjab Legislative Council, *War Speeches of Sir Michael O' Dwyer Lieutenant Governor of the Punjab*, Lahore: Government Printing Punjab, 1918, p. 21, PA.
91. David Page, 1987, *Prelude to Partition: The Indian Muslims and the Imperial System of Control 1920-1932*, Karachi: Oxford University Press, p. 49.
92. David Page, *Prelude to Partition; The Indian Muslims and the Imperial System of Control 1920-1932*, op. cit., p. 49.
93. David Gilmartin, *Empire and Islam*, op. cit., p. 19.
94. L.H. Griffin and C.F. Massy, 1940, *Chiefs and Families of Note in the Punjab*, 2 vols., Lahore: Government Printing Punjab, PA. This is the single most comprehensive account of the social history of the Punjab elite. It contains short stories of the major families of each Punjab district and the Punjab Chiefly States and tells how these families, of peasant origins, achieved the 'elite' status during the rule of the Sikhs and the British. In the Preface to the Original Edition of the 'Punjab Chiefs', Sir Lepel Griffin stated, 'The intention of the work has been to give a picture of the Punjab aristocracy as it exists at the present day. No mention has accordingly made been made of many families, Hindu and Muhammadan, once powerful and wealthy, which fell before the Sikhs. No mention has been made of many old Sikh families, whose *jagirs* were seized by Maharaja Ranjit Singh, and whose descendants are now plain husbandmen. A few notices of tribes and families of no present importance have, for special reasons, been given; but general rule, only the histories of those men have been written who possess, at the present time, rank, wealth or local

influence', L.H. Griffin and C.F. Massy, *Chiefs and Families of Note in the Punjab*, op. cit., p. i.
95. David Gilmartin, *Empire and Islam*, op. cit., p. 18.
96. For a detailed discussion on the British administration and the tribes, see David Gilmartin, *Empire and Islam*, op. cit., pp. 18-38.
97. David Page, 1987, *Prelude to Partition: The Indian Muslims and the Imperial System of Control 1920-1932*, Karachi: Oxford University Press, p. 49.
98. Ibid.
99. Ian Talbot, *Pakistan: A Modern History*, op. cit., p. 58.
100. David Page, *Prelude to Partition*, op. cit., pp. 51-2.
101. Ian Talbot, *Punjab and the Raj*, op. cit., p. 42.
102. See George F. MacMunn, 1979, *The Martial Races of India* [1930], Delhi: Mittal Publications.
103. See Stephen P. Cohen, *The Indian Army: Its Contribution to the Development of a Nation*, op. cit.; S.P. Cohen, *The Pakistan Army*, op. cit.; S.P. Cohen, *Security Decision-Making in Pakistan*, op. cit.
104. S.P. Cohen, *The Indian Army: Its Contribution to the Development of a Nation*, op. cit., p. 54.
105. *Imperial Legislative Council Debates, 1917–1918*, 13 September 1917, pp. 233-4, PA.
106. Ibid.
107. O' Dwyer to Chelmsford, 12 April, and 6 May 1918, Chelmsford papers, MSS Eur. E 264 20, India Office Record [henceforth IOR].
108. Ian Talbot, *Pakistan: A Modern History*, op. cit., p. 61.
109. Ibid.
110. Ibid.
111. See M.S.D. Butler, 1921, *Record of War Services in the Attock District 1914-1919*, Lahore: Government Printing Punjab, PA. (nd), *War Services of the Shahpur District*, Lahore: Government Printing Punjab, pp. 37-50, PA.
112. For the list of tribes listed as 'agriculturist tribes' see S. Gurcharn Singh, 1901, *The Punjab Alienation of Land Act XIII of 1900*, Lahore: n.p., PA. For example in Jhang, the agriculturist tribes included the Jats, Rajputs, Bilochs, Syeds, Koreshis, Kokaras, and Nekokaras. In Multan the list included the Kharals, Awans, Mughals, Pathans, Khokars, Arains, Gujars, Ods, and Mahtams, in addition to Jats, Rajputs, Bilochs, Syeds and Koreshis.
113. Khaild B. Sayeed, *Politics in Pakistan*, op. cit., p. 7.
114. For instance, Pir Sultan Ali Shah, head of the Syeds of Jahanian Shah in Jhang, received five squares as a 'landed gentry' grant, a First Class *Khillat* in 1917, and a Sword of Honour in 1919, and Syed Ghulam Mohammad Shah was given a seat on the Bench of Honorary Magistrate at Sahiwal for their 'hard work to induce the people of their *zail* to enlist, and met with a very fair measure of success', *War Services of the Shahpur District*, op. cit., p. 37.
115. Ian Talbot, *Punjab and the Raj, 1849-1947*, op. cit., p. 60.
116. Ibid., p. 61.
117. For details of these rewards see Chopra, *Chiefs and Families*, vol. 1, pp. 195-6, 220, 250-1, 356, 363-4, 416-17, 468-9, 492, 500; vol. 2, pp. 40, 91, 108-9, 118, 203-5, 224, 234, 238, 248, 276, 290-1, 294, 315, 324, 32, 331, 333-4, 339, 345, 359-62, 369, 376-7, 381, 385, and 1876; *Titled Gentlemen and Chiefs other than Ruling Chiefs*, Lahore: Government Civil Secretariat Press, pp. 100-1, 112-13, PA.

COLONIAL CAPITALISM AND THE PUNJAB   39

118. G. Ouselev and W.G. Davies, 1886, 'Report on the Revised Settlement of the Shahpoor District in the Rawlpindee Division'. Lahore: Government Printing Punjab, p. 43, PA.
119. Revenue Department Proceedings, 3 July 1858, no. 44, PA. In this letter 8 June 1858, G.F. Edmonstone, Secretary to the Govt. of India with the Governor-General, wrote to the Chief Commissioner of Punjab, 'As it is probable that, in rewarding the good services of those who may have distinguished themselves in aiding the British Government during the late disturbances, grants of land, either entirely or in part rent-free, may be made to such persons in perpetuity or for a term of years, I am directed to intimate that, in the opinion of the Right Hon'ble the Governor-General, it is very desirable that these grants should be conferred by a written deed, and that an express condition should be inserted, making the continuance of the grant dependant on the good conduct of the grantee and his successors, the holding being liable to resumption in case of any violation of this condition'.
120. 1866, General Report on the Administration of the Punjab Territories for the year 1865-66, Para 24, Lahore: Government Printing Punjab, PA.
121. For rules for guidance of honorary magistrates, see *Judicial Department Proceedings*, 11 January 1862, nos. 12-12.5, PA.
122. *Judicial Department Proceedings*, 23 November 1867, no. 41, PA.
123. As a Court of Wards, the deputy commissioner was empowered to take charge of the management of the estates of female, minors, idiots, lunatics, and inheritors considered otherwise to be unfit for direct management. In the case of minors the jurisdiction of the Court of Wards extended to the education of wards. Powers of deputy commissioners and commissioners conferred on them under Section 4 (3) of the Punjab Court of Ward Act, II of 1903; see Rules of General Procedure under Section 54 of the Punjab Court of Wards Act, II of 1903; 1935, *Court of Wards, Account Code,* Lahore: Government Printing, Punjab, pp. 29-34, PA.
124. 'Report of the Administration of estates under the charge of the Court of Wards for the year ending 30 September 1895, Lahore: Government Printing, Punjab, 1896, p. 3, PA; and Punjab Departments Annual Reports, L5 VI (3), IOR. For instance the Tiwana family of Kalra estate in Shahpur proved to be the most loyal family of the Raj, Khizr Hayat Tiwana as a minor heir was put under the supervision of the colonial state and his estate Kalra was developed as one of the largest and most influential estate under the control of the Court of Wards Administration.
125. See note 90.
126. Michael O' Dwyer, 1925, *India As I Knew It, 1885-1925,* London: Constable & Company Ltd., p. 214; 1923, *India's Contribution to the Great War,* Calcutta: Government Central Press, Appendix C, p. 276, PA.
127. See 'Speech by Sir Michael O' Dwyer in the Punjab Legislative Council, 26 April 1918', *War Speeches of Sir Michael O' Dwyer Lieutenant Governor of the Punjab,* op. cit.
128. As a reward, generous land grants were given to the servicemen in 'Canal Colonies'. At the end of the First World War, over 420,000 acres of colony land was distributed to just over 6000 commissioned and non-commissioned srmy officers. See B. Josh, 1979, *communist Movement in the Punjab 1921-1947,* New Delhi: Peoples Publishing House, p. 25. Similarly Muslim landowners and Pirs who were instrumental in raising recruits were also given land grants in canal colonies. These land grants became the major tool through which the landed class was created in the Punjab. See Imran Ali, *The Punjab Under Imperialism, 1885-1947,* op. cit.; and *War Speeches of Sir Michael O' Dwyer Lieutenant Governor of the Punjab,* op. cit.

129. Speech of Sir Michael O' Dwyer, Lieutenant Governor of the Punjab, delivered at the Special Durbar held at Dera Ghazi Khan on 18 February 1918, *War Speeches of Sir Michael O' Dwyer Lieutenant Governor of the Punjab*, op. cit., p. 110.
130. Franchise proposals of the Punjab Government, L/Parl./409B, pp. 147-205, IOR.
131. Ibid. In the urban areas the number of seats was restricted to a bare minimum and very high voting qualifications were proposed. These qualifications restricted the vote to 3 per cent of the urban population. Franchise Proposals of the Punjab Government.
132. Ibid., pp. 150-1.
133. GI Reforms Office, Deposit, April 1920, no. 5. Proceedings of the Governor's Conference on the Reforms, 23 January 1920, L/Parl./409B, IOR.
134. Ibid.
135. GI Reforms Office, General, Deposit, Dec. 1919, No. 12: Memorandum by Umar Hayat Khan Tiwana, July 1919, L/Parl./409B, IOR. His son Khizr Hayat Tiwana became the second premier of the autonomous Punjab in 1942. F. Popham Young, the commissioner of Rawalpindi, writes in his comments 'the Tiwana Maliks feel, what is indeed the truth, that Government has made them what they are, and they have responded by proving themselves to be loyal supporters of Government not with mere passivity but with real activity'. Comments of F. Popham, Register of Landed Gentry grants, Rawalpindi Division, 15, Punjab Board of Revenue, file 301/1176KW.
136. Ian Talbot, *Punjab under the Raj*, op. cit., p. 46.
137. According to the 1921 census, the communal ratio of population was; Muslims 55.33 per cent; Hindus 33.58 per cent; and Sikhs 11.00 per cent. The ratio of Muslim voters was highest in rural areas having a record of recruiting servicemen, i.e. voters in Jhelum and Rawalpindi comprised 14 per cent of the Muslim electorate in the Punjab. See Reports of Indian Statutory Commission, 1930, Vol. 2, London: His Majesty's Stationary Office. [Survey CMD 3568] IOR, p. 42.
138. Andrew J. Major, 'The Punjabi Chieftains and the Transition from Sikh to British Rule', in D.A. Low (ed.), op. cit., p. 53.
139. Andrew Major, 1996, *Return to Empire: Punjab Under the Sikhs and British in The Mid-Nineteenth Century*, Karachi: Oxford University Press, pp. 127-33.
140. S.S. Thorburn, 1971 *The Punjab in Peace and War*, New York: AMS Press, p. 229.
141. Khushwant Singh, 1963-6, *History of the Sikhs, vol. 2, 1839-1964*, Princeton: Princeton University Press, p. 94.
142. Forty-nine British civil and military officers of the company were chosen to serve under the board headed by Henry Lawrence.
143. Civil and criminal justice, and land revenue administration, were based upon codes, circulars, and rules issued by Dalhousie to the Board of Administration. See Dalhousie's instructions to the Board of Administration, 1871. Selected Circular Orders of the Board of Administration in the General and Political Departments, Lahore: Government Printing, Punjab, PA.
144. Erick Stokes, 1959, *The English Utilitarians and India*, London: Oxford University Press, p. 268.
145. 1871, Selected Circular Orders of the Board of Administration in the General and Political Departments, Lahore, Government Printing Punjab, PA.
146. Sir Edward Blunt, 1937, *The I.C.S.: The Indian Civil Service*, London: Faber, p. 14.
147. S.S. Thorburn, *The Punjab in Peace and War*, op. cit., p. 165.
148. The distinction between regulatory and non-regulatory systems was simple. In regulatory system, the province was to be regulated by an Act of Parliament or

Regulations of the Government of India. In 1793, Lord Cornwallis issued a revised code of forty-eight regulations for the presidency of Bengal. This body of legislation, subsequently amended, was known as the Bengal Regulations. In the Regulation provinces the head of a district was a judge and magistrate, with powers to adjudicate civil disputes and minor criminal cases. More serious cases were handled by the provincial courts of appeal and circuit. The chief civil and criminal courts at Calcutta controlled these courts. In the non-regulation provinces, the procedures were simple, providing discretionary powers to the official in the conduct of administration.

149. Sir Patrick Fagan, 'District Administration in the United Provinces, Central Provinces and the Punjab, 1818-1857', in H.H. Dodwell (ed.), 1932, *The Cambridge History of India Volume VI: The Indian Empire 1858-1918*, Cambridge: Cambridge University Press, p. 87.
150. *Punjab Administrative Reports 1922-23*, Lahore: Government Printing Punjab, p. 17, PA.
151. See Punjab Legislative Council Debates, 1897-1936, V9 3419-V9 3455, IOR.
152. Ibid.
153. Ibid.
154. For a detailed discussion on the British administration and the tribes, see David Gilmartin, *Empire and Islam*, op. cit., pp. 18-38.
155. Khalid Bin Sayeed, *Politics in Pakistan*, op. cit., p. 8.
156. Hamza Alavi, 'India: Transition form Feudalism to Colonial Capitalism', op. cit., p. 371.
157. Khalid Bin Sayeed, *Politics in Pakistan*, op. cit., p. 5.
158. Proceedings of the Lieutenant Governor, 29 February 1872, Punjab Board of Revenue, file 61/142.
159. Leslie S. Saunders, 1873, *Report on the Revised Land Revenue Settlement of the Lahore District in the Lahore Division of the Punjab, 1865-69*, Lahore: Government Printing Punjab, pp. 68-9, PA.
160. K.B. Sayeed, *Politics in Pakistan*, op. cit., p. 5.
161. See C.L. Tupper, 1880, *Punjab's Customary Law: Statements of Customary Law in Different Districts*, Vol. II, Simla: Government Central Branch Press, pp. 1-37, PA; David Gilmartin, 'Kinship, Women and Politics in Twentieth Century Punjab', in Gail Minault (ed.), 1981, *The Extended Family: Women and Political Participation in India and Pakistan*, Columbia: Columbia University Press, pp. 151-73.
162. David Gilmartin, 'Kinship, Women and Politics in Twentieth Century Punjab', in Gail Minault (ed.), op. cit., pp. 153-7.
163. Government letter to Settlement Commissioner, Delhi division, 30 June 1873, Punjab Board of Revenue, file 61/142.
164. P.J. Fagan, Jr., 25 October 1890 Secretary to Financial Commissioner to Revenue Secretary, Punjab Board of Revenue, file 61/134.
165. Shahpur District Gazetteer, 1917, p. 243, PA.
166. 'Agricultural Tribes' were gazetted by name in each district. Status of these tribes was to be determined by their agricultural character and by their political importance to the British. N.G. Barrier, 1966, *The Punjab Alienation of Land Bill of 1900*, Durham: Duke University Press, p. 112.
167. K.B. Sayeed, *Politics in Pakistan*, op. cit., p. 7.
168. Michael O' Dwyer, *India as I Knew It, 1885-1925*, op. cit., p. 39.
169. I. Talbot, *Punjab and the Raj 1847-1947*, op. cit., p. 40.

170. See Note by Sir Michael O' Dwyer, 8 August 1913, Lieutenant Governor, on the Lower Bari Doab colonization scheme, Punjab Board of Revenue, file 301/1176.
171. See Register of Landed Gentry grants, for grants to the Tiwanas Rawalpindi division, p. 15; for grants to the Dera Ghazi Khan Baloch), Multan division, pp. 14–19, PA.
172. Imran Ali, 'Punjab and the Retardation of Nationalism', in D.A. Low (ed.), op. cit., p. 44.
173. Ibid.
174. Ibid.
175. Imran Ali, *The Punjab under Imperialism, 1857-1947*, op. cit., p. 242.

2

Constructing the Post-colonial State

CONSTRUCTION OF A POST-COLONIAL STATE IN THE CONTEXT OF THE AMERICAN POWER SYSTEM: A NEO-COLONIAL MODEL

In Chapter 1, colonial capitalism and its impact on the political economy of India was examined, particularly the province of Punjab. In this chapter, the construction of the post-colonial state in the context of the American Power System, or Neo-Colonialism, that evolved during the period following the Second World War, will be explored. Although the country got its freedom from British colonialism in 1947, its representatives—the civil bureaucracy, army, and the landed class—operating within the imperatives of neo-colonial capitalism, continued to dominate the national scene and the representative institutions were never allowed to develop. Soon after its birth, the new state of Pakistan was subjected to neo-colonialism in the shape of the 'American power system' and the British colonial capitalism was replaced 'American neo-colonial capitalism'. In this process, the alliance of elite groups, rather than representative institutions, became the key to exercising political power in Pakistan.

This chapter focuses on the dialectic between state construction and political process in Pakistan in its early years, and examines how international political and economic factors, coupled with the domestic and regional factors, shaped the structure of the state in order to protect the interests of the players of the neo-colonial world in the Cold War era.

Pakistan inherited the legacy of a 'security state', a colonial legacy which dominated her colonial past and continued to shadow the process of nation-building in the post-colonial state. Strategic and economic consequences of the partition placed the rulers of the new state into a challenging situation where they were forced to make some vital decisions: Either to declare their independent policy by delinking themselves from the historical baggage of the colonial past, or to continue with the colonial legacy of the obsession with the Soviet invasion, and be included in the 'free world of capitalism', protected and safeguarded by the 'American system of power'. Since the democratic structure on which the new state was to be built was very fragile, it crumbled under the heavy burden of the pressures generated by the Cold War, even before its birth-proper.

The colonial legacy of 'a security state' in the region was reinforced by the minds of a select group of civil and military bureaucracy, trained by the colonial strategists. This elite group became the influencing force of the nation-building process in the formative years of the new state's life, at the expense of the representative institutions. As a result, the security of the new state was tied with the US, the new custodian of the 'free world', in its 'Cold War' against the Kremlin design 'of a world dominated by its will'. Directing the actions of the defence establishments in the Third World, dependent on the economic and military assistance of the US, was a vital part of the US strategy during the Cold War. To strengthen the position of the military elite in these countries, the US had been increasingly 'stressing the necessity for training and education in more than narrowly military skills.'[1] This training, whether political or military, was done primarily under the United States Military Assistance Program (MAP Training). MAP trained over 300,000 officers and other ranks in the US or overseas, from over seventy countries during 1950-1971.[2] Defence establishments in Third World countries, which are often larger than required, have not only created underdevelopment but also encouraged various forms of authoritarianism, which replaced the participation of people with 'elite's government'—civil-military control, absolute monarchy and civilian dictatorship. All these elite governments were dependent on, or linked to, the 'American system of power'. The new, poor nation-states of the 'free world' were forced to enter into all kinds of economic and military agreements to fight the 'created' fear of communism, and thereby, protect the capitalist economy of the free world. 'A stage was reached when the fight against the USSR was equivalent to the fight for control of the world's natural and human resources of the benefit of the "Free World" against those of the East led by the USSR. Oil, strategic materials, and mineral wealth as well as trade and investment outlets became vital strategic areas to defend.'[3]

Many writers concerned with the issue of development view the 'American system of power' as a new form of colonialism which ensures political and economic control over the 'free world'.[4] The 'free world' was persuaded to opt for the capitalist model of development, which favours growth over distribution. The elite governments were less concerned with the poverty of the people and more willing to spend on large defence establishments. The capitalist model of economic growth, along with large defence establishments, has not only drowned the majority of people of these nation-states into an ocean of absolute poverty but also trapped their future generations into a web of 'dependency'. Before we continue this discussion, it seems necessary to understand the background of the Cold War era and the resulting American system of power.

THE BACKGROUND OF THE COLD WAR ERA AND THE RESULTING AMERICAN SYSTEM OF POWER

This phenomenon can be understood in the theoretical framework of the holistic and historical approach of the 'dependency paradigm'. This perspective argues that the development of national or regional economies should be associated with the history and nature of imperialism. Furthermore, it suggests that we need to examine the underdevelopment of the Third World in the context of the Cold War, when the world was divided between capitalism and communism. This perspective views the 'free world' as the new form of colonial capitalism, whose champion is the United States with its new system of power. The American system of power began to take shape during the last few years of the Second World War, when the colonial powers were shrinking and the Soviet Revolution was sweeping the world. Reflecting on the period, Perry Anderson writes:

> Between 1943 and 1945, the Roosevelt administration worked on the shape of the American system of power, which it could see that victory over Germany and Japan, amidst mounting Russian casualties and British debts, was bringing. From the start, Washington pursued two integrally connected strategic goals. On the one hand, the US set out to make the world safe for capitalism. That meant according top priority to containing the USSR and halting the spread of revolution beyond its borders, wherever it could not directly contest the spoils of war, as in Eastern Europe....On the other hand, Washington was determined to ensure uncontested American primacy within world capitalism.[5]

The United States and the Soviet Union emerged as the two main players of the Cold War game, which began at the end of the Second World War, with the Yalta Conference. This meeting of the 'Big Three',[6] at the former palace of Czar Nicholas on the Crimean southern shore of the Black Sea, took place between 4-11 February 1945. The Soviet army had reached the Oder River and was poised for the final attack on Berlin but on 3 February, Stalin had ordered Zhukov to pause while the conference was in session. His occupation of Poland was complete, and he possessed command of the largest army in Europe; twelve million soldiers in 300 divisions. Eisenhower's four million men in eighty-five divisions were still west of the Rhine.[7] Within two months of the Yalta Conference, Roosevelt died of massive cerebral haemorrhage. Critics accused Roosevelt of being a 'sell-out' at Yalta, of giving away Eastern Europe to Stalin; of 'secret deals' with a ruthless dictator; Russia's demand for twenty billion dollars in reparations from Germany; for agreeing to Russian occupation of territory up to the Curzon line; for three seats in the United Nations; for territory on the Far East including Outer Mongolia, South Sakhalin Island, the Kuriles.[8]

Whatever the truth, the fact remains that both Roosevelt and Churchill recognized the reality of Soviet power in 1945.[9] The year 1946 is marked with Cold War demonstrations when US President Harry Truman declared 'no more recognition of communist governments' and 'I'm sick of babying the Soviets'.[10] This declaration was followed by Churchill's visit to the United States on 9 February 1946. Churchill argued for a hard-line response and the need to create a unified Anglo-American opposition to Stalin. In his famous speech 'Sinews of Peace' on 5 March 1946, at Westminster College (Fulton, Missouri), Churchill, expressing the need for a special relationship between the British Commonwealth Empire and the United States, stated, that it should include:

> The continuance of the intimate relationship between our military advisers leading to common study of potential dangers, the similarity of weapons and manuals of instructions, and to the interchange of officers and cadets at technical colleges'. He further declared that the method of realizing 'our overall strategic concept should carry with it the continuance of the present facilities for mutual security by the joint use of all Naval and Air Force bases in the possession of either country all over the world.[11]

In March, Truman demanded that Russia get out of Iran, and in August, he supported Turkey's opposition to Stalin's demands. Under the influence of his advisors, especially George Marshall, Truman supported their hard-line advice and policies. By 1947, these policies came to be known as 'containment'. George Kennan became the 'father of containment' with his 'long telegram' on 22 February.[12] Kennan's depiction of communism as a 'malignant parasite' that had to be contained by all possible measures became the ideological foundation of the Truman Doctrine, the Marshall Plan, and the National Security Act in 1947. In his inaugural address on 20 January 1949, Truman made four points about his 'program for peace and freedom': to support the UN, the European Recovery Program, the collective defence of the North Atlantic, and a 'bold new program' for technical aid to poor nations.[13] It was believed that because of his programs, 'the future of mankind would be assured in a world of justice, harmony and peace'.[14] Thus containment was not just a policy, it was a way of life. The probable fission bomb capacity of the Soviet Union greatly intensified the Soviet threat to the security of the United States, which culminated in NSC 68 that declared:

> In particular, the United States now faces the contingency that within the next four or five years the Soviet Union will possess the military capability of delivering a surprise atomic attack of such weight that the United States must have substantially increased general air, ground, and sea strength, atomic capabilities, and air and civilian defences to deter war and to provide reasonable assurance, in the event of war, that it could survive the initial blow and go on to the eventual attainment of its objectives. In turn, this contingency requires the intensification of our efforts in the fields of intelligence and research and development.[15]

Fearing the threat of Soviet atomic capabilities, it was felt that the US programs and plans were dangerously inadequate, in both timing and scope to accomplish the rapid progress towards the attainment of the United States' political, economic, and military objectives. It was argued that the:

> continuation of...[present] trends would result in a serious decline in the strength of the free world relative to the Soviet Union and its satellites... These trends lead in the direction of isolation not by deliberate decision but by lack of the necessary basis for a vigorous initiative in the conflict with the Soviet Union.[16]

Europe was defeated and the US assumed the 'centre of power in the free world'. This was reflected in the conclusion, which stated:

> we must organize and enlist the energies and resources of the free world in a positive program for peace which...[would] frustrate the Kremlin design

for world domination by creating a situation in the free world to which the Kremlin...[would] be compelled to adjust.'[17]

It was believed that without such a cooperative effort, led by the United States, the free world would have to make gradual withdrawals under pressure until they discover one day that they had sacrificed positions of vital interest.[18] To secure this 'position of vital interest', a much more 'rapid and concerted build-up of the actual strength' of both the United States and other nations of the free world was suggested in the analysis. The program envisaged 'the political and economic measure with which and the military shield behind which the free world...[could] work to frustrate the Kremlin design by the strategy of the Cold War'.[19]

Avoiding a direct war with the Soviet Union, the Cold War was conceived with the aim of frustrating 'the Kremlin design by the steady development of the moral and material strength by the free world and its projection into the Soviet world in such a way as to bring about an internal change in the Soviet system.'[20] The conclusion summarized that 'by means of a rapid and sustained build-up of the political, economic, and military strength of the free world, and by means of an affirmative program intended to wrest the initiative from the Soviet Union,' the United States would be in a position to 'confront with convincing evidence of the determination and ability of the free world to frustrate the Kremlin design of a world dominated by its will.'[21] It was thought that 'such evidence...[was] the only means short of war, which eventually...[might] force the Kremlin to abandon its...[existing] course of action and to negotiate acceptable agreements on issues of major importance.'[22]

For American policymakers, the Cold War was, in fact, a real war in which the survival of the free world was at stake, and Pakistan, before its birth, was destined to enter into this war. Pakistan's proximity to the Soviet Union and China—which formed the emerging communist bloc—and the Middle East and Iran, the centre of oil resources or 'wells of power', placed it in a very critical position on the 'security map of the free world'. The fear of losing 'a half billion South Asians—including standing armies of over half a million and British trained veterans numbering some two million—to the half billion Chinese...at the disposal of the communist bloc' forced the US National Security Council (NSC) to advise President Truman to approve a government policy NSC 98/1 on 25 January 1951, entitled 'The Position of the

United States with respect to South Asia', following the line of the 'Containment Doctrine'.[23] Pakistan was a 'strategically important country...which could contribute substantially to the defence of the Middle East'[24] and had to be made an integral component of the 'American Power System'. Pakistan's adherence to the American power system can only be explained by examining the colonial legacy of a 'security state' in the framework of the 'containment doctrine'.

Continuation of the Colonial Legacy of a Security State

The vital strategic location of Pakistan made it the only logical base from which to launch an attack on the southern and eastern areas of the USSR.[25] British strategists, to secure their colonial interests, had exploited this location and it continued to be exploited by the neo-colonial interests in the Cold War era.

> The Mesopotamian campaign of the First World War, and the strategic movements of the allies in Iraq and Persia in the Second World War, were made possible from the Indian base.[26]

British strategists were worried about the Indian defence in case of the Soviet invasion after their departure, and the partition of colonial India into Pakistan and Hindustan. The British chiefs of staff's main concern was the continued use of the air bases of the North West Frontier by entering into a defence agreement with the new successor state. American strategic planners equally shared this concern during the foreign ministers' conference held in London in November 1945, when the Secretary of State, James Byrnes, requested for American control of these bases and pursued the request throughout 1946.[27] At the end of the Second World War, exhausted Britain 'had little energy remaining to retain' its Indian Empire 'that had already come apart', and was at the verge of a communal war.[28] In the aftermath of the Second World War, 'it was clear to Whitehall and the Downing Street that British power in the world had been superseded by the Americans' and with the beginning of Cold War era 'a *Pax Americana* had settled over the planet.'[29]

With the Partition in sight, 'neither Mountbatten nor Field Marshal Auchinleck wanted to see the division of the Indian Army.'[30] The fear of dividing the Indian army 'for the first time', forced the British strategists to publicly introduce the 'subcontinent's strategic needs into the deliberations, especially the British perception of the region's geographical position with the onset of the Cold War.'[31] Discussing 'defence implications of a partition of India', Lt.-Gen. Arthur F. Smith (chief of the general staff in India), showed his deep concern for the future defence strategy of Pakistan and Hindustan and suggested 'a common strategy, a common military administration, and a common higher direction as the only sound military solution.'[32]

It was feared that no state could afford to remain indifferent in case of a Soviet threat to either state. Pakistan's defence was more significant since it was considered a buffer between Hindustan and any likely communist invasion. Therefore, Hindustan needed to be 'vitally concerned that Pakistan should not be subdued.' It was clearly stated that in case of a Soviet invasion, even united India was not in a position to defend itself 'without outside assistance', and to save Pakistan from Soviet attack, Britain and Hindustan had to combine their forces.[33]

The other argument for the common defence strategy presented by the British chief of the general staff was that Pakistan's financial resources would not allow it to maintain an effective defence establishment. A large defence establishment would exhaust the new state's scarce financial resources and create 'political and internal defence problems'. A separate defence establishment for Pakistan was not only considered 'economically wasteful and quite impracticable but a threat to its political stability.'[34] Before their departure, British military strategists wanted to secure the continued use of the Indian subcontinent by the Western Allies. Their main concern was to protect Indian soil from being used against the interests of the neo-colonial world, and to frustrate the Kremlin design of a world dominated by its will.

After the hopes of a joint defence establishment vanished, British strategists pinned down their aspirations to woo Pakistan on towing the line, and felt that 'an arrangement with Pakistan alone' would meet their strategic requirements. The 'arrangement' was that Pakistan should 'maintain a defence organization larger than what it would need for its own purposes.'[35] To achieve this end, Britain was ready to offer any 'inducements, material, financial, or political' to persuade Pakistan 'to do what...[she] wanted.'[36] It is shocking to see how British strategists changed their line of argument from common defence establishment to persuade Pakistan to 'maintain a defence organization larger than what it would need for its "own purposes" which was earlier considered as "suicidal", "ruining itself",' economically wasteful and quite impractical.

Considering the military commitments of India and Pakistan, immediately after the partition of the Indian army, British defence strategists concluded that:

> '...besides the normal commitment of maintaining law and order, India [had]...the Kashmir commitment which absorb[ed] a large part of her military forces. This commitment...[was] one which India...[could] increase or limit as she desire[d]...India...[had] no other military commitments at...[the moment]'. While Pakistan's 'military commitments and responsibilities' were viewed as 'unquestionably complex and of great importance', it was concluded that 'it seem[d] clear that unless Pakistan... [was] able to fulfil these commitments she...[would] be unable to maintain the integrity of her frontiers, her position within the Commonwealth and her influence and prestige in the Muslim World.[37]

Pakistan's 'influence and prestige in the Muslim World' were significant factors, which had to be exploited in favour of British and American strategic interests, especially in the Middle Eastern region which was rich in oil resources. Identifying the strategic significance of Pakistan for the defence of the Middle East against the threat of Russian's control of their oil fields, Sir Olaf Caroe, a member of the British India Civil Service, while giving his policy recommendations for the US in the late 1940s, stated that:

> the establishment of independent states on the Indian Peninsula entail[ed]... a new approach to old problems. In this quarter, as on the Northwest Frontier, Pakistan...[had] succeeded to much of India's responsibility... India...[was] no longer an obvious base for the Middle Eastern defence. It stands on the fringe of the defence periphery; Pakistan on the other hand lies well within the grouping of South Western Asia.[38]

Realizing that as an end result of the Second World War, the United States was going to assume the role of the policeman of this region, Sir Caroe reminded Americans that:

> it...[was] as if American concern had been enlisted just in time to share in the results of the enterprise and experience of Englishmen before they quitted the position of authority which had been held against every challenge for more than a century in India, and on its confines.[39]

The basic line of argument was that, 'both...faced the imminence of Russia towering over these lands.'[40] The imperial defence policy was going to become the American policy of containment in the Cold War era. The March 1947 Truman Doctrine, which established the American containment policy, 'cantered on checking the spread of Soviet influence...had suddenly become a factor in the equation of Indian independence.'[41]

After the Chinese Revolution, Pakistan and India had to be protected from 'ultimate communist control' due to the 'political and economic dangers of communist encirclement of the Indian and Pakistan land frontiers.' It was feared that, 'if the Indian sub-continent also became communist it would be unlikely that South East Asia could hold out for long against communist infiltration.' Furthermore, it was calculated that, 'in war the loss of the facilities and resources of India and Pakistan, quite apart from their possible use by the Russians, would be a most serious disadvantage.'[42] The British Foreign Office (London) was engaged in appreciating the consequences of a communist domination of the whole, or, at the very least, a very large part of China, as early as November 1948. The minutes of a secret meeting held at the Foreign Office (London) on 10 November 1948, reveal that the Foreign Office, London, was given the task to provide an appreciation of the situation in the aftermath of communist domination of China.[43] In addition to the Foreign Office's appreciation of the situation, the officials in the Ministry of Defence (London) decided to prepare a memorandum to discuss the political and strategic effect on both India and Pakistan of the communist domination of China.[44] The considerations to be taken in account included the fear of 'a greatly increased risk of communist agitation in India and Pakistan', particularly 'in the Near East Frontier area, and Bengal (tea gardens and jute), and Kashmir.'[45] In Kashmir, Sheikh Abdullah's government was seen as being sympathetic to communist elements, and being adjacent to Sinkiang, which was governed by the communists, it posed a serious threat. This forced the military strategists in London to suggest securing 'a settlement of the quarrels between India and Pakistan, particularly in relation to Kashmir.'[46] It was calculated that in the absence of a resolution in Kashmir, 'Pakistan would in the last resort prefer to accept Russian help at Russia's price rather than submit to Hindu domination.'[47]

The Chinese Revolution forced the British strategists to suggest that the 'defence of the Indian sub-continent...[could] be effectively undertaken only by the joint efforts of India and Pakistan.' To achieve this purpose it was proposed that India had to '...[compose] her differences with Pakistan'. Due to Pakistan's strategic location, the protectors of the 'free world' could not afford its inclusion in the communist bloc, 'there...[was] no question about Pakistan's responsibility for the North West Frontier watch and ward and for coastal protection.'[48] It was felt that 'the burden of the North West Frontier on anything approaching the scale which was customary when the British government controlled India would be almost certainly too great to be borne by Pakistan in the absence of assistance from India or this country'. This was the view of the British Defence Ministry on the question of providing military aid to Pakistan.[49] A report of the Joint Planning Staff dated 12 January 1949, concluded 'to continue to give all possible military support to Pakistan giving her special considerations over the claims of India in view of her lack of productive capacity and of her present military commitments.'[50] This conclusion was based upon the observation of the Commonwealth Relations Office, which stated:

> We feel that the defence of Indian sub-continent is a task which can be undertaken effectively only by the joint co-operation of India and Pakistan. We also feel, in view of Pakistan's considerable military commitments for the defence of this area from external aggression and in view of her total lack of productive capacity for warlike stores, it is particularly desirable that we should afford her all possible military assistance.[51]

With regard to India, it was suggested that 'the case of Pakistan might perhaps with advantage, receive more emphases'.[52] In a draft report prepared by the Joint Planning Staff for the Chiefs of Staff Committee, with the objective to examine the 'contribution, which Pakistan could make to Commonwealth defence in a war with the Soviet Powers', various possibilities of a Soviet attack were considered. It was concluded that 'the maximum contribution Pakistan could make in war' would include:

> (a) to ensure her internal security and undertake responsibility for her defence on land and for defence of her ports and coastal communications; (b) provide the necessary bases and communications for defence and offence and in particular, strategic air bases; and (c) provide some land and sea forces for operations beyond her frontiers.[53]

Pakistan's defence was vital for the 'capitalist world' to safeguard its control over the Middle East's oil and while reflecting this concern, the draft report noted, the land communications between the Middle East oil areas and Egypt are very meagre compared with the sea communication to India. From this aspect, therefore, the Indian subcontinent and in particular Western Pakistan forms the best base from which to conduct the defence or recapture these oil areas.[54]

Earlier, in March 1948, the chief of staff (COS) wrote a letter to the government of Pakistan in which 'they gave certain points which they thought should be considered in any defence talks when they took place.' Those certain points were similar to the ones stated in the draft report prepared by the Joint Planning Staff for the Chiefs of Staff Committee dated 27 April 1949, with the objective of examining the 'contribution which Pakistan could make to Commonwealth Defence in a war with the Soviet Powers'. In September 1948, General Cawthorn, while informing the British government that Prime Minister Liaquat Ali Khan was anxious to have the assurance before the opening of the Commonwealth Prime Ministers' Conference in London, said, that 'we should welcome an approach by Pakistan to open defence talks with us.'[55] After the conference in October 1948, General Cawthorn informed the British government that 'Mr Liaquat Ali now regarded the COS letter as dead'. However, he added that:

> Pakistan would forward their suggestion as asked for in the paper on Commonwealth Consultation but if, in the meantime, HMG in the UK indicated a wish to proceed with unilateral discussions with Pakistan on a basis similar to that set out in the COS agenda, applied to Pakistan alone, Pakistan would gladly agree.[56]

There was no official request from the government of Pakistan asking what 'contribution she [could] make to Commonwealth defence' and it was considered that 'General Cawthorn [might have] expressed such sentiments unofficially to the members of the COS Committee.'[57] On 16 April 1949, the following letter was handed to Liaquat Ali Khan:

> HMG in the UK would be glad to open defence discussions with the Government of Pakistan at some time during the current year. Before suggesting a firm date for these discussions, which would cover a wide field in subjects of a top-secret nature, the UK Government would be glad to know whether this proposal is acceptable to the Government of Pakistan.[58]

The Joint Planning Staff's draft report of 27 April 1949, took into consideration the note prepared by the secretary of defence of the

CONSTRUCTING THE POST-COLONIAL STATE

British government dated 19 April 1949, expressing the expectations of British strategists with regard to the contribution of Pakistan to Commonwealth defence, which included:

(a) Pakistan should aim to ensure her own internal security and to provide for her own land and sea defence.
(b) The allies would wish to have the right to use strategic bomber bases in Pakistan should the need arise.
(c) Pakistan should be asked to plan...for the defence of Middle East oil areas....
(d) Should the Middle East oil areas be lost to the Allies, they would request to use the Karachi base from which to mount an expedition for their recovery.
(e) Pakistan should agree to raise in war, within the limits of her manpower, ancillary units such as pioneer battalions, and transport companies to supplement the Allied land forces.
(f) She should aim to be capable of taking and sharing the control of sea communication in the Indian Ocean, particularly in the Arabian Sea and the Bay of Bengal.
(g) She should aim to be capable of carrying out docking, refitting, and repair requirements for her own ships and the Commonwealth ships operating in the area.
(h) The Allies would require air transit facilities for military aircraft across Pakistan territory.[59]

In his note sent on 3 May 1949, the secretary of defence re-emphasized the 'value of Pakistan as a main base', arguing that 'Pakistan is well situated to assist in the defence or recapture of the Middle East Oil area and could provide air fields for the strategic bomber offensive.'[60] His analysis was echoed in many recommendations and policy papers of the British Ministry of Defence and Commonwealth Relations Office, suggesting a combined American and British military assistance program for Pakistan and Afghanistan, considering their defence needs.

> It...[was] improbable that the defence needs of Afghanistan, Pakistan and India...[could] be met otherwise than from joint United States and United Kingdom resources. Of these needs...those of Afghanistan and Pakistan are, to us, and the USA, the more important...and we do not wish to drive these countries into asking Russia to provide these needs.[61]

These views were shared by an internal report prepared by the South Asia section of the State Department in November 1949. In the report,

Pakistan was seen as the strongest military power to emerge in Asia between Japan and Turkey. The report considered Pakistan's vital strategic position, its proximity to the oil fields of the Middle East and the Soviet heartland. It was pointed out that Pakistan offered the best possibility of the closest base available to the Soviet Union, in addition to possessing many of the best units of the Second World War, and was having to shoulder the entire burden of defence against the Soviet Union for the whole subcontinent.[62] Later, in December 1950, the US embassy in Pakistan, in its report 'US Strategic Interests in Area', which it submitted to the conference of American ambassadors, held in 1951 in Ceylon, endorsed these views.[63] The report recognized that Pakistan's vital strategic location made it the 'only logical base' from which to launch an attack on southern and eastern areas of the USSR. Therefore, it was considered essential to assure 'the control or cooperation of... Pakistan and deny bases...in this area to the USSR', since otherwise the 'entire East-West line of communication would be...[endangered]'.[64] Earlier in the beginning of 1950, in a top secret letter, the US embassy (Karachi) had asked the Pakistani Inter-Services Intelligence Directorate for detailed information on: (1) airfields in Pakistan, (2) the actual spread of its railway system, (3) classification of major bridges, and (4) facilities for stationing standard divisions in the western border areas of West Pakistan.[65]

In accordance with the role assigned to Pakistan in the Cold War era, in February 1949, General Gracey, the Pakistan army chief, directed Major General Tottenham, then serving as divisional commander in the Pakistan army, 'for moving a Pak[istani] Division into the Iranian Oil Fields to lend a hand in case the British or Americans needed it.'[66] The dispute over the nationalization and control of the Anglo-Iranian oil companies in Iran could lead to a military solution, therefore, they felt it was necessary to fortify Pakistan's defences in Balochistan, along with the Khojak Pass. General Gracey had apparently conceived a war game entitled 'Exercise Stalin', in which the Pakistan army was to fight against the Soviet Union.[67] Apart from the external Soviet threat, building a military establishment was considered essential 'for maintenance of internal security' of Pakistan's territories.[68] It was feared that 'the Soviet Union would stir up as much internal unrest as possible in India and Pakistan, particularly by infiltration and by exploiting local movements such as the Red Shirt of the North West Frontier Province.'[69] It was also assumed that the Soviets 'would endeavour to cause the maximum irredentism and by stirring up the frontier tribes.'[70]

East Bengal was perceived as potential land for germination of communist seeds and had no share in the defence establishment. Due to these 'sins', there were deliberate efforts on the part of Punjab, which emerged as the major partner of the neo-colonialism, to check East Bengal's claim in the state-formation process.

Building of the Defence Establishment at the Cost of Economic Development

There is a strong argument that the Kashmir conflict was deliberately created by the British military strategists in alliance with the Congress leader Jawaharlal Nehru, who was under the strong emotional influence of Lady Edwina, the wife of Lord Mountbatten, the last viceroy of colonial, and the first governor-general of independent India. Creating a 'mutilated, truncated and moth-eaten Pakistan', under the constant threat of siege by an aggressive India, and a strong central government in India led by Nehru, under the close monitoring of Mountbatten, was a two-pronged strategy to provide a rationale for 'defence establishments' in Pakistan and India at the end of their colonial rule after the British lost hope of a common defence establishment to act as a resistance force against the Soviet expansionist designs. Lawrence Ziring notes that 'the British had set the scene for what was to become one of the more intractable, long-term problems of modern diplomacy'.[71] The Kashmir dispute helped the British strategists in alliance with Nehru to keep alive the animosity between India and Pakistan, and a feeling of insecurity amongst people of the newly-created, 'moth-eaten and truncated', Muslim state. Those feelings gained strength by Mountbatten's statements, like the one he had made in a cabinet meeting shortly before Partition, that a truncated Pakistan 'if conceded now was bound to come back later'.[72] Under Mountbatten's influence, Nehru was made to believe that:

> Kashmir...[was] of the most vital significance to India.... [H]ere lies the rub.... We have to see this through to the end...Kashmir is going to be a drain on our resources, but, it is going to be a greater drain on Pakistan,

he wrote to his high commissioner to Pakistan, Sri Prakasha, who admitted to Mountbatten that 'for the sake of peace of all round' the 'best thing' India could do was to hand over Kashmir to Pakistan.[73]

The Kashmir dispute provided the opportunity for General Frank Messervy, commander-in-chief of the Pakistan army, to convince the chiefs of staff that 'the long-term policy of the Government of India would be to seek the subjugation of and incorporation of Pakistan into India' and it was felt obligatory to provide 'every assistance...to the Pakistan armed forces' and build a defence establishment in Pakistan.[74] But surprisingly, when that moment came, just a week after this observation, the acting commander-in-chief of the Pakistan army, General Douglas Gracey, refused to send his men to fight the Indian army marching towards Pakistan after having forcefully occupied the Kashmir valley against the wishes of its people and the maharaja. If General Gracey had obeyed Jinnah's orders, the fate of Kashmir might have been decided according to the wishes of the majority population, and the upkeep of a defence establishment beyond Pakistan's means, which has crippled the national economy, would not have been required. The important question to probe is why the commander-in-chief of the Pakistan army felt obliged to stall instead of obeying Jinnah's orders. The answer lies in the strategic implications of the origin of the Kashmir conflict, which has its seeds in the Partition Plan which was announced on 3 June 1947.

Alex von Tunzelmann claims that the plan announced on 3 June 1947 was not the original plan conceived by Mountbatten and approved by the British government, rather it was a plan smoothed by Jawaharlal Nehru, V.P. Menon, and the then governor of Punjab, Evan Jenkins.[75] Nehru was invited by Mountbatten and his wife Edwina to accompany them for a stay at Simla in May 1947, where he was shown the secret plan of transfer, by Mountbatten. Nehru rejected the plan outright, terming it 'as a picture of fragmentation, and conflict and disorder'. Nehru was assigned the task to smooth the plan into an acceptable shape in consultation with V.P. Menon and Evan Jenkins. Tunzelmann confirms that by that time, Nehru and Edwina were having an 'affair' which could be a great embarrassment for the British government and the Congress if known to the general public. The founding principle of the Partition Plan was the reappointment of Mountbatten as the joint governor-general of the two new dominions to be established as a consequence of the plan, India and Pakistan. 'Telephone calls were made to Congress potentates.... Neither the Muslim League, the princes, nor any other body in India would be given the chance to review the plan before its announcement'.[76] On 18

May, Mountbatten and V.P. Menon left Delhi for London 'to sell the plan to the British government'.[77]

On 2 June 1947, Jinnah and other leaders of the Muslim League came to know about the plan when they were 'summoned' by the viceroy to discuss it along with the leaders of the Congress who were already familiar with the plan. Mountbatten told Jinnah 'that there could not be any question of a "No" from the League'.[78] The next morning, the League and the Congress, both gave their acceptance to the plan of transfer which was announced the same afternoon. According to the plan, power was to be transferred by 15 August 1947—ten months in advance of the June 1948 deadline—and British India was to be divided into two states, Hindustan comprising Hindu majority areas, and Pakistan the Muslim majority areas. Following the principle of the Partition plan, it was decided that the provinces of Bengal and Punjab would also be divided. This was against Jinnah's demand of Pakistan consisting of all the Muslim majority provinces; Sindh, Punjab, North West Frontier Province, Balochistan in the west, and Bengal and Assam in the east. In a press conference held on 13 April 1947, Jinnah had categorically declared that anything less, any partition of Bengal or the Punjab would be a 'truncated or mutilated, moth-eaten Pakistan', which would not be acceptable to the Muslim League.[79] This was the stand Jinnah took in his meetings with Mountbatten, when he 'raised the possibility of partitioning the provinces' arguing that:

> those provinces had strong internal identities: that Hindus identified themselves more strongly as Bengalis or Punjabis than as Hindus or Congress supporters, and that the integrity of their provinces ought to be preserved above all.[80]

Two Boundary Commissions were established, one for each province, 'with the terms of reference to demarcate the boundaries of the two parts of the respective provinces on the basis of ascertaining the contiguous majority areas of Muslims and non-Muslims'.[81] Along with the division of Bengal and Punjab, 600 autonomous princely states were given the choice to accede to any dominion. Ambiguous over their future, 'the princes were forced to vacate their lands'[82] and by 15 August 1947, with the exception of Hyderabad, Junagadh, and Jammu and Kashmir, all the other princely states had acceded to India. In consolidating a perfect Indian union, the 'British role…was not insignificant…[rather] it could be argued that the British set the scene', by their 'diplomatic silence' on the choices given to 600 autonomous princes to join any dominion.[83] It was not made explicit whether the princes were 'required to yield to the preferences of their erstwhile subjects, or were they free to determine their futures in accordance with traditional royal prerogatives'.[84]

Mountbatten's role in the partition of India needs to be investigated in the light of new evidence available. Many historians question Mountbatten's impartiality in determining the crucial issues of the partition and its alliance with the Congress leadership.[85] 'It need only be mentioned that Mountbatten as India's Governor-General presided over the initial phase in formation of a more perfect Union'.[86] Mountbatten established a state department in July 1947, with the aim 'to help India achieve its aim of leaving no state behind'.[87] Vallabhbhai Patel was made the head of this department which had no Muslim League representative. Siding entirely with Congress, Mountbatten 'agreed to help Patel and pledged to deliver "a full basket of apples" before 15 August'.[88] Using his 'royal connections to exert pressure' on the princes, Mountbatten succeeded in getting the majority of states to accede to India except the most important states—Hyderabad, Kashmir, Bhopal, Travancore, and Junagadh a small state.[89] In the remaining hold outs, Hyderabad, Bhopal, and Junagadh, the population was largely Hindu but the princes were Muslims. Although, historically these states were seats of Muslim civilization, geographically, they were too far from the areas which were going to be included in Pakistan. Bhopal and Junagadh were quickly overrun and incorporated into the Indian union without giving any consideration to Pakistani protests.[90] Hyderabad suffered the same fate in September 1948, on the day of Jinnah's funeral. Forceful occupation of these states by the Indian army, despite the decision of their princes not to accede to the Indian dominion, did hurt the sentiments of the people of the newly-created state of Pakistan, but all was overshadowed by the occupation of the Jammu and Kashmir state.

India's argument for the occupation of Hyderabad, Bhopal, and Junagadh, was that following the principle of partition, Hindu majority states had to accede to India. Negating its own argument, the Indian troops who arrived by air in Srinagar on 27 October 1947, deprived the predominantly Muslim population of Jammu and Kashmir from determining their own future, according to the wishes of the majority population. Kashmir was not an isolated pocket, rather it had geographical and historical links with western Punjab. All of West

Pakistan[91] was dependent on the Indus and its tributaries for existence as a civilized and populous state.[92] At the time of Partition, the irrigation canals of the Indus system watered approximately 34 million acres of land in West Pakistan. Out of this only 5 million acres were in Indian Punjab. The catchments of the five main left bank tributaries of the Indus all lay in the Indian Hill States, or in Kashmir. Kashmir contains most of the catchments of three major rivers, the Jhelum, Chenab, and the Ravi. With the partition of Punjab, the control of the three rivers, the Ravi, Beas, and Sutlej went to the Indian dominion, causing a loss of several acres of land in West Punjab. The inclusion of Kashmir in India meant that control over the Jhelum and Chenab rivers would also pass to India thus depriving West Pakistan of its main sources of life.[93] Moreover, Kashmir had great strategic importance, owing to its closeness to Russia, China, Afghanistan, and Tibet. The only road linking India and the state was via Pathankot, a non-Muslim tehsil of Gurdaspur district, which was a Muslim majority district, and contiguous with western Punjab.

The Boundary Commission's decision to award Gurdaspur—a district with a Muslim majority to East Punjab, which was to be a part of India, set the scene for blocking Pakistan's claim to Kashmir. This enabled New Delhi to dispatch troops to the predominantly Muslim state after having secured, and not without some help from Mountbatten, the maharaja's controversial letter of accession.[94] 'At a Hindu Maharaja's choice, but with a British Governor-General's backing three million Muslims in region always considered to be vital to Pakistan, if she were created, were legally to be made Indian citizens.'[95] Linking the Radcliffe Award with the occupation of Jammu and Kashmir by Indian troops, Ziring writes:

> The Radcliffe Award had given the Punjabi Muslim district of Gurdaspur to India with the full knowledge that New Delhi would thereby have road access to the mountain state. Thus, by air and then by land, Indian troops occupied Jammu and Kashmir, soon after the transfer of power, even while the Maharaja's accession to India revealed serious legal flaws that New Delhi refused to clarify.[96]

Sir Cyril Radcliffe, the chairman of the commission, who had never visited India and had no understanding of Indian demography or culture, was the choice of Mountbatten. Sir Cyril Radcliffe was given just three weeks to complete his task. He was bound to consult the viceroy. Radcliffe hardly attended any meeting of the boundary commissions and preferred to stay in contact more with Mountbatten than members of his committees, 'as his office was just down the hall from that of the Viceroy.' Radcliffe's reviews of the committee's deliberations and examinations of the maps and other records, were conducted in the presence of Mountbatten. 'Thus when the committees failed to agree on the drawing of boundaries between the two dominions, Radcliffe pre-empted their work and made all the decisions for them.'[97] The Award was handed over to Mountbatten on 13 August 1947, but he did not make it public until the 17th.[98] The award did not satisfy any party, but Radcliffe's decision to award Gurdaspur to India led to suggest that 'some strategic concerns' were at work. 'The Gurdaspur manoeuvre merely prepared the ground for a display of arms in which India and Pakistan were provoked to make war on one another the very day they became free of imperial rule'.[99] Wolpert writes that, 'On October 22nd, several thousand armed Pathan tribesmen invaded Kashmir in British army trucks, capturing Muzaffarabad' forcing the maharaja to flee to Jammu where he 'refused to sign the instrument of accession to India's union that V.P. Menon brought with him'.[100] This tribal movement according to Stephens's account:

> opened suddenly on October 19th, when 900 Mahsuds set off in motor trucks from Waziristan. Others from nearby soon followed; Wazirs, Daurs, Bhittanis, Khattaks, Turis, and some Afridis from farther north, and before the leading British personages on the Frontier—governor, chief secretary, and divisional commanders—knew what was happening, the spearhead of the forces, about 2000 strong, had slipped across the strategic bridges on the Indus at Khushalgarh and Attock, and was away towards the Kashmir border at Domel.[101]

On 26 October, 'all of north India's more than 100 civil and military transport planes' were ready 'to fly India's First Sikh Battalion to Srinagar from Delhi's airport'.[102] Ian Stephens, the editor of the *Statesmen*, who was invited for a dinner by Lord and Lady Mountbatten on 26 October 1947, noted:

> I was startled by their one-sided verdicts on affairs. They seemed to have become wholly pro-Hindu. The atmosphere at Government House that night was almost one of war. Pakistan, the Muslim League, and Mr Jinnah were the enemy. This tribal movement[103] into Kashmir was criminal folly. And it must have been well organized. Mr Jinnah, Lord Mountbatten assured me,

was sitting at Abbottabad, ready to drive in triumph to Srinagar if it succeeded.[104]

Stephens writes that 'subsequent inquiries showed that Mountbatten was wrong and Jinnah was in Lahore'. On learning what the Indians had done Jinnah issued orders 'on the evening of 27th October (1947) at Lahore' to send in Pakistani troops, but, General Gracey who was then acting commander-in-chief of the Pakistan army, 'felt obliged to stall' and decided to 'consult Field Marshal Auchinleck, the Supreme commander of...both dominions' forces',[105] who flew to Lahore and threatened Jinnah 'that unless he withdrew his order every British officer in Pakistan's army would be ordered to immediately to "stand down". That stand down would begin with General Gracey'.[106] Field Marshal Auchinleck, the supreme commander of both dominions' forces could request Lord Mountbatten to order the Indian army to halt but he did not do so. His threat to Pakistan resulted in the 'cancellation of Mr Jinnah's orders and an arrangement with Mountbatten for a conference of the political heads of both Governments at Lahore on October 29th'.[107] Nehru refused 'to discuss anything with Jinnah'[108] and 'when after a three-day postponement, Lord Mountbatten alone attended it and he could do no more than undertake to refer to his absent colleagues the proposals Mr Jinnah put forward', which included a ceasefire within 48 hours, withdrawal of Indian troops and the tribesmen and empowering the two Governor-Generals to administer the State and arrange a plebiscite.'[109] The Indian government's rejection of these proposals, in spite of Mountbatten's promise that official acceptance of the maharaja's accession would be followed by a referendum, initiated the never-ending battle between Pakistan and India.[110] Before his death, Jinnah told his nation that 'We have been the victims of a deeply-laid and well-planned conspiracy with utter disregard of the elementary principles of honesty, chivalry, and honour'.[111]

The fragility of Pakistan's sovereignty made it easy for the British military strategists to forget all the previous arguments about Pakistan's inability of bearing the burden of building a large defence establishment and convince Pakistan's early managers to refurbish the army, at whatever cost, to the central exchequer. The Kashmir dispute exposed the vulnerability of the newly-created state, and the fear of subjugation by the Indian army forced the financially-constrained state to think in terms of 'security needs' at the cost of building a new central government apparatus, rehabilitating millions of refugees, and setting up a handful of basic industrial units. Pakistan's share of assets was calculated as 17.5 per cent of the total assets of undivided India, and a third of the defence forces. In addition to the Rs 200 million made available in August 1947, for its initial cash-flow requirements, Pakistan received Rs 550 million as its final share of the rupee cash balances. Pakistan's share of the Sterling balance came to a total of £147 million out of a total of £1,160 million Sterling balance held by the Reserve Bank.[112] With this share of the balance, Pakistan was not financially capable in opting for a defence establishment, but the strategic consequences of the Partition, forced it to look for 'allies' who could offer some financial assistance for meeting its 'security needs' while still on the birth bed. Britain, itself crippled with the heavy debt accrued in the Second World War, was not in a position to lend this 'helping hand'. However, military strategists in London were all convinced to provide 'every assistance to the Pakistan armed forces' and build a defence establishment in Pakistan.[113] It was concluded that:

> the defence needs of Afghanistan, Pakistan and India...[could] be met otherwise than from joint United States and United Kingdom resources. Of these needs...those of Afghanistan and Pakistan...[were] to...[Britain] and the USA, the more important. This apart from the fact that both these countries...[had] no production capacity whatsoever.[114]

During the Kashmir war, when the United States withheld the arms supply for India and Pakistan to stop the armed conflict between the two dominions, British military strategists advised the US government to reconsider its decision about the embargo of arms arguing that:

> the United States embargo on the supply of arms to either Dominion would, taken together bring about a situation in which there [would] be a serious shortage of the means required in this area, where Russia's influence...[was] dominant, to meet any sudden attack by the USSR.[115]

It was further argued that the UK government 'could possibly reach an agreement with the United States Government to meet jointly the requirements of Afghanistan, Pakistan and India, but only jointly'.[116] It was re-emphasized that:

> it seem[ed] improbable that the defensive needs of Afghanistan, Pakistan and India...[could] be met otherwise than from joint United States and United Kingdom resources and...[they did] not wish to drive these three countries into asking Russia to provide their needs.[117]

However, the conclusion reached was that, 'in the circumstances...the priorities of allocation between India and Pakistan...the priority...over India...should be given to Pakistan'.[118]

Equipped with these imperial strategic arguments, just after a month of its birth, Pakistan's first finance minister, Ghulam Mohammad, approached Washington to lend a 'helping hand' to Pakistan to build its defence establishment against the Soviet threat. The first budget of Pakistan, announced on 28 February 1948, reflected the priorities of the new state. More than 70 per cent of the total revenues of the central government were allocated for defence. An apologetic finance minister had to defend the allocation of such a huge amount of central exchequer for defence in view of multiple dangers to the security of the state. He confessed that he had been 'reluctantly constrained to spend on the Armed Forces money' which should have gone into 'social, industrial and economic development of the country'.[119] The trend set by the first budget of Pakistan, giving priority to the state's defence over the people's real needs, could never be reversed with an expanding defence establishment. Table 3 shows the defence expenditure between the years 1947 to 1959.

Table 3: Defence Expenditures 1947-59		
Year	Defence expenditure (In million Rs)	Percentage of the total Government Expenditure
1947-48	236.0	65.16
1948-49	461.5	71.32
1949-50	625.4	73.06
1950-51	729.4	51.32
1951-52	725.7	54.96
1953-54	633.2	56.68
1954-55	640.5	58.7
1955-56	917.7	64.0
1956-57	800.9	60.1
1957-58	854.2	56.1
1958-59	996.6	50.9

Source: Hasan-Askari Rizvi, *The Military and Politics in Pakistan, 1947-99*, Lahore: Sang-e-Meel Publications, 2000, pp. 57-58.

Pakistan's defence expenditure in the years 1947-51 was more than 70 per cent of its total expenditure. 'Pakistan was spending more on defence than its resources could afford.' To equip her defence forces, Pakistan used a large part of her Sterling reserves and foreign currency earnings. To get resources for defence purposes, the central government had to exploit the revenue sources of the provinces, against their wishes, by expanding the state's administrative mechanism to ensure the centre's control over the provinces' finances.[120] The required sum could only be made available by diverting resources from nation-building activities thus placing the provincial governments in a financially tight situation. This process not only resulted in enlargement of non-representative institutions of the state—the bureaucracy and the army—at the cost of political accountability but also initiated a tussle concerning the conflict of interests between the central and the provincial governments. This conflict was observed by the British high commissioner who wrote in 1948, 'the Central Ministries...[had] continued to work hard on plans for extending the defence services', however, there was 'some doubt, if the Pakistan provinces...[were] taking matters as seriously as the Centre.'[121] At the time when the state construction was in its initial stages, this conflict proved to be the most disintegrating force. 'Economies of scale and the sitting of the federal capital in West Pakistan perpetuated the inter-wing imbalance.'[122] In the later years the conflict sharpened because of the absence of representation of East Pakistan and the three smaller provinces of West Pakistan from the defence establishment and the continued concentration of colonial recruitment patterns in the province of Punjab, which resulted in destabilizing political repercussions.[123]

The concentration of state authority in the province of Punjab created a sense of alienation in East Pakistan and the three smaller provinces of West Pakistan, which were kept out of the decision-making process. In 1953 the Economic Appraisal Committee conceded that Pakistan's annual expenditure on defence and civil administration was wholly out of line with available resources. No matter how much Pakistan skewed its economy and politics to meet its strategic defence requirements, it could not match, unaided, the resources of India. Using this pretext, the bureaucracy and their military allies became increasingly locked into a dependent relationship with the United States, which provided them with both the motives—the exclusion of political interference on foreign policy issues and increasing resources—to tilt the balance of power away from representative parties and politicians.

It is startling to note that in the summer of 1952, when the country was facing a worsening shortage of food grains, Pakistan's representatives were busy purchasing arms in Washington. On the one hand they had an appeal for a one million ton wheat grant and on the other they were carrying a shopping list for military equipment worth $45 million.[124] Jalal claims that:

> even before the central cabinet had acquiesced to giving the go ahead for the defence expansion, army headquarters in complicity with officials in the ministries of defence and foreign affairs had worked out various arrangements to obtain warlike materials from foreign governments as well as arms dealers, both at home and abroad.

She asserts that 'the central government was simply giving official sanction to a process that was already well under way'.[125]

This reveals that from the very beginning, the national leadership was made hostage to the interests of the American power system, which was being protected by a powerful group of civil servants located in the ministries of defence, finance, and foreign affairs. It needs to be remembered here that the persons in charge of military affairs were either British army officers or those brains who had been trained by them, and whose major aim was to maintain the concept of a security state at any cost. In this scheme of things the army became the main focus of attention. In 1950, Ayub Khan's selection as the first Pakistani commander-in-chief replacing General Gracey, was a matter of great calculation and an insurance that under his leadership, the Pakistan army would play the role which the British Indian army had been playing before. Ayub's selection as the first Pakistani commander-in-chief was the result of the 'nationalization policy' of the army, initiated by Liaquat's government under immense pressure from the people of Pakistan, who were not happy with the performance of the British army officers during the Kashmir war. It needs to be mentioned here that the majority of army officers at the time of independence were either British or non-Muslims, despite the fact that the Muslim soldiers made the bulk of the Indian army, and thus, were mostly not available for service in Pakistan.[126] On 1 July 1947, the British government decided that independent India and Pakistan would have operational control over their respective armed forces by 15 August, but the administrative control was to continue under the 'Supreme Command', until the respective governments were in a position to control and maintain their own forces. This supreme command was headed by Field Marshal Auchinleck, who later appointed Generals Lockhart and Messervy of the (British) Indian army as commanders-in-chief of the Indian and Pakistan armies, respectively. In addition to such appointments, it was made possible through the supreme command to assign about 500 British army officers to the operationally-independent Pakistan army, of which at least 480 were still present in Pakistan in 1951.

British military strategists had their reservations about the hasty process of nationalization and believed that 'it would be several years before Pakistanis would be fit to take over the commands, for example, of the Divisional Artillery and engineer units and it would be at least 1958 before they could manage their own staff college.'[127] Against the wishes of the commander-in-chief and other senior military staff of British origin, Liaquat was:

> forced by outside pressures to speed up the process of nationalization so that it was completed by 1950 as far as the non-training appointments, including of course, the C-in-C, and Principal Staff Officers, were concerned.[128]

This situation was not very pleasant for British security concerns. To keep the nascent Pakistani military establishment under their influence and control, General Douglas Gracey, the British-origin commander-in-chief 'pressured' Liaquat to:

> consider the early appointment of a strong body of Military advisors, to be composed of some of the senior [British] officers...holding key appointments who would be at hand both to assist their Pakistani successors and to ensure no break in the continuity of business.[129]

Under these circumstances, hopes were expressed that 'Liaquat... [would] do nothing to weaken the efficiency of the Army.'[130] The selection of the commander-in-chief was considered 'the occasion for considerable heart burning' since it had to be done ignoring the many talented officers and choosing the one who was most suited to ensure 'no break in the continuity of business' in a 'period in which the dangers to the British and Commonwealth connections should not be underestimated.'[131]

General Ayub Khan was groomed to lead a pro-West army under the close supervision of the defence secretary, Iskandar Mirza, which could contribute substantially to the defence of the Middle East. According to the State Department's policy statement on Pakistan, in the light of NSC 98/1 (The Position of the United States with Respect to South Asia) approved as US governmental policy on 25 January 1951, it was made explicit that the 'kingpin' of US interests in Pakistan was its army. The State Department argued that as a 'strategically important country, Pakistan could contribute substantially to the defence of the Middle East and should be regarded as a potential member of a Middle East Command.'[132]

SUBVERTING STALIN'S INITIATIVE—FIRST MAJOR SUCCESS OF THE AMERICAN POWER SYSTEM

In May 1949, Stalin invited Prime Minister Liaquat Ali Khan and his wife to visit Moscow. This invitation provided an opportunity for the political leadership in Pakistan to rethink security arrangements without the historical baggage of its colonial legacy of a 'security state'. This could check the ambition of an emerging and powerful, pro-West group in the civil and military bureaucracies that wanted to align with the Anglo-American bloc in the Cold War era, and in order to continue the 'concept of a security state'. This invitation gave Liaquat a chance to trawl support from all quarters in a situation where he had failed to turn the Commonwealth connections to Pakistan's advantage on the Kashmir issue.[133] At the Commonwealth Prime Ministers' Conference of April 1949, Liaquat Ali Khan warned the London Press that 'Pakistan could not be taken for granted and treated like a camp follower'.[134]

The Pakistan government's announcement on 8 June 1949, that the prime minister and his wife had accepted an invitation from Stalin to visit Moscow clearly indicated Liaquat's desire to stay neutral in the emerging Cold War scenario, in following the footsteps of Nehru. Liaquat, who was being portrayed as pro-American and seen 'not as anti-British as some of his colleagues', in spite of his strong criticism of British policies, had returned disillusioned from London after attending the Commonwealth conference.[135] Liaquat who was struggling to grip the internal politics of the landed aristocracy and its emerging alliance with an ambitious pro-West group in the civil and military bureaucracies, found an opening in the coming visit to Moscow, and to shed the image of belonging to the pro Anglo-American bloc, and thereby, capture the aspirations of the people of Pakistan. It was reported that 'the announcement was most favourably received by the Pakistani press, which welcomed the invitation as a sure sign of Pakistan's proud position in the world affairs, and as an opportunity to show that Pakistan was not aligned with any power.'[136] These feelings were expressed by many Muslim League deputations in a meeting with the minister of Kashmir Affairs, who reportedly told the British high commissioner that:

> in every case these people demanded an end of membership of the Commonwealth because HMG [had] sold out to India…and Muslim Leaguers pressed for association with Russia on the grounds that Pakistan was not strong enough to go around being rude to powerful neighbours who had so far done her no harm.[137]

Concerned over these pro-Russian feelings amongst the members of the ruling political party, the high commissioner hoped in utter despair that:

> Liaquat's acceptance of the Russian invitation to visit Moscow…[might] be merely another kick of his heels in the air, like the "camp follow" speech… [might] equally well be a clever move to satisfy the party…and others that he…[was] not permitting Pakistan to be tied to the United Kingdom's apron strings.[138]

Liaquat's acceptance of the Russian invitation to visit Moscow was seen as a 'manoeuvre' on Liaquat's part, 'to appear to retain the country's freedom of choice in foreign affairs.'[139]

On the other hand, Liaquat's proposed visit was viewed as an intelligent move to give a strong signal that Pakistan was ready to have an alliance with any power that could guarantee Pakistan's security against India, and it should not be 'taken for granted as good boys; good boys who would not play ball with communism or flirt with the left; boys who would starve and die rather than even talk to the communists.'[140] This signal was undoubtedly taken up by the American intelligence network, which warned that if Liaquat felt that Pakistan 'was being sold down the river in favour of India by the UK and the US, he might be tempted to use the USSR as a counter.'[141] According to Sajjad Hyder, after the announcement there was 'sudden warmth in America's attitude towards Pakistan and its Mission in Washington after the Soviet Union invitation.'[142] After Nehru's visit to the United States in 1949, officials at the Pakistan embassy in Washington and its foreign ministry, who were more than keen to tie their knots tightly with the

US interests, and in return wanted financial help for their military requirements, saw this as an opportunity to demand immediate attention. Pakistan's ambassador in Washington, reflecting their thoughts wrote to Liaquat that:

> your acceptance of the invitation to visit Moscow was a masterpiece in strategy,...every effort...[is] being made to rid us of our suspicions and to impress on us that we shall be accorded just treatment and the attention we deserve.[143]

G.W. Choudhury observes that Nehru's visit to the United States had 'prompted an unexpected and spectacular development in Soviet-Pakistani relations.' He writes, 'Nehru's first trip to the United States in 1949 at the invitation of President Truman, as well as of his speeches in North America brought more harsh comments from the Soviet press; he was virtually dubbed as an American stooge.'[144] G.W. Choudhury claims that disappointed with India, Kremlin found it necessary to make friendly gestures to Pakistan for maintaining the regional balance. The invitation followed with the announcement of a Trade Mission. 'The combination of the Mission and the visit' was seen as an 'increased interest on Russia's part in the affairs of the dominion.'[145]

The proposed visit of a Pakistani prime minister to Moscow created an uproar in diplomatic circles. 'The news of the Soviet invitation, a countermeasure to Truman's invitation to Nehru surprised Pakistanis as much as the world.'[146] Immediately after the announcement, desperate efforts were made to investigate why and how Liaquat got the invitation. The fortnightly summaries of communist developments in Commonwealth countries prepared by the Commonwealth Relations Office suggested that:

> precise information of how the invitation came to be given...[was] still lacking. It...[was] known that when Liaquat Ali Khan was in Tehran on his way back from London to Pakistan, he met and conversed with the Russian Charge d' Affaires. At that time, the Prime Minister was fresh from his London disappointment and the "camp follower" statement he had made before he left England. He was also probably aware of the developments in Pakistan since his departure and the difficulties which would confront him on his return. He...[might], therefore,...[had] been in a mood which prompted him to angle for a Soviet invitation. On the other hand, he...[might] merely have spoken in a way which gave the impression when the inevitable report went back to Moscow that the moment had arrived at which to act.[147]

Commenting upon the reactions within 'the official circle', it was observed that 'feeling...[was] mixed about the visit', and 'it was believed that the foreign minister regard[ed] it as a most unfortunate development.'[148] However, 'the general public in the majority,... appear[ed] to look on it as rebuke which the United Kingdom Pro-India attitude rightly deserv[ed].'[149]

It was felt that Liaquat had accepted the invitation to visit Moscow due to these reasons: firstly, 'feeling that in the dispute between Pakistan and India, Western Democracies tend to take the side of India in hope of thus gaining Indian support against communism.'[150] It was seen as a gesture to persuade the American power system players that 'Pakistan support cannot be assumed and must be paid for.'[151] The role of the United Nations Commission for India and Pakistan, in giving in 'to Indian procrastination regarding Kashmir' and Nehru's success in the London conference regarding India's place in the Commonwealth, were believed to bring 'this feeling to a head.'[152] Secondly, the internal political crisis in Pakistan was assumed to be out of Liaquat's control who, was alleged as 'too subservient to United Kingdom and USA,' and it was thought that 'the announcement may be designed by Liaquat to steal his critics' thunder.'[153] The other major reason given was that 'Nehru... [had] been invited to visit Washington whereas no similar invitation... [had] been given to Liaquat.'[154]

These reasons reinforced the view taken up by the pro-West group within Pakistan's hierarchy that the proposed visit did not represent a 'move by Pakistan towards friendship with the communist bloc.'[155] The Commonwealth Relations Office, London was quick in reassuring its allies that 'there...[was] no reason to suppose that the Pakistan's Prime Minister's decision portends any realignment of Pakistan foreign policy.'[156] It was a question of critical importance if 'the initiative came from Pakistan or Russia'. It was calculated that to ensure his hold over internal politics, Liaquat 'fished' the invitation 'for obvious value of the invitation to Pakistan Government in internal political field.'[157] The Anglo-American forces believed that 'the Soviet motive in issuing the invitation was to fish in troubled waters.' They wanted to assure their partners in Pakistan 'that a development which came as grist to the Soviet mill was hardly likely to be of great benefit to Pakistan or to the Commonwealth generally.'[158] In reality, the protectors of 'a free world' were worried about the possible collaboration between Pakistan and the Soviet Union and its impact on the whole region. Liaquat was seen too eager to come to Soviets' terms to solve his internal political crisis and could not be trusted. It was observed, 'Pakistan Prime Minister would not be prudent in Moscow and he no doubt realized the need for a long spoon when supping with Stalin.'[159]

Liaquat's proposed visit to Moscow brought all kinds of worries to the surface. The fear was expressed that, 'Pakistan might raise the Afghan question in Moscow and then try to frighten the Afghans with the bogey of Russian annexation of northern Afghanistan.'[160] The most alarming consequence of the visit was expected to be that 'the Russians might play on Pakistan vanity by treating them as a leading Moslem nation and might even hint at a new Soviet alignment in favour of the Moslems and Arabs throughout the Middle East.'[161] This could mean a victory for the Kremlin design, which could not be allowed to happen. Therefore, Liaquat's visit to Moscow had to be stopped. Soviet control over Middle Eastern oil producing countries was the greatest fear of the American power system. Liaquat's visit to Moscow could initiate this process. It was feared that Liaquat might 'take the opportunity to use Russia as a buffer against the Anglo-American bloc.'[162]

The reaction, which developed in India to Liaquat's acceptance of a state visit to Moscow, was similar to that of the Anglo-American opinion-makers. The Indian press expressed similar fears regarding the expected outcome of Liaquat's proposed visit. The *Searchlight* said that 'Pakistan...[had] not followed and never...[would] follow a settled foreign policy.' It voiced the Congress' concern that:

> as Nehru decided not to leave the Commonwealth and the British Government did not help in presenting the Kashmir valley to Pakistan, Liaquat...[was] apparently reviving Pakistan's old plan of an Islamic Block in the Middle East with Pakistan as leader but with Russian blessing.[163]

Threatened by the Russian move to invite Pakistan's prime minister to Moscow, the Indian government was feeding the pro-Congress Indian press to highlight the 'extreme opportunism of Russian foreign policy.'[164] Following this official line of thinking, the *Searchlight* warned that extreme opportunism of Russian foreign policy would be at work 'in the Middle East where after backing Israel, Russia may now be veering round to flirtations with the Arab States.'[165] The other concern showed by the Indian press was that Liaquat might think that he could defy Afghanistan, 'provided Russian support moral or material was assured.' The major concern expressed was that Liaquat would use the Russian influence 'to settle relations between Afghanistan and Pakistan.'[166] At the same time, a reassurance was felt through the fact that in presence of 'so effective a part of her defence forces and civil administration under British control,' Liaquat's visit would not 'lead to a foreign policy at Karachi oriented to Moscow.'[167]

On 2 August 1949, the government of Pakistan announced that the prime minister would visit Moscow in the first week of November. 'The USSR [was] sending a private plane to Karachi for the use of the Prime Minister.'[168] It was also announced that Mohammad Ali, the secretary general of Pakistan, would be included in the official party. This was in line with the popular mood in the streets of Pakistan, but it caused a panic among the protectors of the free world. Using all kinds of influences, Liaquat's visit to Moscow was postponed and instead an invitation from the US government was sought. The Commonwealth Office in London was a keen player in sounding off the State Department for extending a similar invitation to Liaquat. It was believed that such an invitation would 'take a good deal of the sting of any visit…Liaquat Ali Khan actually makes to Moscow.'[169] Britain took the Pakistani move towards Moscow 'as a loosening of ties with London.'[170] In a letter to the prime minister of Pakistan, the British high commissioner in Pakistan, relaying the displeasure of the British government over his planned visit to Moscow, wrote that the British ambassador 'may be prevented from showing the courtesy, which he deserves.'[171] Due to the close association of Pakistani officials in the foreign and defence ministries with the Commonwealth Office in London and the State Department in Washington, Liaquat was not only forced to postpone his visit to Moscow but also had to board a plane to the United States instead.

Liaquat's Visit to the United States—A Quest for Territorial Guarantees

Liaquat's visit to the United States on 3 May 1950 was planned to subvert his scheduled visit to the Soviet Union in November 1949.

The desirability of offsetting the impact of Liaquat's anticipated travel to the Soviet Union, along with balancing Nehru's state visit to the United States, were the main arguments that Assistant Secretary McGhee used successfully to request an invitation for the Pakistani leader. Truman gave his final approval on 17 November 1949 and a month later, McGhee personally presented the invitation to Prime Minister Liaquat during the first trip of an American assistant secretary of state to the subcontinent.[172]

As a result of this persuasion and the presence of a powerful lobby in Liaquat's cabinet, which included the foreign and finance ministers, Liaquat was denied the opportunity to be the first South Asian leader to land in the Soviet capital and write the history of this region in accordance with the people's aspirations. Liaquat's acceptance of a visit to Washington before travelling to Moscow cooled off the relationship between Pakistan and the Soviet Union, which took a hostile turn in the later years, when Pakistan joined in defence pacts against the Kremlin. On the other hand, Liaquat's visit to the US was also not up to the expectations of those who wished to win over Americans for military and financial assistance. 'Liaquat's schedule in Washington was light. There was no separate business meeting with President Truman', who greeted Liaquat and his wife at Washington's National Airport and hosted a formal state dinner at their residence.[173]

Contrary to wishes of the pro-West group in the Pakistani bureaucratic hierarchy,

> Liaquat's basic approach during the trip was of a goodwill salesman. It was not a Cold War-oriented visit...Although Liaquat maintained Pakistan's interest in receiving military equipment he did not stress the subject or urge closer ties with the United States during public appearances.[174]

His idea of a 'territorial guarantee' stirred the media's interest in the security issue. Answering to a reporter's question on the size of the standing army the prime minister wanted, Liaquat surprised the audience by suggesting that there was no further need to maintain an army if the US could provide a territorial guarantee. He stated that 'it depended on this great country of yours...if your country will guarantee our territorial integrity, I will not keep any army at all.'[175] This was not a new stance, as early as June 1949, Liaquat was thinking in terms of a 'territorial guarantee for both Pakistan and India underwritten by Britain and USA.'[176] He reiterated this idea in an interview given to *The New York Times* in April 1950 and argued that 'it was the best if not the only way of both Dominions now spent for less sterile and more constructive expenditure.'[177] The idea of a territorial guarantee was beyond the scope of a security state and caused much concern amongst those military strategists who wished to build a defence establishment at any cost.

By inviting Pakistan's prime minister to Moscow at the time when 'Pakistan felt frustrated over Truman's invitation to Nehru and over the special provision to keep India in the Commonwealth even as a Republic, the Soviet Government in spite of consistently unfriendly attitude of Pakistan,' showed its interest in solving the domestic and external problems of Pakistan.[178] The Kremlin did not favour Nehru's non-aligned policies and by extending a friendly hand to Pakistan, the largest Muslim country, Soviets wanted to maintain the regional balance in their favour. Pakistan could have exploited this situation and asked for a territorial guarantee against India. This was not in the interest of 'the powerful clique...that was accustomed to making decisions on external relations.'[179] Trained in a colonial environment, this group was apprehensive about the Kremlin's intentions and motives. 'Its members regretted that the partition of India had exposed Pakistan to Soviet attention.' Relying on the colonial thesis, they 'discerned clear links between present policy and the traditional Russian interest 'in the general direction of Persian Gulf.'[180] Therefore, they were not in favour of having a friendly relationship with the Soviet government—a policy, which harmed Pakistan more than it helped in solving its multiple problems. In their keenness to become an ally of the Anglo-American bloc, they did not take into account the national interests of the country, which could not afford a large defence establishment. For them continuation of the concept of a security state was essential for consolidating the state authority in their hands. For that they had to be allied with the neo-colonial forces thus ignoring the popular mood of the people that considered 'western nations imperialistic', and was against any such alignment.[181]

Interestingly, the people of Pakistan were more 'enthusiastic' about having a relationship with Soviet Union. These feelings were reflected when Liaquat announced his visit to Moscow. Endorsing this fact, the Commonwealth Relations Office reported in its fortnightly reports:

> although there...[had] been one or two lone voices in Pakistan asking suspiciously what Russia hop[ed] to get out of the Prime Minister, public opinion...[had] generally remained enthusiastic about the proposed visit. Since news about the visit was made public, a tendency...[had] been noticeable in the Pakistan press to view the Soviet regime more favourably than...[had] recently been the case.[182]

On the other hand, the US policy on the Palestine issue 'occasioned widespread press criticism and demonstration' and the US was being 'criticized for too great a leniency towards India in the Kashmir dispute and for favouring India at the expense of Pakistan.'[183]

For the masses of Pakistan, security against India was vital and the idea of territorial guarantee presented by Liaquat answered their worries. Symonds wrote in 1949,

> ...if it came to a war with India in which Pakistan's back would be against the wall of the Himalayas, many Pakistanis...[had] told the writer that religious sentiments would completely outweigh economic considerations; that an emotional fear of Hindu domination would obliterate apprehensions of the consequences of a Marxist regime; and that help would be sought from behind the mountain wall if it were not available from the Western forces... And it...[was] against this background that Liaquat Ali's visit to Moscow has been welcomed in Pakistan, even by those classes which would have most to lose under communism.[184]

The idea of a territorial guarantee had received an enthusiastic response from the people of Pakistan who would have welcomed it 'with fierce joy throughout the country' even if the Soviet Union offered it.[185] However, the possibility that Soviets might be willing to make such an offer to Pakistan was very disturbing for Indians as well as the British strategists. The hue and cry raised by the Indian press over Liaquat's visit to Moscow reflected this concern. We have earlier discussed the fears expressed by the Indian press in this regard.

The signals of the 'danger' of the Soviets making a tempting offer which could free Pakistan of the bondage it had inherited from the British Raj, was in the air when Liaquat visited the US in 1950. The Americans learnt, through Henderson, of a Soviet offer to Pakistan of one thousand of its latest tanks, as many fighter aircraft as Pakistan could maintain and large shipments of machinery which would enable Pakistan to industrialize rapidly. In return, they wanted Pakistan's alliance with the Soviet bloc. Henderson believed that the Pakistani government had refused the offer; however, he showed his concern about the Soviet intentions that in his opinion were to tempt Pakistan by almost 'inconceivable and stupid offer.'[186] He speculated that the Pakistani government was circulating such stories to put pressure on the US. But, for a politician like Liaquat, the cost of building a defence establishment was becoming heavier with every passing day, creating a cleavage between the centre and the provinces. The increasing cost of defence was out of proportion to the resources available to the state. 'A territorial guarantee would release financial resources for various development schemes and perhaps pave way for reconciliation of the centre with the provinces.'[187] But it was not in line with the strategic designs conceived for the containment of communism by the US strategists and the role Pakistan had been assigned to play in the emerging American power system.

NOTES

1. Amos A. Jordan, Jr., 1962, *Foreign Aid and Defence of South Asia*, New York: Preager, p. 209.
2. Amos A. Jordan, Jr., 1962, *The Role of the Military in Underdeveloped Countries*, Princeton: Princeton University Press, pp. 40, 208.
3. W. Nabudere Dani, 'The Role of the United States in the Global System after September 11th', Social Science Research Council, retrieved 25 June 2004 from http://conflicts.ssrc.org/.
4. Perry Anderson, September-October 2002, 'Force and Consent', *New Left Review*, 17: 5-30.
5. Ibid., pp. 5-6.
6. Stalin, Roosevelt, and Churchill.
7. Cold War Policies, retrieved 9 December 2002 from http://history.sandiego.edu/gen/20th/coldwar0.html.
8. The criticism of Yalta is discussed in Athan G. Theoharis, 1970, *The Yalta Myths: An Issue in U.S. Politics, 1945-1955*, New York: University of Missouri Press.
9. The interpretation of Yalta as a product of power politics rather than ideology can be found in John Gaddis, 1982, *Strategies of Containment: A Critical Appraisal of Post-war American National Security*, New York: Oxford University Press; and Melvyn P. Leffler, 1992, *A Preponderance of Power: National Security, The Truman Administration and Cold War*, Stanford: Stanford University Press.
10. Harry Truman's letter to James Byrnes, 5 June 1946; Cold War Policies, retrieved 21 December 2002 from http://history.sandiego.edu./truman46.html.
11. Cold War Policies, retrieved 17 September 2003 from http://history.sandiego.edu/gen/20th/coldwar0.html.
12. See Thomas Paterson, *Meeting the communist Threat*, New York, 1988. Paterson's vivid account of America's cold war policies argues that while Americans did not invent the communist Threat, they certainly have exaggerated it, nurturing a trenchant anti-communism that has had a devastating effect on international relations and American institutions.
13. Cold War Policies, retrieved 21 December 2002 from http://history.sandiego.edu./gen/20th/truman46.html.
14. Ibid.
15. Cold War Policies, retrieved 19 December 2002 from http://history.sandiego.edu./gen/1950s/nsc68.html.
16. Ibid.
17. Ibid.
18. Ibid.
19. Ibid.
20. Ibid.
21. Ibid.
22. Ibid.

23. Copy of the Third Progress Report on NSC 98/1, 23 April 1952, submitted by Dean Acheson to James S. Lay, Executive Secretary, National Security Council, NND 959417, Record Group [henceforth RG] 59, National Archives and Record Administration, Washington [henceforth NA].
24. Ibid.
25. 'U.S. Strategic Interests in Area', submitted by the American Embassy (Karachi) to Secretary, State Department, Washington, 28 October 1950, NND. 842423, RG 84, NA.
26. Ibid.
27. Richard Aldrich and Michael Coleman, October 1989, 'Britain and the Strategic Air Offensive against the Soviet Union: The Question of South Asian Air Bases—1945/9, *History*.
28. Lawrence Ziring, 2003, *Pakistan in the Twentieth Century: A Political History*, Karachi: Oxford University Press, p. 37.
29. Ibid., p. 39.
30. Ibid., p. 51.
31. Ibid., pp. 51-52.
32. 'Defence Implications of a Partition of INDIA into PAKISTAN and HINDUSTAN', 1 April 1946, L/WS/1/1029, IOR.
33. Ibid.
34. Ibid.
35. Correspondence between Commonwealth Relations Office, London [henceforth CRO] and the Ministry of Defence on the Provision of Warlike Stores for Pakistan, L/WS/1/1132, IOR.
36. Ibid.
37. Ibid.
38. Sir Olaf Caroe, *The Wells of the Power: The Oilfields of South-Western Asia*, op. cit.
39. Ibid.
40. Ibid.
41. Lawrence Ziring, *Pakistan in the Twentieth Century: A Political History*, op. cit., p. 52.
42. General Strategic Implications of the Situation in China as foreshadowed in the Foreign Office, London [henceforth FO] Appreciation, 20 January 1949, Strategic Papers, Chiefs of Staff, L/WS/1/1198, IOR.
43. Minutes of meeting held at FO, 10 Nov. 1948, L/WS/1/1198, IOR.
44. Ibid.
45. Ibid.
46. Ibid.
47. Ibid.
48. Correspondence between CRO and the Ministry of Defence, London, on the Provision of Warlike Stores for Pakistan, L/WS/1/1132, IOR.
49. Ibid.
50. Strategic Implications of the Situation in China, Report by the Joint Planning Staff, London, 12 January 1949, L/WS/1/1198, IOR.
51. A letter from CRO, 7 January 1949, L/WS/1/1198, IOR.
52. Ibid.
53. 'Contributions of Pakistan to Commonwealth Defence', draft report by the Joint Planning Staff for Chiefs of Staff Committee, Joint Planning Staff, London, 27 April 1949, L/WS/1/1236, IOR.

54. Ibid.
55. Minutes of the meeting of the Chiefs of the Staff Committee, Joint Planning Staff, London, 7 May 1949, L/WS/1/1236, IOR.
56. Ibid.
57. Ibid.
58. Ibid.
59. 'Contribution of Pakistan to Commonwealth Defence', note by the Secretary, for Chiefs of Staff Committee, Joint Planning Staff, London, 19 April 1949. L/WS/1/1236, IOR.
60. Note by the Secretary of Defence entitled 'Value of Pakistan as a Main Base', L/WS/1/1236, IOR.
61. Correspondence between CRO and the Ministry of Defence, L/WS/1/1132, IOR.
62. Matthews to McGhee, Internal Memo, 1 November 1949, NND. 842423, RG 84, NA.
63. 'US Strategic Interests in Area', submitted by the US Embassy at Karachi, 28 December 1950 for the conference of American ambassadors in Ceylon held in December 1950, NND. 842423, RG 84, NA.
64. Ibid.
65. Secretary, Rawalpindi Case Trial Committee to Louis Saillart [general secretary] and Serge Rostovsky [secretary], World Federation of Trade Unions, Vienna, 7 September 1951, intercepted by the American Legation in Vienna, 2 October 1951, 350-Pak.Pol. 10-2-51, NND. 842430, RG 84, NA.
66. Ibid.
67. Ibid.
68. 'Contribution of Pakistan to Commonwealth Defence', note by the Secretary, for Chiefs of Staff Committee, Joint Planning Staff, 19 April 1949, L/WS/1/1236, IOR.
69. Ibid.
70. Ibid.
71. Lawrence Ziring, 2003, *Pakistan in the Twentieth Century: A Political History*, Karachi: Oxford University Press, p. 89.
72. Cited in Allan McGrath, 1996, *The Destruction of Pakistan's Democracy*, Karachi: Oxford University Press, 1996, pp. 27 and 35ff.
73. Nehru to Sri Prakasha, 25 November 1947, *Selected Works of Jawaharlal Nehru*, ed. S. Gopal, Second Series, 16 Vols., New Delhi: Orient Longman, pp. 346-7.
74. Minutes of the Chiefs of Staff meeting, London, 21 October 1947, L/WS/1/1133, IOR.
75. Alex Von Tunzelmann, *Indian Summer*, op. cit., p. 191.
76. Ibid., pp. 191-2.
77. Ibid.
78. Ibid., p. 198.
79. Cited in *The Times*, 2 May 1947, p. 4; Transfer of Power, vol. x, p. 543.
80. Alex Von Tunzelmann, *Indian Summer*, op. cit., p. 182.
81. V.P. Menon, 1957, *Transfer of Power in India*, Princeton: Princeton University Press, pp. 401-2.
82. Lawrence Ziring, *Pakistan in the Twentieth Century: A Political History*, op. cit., p. 91.
83. Ibid., pp. 89-90.
84. Ibid., p. 90.

85. For criticism of Mountbatten's role see Andrew Roberts, *Eminent Churchillians*, 1994, (London: Oxford University Press. A. Roberts has reopened the controversy concerning Mountbatten's role in the award of the Muslim majority *tehsils* of Ferozepur and Zira to India with the consequent control of the Sutlej river canal headworks, pp. 93ff.
86. Ibid., p. 91.
87. Alex Von Tunzelmann, *Indian Summer*, op. cit., p. 218.
88. Ibid.
89. For a detailed account of Mountbatten's 'heavy-handed strategy' of coercing the princes of States to accede to India, see Alex Von Tunzelmann, *Indian Summer*, op. cit.
90. In Junagadh the situation was opposite to that in Kashmir as it was a Hindu majority state with a Muslim ruler. He decided to accede to Pakistan, but the Indian army took over the state and arranged a plebiscite, which recorded a 90 per cent vote in favour of accession to India. This process was not repeated in Kashmir where India never allowed arranging of a plebiscite to decide the fate of that state.
91. Present-day Pakistan.
92. Note on the result of control by the Indian dominion on the waters of the Indus tributaries in Kashmir, L/WS/1/1204, IOR.
93. Ibid.
94. Ayesha Jalal, *The State of Martial Rule*, op. cit., p. 57. L. Ziring writes, 'Indian forces had entered Kashmir prior to receipt of the Instrument of Accession, and it is doubtful that there ever was such a document', *Pakistan in the Twentieth Century: A Political History*, op. cit., p. 95.
95. Ian Stephens, 1964, *Pakistan*, London: Ernest Benn Limited, p. 204.
96. Lawrence Ziring, *Pakistan in the Twentieth Century: A Political History*, op. cit., p. 92.
97. Ibid., p. 59.
98. See V.P. Menon, *Transfer of Power in India*, op. cit., p. 402.
99. Lawrence Ziring, *Pakistan in the Twentieth Century: A Political History*, op. cit., p. 63.
100. Stanley Wolpert, 2006, *Shameful Flight*, Karachi: Oxford University Press, p. 184.
101. Ian Stephens, *Pakistan*, op. cit., for a detailed account see pp. 192-211.
102. Stanley Wolpert, *Shameful Flight*, op. cit., p. 184.
103. Ian Stephens, *Pakistan*, op. cit., for a detailed account pp. 192-211.
104. Ian Stephens, *Pakistan*, op. cit., p. 203.
105. Ibid., p. 205.
106. Stanley Wolpert, *Shameful Flight*, op. cit., p. 186.
107. Ibid.
108. Ibid.
109. Ibid., p. 206.
110. Ian Talbot, *Pakistan: A Modern History*, op. cit., p. 116. 'In the 1948-49 Indo-Pakistan war, India's failed attempt to indict Pakistan before the United Nations Security Council for violating her sovereignty and continued Pakistani military occupation of Azad Kashmir ... Nehru to conclude that the circumstances were not right for a plebiscite to be held, despite the passage of a United Nations resolution calling for a plebiscite to be conducted by its nominee administrator.'
111. Stanley Wolpert, *Shameful Flight*, op. cit., pp. 186-87.
112. L/E/9/362, IOR.

113. Minutes of the Chiefs of Staff meeting, 21 October 1947, L/WS/1/1133, IOR.
114. Correspondence between CRO and the Ministry of Defence on the Provision of Warlike Stores for Pakistan, 13 May 1948, L/WS/1/1132, IOR.
115. Ibid.
116. Ibid.
117. Ibid.
118. Ibid.
119. See finance minister's budget speech, budget of the Central Government of Pakistan, 1947-48 (15 August to 31 March), and 1948-49.
120. Ibid.
121. British High Commissioner's fortnightly report, 8 November 1948, L/WS/1/1204, IOR.
122. Ian Talbot, *Pakistan: A Modern History*, op. cit., p. 25.
123. As a result of the process set in motion in the early years of the formation of state of Pakistan, East Pakistan lost its faith in the federation of Pakistan and ultimately declared its independence in 1971 after a long and bloody army operation which led to a war between India and Pakistan which resulted in Pakistan army's defeat and creation of Bangladesh.
124. British Embassy in Washington to the FO, telegram, 28 July 1952, DEFE7/152, the National Archives: Public Record Office [henceforth TNA: PRO].
125. Ayesha Jalal, *The State of Martial Rule: The Origins of Pakistan's Political Economy of Defence*, op. cit., p. 77.
126. Hasan-Askari Rizvi, *The Military and Politics in Pakistan, 1947-1997*, op. cit., notes that 'by 1947 only a few Indians attained the substantive rank of Lieut.-Colonel. During Second World War, a large number of Indians were given Emergency and Short Commissions to meet the need of rapid expansion of the Army.' According to Rizvi's calculations there were 4 Muslim and 5 non-Muslim in the rank of Lt.-Colonel, 42 Muslims and 61 non-Muslims in the rank of Major, and 114 Muslims and 218 non-Muslims in the rank of Captain. See Table IV, p. 45.
127. From the office of the High Commission [Karachi] for the United Kingdom, 14 June 1949, L/WS/1/1188, IOR.
128. Ibid.
129. Ibid.
130. Ibid.
131. Ibid.
132. Third Progress Report on NSC 98/1, 23 April 1952, submitted by Dean Acheson to James S. Lay, Executive Secretary, National Security Council, NND 959417, RG 69, NA.
133. Ayesha Jalal, *The State of Martial Rule*, op. cit., p. 110.
134. CRO Fortnightly Summaries of communist Developments in Commonwealth countries, L/WS/1/1207, IOR. See also Richard Symonds, *Making of Pakistan*, 1966, Karachi: Allied Books Corporation, p. 170.
135. CRO Fortnightly Summaries of communist Developments in Commonwealth countries, first half of June 1949, L/WS/1/1207, IOR.
136. Ibid.
137. From the office of the British High Commissioner [Karachi], 14 June 1949, L/WS/1/1188, IOR.
138. Ibid.
139. Ibid.

140. A letter from A.H. Ispahani, Pakistan's ambassador in Washington to Liaquat Ali Khan, cited in G.W. Choudhury, 1975, *India, Pakistan, Bangladesh, and the Major Powers*, New York: Free Press, p. 12.
141. Intelligence Report, State Department Lot File 57 D 421, 3 April 1950, RG 59, NA.
142. Sajjad Hyder, 1987, *Foreign Policy of Pakistan: Reflections of an Ambassador*, Lahore: Vanguard Books, p. 10.
143. A letter from A.H. Isphani, Pakistan's ambassador in Washington, to Liaquat Ali Khan, cited in G.W. Choudhury, *India, Pakistan, Bangladesh, and the Major Powers*, op. cit., p. 12.
144. Ibid., p. 11.
145. CRO Fortnightly Summaries of communist Developments in Commonwealth countries, first half of June 1949, L/WS/1/1207, IOR.
146. A letter from A.H. Ispahani, Pakistan's ambassador in Washington, to Liaquat Ali Khan, cited in G.W. Choudhury, *India, Pakistan, Bangladesh, and the Major Powers*, op. cit., p. 12. Ibid., p. 12.
147. CRO Fortnightly Summaries of communist Developments in Commonwealth countries, 15 September 1949, L/WS/1/1207, IOR.
148. Ibid.
149. Ibid.
150. Outward Telegram from CRO to Acting UK High Commissioner in Canada, UK High Commissioner in Commonwealth of Australia, Acting UK High Commissioner in New Zealand. UK High Commissioner in South Africa, RPTD: to UK High Commissioner in India, UK High Commissioner in Pakistan, Acting UK High Commissioner in Ceylon, Acting UK Representative to Republic of Ireland, 24 June 1949, L/WS/1/1198, IOR. See also report of the first half of June 1949, CRO Fortnightly Summaries of communist Developments in Commonwealth countries, L/WS/1/1207, IOR.
151. Ibid.
152. Ibid.
153. Ibid.
154. Ibid., See also Inward Telegram to CRO, from Acting UK High Commissioner in Ceylon, 17 June 1949, L/WS/1/1198, IOR.
155. Ibid.
156. Outward Telegram from CRO to UK High Commissioner in India, Acting UK High Commissioner in Ceylon, Acting UK Representative to Republic of Ireland RPTD: UK High Commissioner in Pakistan, Acting UK High Commissioner in Canada, UK High Commissioner in Commonwealth of Australia, Acting UK High Commissioner in New Zealand. UK High Commissioner in South Africa, 24 June 1949, L/WS/1/1198, IOR.
157. Inward Saving Telegram to CRO from UK High Commissioner in Pakistan, 6 July 1949, L/WS/1/1198, IOR.
158. Inward Telegram to CRO from UK High Commissioner in India, 16 June 1949, L/WS/1/1198, IOR.
159. Ibid.
160. Ibid.
161. Ibid.
162. Ibid.
163. Ibid.
164. Ibid.

84   AUTHORITARIANISM AND UNDERDEVELOPMENT

165. Ibid.
166. Ibid.
167. Ibid.
168. Inward Telegram to CRO from UK High Commissioner in Pakistan, 2 August 1949, L/WS/1/1198, IOR.
169. H.A.F. Rumbbold [CRO] to R.H. Scott [FO], 13 June 1949, DO35/2981, TNA: PRO.
170. G.W. Choudhury, *India, Pakistan, Bangladesh, and the Major Powers*, op. cit., p. 13.
171. Cited in ibid., p. 14. At that time, the British ambassador was representing Pakistan in Moscow, since no exchange of ambassadors had taken place by that time between the two countries.
172. Dennis Kux, 2001, *The United States and Pakistan, 1947-2000: Disenchanted Allies*, Karachi: Oxford University Press, p. 32.
173. Ibid., p. 34.
174. Ibid., p. 35.
175. Cited in ibid.
176. Ayesha Jalal, *The State of Martial Rule*, op. cit., p. 111.
177. Liaquat's interview, *The New York Times*, 18 April 1950.
178. G.W. Choudhury, *India, Pakistan, Bangladesh, and the Major Powers*, op. cit., p. 12.
179. See ibid., p. 13. Pakistan's first Foreign Minister Chaudhry Mohammad Zafarullah, Secretary Foreign Affairs Mohammad Ikramullah, and Finance Minister Ghulam Mohammad, were powerful members of this clique. General Iskandar Mirza, the Defence Secretary, was another powerful member of this clique.
180. Ibid.
181. Memorandum prepared by the State Department for Liaquat's visit, cited in Dennis Kux, *The United States and Pakistan, 1947-2000: Disenchanted Allies*, op. cit., p. 34.
182. 15 September 1949, CRO Fortnightly Summaries of communist Developments in Commonwealth countries, L/WS/1/1207, IOR.
183. Memorandum prepared by the State Department for Liaquat's visit, cited in Dennis Kux, *The United States and Pakistan, 1947-2000: Disenchanted Allies*, op. cit., p. 34.
184. Richard Symonds, *Making of Pakistan*, op. cit., p. 174.
185. See article 'Pakistan May Cut its Links with Crown', *Sunday Observer* (London), 14 August 1949, cited in ibid., p. 112.
186. Henderson to Secretary of State, 8 May 1950, 790D.5/5-850, State Department Central File, RG 59, NA.
187. Ayesha Jalal, *The State of Martial Rule*, op. cit., p. 111.

3

Emergence of the Institutional Imbalance

BUREAUCRACY, ARMY, THE FEUDAL NEXUS, AND PURSUANCE OF A NEO-COLONIAL MODEL

In previous discussions, an analysis of the growth of representative institutions of colonial capitalism was given with the primary aim of understanding how these representative institutions of a colonial state continued to dominate the formation of a post-colonial state and jeopardized its evolution. Why the new state was not allowed to develop democratic institutions and introduce a social and economic reform program has been investigated. It was seen that from the very beginning the new state was forced to invest in the defence establishment at the cost of economic development, which in turn created tension between the central authority and provincial autonomy. The continuation of the colonial legacy of a security state, in the context of the American power system, not only hampered the development of political institutions and democratic processes but it was also accompanied by underdevelopment.

In this chapter, how the civil bureaucracy and the army representing the central authority, rose to prominence in Pakistan, and how their alliance succeeded in aligning Pakistan with the neo-colonial world, will be explored. As a consequence, in the initial and most critical stage of its growth, the new nation-state witnessed the non-representative institutions assuming dominance over the representative institutions, and adopted of a western model of development, which was a new form of colonial capitalism, which in turn produced poverty and underdevelopment. The post-Second World War period is characterized by the notion of 'liberating' the governments in economically-backward countries in the Third World and then forcing them to take part in a competitive world system in order to develop economically. Justice notes that:

> following the Second World War, as the colonial period ended and new independent nations emerged through the Third World, large scale economic assistance from developed countries to developing or Third World countries became an important part of international diplomacy.[1]

Escobar observes that the era 1945-55 is characterized by post-war transformations and witnessed the emergence of a new strategy to manage the problems of what came to be known during this period as the 'underdeveloped world'.[2]

Although the concept of 'developing others' countries can be traced to the colonial period, its impetus, and its stress on economics, culminated after the Second World War. The success of the Marshall Plan and Recovery Programs in Europe suggested that a similar model of economic aid to Third World countries would soon lift them out of their 'backward' conditions. This new strategy encompassed all aspects of the economic, social, political, and cultural life and included the populations, the process of capital accumulation, agriculture and health, natural resources, administration and cultural values, etc., of the former colonies, or underdeveloped countries. This strategy was exhibited in the first 'missions' sent to the underdeveloped world by the International Bank for Reconstruction and Development during the late 1940s and 1950s. These missions were tasked with formulating comprehensive development programs, based on the assumption that the developed world had the financial and technological capacity for helping 'backward' countries to develop.

This economic model drew its inspiration from the early modernization theories that presented a culturalist thesis, in which a set of stereotypical notions of 'character' and 'personality' are found. According to these notions, colonial peoples were 'primitive' and 'barbarous', and untouched by civilization, until they came in contact with colonialism. Two schools, evolutionism and diffusionism, representing the broader 'functional school' in particular, present this thesis.[3] Both evolutionists and diffusionists view societies of the Third World as 'traditional' and 'static' before their contact with the West, lacking any 'endogenous dynamic for development and progress'. Without discussing the destructive role of colonial impact, they see colonialism as a modernizing force, responsible for the transformation of a traditional society into a modern one. Discussing the 'self-legitimating ideas of colonial domination,' K.S. Singh shows that there is not a 'hint or acknowledgement of the destructive role of the colonial impact in India'.[4] Most notable amongst the authors of functional schools are Gabriel Almond, Joseph La Palombara, Myron Weiner, Leonard Binder, and Samuel P. Huntington. All these distinguished political scientists were members of the ten-men Committee on Comparative Politics, constituted in 1954, with the task to analyze and recommend for the newly-liberated states in Africa and Asia. The theme of their analysis was in terms of 'crises of development', 'national integration', 'moderation', etc. They advanced the pro-establishment school of development.

These early writers of the modernization paradigm reject any connection between the poverty of the underdeveloped world and the wealth of the developed world and do not address the question of colonialism directly. They presented a concept/model in which the villain is the 'non-western world', and its 'cultural strains', which, should wait for deliverance through the 'diffusion of world culture'. This model led towards a linear development path ending in 'Western-style', market-oriented societies. The underlying belief was that the cultural diffusion of Western economic/technological processes and the compatibility of social structures, would force the developing countries in the long run to adopt the characteristics of the developed nations. This economic theory was best described by Rostow's model of five stages of development. These five stages were: traditional society, precondition for takeoff, the takeoff process, the drive to maturity, and high mass consumption.[5] In this linear progress, the prediction was that traditional societies would eventually advance through the stages that have been achieved by developed societies. It was assumed that lack of human skills and investment capital were the major problems, therefore, the system of banks and development-assistance agencies, such as the IMF and the World Bank, were designed to provide capital for investment to developing countries who were trailing in these policies. Assistance was provided for reasons that ranged from humanitarian to economic, political, and military concerns.[6]

The main focus of most foreign aid appears to have been either political or economic.[7] There is a concealed connection between foreign 'assistance' to the 'less developed' world by the industrialized nations via aid organizations and those nations' political agendas, particularly in the 'Cold War Era'.[8] The alliance between the civil and military bureaucracies in Pakistan, and centres of the international financial system in London and Washington, is of special importance in this context. In the 'Cold War Era', the rise of military dominance resulted in political instability in the majority of Third World countries, which led to various forms of authoritarianism, replacing the representative governments with elites' governments. All these elite governments were dependent, or linked, to the industrial world order, and special military blocks were established to fight any signs of dominance of communism. This idea of economic development enforced the new and extraordinary changes of social and administrative centralization, in addition to repressive work disciplines, social upheaval, and revolutions, in these societies. For most of the newly-liberated countries of the Third World, these new disciplines turned out to be equally as bad than those, or even worse, imposed by the former colonial rulers because national liberation was equated with competition in the capitalist world economy.[9]

In the following discussion, how the development of the institutional imbalances, which plagued Pakistan's history, was due to the crafty approach of the international managers of the Cold War will be examined. They allied themselves with the domestic actors to continue the colonial legacy of 'controlling the democratic institutions' through an authoritarian administrative structure. 'Effective power within the state apparatus lay in the hands of a [feudal-] military bureaucratic oligarchy from the inception of the state, rather than with the political leadership'.[10] This oligarchy—a select group of civil and military bureaucracy—trained by the colonial strategists in league with their international connections, pursued the colonial policy of a 'security state' in the region. Such a security state could guarantee the 'Containment of communist Revolution' and protect the neo-colonial interests as well. With this mindset, any chance of building democratic institutions was very remote.

Role of the Civil Bureaucracy

On the eve of independence, the new state started off with a colonial legacy in the institution of the governor-general, who was totally in control of the administrative authority. Jinnah, in his person, was the supreme authority of the new nation-state. His personal authority introduced a legendary character to the office of the governor-general. The prime minister and the cabinet were his selection, and were answerable to him only. It has been argued that Jinnah's choice of becoming the governor-general instead of the prime minister set the trend for continuation of the colonial tradition of consolidating power in a non-representative office.[11] These historians claim that if Jinnah had chosen to be the leader of the parliament, the parliamentary history of Pakistan would have been different. It has also been suggested that this imbalance of power distribution, between the governor-general and the prime minister, in a new state, not only complicated the process of state construction but brought to surface the differences between the two powerful personalities of the independence movement.[12] As a consequence, the civil bureaucracy began asserting its role in the state-formation process. It is a known fact that Jinnah was very ill at the time of achieving his goal—the creation of Pakistan.[13] He did not have enough time at his disposal to run the affairs of the government on a daily basis. He selected a team of his choice to run the government under the leadership of Liaquat Ali Khan as the prime minister. He, himself, headed the new state as the governor-general, to serve as a symbol of unity and sovereignty to the new nation. 'Mohammad Ali Jinnah's decision to preserve the British-installed viceregal system was a decision made out of necessity as much as choice.'[14]

The Indian Independence Act amended the Government of India Act of 1935 and made it the basic constitutional document of the dominions of India and Pakistan.

> On 15 August 1947, Pakistan, like India came into existence specifically identified as an independent dominion with a constitution created by Parliament and modelled on the Westminster form of parliamentary cabinet government.[15]

The legislative functions of the federal legislature of British India were to be carried out by the constituent assemblies of India and Pakistan. In addition to these functions, the two assemblies were given full constituent powers, each bearing the initial responsibility of drafting any new constitutions, and making any changes to the Government of India Act of 1935 and the Indian Independence Act. The newly-created Constituent Assembly of Pakistan was 'made up of the representatives elected in 1946 to the Constituent Assembly of undivided India from the areas which, after independence, constituted Pakistan'.[16] Jinnah estimated that the drafting of a new constitution would be a 'stupendous task', taking anywhere from eighteen months to two years after independence. He declared that 'until we finally frame our constitution, which of course can only be done by the Constituent Assembly, our present provisional constitution based on the fundamental principles of democracy not bureaucracy or autocracy or dictatorship must be worked'.[17] It was unthinkable that the constitution-making process would be a lengthy one and as a consequence, the new state would be subjected to 'authoritarian rule', imposed by the feudal-military-bureaucratic oligarchy.

It was unfortunate for the new state to lose its mentor and leader merely a year after its birth. After Jinnah's death on 11 September 1948, though Liaquat Ali Khan could not fill the gap, he was able to run the affairs of the government very smoothly and assert his position as the prime minister in accordance with the parliamentary traditions. Khwaja Nazimuddin, Jinnah's successor as governor-general never overstepped his constitutional limits and facilitated Liaquat in asserting his authority as the prime minister. From 1948 to 1951, the centre of power was the prime minister and his cabinet. The imbalance between the offices of the governor-general and the prime minister emerged in the years following Liaquat, and cannot be attributed to the extraordinary powers vested in Jinnah as the first governor-general of Pakistan, as seen by some historians. On the contrary, there is convincing evidence to indicate that the international forces should be seen as the determining factors for strengthening the civil bureaucracy and the military, to safeguard their strategic interests in the Cold War Era.

'Pakistan did not begin its independent existence with a blank slate. It inherited a system of government highly dependent upon the civil bureaucracy', which was groomed in an authoritarian culture not responsive to democratic forces.[18] By training, the colonial civil bureaucracy was not meant to accept the supremacy of representative institutions, especially in the north-western security zone.

> Those officers who managed this inherited administrative system had not been trained to accept the concepts of citizen participation in government decision-making, the domination of elected leadership in government policy-making, or public scrutiny of government operations.[19]

The bureaucracy, which was trained under the colonial rule, was reluctant from the beginning, to submit to the authority of the parliament and the politicians. The ICS was reincarnated in Pakistan in the form of the CSP (Civil Service of Pakistan). 'The tradition [of Indian

Civil Service] had deep roots in a different culture and a different era...and that the structure was designed for the rule of the conqueror over the vanquished'.[20] It was not designed to promote citizens' participation in the affairs of the government, nor was it meant to put a great deal of emphasis on economic development. Those factors needed to be considered 'ill at a time when a nation had to be formed quickly from two patches of land on the subcontinent'.[21] Instead, surprisingly, the new state chose to continue the structures and the tradition of the Indian Civil Service and most of the task of the nation-building was assigned to it, an inherent contradiction in itself. The members of the ICS were trained to protect colonial interests and were anathema to any form of nationalism.

Originally, the ICS consisted of a class of British administrators who were considered the best breed, 'guardians of the Empire', and the 'steel frame' of the Raj. With the increasing demand of opening up the doors of the ICS for Indians, the colonial recruitment policy was changed to accommodate Indians in the ICS through a highly competitive process.

> Pakistan inherited this system, with some qualification in 1947. The administrative core...numbered less than a hundred Muslim ICS Officers and Jinnah filled vacancies in the administrative cadre with hand-picked British ICS and military officers. The system has been described as viceregal in that civil servants made major policy and decisions relating to the implementation of policy.[22]

In colonial India, for the first time, members of the ICS were put under the authority of Indian ministers, who were appointed at the provincial level, under a system known as Diarchy, introduced by the Government of India Act of 1919. Though the Indian ministers were to hold certain minor portfolios in provincial governments, still most of the British members preferred to resign rather than submit to their authority.[23] This showed the racist attitude of the colonial rulers, who did not consider an Indian fit to govern. The 1919 Act, which introduced the concept of 'controlled democratic institutions' at the provincial level, was meant to satisfy the demand of Indian political parties for 'self-rule'. To pacify this situation, procedural methods, governing the relationship between senior civil servants and ministers, were introduced to resolve the question of a 'proper relationship' between Indian ministers and the members of the ICS. The relationship was an issue of widely-held discussions on the 1919 Reforms Proposals. These discussions were pigmented with paternalistic ideas of the colonial rulers who indicated, very specifically, that the Indian ministers would be protégés of the senior British civil servants, and learn the art of self-government from them.[24] This reversed the normal relationship between a minister, and the secretary of his ministry, that existed in any responsible form of government. The provision that the secretary could bypass the minister and obtain orders directly from the governor of the province, in case of a dispute between them, not only established the supremacy of the bureaucracy over the limited powers of the minister, but also hampered the growth of the representative institutions. This provision was kept intact in the post-colonial state, knowing that the bureaucracy was never fully accountable to the representative institutions.

The colonial system of government and the rules of business were altered in independent India, where a political leadership was able to assert itself. In Pakistan, however, these colonial procedures found a new life in the form of a secretary-general post of the government of Pakistan, 'an overlord of the bureaucracy who was to have direct authority over every secretary of every ministry, independently of the cabinet'.[25] The colonial pattern of a centralized organization, with the central secretariat playing critical roles in policy-making, and coordination of ministries and divisions, was also continued in the post-colonial state under the authority of the secretary-general giving the bureaucracy unlimited powers without being responsible to the people of Pakistan. This post was proposed by Chaudhry Mohammad Ali, who was the first and the last secretary general of the government of Pakistan and was the chief advisor to Liaquat Ali Khan. When he left this post in 1951 to become the finance minister in Nazimuddin's cabinet, the post was abolished.

It has been discussed in the previous chapter, how an ambitious group of the civil and military bureaucracy, subverted Liaquat's plan to visit Moscow and instead forced him to land in Washington. A civil servant's appointment as the finance minister was a clear violation of democratic rules. But this action was not condemned because the manner in which the whole government was changed after Liaquat's assassination could not be justified in any democracy. It will be further discussed in the following sections.

After independence, the new state was challenged with gigantic problems of rehabilitating million of in-coming refugees, restoring the law and order in cities and villages burning with the fires of hatred, and building an infrastructure of the new government with literally nothing in its hands. The civil bureaucracy had the opportunity to create its apparatus in accordance with the aspirations of its founder, on the basis of a modern, progressive, and democratic state, and to establish, the 'peoples' government, responsible to the people, more or less, on democratic lines and parliamentary practices'.[26] For that it had to come out of its colonial mould by accepting the authority of the people of Pakistan and had to assist the political leadership in building a nation-state. Instead, it chose to collaborate with the strategic interests of neo-colonialism and preferred to continue the colonial administrative structures embedded in authoritarian traditions, against the wishes and instructions of Jinnah. Mr Jinnah was a constitutional lawyer, who, throughout his life struggled for a constitutional solution for the Indian Muslims, and finally won a Muslim state through a democratic battle. Under his leadership, the Muslim League scored a victory in the 1946 elections and on whose basis he, later, advocated the case of Pakistan. He had a firm belief in the supremacy of the people and a constitution. His numerous speeches and statements, at various occasions in the last year of his life, should have served the guiding principles for laying down the foundation of the state. He declared to a gathering of civil bureaucrats in Sibi, Balochistan, on 14 February 1948 that, 'Pakistan is now a sovereign state, absolute and unfettered, and the Government of Pakistan is in the hands of the people'.[27]

In a similar vein, when addressing the officers at Chittagong in East Pakistan the following month, he declared, 'those days have gone when the country was ruled by the bureaucracy. It is people's government, responsible to the people more or less on democratic lines and parliamentary practices'.[28] 'Do your duty as Servants', he advised the civil bureaucracy. If the bureaucracy had followed his advice, Pakistan's history would have been different.

Role of the Army

The other domestic partner in this nexus was the army, which was again a creature of colonialism. Like the civil bureaucracy, the army was brought up to be the custodian of 'law and order'. In the colonial state, 'for the army, the nationalist politicians were the greatest threat to law and order,'[29] a tradition which was reinforced in the post-colonial state. Earlier on it was discussed how the security of the new state was tied to the US, the custodian of the 'free world', in its Cold War against the Kremlin. One of the vital strategies of the Cold War was to build defence establishments in the Third World, which were dependent upon the economic and military assistance of the US. Due to the confrontation with India over Kashmir, the army in Pakistan was given a position of the 'final guarantor of the integrity and survival of the country,' placing it in a focal position to steer the state-formation process in its desired direction.

According to Jalal, the Rawalpindi Conspiracy, disclosed in April 1951, and Liaquat's assassination in October 1951, are watersheds of Pakistan's history, when the pendulum of power shifted in favour of non-representative institutions.[30] Liaquat's death paved the way for the bureaucracy-military-feudal alliance to dominate state policies in line with the 'containment doctrine'. It can be speculated that Liaquat Ali Khan was removed from the scene due to his increasingly independent stance and unwillingness to cooperate with the US to playing any role in the Middle East defence until he was given assurances that the US would play a role in resolving the Kashmir conflict. Liaquat's efforts to formulate an Egyptian-Iranian-Pakistan bloc to safeguard the interests of the Muslim world, especially the wealth of oil, were seen as dangerous signs. This speculation is given weight by the observations made by the American ambassador to Pakistan in his secret telegram dated 15 November 1951, sent to the secretary of state in Washington, after the assassination of Prime Minister Liaquat Ali Khan. The American ambassador reported[in]: Developments Iran and Egypt are seriously affecting Pakistan['s] popular position [with] reference [to the] United States and we should now expect [a] period of critical attitudes. This change may imperil parts of [the] information programs. Clearly any revelation of my private understanding with top Government of Pakistan (GOP) officials will create [the] greatest embarrassment to them.[31]

In this background, Liaquat's decision of not sending Pakistani troops to Korea to assist the American forces in 1950 despite the pressure generated by Ghulam Mohammad. The latter had threatened the prime minister 'to govern or get out', and also described the cabinet as a 'stable of mules',[32] was not to be appreciated by the 'top GOP officials', who had a private understanding with the American ambassador. Liaquat demonstrated his statesmanship by convincing the parliament to pass a resolution which condemned North Korean aggression, but offered 5,000 tons of wheat instead of ground troops. The resolution was an effort 'to dispel any doubts that the national parliament was toeing the American line', by declaring that Pakistan was not 'aligning herself inextricably with any power bloc'.[33] Earlier, by accepting Stalin's invitation to visit Moscow, Liaquat had shown his willingness to stay neutral in the Cold War. The Colombo conference held between 26 February and 2 March 1951, in which all the American ambassadors and the State Department officials participated, noted that although Pakistan was willing to provide troops for the defence of the Middle East, it would in exchange insist on military guarantee against India.[34]

> Although Pakistan under Liaquat's leadership was pro-Western, he was unwilling to align with the United States and her allies against the communists unless Washington guaranteed Pakistan's security against India. This was a step that Truman's administration was not ready to take.[35]

In speeches during his tour of West Pakistan in the month of September 1951, a few weeks before his assassination, Liaquat expressed his displeasure and dissatisfaction over the efforts of the United States in resolving the Kashmir issue. 'Aware of the public sentiment' on the Kashmir question, Liaquat asserted that 'Kashmir's place must be with Pakistan...[and] demanded the withdrawal of Indian troops from Kashmir and the cessation of Indian control as a prerequisite for a fair and impartial plebiscite'.[36] It was not in Washington's interest to offend India by supporting Pakistan's case. The United States was in the process of getting Indian and Pakistani signatures for a technical and economic assistance program under the Mutual Security Act of 1951, which would have blocked their entry into the communist orbit.[37] Liaquat's bargaining on a 'territorial guarantee' against India, before signing the Mutual Security Act, was not acceptable in the situation, at a time when the US was engaged in a war in Korea, and was becoming extremely concerned about rapidly-spreading influence of the communist elements in South Asia. The other major concern was the defence of the Middle East in view of Britain's declining grip.

The emerging nationalist feelings in Egypt and Iran were also a matter of serious concern and threat to the imperialist interests. Egypt's refusal to renegotiate the treaty of 1936, under which British had the right to maintain troops in the country and its blockade of the Suez Canal came at a time when in Iran, Prime Minister Mohammad Mossadeq was in the process of nationalizing the British-owned Anglo-Iranian oil company. Similar nationalist anti-imperialist feelings were appearing in Pakistan too. Such feelings were developing within the rank and file of the army also. Major General Akbar Khan and other officers during the Rawalpindi Conspiracy trial 'argued that the British officers serving in the Pakistan army were indifferent, if not inimical, to the aspirations of the country'.[38] These officers contended that 'the British officers were preoccupied with the protection of British interests in Iran and the containment of Russia, rather than with addressing the security concerns arising from the Indian aggression in Kashmir'.[39] In this regard, Brigadier Habibullah's statement before the tribunal needs special attention, in which he admitted that in October or November 1948, during the days of intensive fighting in Kashmir, Major General Tottenham 'had prepared an appreciation, under instruction of the GHQ, on the deployment of a brigade of Pakistanis in Iran to protect the oil fields there'.[40] This admission supports the plea of the secretary of the Rawalpindi Case Trial Committee, which was sent to Louis Saillart [general-secretary] and Serge Rostovsky [secretary] of the World Federation of Trade Unions in Vienna on 7 September 1951, which took the stand that the conspiracy was engineered by the British and American intelligence agencies to kill the growing discontent over the anti-Moscow and pro-West policies.[41] In this connection, a conversation between Iskandar Mirza, the defence secretary of Pakistan, with the army attaché of the American Embassy on 10 March 1951, becomes significant. Iskandar Mirza asked the army attaché that 'if in...[his] opinion there...[was] any connection between this episode [Rawalpindi Conspiracy] and those which happened...in Morocco...and Iran,' the army attaché replied, 'I had no opinion'.[42]

Pakistan joining hands with Iran and Egypt meant that Western powers had to lose the most strategic location to control the rich, Middle Eastern oil wells. Furthermore, it could lead to a nationalist movement in the Muslim world, particularly in those countries, which were rich in oil resources and thus, alter the balance of power. With its hands full with the Korean War and 'massive build up of communist China Forces along northern side of Yalu'[43] (the border between Korea and China), Truman's administration was initially cautious especially in Iran. 'This restraint was dictated by the need to avoid provoking the Soviet Union because an invasion or even a communist coup could have meant the irrevocable loss of Iran's oil resources to the West'.[44]

The perceived threat from the Soviet Union forced the US policy-makers to follow a more aggressive plan to pursue its interests. The Colombo conference was held in accordance with the new role America was to play in the Cold War era, when President Truman presented his budget in early January 1951, which intended to double the military's share to pay for increased American commitments around the world. American interests in Asia were to receive special attention, as the National Security Council advised that the US should take 'calculated risks' in South Asia as envisioned in NSC 98/1, entitled 'The position of the United States with respect to South Asia'.[45] The most significant calculated risk was to ensure that all was done to win India and Pakistan over to the side of the West during the Cold War.[46] The Colombo conference, which was aimed at 'how to proceed' in defending American interests, noted that the Persian and Iraqi sectors could not be defended without Pakistan's assistance, and moves would have to be made to secure it.[47] The conclusion of the conference backed the huge increase in American military spending, which was a clear signal of how America planned to secure Pakistan's help without giving any security guarantee. Pakistan was supposed to take a 'constructive interest in international affairs' that included, 'behind-the-scene efforts to counsel moderation on the part of its more nationalistically inclined Muslim neighbours, notably Egypt and Iran'. Against:

> Pakistan's official attitudes on political issues in the Muslim world was not paralleled by the bulk of the Pakistani Press and other public media which denounced "Anglo-American Imperialism" in customary language and with unaccustomed vigour in some quarters.[48]

Some of these 'quarters' belonged to the Pakistan army, who were not happy with the Kashmir policy and wanted direct action in Kashmir. These quarters were seen as being under the communist influence.[49]

Rawalpindi Conspiracy

To pursue an active pro-west foreign policy, it was necessary to clear the Pakistan army of any communist influence and make such persons in charge of military affairs who had undoubted loyalty for protecting American interests. As discussed earlier, Ayub Khan was selected for this role, though he was quite junior. He was made the first Pakistani commander-in-chief of the Pakistan army, ignoring many capable and senior generals.[50] Trained by General Gracey and patronized by Iskandar Mirza, he was the best choice as far as the Americans were concerned. Immediately, after assuming command, Ayub was involved in a major political and military crisis, which became known as the 'Rawalpindi Conspiracy', and which was seen as a 'communist plot' to overthrow the government. This 'conspiracy' helped Ayub tighten his grip over the army, by getting 'rid of the doubtful ones' after he had 'examined the antecedents of officers'.[51] Zaheer observes that 'for Ayub Khan, whose appointment as commander-in-chief was somewhat controversial in the higher echelons of the army, it was a good opportunity to take advantage of the general scare among the officers and to strengthen his position'.[52] Major General Akbar Khan, the then chief of staff, along with other military officers were accused of plotting a coup against the government with the help of the Communist Party in Pakistan. In a statement issued by the prime minister on 9 March 1951, while on an election tour in the Punjab, it was revealed that a conspiracy had been planned 'to create conditions in the country by violent means and to subvert the loyalty of Pakistan's defence forces'.[53] The prime minister 'could not disclose publicly the details of the plans of those who were implicated in the conspiracy…[for] reasons of national security'.[54] On 10 March 1951, the defence secretary, Iskandar Mirza, told D.W. Hickey, the army attaché to the American Embassy in Karachi, that 'the Russian Embassy to Pakistan had something to do with the plot…and the Embassy had spent considerable money on the Punjab, to the extent of giving cameras to people'.[55] Mirza told the army attaché that 'Major General Akbar Khan is 100 per cent communist and has been in contact with communists since he took up his job as Chief of Staff at Rawalpindi'. The American army attaché reported that 'in the personal opinion of Col. Mirza, conspirators motivated by dissatisfaction with the Government of Pakistan's handling of the Kashmir issue and feeling that Pakistan should turn away from Western powers and toward Soviet Union'.[56] It was reported by the American ambassador that:

> Brigadier Hussain, Director Inter Services Intelligence, expressed opinion to Army Attaché that there…[was] some unrest in Pak Army especially among junior officers and enlisted men, because of failure to settle Kashmir issue. Some members of Army strongly believe a change of Govt…[was] only solution.[57]

The manner in which Major General Akbar Khan's coup plan was linked with the Communist Party in Pakistan and the subsequent establishment of a special tribunal, raised some serious questions about the actuality of a conspiracy. Writing about the conspiracy, Ayub comments that at the time of his leaving, General Gracey:

> did mention to...[him], somewhat vaguely, that there was 'Young Turk' Party in the army....[He] wanted to know what...[General Gracey] meant by that....[General Gracey] was not very explicit, but did say that there were some peculiar people, like Akbar Khan. Two or three months later the Akbar Khan conspiracy, which came to be known as the Rawalpindi Conspiracy, was discovered.[58]

Ayub thought that the conspiracy 'grew in the soil of discontent and distrust and it was able to develop for several reasons'.[59] One of the reasons Ayub offered was 'considerable unrest among the officers caused by a spate of swift promotions'. He wrote that 'every officer felt that unless he was made Commander-in-Chief no one would believe that he had done well in life'. The other reason stated by Ayub was the fighting in Kashmir 'with little directions from the headquarters which placed considerable responsibility in the hands of junior officers'. But the main reason for the discontent, Ayub thought, 'was that we had a government which failed to discharge its functions properly'. Ayub used similar reasoning for overthrowing a civilian government in 1958 and imposing the first Martial Law in the country. Surprisingly, in his autobiography, which was published in 1967, Ayub did not refer to any connection of the communist party with the conspiracy, except the peculiar character of some people. It can be assumed that by then the need to link the conspiracy with the communist factor was no more there, since the establishment felt betrayed at the hands of its American allies. It was an irony of global politics that the America's most trusted 'man' was the first Pakistani head of state to land in Moscow and seek the Soviet's help in negotiating a ceasefire agreement with India in 1965.

However, in the 1950s by connecting the communist party with the conspiracy, the government was handed an 'opportunity to ban the organization, smash its cadres, and scatter its sympathizers and front organizations for all times to come'.[60] Under the pretext of the 'conspiracy', American and British intelligence networks joined hands with the Pakistan intelligence agencies, and the state, using colonial safety acts, wiped out all those progressive and liberal forces, which could have posed a threat to the power structures of a neo-colonial state. Any progressive forum or organization could be declared a 'front organization' of the communist party and faced the wrath of the intelligence agencies. The organizations identified by the central intelligence department as the 'front organizations' of the communist party of Pakistan and considered a threat to the state, included: Peace Committee, Azad Pakistan Party, Democratic Women's Association, Kisan Committee, Sindh Hari Committee, the Punjab Union of Journalists, Azad Pakistan Students Federation, Democratic Students Federation, Peoples Publishing House, Pakistan Trade Union Federation, Pak-Soviet Cultural Association, Pak-China Cultural Association, Civil Liberties Union, and the Progressive Writers' Association.[61] By involving Faiz Ahmed Faiz, who was not only a respected and beloved name in Urdu literature but also one of the leading personalities of the Progressive Movement in Pakistan, along with Sajjad Zaheer, the secretary-general of the communist party, in the Conspiracy, the central intelligence department was given 'an excuse to hound and hunt down prominent writers, trade unionists, and members of the Muzdoor-Kisan, and communist parties of Pakistan'.[62] Jalal writes, 'by accusing budding patriots of pro-communist leanings and government critics of sabotage, the security authorities adopted the postures of holy warriors entrusted with the responsibility to metamorphosis the land of pure into a veritable intellectual wasteland'.[63]

It can be argued, that the fear of Pakistan going into the Soviet orbit provided the 'clue to the complex influences that served as a background' to the conspiracy.[64] No one can deny the fact that:

> until the exposure of the conspiracy, the [communist] Party had been doing fairly well on its own, through its regular cadres and a large number of front organizations in the social, political, and the intellectual fields.[65]

It was believed that all these organizations were operating under the direct inspiration of the Soviet embassy, which was established in March 1950, and was supposed to be providing them with finances and propaganda material.[66] The 'peace campaign' was considered 'a sounding board for Soviet propaganda',[67] which was sweeping the country like a wild fire. It was feared that the Soviet propaganda had a 'very great appeal to the people of Pakistan whose one wish…[was] to be allowed to remain outside the entanglement of the "cold war"'.[68]

Under the threat of the spreading influence of communism, as early as March 1949, the joint services intelligence was circulating reports about alleged plans of the communist party to destabilize the state.[69] According to the office of the high commissioner,

The other document I was shown was entitled "Organizational Plan of the communist Party in Pakistan", a most hair-raising leaflet,...which talked in terms of subterranean armies of shock troops already formed, planned attacks on nerve centres, shadow governments and so on.[70]

Looking at the popularity graph of the progressive organizations, it was highly probable that the communist party would have gained the status of a major mainstream political party, 'capable of playing a secular and socially progressive role'[71] to replace the colonial-feudal political culture of Pakistan. That would have gone against the interests of the American power system. Any such development was likely to affect the Muslim world, especially the Middle Eastern states, where a wave of nationalism was already sending danger signals for the Anglo-American bloc. The fear that through Pakistan, the Soviet Union could spread its influence to the warm waters of the Persian Gulf, had to be countered by all means. This fear was dealt with through the conspiracy, a fact confirmed by a dispatch sent by the American vice-consul in Lahore on 26 July 1951, which stated 'that the central intelligence department is confident that no important communists are at large in Pakistan and that any threats from the organization has ceased for an indefinite period'.[72] In a CIA weekly report sent on 10 July 1953, giving the 'current situation of communism in Pakistan', it was stated that:

In March 1951...discovery of communist implication in the so-called 'Rawalpindi Conspiracy' by high-ranking army officers to overthrow the government led the regime to take stringent anti-communist measures. All important communists were jailed and the influx of communist propaganda from abroad was limited....The assassination of Prime Minister Liaquat Ali Khan in October 1951 gave the government further excuse for repressive action, though there was no firm indication that the communists were connected with the killing.[73]

Faiz Ahmed Faiz, who was then the editor of the *Pakistan Times*—a pro-Moscow newspaper in the eyes of the intelligence agencies—in his statement before the tribunal, accused the Punjab police of falsely implicating him in the case. He claimed that his arrest was due to his editorials which had exposed the establishment of an intelligence system in Pakistan by Jenkins, the DIG of Central Intelligence Department (CID), with the assistance of the British intelligence network.[74] A report sent by the American ambassador as early as 29 September 1949, confirmed the establishment of an intelligence system in Pakistan with the assistance of the British intelligence network. He reported that:

> The United Kingdom High Commissioner informed me that the Foreign Office was planning to send him for discreet distribution background material designed to combat communist propaganda. He said that he had discussed this matter confidentially with the DIG-CID, Anwar Ali of the Punjab Police and that the latter had expressed great interest in such material and had said that he would be willing to distribute the material. He said that he fully understood the circumstances and was prepared to distribute the material in such a way as to make it appear that it emanated from the Punjab police and was even prepared to refrain from disclosing to other members of the Pakistan Government the source of the material.[75]

According to a fortnightly report of the Commonwealth Relations Office, 'Pakistan Times was the main culprit being the Muslim League Paper' in increasing the communist propaganda.[76] However, 'it...[was] thought that responsibility for this lie[d][lay?] on an individual, and not on the party'.[77] And that individual was the editor of the paper, Faiz Ahmed Faiz.

Another fortnightly report observed that:

> in Western Pakistan stern action continu[ed] to deprive the communists of political license. In view of this latitude being allowed to the press...[was] all the more remarkable. The tone of Pakistan Times...[had] become more markedly communistic than ever, and Dawn, a paper reportedly in the Pakistan's Government's confidence,...[had]...been showing increased favour to Russia in the presentation of World news.[78]

It was felt that because of their limited circulation, those two English language papers were not of much concern if the lead was not followed by the Urdu press, 'a position made worse by an increasing tendency of papers published in Pakistani languages to follow their example'.[79] Faiz's activities were being watched with great concern and being reported in fortnightly summaries prepared by the Commonwealth Relations Office about the communist developments in Commonwealth countries. 'The Pakistan Trades Union Federation held a two-day meeting in Lahore, again with the Editor of the Pakistan Times in the Chair'.[80] The summary went on to say that the communists under his leadership were 'making a new bid to attract labour support'.[81]

Although, the tribunal rejected Faiz's defence, the allegation that an intelligence system was being established in Pakistan with the help of British and American agencies to fight communist threat proved true.

> The Cold War in South Asia also had a domestic front. As the internal vulnerabilities of Pakistan and India became more evident (especially in light of the Comintern's 1949 call for revolutionary uprisings throughout the world), Washington mounted a variety of developmental, intelligence, and information programs in South Asia....America cooperated with Indian and Pakistani governments in countering local communist parties.[82]

There is need to analyze the consequences of the conspiracy in the context of 'McCarthyism'—an important strand in American politics of that time. 'Named after the Wisconsin Senator, Joseph McCarthy, this was a period of intense anti-communism which lasted from 1948 to about 1956. The government of the United States actively persecuted the communist party in the USA, its leadership, and others suspected of being communists'.[83]

The manner in which the Rawalpindi Conspiracy provided General Ayub Khan the opportunity to 'tighten its grip' over the army and steer it towards the Western bloc against the popular feeling, is reflected in his conversation with the American consul general on 13 February 1953. Ayub reportedly told the consul general that:

> he had a strict control over the Army officers and with the efficient intelligence of GHQ. He did not feel that any military leader would be successful in inciting others to take action....the failure of Rawalpindi Conspiracy Case would keep military officers from attempting any action.[84]

In making Pakistan a client state of the United States, Ayub's role needs special attention. By December 1952, Ayub was in a position to advise 'the leading politicians of Pakistan that they must make up their minds to go whole-heartedly with the West', and assure the American consul general that the 'Pakistan Army was friendly to the United States and...[would] not allow the political leaders to get out of hand, and the same...[was] true regarding the people of Pakistan'. Assuming the role of the protector, Ayub declared that 'he realized that the army was taking on a large responsibility, but that the army's duty was to protect the country'.[85] As early as February 1953, General Ayub was ready to install 'a Military Government in order to secure stability for Pakistan, stating that the Pakistan Army would not allow either politicians or the public to ruin the country.'[86] This fact was confirmed by the American embassy which maintained regular contact with General Ayub and his senior colleagues, and which had concluded in February 1953 that General Ayub was in complete control of the army and 'the army...[was] definitely ready to take control should Civil Government break down, although they would be reluctant to do so'.[87] In October 1954, the American ambassador reiterated his observation about the 'army's 'ability to step in any time as, if and when necessary'.[88]

Punjab's Role in Creating the Institutional Imbalance

At the time of its birth, Pakistan had the fifth-largest population in the world, and was the world's largest Muslim state, in terms of population. The areas of British India, which constituted the state of Pakistan, each had a different colonial heritage and so each one viewed the emergence of Pakistan from a different angle. The provinces of north-west India including West Punjab, Sindh, British Balochistan, NWFP, along with the tribal agencies and the ten princely states, including Bahawalpur (in the Punjab province), Khairpur (in Sindh), Swat, Chitral, Dir, Amb (in the NWFP), and Kalat, Kharan, Mekran and Las Bela in Balochistan, constituted the western wing of Pakistan, while East Bengal and the district of Sylhet, comprised its eastern wing. The distance was not the only dividing factor between the two wings of Pakistan; the geography, and the colonial inheritance, were two other major factors which contributed towards producing a different political culture. Bengal, which was the first Mughal province to be annexed by the East India Company, had a very strong tradition of independent rule and a long record of struggle for the freedom movement, 'By the victories of Plassey and Buxar (1757 and 1764), the East India Company...in the following half century extended its control over the greater part of the subcontinent'.[89] The company annexed Bengal to monopolize trade and to control the resources of the richest province in India. On the contrary, in north-west India colonial rule was 'prompted by strategic rather than commercial considerations' on a piecemeal basis.[90] When Bengal became the Crown's province after the 1857 Revolt, it was the first province to taste British democracy. Under the Indian Councils Act of 1861, a legislative council was set up in the province, and Bengal became the first 'regulation province' of India, working under the jurisdiction of a High Court. As a result of the introduction of the political reforms and higher educational attainment of its population, political consciousness developed much earlier in Bengal than in the other provinces of India thus placing it on the forefront of constitutional, agitational, and revolutionary politics, especially from 1905 onwards.[91] Muslim League was formed in Dhaka in 1906 and Bengali Muslims played a leading role in Muslim politics.

Since, Bengal was not a part of the British security state of the north-west India it did not go through the same experience of colonialism. As a consequence, the three representative institutions of British colonialism; the army, civil bureaucracy, and the landed class, which were created in the north-western provinces of British India 'to establish a security state', were absent in Bengal. Bengal was the first 'regulation province', where democratic institutions were more developed in comparison to 'non-regulation' provinces of the North West Frontier, Sindh, and the Punjab. The provinces forming the west wing of Pakistan inherited a tradition of bureaucratic authoritarianism. The hallmarks of this tradition were paternalism, wide discretionary powers, the personalization of authority, and the supremacy of the executive over representative institutions. Political institutions were deliberately left weak to patronize the local rural elite in the north-west security state area. This not only retarded political institutionalization, but also placed an insurmountable deterrent in the way of any future socio-economic reform by creating a structure for the dominant feudal political interest, 'The autocratic traditions attendant on the early period of British rule thus persisted within them well beyond the high noon of Empire'.[92]

In colonial Punjab a special bond was established between the peasantry and the army, which proved to be a vital factor in the military dominance in independent Pakistan.[93] Talbot argues that in reinforcing autocracy, there were two important factors which should be considered for evaluating the colonial policies of expansion in the north-west region of India. These included the tribal composition of these regions, and the threat of Russian expansion from Central Asia and Afghanistan. In the post-colonial state-formation process, Punjab, the largest province of West Pakistan, which enjoyed the reputation of the 'loyal' province of the Raj and was represented by three bases of colonial power—the army, civil bureaucracy and the landed class—emerged as the most powerful negotiator, 'the arbiter of national authority'.[94] 'It was difficult for a national government to remain in office without keeping its bridges with the Punjab in good repair'.[95]

The population of East Bengal in 1951 was 41.9 million and that of West Pakistan 33.7 million, as shown in Table 4, below.[96]

Table 4: Population of Pakistan in 1951

	Population (000)	Total (%)
Punjab	18,815	24.9
Sindh	4,606	6.1
NWFP	3,223	4.3
Bahawalpur	1,822	2.4
Khairpur	319	0.4
Balochistan States Union	552	0.7
Balochistan	602	0.8
Karachi	1,123	1.5
NWF Agencies	2,642	3.5
Total West Pakistan	33,704	44.6
East Bengal	41,932	55.4
Total	75,636	100.0

In 1948, the official strength of the constituent assembly was as follows:

East Bengal	44
Punjab	22
Sindh	5
NWFP	3
Balochistan	1
Balochistan States	1
Bahawalpur State	1
Khairpur State	1
NWFP States	1
Total	79

East Bengal had the right to decide the major state policies and determine the shape of the future constitution, having the majority in the constituent assembly on the basis of the majority population. These traditions were sacrificed at the altar of the colonial legacy of a security state, since East Bengal did not have any representation in the defence establishment or civil bureaucracy, two prerequisites for continuation of the concept of a security state in the aftermath of the beginning of the Cold War. Furthermore, East Bengal lacked a landed class and was in direct conflict with the interests of the landed class of West Pakistan's provinces, particularly of the Punjab. Denying the role of East Bengal in Pakistan's defence, General Gracey declared that 'the battle for East Bengal would be fought in the West Punjab'.[97] Because of the continued colonial recruitment policy, highly concentrated in the Rawalpindi division of the Punjab, and a few adjoining poor districts of the NWFP, Punjab was able to maintain the largest share in the defence establishment, which placed it in central position to monopolize the state authority.

East Bengal was perceived, potentially, as a fertile land for germination of communist seeds, and therefore, it had no share in the defence establishment.[98] Due to these 'sins', there were deliberate efforts on part of the Punjab, which emerged as the major partner of neo-colonialism to check East Bengal's claim in the state-formation process. Punjab monopolized the central authority through a group of powerful men, all trained in the autocratic bureaucracy of British India, and who disliked democracy and politicians alike. These representatives of the civil bureaucracy, the 'guardians of the British Empire', were trained in colonial-authoritarian culture, and were used to work in an environment of 'controlled democracy'. They had a special dislike for any feelings of nationalism and politicians. The chaotic circumstances of the partition, in the international context of the Cold War, had put them in charge of the affairs of the new state, 'Officers at the top echelons of the non-elective institutions—the military and the bureaucracy—began to skilfully manipulate their international connections with London and Washington', in order to maintain their control over the state authority.[99] The most powerful man of this 'top echelon' was Malik Ghulam Mohammad (1895-1956), the first finance minister in Liaquat's cabinet, who made a successful bid for power by elevating himself as the governor-general in 1951, after Liaquat's assassination. Nazimuddin was made to step down as the governor-general and was given the post of the prime minister.

> Nazimuddin was a Bengali; Ghulam Mohammad was a Punjabi. Nazimuddin was regarded as weak; therefore the Punjabis discounted him.... Ghulam Mohammad was known to be tough and unyielding; but he was a sick

man.... In taking this decision, the Pakistan cabinet unwittingly terminated the parliamentary experiment in their country.[100]

This decision was not taken by the cabinet as a whole but rather by a group of powerful men. It is interesting to note that the American embassy was aware of this elevation before its announcement in the cabinet meeting. A despatch from the Karachi embassy to the US secretary of state in Washington stated:

> Embassy informed Cabinet meeting tomorrow to be presided over by Governor-General who will probable step down as GG and take over temporarily as PM,' Reference Emb. Des. 409 October 4.[101]

In this message, a reference to the embassy despatch dated 4 October appears intriguing, and could not be traced. Liaquat had decided to remove Ghulam Mohammad from his cabinet and send him to the United States as an ambassador 'where he hoped to recoup his health'.[102] Abdur Rab Nishtar was:

> the man believed to be Liaquat's chosen successor...a jovial but masterful Punjabi landlord, with long political experience stretching back to the days of Khilafat movement. Since July 1949, he had governed West Punjab, but Liaquat was known to have thought of bringing him into the cabinet as deputy Prime Minister.[103]

Nishtar did not succeed Liaquat as prime minister but had to be included in the cabinet due to his influence in the Punjab Muslim League as minister for industries, along with Chauhdry Mohammad Ali who was inducted as the finance minister. Mushtaq A. Gurmani was moved from the Ministry for Kashmir Affairs to the Ministry for Interior due to his influence. This was the most influential group of ministers in the cabinet, and all belonged to the province of Punjab. Nishtar was later dropped from the cabinet when Prime Minister Nazimuddin was dismissed.

> As early as 1948, an American official in Pakistan reported that Ghulam Mohammad viewed himself as Jinnah's successor, had gained "unlimited power" within Liaquat's cabinet and had acquired many followers.[104]

Liaquat's assassination cleared the way for Ghulam Mohammad to become 'Jinnah's successor', although he had no qualification to be in this position. Belonging to a middle class family of Lahore, a civil bureaucrat having 'conservative financial views', and known for his disliking of parliamentary democracy, Ghulam Mohammad considered politicians 'unprincipled and undisciplined' and found 'the ways of party politics alien and distasteful'.[105] His actions as the governor-general demonstrated his dislike for democratic procedures, norms, and traditions which ultimately set the scene for 'failure' of democracy in Pakistan. Strangely, Ghulam Mohammad's elevation to post of the governor-general, negating all democratic norms, was appreciated by the US officials who considered him 'very definitely pro-western and one of the ablest men in the government of Pakistan', who 'had no desire to die before organizing the Muslim World against communism'.[106]

Ghulam Mohammad had a close personal relationship with McGhee, the assistant secretary of state, as revealed by the American ambassador in his correspondence with the State Department. The American ambassador wrote to McGhee on 18 October 1951, after having tea with Ghulam Mohammad and several members of the cabinet:

> I have just talked with Ghulam Mohd. who asked me to send you his affectionate greetings. He said he is bearing up very well under shock of Liaquat's death and necessity for taking immediate decisions that have resulted in his appointment and Nazimuddin's Premiership.[107]

In an earlier correspondence, the American ambassador wrote to McGhee on 7 September 1951:

> Ghulam Mohammad was much moved by your message when I had tea with him this P.M....He requests I deliver you the following message: Please receive Zafrullah[108] when he comes to Washington next week. He hopes you will have him to your home because he wants you to know him better and he hopes you will arrange appointment for Zafrullah for Harriam.[109]

Ghulam Mohammad was one of the favourite officials in the government of Pakistan who had 'a private understanding' with the American ambassador and officials in the State Department. He had 'visited the United States several times in connection with affairs of the International Monetary Fund and the International Bank...and was the prime mover in the formation of a permanent organization of Islamic countries' for economic and political cooperation. He had also 'asked the support of the United States in establishment of an Economic Commission for the Middle East...similar to the Economic Commission for Asia and the Far East'.¹¹⁰ His pro-Western views and his 'influence' in Islamic countries, to be used to the advantage of the United States, was a vital factor in his elevation to the governor-generalship. Pakistan was expected 'to be assiduously cultivated by any and all Muslim countries for support in various controversial Middle East and Asian issues'.¹¹¹ It was observed that it would:

> undoubtedly heighten his already large influence in the cabinet and... [would] tend to counter-balance by a vigorous pro-Western outlook, any compromising tendency in the other direction which may be expressed by Nazimuddin from time to time under domestic political pressure.¹¹²

Prime Minister Nazimuddin, the successor to Liaquat 'as chief of state', was seen as a mere coordinator and 'estimated to lack the drive and imagination to be a policy-career'.¹¹³ The new prime minister was confronted with many troubles, 'squabbles in provincial circles, the Kashmir dispute, and Pakistan's relations with other countries'. However, the American embassy was assured that 'in decisions on these problems, the new Governor-General, Ghulam Mohammad...[had] taken a hand, indicating a desire on his part to transcend the constitutional limits of his position'.¹¹⁴ As expected, within a period of less than two years, the governor-general, transcending his constitutional limits, dismissed the prime minister in a 'coup', when he felt that Nazimuddin was getting political strength and could pose a threat to American interests. In similar vein, the popular ministry of the United Front in East Bengal, which was elected through an election after defeating the ruling party, the Muslim League, was dismissed in May 1954. This happened less than four months after it began working on the pretext of 'communist activities', and the province was placed under governor's rule. The United Front, an alliance of all major political parties of East Bengal, was against the Mutual Defence Agreement which was going to be signed between Pakistan and the United States.

Ghulam Mohammad's most horrendous sin was the dissolution of the first constituent assembly when it revolted against his excessive powers, in October 1954, in a 'constitutional coup'. The assembly was dissolved at a time when, after a long period of seven years, it had successfully reached a consensus on the constitution of Pakistan. A constitution was badly needed for the new state, whose complete authority had yet to be asserted. British Balochistan was deprived of the governor's province status like the other four provinces. Similarly the princely states and tribal frontier areas were operating under colonial rules and regulations. Most importantly, the constitutional rights of the federating units (provinces), and their relationship with the centre in a federation, was yet to be resolved. On the contrary, Indian leaders, within two years, 'liquidated two thousand years of history, overthrowing dynasties which the British had accepted as sacrosanct' and brought them under the Indian constitution, which came into effect on 26 January 1950. 'For several years, administration in the former princely states retained some of its peculiar and unique qualities; but quite rapidly law and administration took on an overall uniformity and unity'.[115] In Pakistan, however, the assembly's dissolution was legitimized by Chief Justice Munir's 'Law of Necessity', which overruled the decision of the Sindh High Court declaring the governor-general's action illegal. A Punjabi chief justice rescued a Punjabi governor-general through his life's most controversial legal decision, which became the basis for such unconstitutional actions to be repeated again and again, sabotaging democratic culture. The Law of Necessity haunts Pakistan till today.

During Ghulam Mohammad's tenure as governor-general, the Pakistan army started to influence both the country's political development and the foreign policy issues confronting it. The Pakistan army was the force behind Ghulam Mohammad's illegitimate coups, first against Nazimuddin, and then against the assembly. After dissolving the constituent assembly in 1954, Ghulam Mohammad invited the army to take over. The Americans did not approve of the army's take over at a time when they were in the process of signing a mutual defence agreement with Pakistan. A civilian government, no matter how authoritarian and dictatorial, was the need of the hour, and the army was to stay behind the scene.

The second name of this 'top echelon' described by Alavi as 'military-bureaucratic oligarchy', and 'the executive group' by the State Department in Washington, was the defence secretary, Major General Iskandar Mirza,[116] who, despite his military designation, was a career bureaucrat. He was backed by his close contacts with the US officials, which helped him succeeded Ghulam Mohammad as the governor-general, when the latter was forced to resign on 6 October 1955, due to his prolonged illness. Mirza was included in the cabinet as the interior minister when Ghulam Mohammad dissolved the assembly in 1954, though, being a civil servant, he could not be appointed in this post. Mirza's letter of retirement was issued post-dated, although no one was bothered about such a violation of the rules when the whole government machinery was involved in illegal methods, 'According to the Gazette of Pakistan dated 21 January 1955, Major General Iskandar Mirza, CSP, retired from Government Services with effect from 24 October 1954'.[117] The notification was issued 'to remove the onus having been appointed to a cabinet post while, still a member of the civil services' because this point was 'raised indirectly by [Maulvi] Tamizuddin his court petition challenging the Government action of 24 October,' of dissolving the constituent assembly.[118] The inclusion of General Ayub, the army's commander-in-chief, in the cabinet, as the minister of national defence, was another gory example of this unholy play which was aimed at depriving the political forces of their legitimate share in the affairs of the government.

Known for his dislike of politicians and democracy, Mirza was appointed the governor of East Bengal in addition to his assignment as the interior minister for 'firm action', when the provincial government of the United Front was dismissed by Ghulam Mohammad in May 1954. Due to his international connections, Iskandar Mirza became the first president of Pakistan after the approval of the 1956 constitution. General Iskandar Mirza's son, Humayun Mirza, married Dodie, the daughter of the American ambassador to Pakistan, during the crucial negotiations of the mutual defence agreement between Pakistan and the United States, in the year 1954. Mirza played a leading role in these negotiations, aided by his 'protégé' General Ayub Khan. This marriage of alliance, which took place on 23 October 1954, had a significant political importance which was not publicized at that time due to the fear of an unfriendly public reaction. H.A. Hildreth, the American ambassador, was concerned 'about any reaction in Pakistan resulting from a Christian wedding'. This concern was shared with the Pakistani ambassador in Washington, who advised, 'if there were nothing in our announcement saying what kind of ceremony was going to be held, he did not think there would be any amount of discussion in Pakistan'.[119] The extent to which this marriage affected the relationship of two governments, can be measured by the reasons the American ambassador gave in convincing Dulles, the secretary of state to invite General Mirza on an official visit to Washington. He wrote:

> Ever since General Iskandar Mirza became Governor-General of Pakistan in the fall of 1955, I have received hints from Pakistan sources and direct suggestions from Americans on my staff that considering General Mirza's

stout adherence to a pro-free world and pro-US foreign policy, he should be invited on an official visit to the United States. General Mirza is the stoutest supporter of the United States in high offices in Pakistan today and I am positive that no hints have been inspired by him. Last night, I learned from reliable sources that Prime Minister Suhrawardy would have refused to let his new Foreign Minister, Firoze Khan Noon, go to the 'Users Conference' in London if Mirza had not insisted by phone to the Prime Minister in East Pakistan that the Prime Minister had agreed there would be no change in foreign policy.

After producing proof of Mirza's loyalty to the United States, the ambassador wrote:

Finally, because of my personal relationship with my son-in-Law, Humayun Mirza, the President's Son, I know that Humayun does not expect to return to Pakistan until he has finished the two year course at Harvard Business School. Because his decision to go to Harvard Business School was hard one for both him and his father, his parting request to his father was that his father visit him while he was in the States....This is all that Humayun has ever mentioned to me and it was said at the airport when I was saying goodbye to him....Therefore, I think it behoves the United States to be in time with its invitation rather than too late.[120]

The 1956 constitution was formulated under the 'watchful' eyes of Iskandar Mirza, who ensured that the office of the president was more powerful than that of the prime minister, and had the authority to dismiss him. Under this authority, General Mirza dismissed four prime ministers within a period of two-and-half years. Mirza played havoc with the politicians and the political system of the country. In East Pakistan, the Muslim League was abolished in the 1954 elections and was officially finished in West Pakistan with the creation of the Republican party under Mirza's tutelage. General Mirza was the one, who first declared martial law in Pakistan on 6 October 1958 by abrogating the 1956 constitution—his own creation—and invited General Ayub to form the government.

The third member of this 'oligarchy' or the 'executive group' was Chaudhry Mohammad Ali, the secretary-general—the overlord of the civil bureaucracy, a special post created on his own advice, and 'later came to be identified with...[him].... This impression was strengthened when the post of Secretary General was not filled, but was allowed to lapse when...[he] became Finance Minister in October 1951,'[121] and later was selected as prime minister in 1956. As discussed earlier,

Chaudhry Mohammad Ali's induction in the cabinet, while he was still in the civil service, is a sheer example of abuse of power and authority, and of disrespect for democratic norms. Setting such examples in the formative years of the nation's life proved to be fatal for the growth of democracy in Pakistan. Again, his selection for the post of the prime minister was not in accordance with the parliamentary traditions.

The fourth name is of General Ayub, the most important member of this oligarchy, which became the 'decision-making body' of Pakistan in alliance with its international patrons, during the first decade of Pakistan's history.

It can be argued that this oligarchy was in alliance with the three dominant economic classes—the metropolitan bourgeoisie, the domestic bourgeoisie, and the feudal class—which were located together within the structure of neo-colonialism. There was no structural contradiction between them and together they constituted a 'block in power' in the post-colonial state.[122] This block was strengthened by the new leader of neo-colonialism, the United States, through the liberal grants of loans, supply of experts, and training of civil and military officials. Pakistan's neo-colonial alliances facilitated the development of an over-sized military and bureaucratic state apparatus; this apparatus in turn, preserved the relations of production to allow the domestic bourgeoisie and the feudal class to appropriate surplus value through the exploitation of the country's material and human capital.[123] The capitalist mode of production led not only towards growing inequalities within the country, but also produced a heavy debt burden, which helped further consolidate Pakistan's dependence on the global imperialist powers.

The axis of the civil bureaucracy and the army that appeared in Liaquat's time, has been discussed, and many observers speculate that Liaquat's murder paved the way for their ascendancy. Liaquat's death in 1951 facilitated this alliance to maintain its control over the democratic institutions through unconstitutional methods.[124] Jalal argues that this process started with the appointment of General Ayub Khan, as the first Pakistani commander-in-chief of the army, and its roots should be traced to the Rawalpindi conspiracy case.[125] General Ayub Khan's appointment surprised most speculators, since he was quite junior, and did not possess any 'superior' qualifications. It is believed that 'undoubtedly General Graccy had a hand in the decision. Even the Americans seemed reassured'.[126] Ayub Khan's appointment was another victory for the pro-Western and anti-communist group of bureaucrats and politicians belonging to the province of Punjab, which later came to dominate the political decision-making process in the country and thus began the eclipse of the parliamentary forces.

Under the banner of parliamentary democracy, a small elite born in colonial capitalism, in partnership with the forces of neo-colonialism, continued to dominate state resources and its policies, keeping away the majority of people from sharing the benefits of independence. The capitalist model, accompanied by the concept of a security state, deprived the people of their freedom to choose an economic model in accordance with their needs. Under the pretext of a communist threat, the state took the shape of a 'garrison state' where any activity concerning people's participation, ranging from students' associations to trade unions and opposition political parties, was considered anti-state. Moreover, the kinds of elite groups which emerged during colonial rule, continued to exist and kept on shaping the contours of the post-colonial state.

The colonial economic structures were not altered, rather, new exploiting forces, in the form of an indigenous bourgeoisie, were added to the institution of a feudal class, in the name of industrial development. Furthermore, the recruitment patterns of the army were not modified, which continued to be concentrated in the western arid zone of the Punjab. The theory of martial races was reinforced by the military authorities that found justification in propagating this theory for the over-representation of certain ethnic groups and the under-representation of others. Like the colonial state, the post-colonial state used land settlement policies for the fulfilment of military needs and maintained the rural bases of military recruitment patterns. The penetrating process of the military into the seminal sources of society's authority, the control and possession of agricultural land, proceeded in the post-colonial period, which resulted in a strong alliance with the landed interests. This alliance, joined by religious factions, became a barrier in adopting any anti-*zamindari* legislation despite the Muslim League's declared policy of agrarian reforms.

An examination follows of the role of religion in strengthening the military-civil bureaucracy-feudal nexus in the early years of the state-formation process, when with the Chinese Revolution the spread of communism in Asia became a nightmare for the planners of the neo-colonial world.

Islamic Ideology—A Shield against Communist Ideology and a Guardian of Neo-colonial Economic Policies

In addition to building a large defence establishment, the powerful ruling clique of Pakistan, in alliance with the British and American intelligence networks, contrived the wall of religion as a shield in the form of 'Islamic Ideology', to promote the fear of communism. The use of religion, as a tool to fight the 'evils' of the communist ideology, was a strategy devised for most of the Muslim countries, especially the 'oil rich countries', vacated by the colonial powers. The strategy was to align these countries into new defence pacts by creating client garrisons which would be ready to move against communist aggression.

The trend encouraged and grouped all the conservative elements of the society, which, along with the shield of Islamic ideology, served as a tool to fight the 'evils' of the communist ideology, and thereby help to preserve the colonial economic structures in the post-colonial state. The Rawalpindi conspiracy was an early manifestation of this process, which helped eliminate the progressive and liberal elements from the society in the name of a threat from communism. This encouraged a continuation of the colonial patronage for the conservative elements to block anti-Western and anti-colonialism sentiments and help promote religious fanaticism.

> Islamic Ideology...forms an important part of the general social, legal and political superstructure which has been constructed to justify and preserve the...social relationships between feudal lords and serfs, capitalists and wage-labourers, based on the semi-feudal and capitalist mode of production, which in itself is linked to international monopoly capitalism.[127]

Anti-Ahmadiya riots in 1953, led to the imposition of the first martial law in Punjab and the dismissal of the second prime minister in an unconstitutional act. This was the result of the ideological structure, created by the ruling elite of Pakistan, in collaboration with their international sponsors. This course started in the aftermath of the Chinese Revolution when, 'exchange of intelligence information on communist activities and the police information' in 'countries interested in the area' was felt necessary, especially in peace-time, to check the spread of communism, besides building up the military.[128] To contain the communist revolution, all the conservative forces in the domestic society were grouped together and promoted. No love for communism could be tolerated and all the progressive elements in society had to be checked. The Foreign Office in London, made every effort to formulate a unified political action with the countries concerned, to control the communist influence. To achieve this objective, the Foreign Office in London, suggested that 'the free exchange of intelligence information about communist activities between the Governments of the countries concerned would lead to co-operation between the security forces in dealing with communist Leaders and their armed bands'.[129] The telegram sent by the UK high commissioner in Pakistan to the Commonwealth Relations Office, dated 25 December 1948, reveals the campaign against communism organized by the Central Office of Information in London. The commissioner informed the Commonwealth Relations Office that 'the material to combat communism…[was] originated by the Central Office of Information, and sent by radio, cable or air mail to the British Information Service here, who endeavoured to place it in as much of the Pakistan Press as possible'.[130] He further wrote that 'arrangements… [were] made locally for translation into Urdu, Pushto and Gujrati'.[131] The commissioner gave the details of the use, 'which might be made of material received from the Information Department recently [then] been established in the Foreign Office for dealing with communist propaganda'. He stated that 'we…[had] decided that for the present [then] an approach should be made to the Editor of one newspaper only, a Karachi English daily on whose co-operation reliance…[could] be placed'. It was assumed that 'material accepted by him…[would] automatically be published in an associated English daily in Lahore, and [then] this material…[would] filter through to the vernacular press'.[132]

The Pakistan government was 'fully conscious of dangers arising from communist conquest of China and [its] suggestion for an early meeting of Commonwealth Ministers, however, unrealistic [reflected] their apprehension'.[133] To meet the communist threat the British government was more than eager to establish a 'complete security intelligence link between London and Karachi'.[134] This suggestion was discussed with the foreign minister of Pakistan, who found it an 'excellent idea' and advised the British high commissioner in Pakistan to discuss it with the foreign secretary, Ikramullah.[135] The British High Commissioner in Pakistan followed the advice and was surprised to find out that 'all this was already working'.[136] Finding fertile ground, it was suggested by the Commonwealth Relations Office that 'it would be unfortunate, if occasion, were not taken…to propose to Pakistan

Government extension of existing co-operation in whatever way suit[ed] UK Government...this...[would] not be limited to suggestions about anti-communist publicity and propaganda, only'.[137]

This is how public opinion in Pakistan was being influenced by the campaign against communism, sponsored by the UK's foreign and information ministries, later joined by the US embassy and USIS (United States Information Services). In August 1949, the US team in Karachi had informed the secretaries of state and defence, 'that senior Pakistani officials were seeking funds and authority "to establish a large secret civilian intelligence agency".'[138] In December 1949, the finance minister shared his fears with the US assistant secretary of state that the newly-appointed Russian ambassador would be accompanied by 'certain trained secret agents' and requested for US help 'in a free interchange of information regarding the activities of the new Russian Ambassador and his staff'.[139] In addition to the British intelligence network in Pakistan, the finance minister was eager to explore the possibility of receiving help from the American intelligence as well, to build up an 'Islamic barrier against communism'.[140] This feeling was shared by the foreign minister, Chaudhry Zafrullah[141] who 'was not greatly concerned with communist influence in West Pakistan' but believed that in 'East Bengal there was always greater danger due to the terrible overcrowding of population'. For him the solution was in orthodox Islam, which 'provides a sure shield against communism'.[142] Similar views were shared by the labour minister, who advised the participants of the Eastern Pakistan Trades' Union Federation Conference held in Dhaka in 1949, that they should base 'their lives on sound Islamic principles and not to look to other countries for guidance in trade union affairs'.[143]

In July 1950, the discovery of 'communists stationed in Lahore'[144] provided the central government an opportunity to involve the American embassy to assist the Pakistani security apparatus in countering the Soviet propaganda effectively. In the campaign against communism, *Nawa-i-Waqt*, the Urdu daily published from Lahore, took the lead. It was supported by the powerful Punjabi alliance of civil bureaucrats and landed politicians. A memorandum of the US State Department reveals how public opinion in Pakistan was being influenced by identifying and encouraging those policymakers and influential individuals who were considered pro-Western. While senior government officials were seen as pro-Western, the press and universities were seen as dangerous zones.[145] In the war against communism, Pakistan was being conceived as assuming the leadership of the Muslim world and to be persuaded to join a Middle East Defence Group. As an initial step, the State Department proposed the organization of an Islamic economic conference in Karachi and establishment of an Islamic University.[146]

In this context it should not be surprising to see the wall of religion being built-up to combat the fear of communism. A pro-West and anti-communist group of bureaucrats and politicians, belonging to the province of Punjab, emerged as the 'custodian' of Islamic ideology and any voice of difference was considered a threat to the 'interests of the state'. Very soon, the target became Prime Minister Liaquat Ali Khan, who was being pressurized to toe the lines of this emerging 'clique'. Supported by the international forces of neo-colonialism, this group had a two-pronged policy: one, attacking the liberal and progressive elements of the society, under the pretext of 'Islamic Ideology', for protecting the interests of the landed elite and the defence establishment. And second, consolidating state power in the hands of the civil and military bureaucracy. USIS was given a special mission of promoting this Islamic ideology with these objectives: (1) 'to show the communists as anti-God and therefore a threat to the continued existence of the Muslim world as a free and independent religio-political entity;' (2) 'to discredit the concept of communism as a panacea or even as an acceptable socio-economic theory'; and (3) 'to promote the Islamic socio-economic concept under which there will be freedom and dignity for the individual and which will provide for the elimination of economic disparities and inequalities.'[147]

It was contested that the foundations of 'Islamic ideology' were laid down by Quaid-i-Azam Mohammad Ali Jinnah's 'two-nation theory', which gave birth to Pakistan. There is no doubt that religious identity was the main contributing factor in the creation of Pakistan and partition of colonial India into two independent nations, however, Jinnah declared, soon after the announcement of independence, that the 'two-nation theory', having achieved its logical conclusion, should be abandoned and Hindus and Muslims living in any dominion should be treated as equal citizens of the state irrespective of their religious identity. Jinnah's address in the inaugural session of the constituent assembly of Pakistan on 11 August 1947, gave clear directions to build the new state on a western democratic pattern, providing a guarantee for social justice and equal status for every citizen. Jinnah declared:

> You are free; you are free to go to your temples, you are free to go to your mosques or to any other place of worship in this state of Pakistan. You may

belong to any religion or caste or creed-that has nothing to do with the fundamental principles that we are all citizens and equal citizens of one State. Now, I think we should keep that in front of us as our ideal, and you will find that in course of time, Hindus would cease to be Hindus, and Muslims would cease to be Muslims, not in the religious sense, because that is the personal faith of each individual, but in the political sense as citizens of the State.[148]

Many historians criticize Jinnah and his colleagues for not giving any 'blueprint for the state they intend[ed] to create'. Ziring has argued that 'the chaos that overwhelmed Pakistan at independence was a consequence of little planning and virtually no conceptualization'.[149] On the other hand he stated that, 'Jinnah devoted all his energy and used all his time in convincing the viceroy that a sovereign Muslim State within the subcontinent was not only justifiable but also feasible'.[150] The fact is that Jinnah not only had to devote his time to convince the Viceroy but to fight the battle on many other fronts also. Jalal suggests that Jinnah deliberately chose not to give any 'blueprint' because of the presence of visible conflicting interests of Indian Muslims scattered all over India. To become the 'sole spokesman' of Indian Muslims, Jinnah required support of every Indian Muslim group, the landed class, the industrials, the students, women, farmers, workers, and the ulema. Jalal argues that Jinnah was using the two-nation theory:

> to negotiate a new constitutional arrangement in which Muslims would have an equal share of power at a centre reconstituted on the basis of a partnership between two essentially sovereign states, Pakistan (representing the Muslim majority provinces) and Hindustan (representing Hindu majority provinces).[151]

Jinnah was leading a party who had its main bases of support in the Hindu majority provinces, if the Muslims of the Hindu majority provinces had to play an effective role in the making of India's constitutional future, then Muslims in the Muslim majority provinces had to come under the umbrella of the Muslim League. Without their support, the League, under the leadership of Jinnah, could not claim to be the sole representative body of Indian Muslims. The League had little organization and support in Muslim majority provinces, especially in the Punjab, which was dominated by the landed class of 'Unionists' and was called the 'corner stone of Pakistan'. Without the Punjab in his lap,

EMERGENCE OF THE INSTITUTIONAL IMBALANCE   121

there was no weight in Jinnah's demand to solely negotiate India's constitutional future on behalf of the Indian Muslims. With a very weak organizational structure, the League was in no position to mobilize the masses of Indian Muslims:

> this is where religion came to the rescue of a politician whose secular leanings had won him the title of ambassador of Hindu-Muslim unity...yet Jinnah's resort to religion was not an ideology to which he was ever committed or even a device to use against rival communities; it was simply a way of giving a semblance of unity and solidity to his divided Muslim constituents.[152]

The interests of Muslims in the Hindu majority provinces were different from those in the Muslim-majority provinces. The most important fact remained that the state of Pakistan, which Jinnah wanted to create, was going to have an undivided Bengal and Punjab, and with a very large non-Muslim population in these two provinces, Jinnah could not afford to alienate any section of the population by announcing future state policies. It was safer to leave it to the future legislators to frame state policies in accordance with their needs and requirements, once the state had been created. However, Jinnah made it very clear that the state he was fighting for was not going to be a 'theocracy', and would be based upon principles of democracy. 'There can be no doubt that Jinnah was a secularist and against theocracy,'[153] and given a chance, he could have led the constituent assembly to form a constitution on secular lines, based upon parliamentary democracy similar to the constitution of Britain, the one he was familiar with. However, soon after Jinnah's death, a debate about the secular or Islamic 'nature of the constitution', shadowed the process of constitution-making in Pakistan. All those religious parties, who were against the creation of Pakistan and Jinnah, now joined hands and formed a 'pro-Shariat lobby', campaigning for an 'Islamic form' of constitution; the only constitutional form acceptable to them. American and British networks funded these religious parties for playing their role in the war against communism. By promoting religious parties the aim was to check the growth and popularity of those groups and political parties, which were leaning towards communism.

Under the pressure of this powerful 'pro-Shariat lobby', Liaquat was trapped into introducing the Objectives Resolution in the constituent assembly on 2 March 1949, which was not only 'quite contrary to the Quaid-i-Azam's conception of the State,'[154] but it also encouraged the 'orthodox elements' within and outside the cabinet. This resolution was introduced at a time when agrarian reforms were being discussed in the Agrarian Committee, specifically established by the Muslim League. The Objectives Resolution became a tool in the hands of the pro-Shariat lobby which wanted to divert the public's attention away from the question of agrarian reforms, and engage them in the controversy of the relationship of Islam and the state and the proprietary rights in Islam. Nawab Mamdot, the chief premier of the Punjab, headed this lobby and was supported by the powerful landed elite, religious parties, and the vernacular press. 'Mamdot increasingly cultivated the religious groups and posed as the upholder of Punjab autonomy'.[155] This lobby had their benefactors in the central government, besides the finance minister, Ghulam Mohammad, who had 'gained 'unlimited power' within Liaquat's cabinet;'[156] it also included Chaudhry Mohammad Ali, the secretary general of the central government, known for his 'right wing' leanings, and the defence secretary, Iskandar Mirza. All these three pro-West bureaucrats were trained in the conservative administrative environment of British colonialism in which religion was used to create local allegiances to cap the growth of representative institutions.

In Chapter 1, it has been discussed, how the ideological structure of the British rule converted *sajjada nashin*s of the shrines into 'agricultural tribes' thus nurturing the religious influence of these local leaders and integrating them into the structures of colonial capitalism, 'The political positions of Islamic religious leaders reflected their places within the larger political and ideological structure of British rule'.[157] This legacy continued in the post-colonial state in order to help establish Punjabi hegemony. As discussed earlier, a number of religious parties, who were not in favour of Pakistan and considered the Muslim League and its leaders 'anti-Islamic', encouraged by this lobby, joined hands to pressurize the government into introducing Islamic laws. Under the banner of Islamic laws this lobby rejected state control over agricultural land and fixation of any limits in ownership rights. It was necessary to do so because of the popularity the Kisan party was gaining in Punjab by voicing the concerns of the millions of incoming refugees, and campaigning for legislation of tenancy rights, and distribution of agricultural land. The big landlords were not only busy obtaining the land left behind by Hindus and Sikhs by all 'unlawful' means, but they were also busy resisting any kind of agrarian reforms. The proposal by the minister of refugees and rehabilitation in the Punjab cabinet for redistributing agricultural land and the tenancy reforms, which were to be pursued in the resettlement program in East Punjab, faced such an opposition that he had to resign from his ministry. His resignation was an indication that the structure of landownership in West Punjab would continue to sustain an agrarian system in which land was 'perceived to be a political rather than a commercial commodity'.[158] The Punjab premier was the most vocal voice against these proposals, which included a 50-acre ceiling on landholdings, the nationalization of basic industries and the exchange of refugee property through officially appointed trustees.[159]

The power of the landed elite was again manifested when the report of the agrarian committee of the Pakistan Muslim League had to be shelved under their pressure. This report appeared in July 1949 and reflected the radical views of the progressive elements in the Muslim League and popular public opinion. The committee recommended a ceiling on landownership of 450 acres of the non-irrigated and 150 acres for irrigated land, and called for greater security for tenants and uncompensated abolition of *jagirs*.[160] The findings of the report generated an opposition more formidable than the prescriptions and 'the central government had to beat a hasty retreat'.[161] Jalal observes that 'even before the report of the Pakistan Muslim League's agrarian reform committee had become public the bigger landlords had taken recourse to religion'. The pro-Shariat lobby was encouraged to denounce the central government and its agrarian policy. The hasty retreat of the central government strengthened the 'old guard' and disheartened many League members, who were now looking for other alternatives. The communist party was such an alternative, which was attracting students, farmers, trade unions, and intellectuals alike. The socio-economic policies of the central government, accompanied by a large defence budget, were creating unrest among the people. The summer of 1950 witnessed an unprecedented agrarian unrest in many districts of the Punjab due to the announcement of the Punjab Protection and Restoration of Tenancy Rights Act. Although the act provided security of tenure under certain conditions, it was far removed from the demands, put forward by the small farmers. Under the influence of big landlords, the League was not in a position to introduce any revolutionary agrarian reforms. This resulted in 'unrest among the urban as well as the rural people', who were getting increasingly disillusioned with the League.[162]

The Objectives Resolution brought to surface the differences of interests between East Pakistan and the Punjab. Objecting to the resolution, the non-Muslim members of the constituent assembly largely from East Pakistan, complained 'that in the state envisaged by that Resolution their position would be that of *Zimis*, contrary to what the Quaid-i-Azam had declared'.[163] The most important question here is to explore why the state deviated from the path of secularism, as clearly laid down by Jinnah, in his inaugural address of the constituent assembly of Pakistan on 11 August 1947. The fact that in the aftermath of the Cold War, it was felt necessary to continue with the colonial legacy of a security state, has already been discussed. In this framework, the province of Punjab was placed in the central position of the state authority since it monopolized the most powerful institutions of both the army and the bureaucracy. By introducing the Objectives Resolution, the constituent assembly initiated a controversy which strengthened the orthodox elements inside and outside the assembly, who attained such a powerful status that the process of constitution-making became a hostage in their hands.

The religious controversy proved to be a vehicle for Punjab's hegemony over other provinces. East Pakistan, having a large Hindu minority and more progressive attitudes, was in direct conflict with the interests of Punjab. The conflict of interest was visible in the debates of the legislative assembly and caused the long delay in constitution-framing. The 'Interim Report', a constitutional draft submitted to the constituent assembly by Liaquat in September 1950, invited a lot of criticism from the Bengali legislators who 'were not granted a legislative majority although they constituted the majority of the population of Pakistan. They saw themselves being turned into a minority by the bicameral provision of the Interim Report'.[164] The working committee of the East Pakistan Muslim League demanded radical changes in the report. Feelings of the East Pakistani people were reflected by the *Pakistan Observer* of Dhaka, which called the report a 'fatal stab and shameless conspiracy against the province by the power drunk ruling clique in Karachi to impose a dictatorship under the camouflage of Islam'.[165]

The report, which was basically a reproduction of the 1935 Act along with some of the amendments made in the Indian Independence Act, and with the Objectives Resolution as the Preamble, was not only given an unfavourable reception in East Pakistan, it disturbed equally those religious elements who believed that it had departed from the principles accepted in the Objectives Resolution.[166] Due to strong opposition, Liaquat had to withdraw the report. With his assassination in October 1951, the task of constitution-making shifted to the shoulders of the new prime minister, Khwaja Nazimuddin, who belonged to East Pakistan. Like Liaquat, he had to face many obstacles in the process of constitution-making. There were strong forces working against the democratic institutions. The *Nawa-i-Waqt* launched a campaign to prove the 'incompetence of the Assembly'.[167] Maulana Maududi, the leader of the Jamaat-i-Islami, declared the beginning of a campaign of public demonstrations for an Islamic constitution.

In November 1952, Nazimuddin submitted the Basic Principles Committee Report to the constituent assembly, which was an elaboration on Liaquat's interim report.[168] A day before the submission of the report, thousands of Maududi's followers paraded in front of the assembly building in Karachi with banners and placards. The president of the assembly was forced to impose Section 144 of the Rules of Civil Procedure and ordered the press not to write about the contents of the report.[169] It appeared that the demonstration against the report had the approval of the governor-general, Ghulam Mohammad, who was not in its favour. The Punjab Muslim League, which had at first supported the report, withdrew it under the influence of the governor-general.[170] The report introduced the principle of parity in representation between the east and west wings in both houses, lower and upper:[171]

> The five to one advantage West Pakistan enjoyed over East Bengal in the upper house, by the equal weight of the units given in the provinces in the Interim Report, was abolished by making East Bengal's vote in the upper house equal to the combined vote of all of the provinces of West Pakistan, sixty to sixty.

These legislative representations were seen as Nazimuddin's policy of increasing the power of East Pakistan vis-à-vis Punjab. The Punjab Muslim League insisted on a unitary form of government instead of a federal one, a thought that form of government was not acceptable to any other province. Punjab feared that the greater number of units in West Pakistan would provide an opportunity for East Pakistan's politicians to form a bloc in alliance with the smaller units of West Pakistan against its interests. *Pakistan Times*, representing the Punjab case, produced editorials against parity.[172]

By giving the voting power to East Pakistan, the interests of the neo-colonial powers had to be sacrificed, since East Pakistan was considered a fertile ground for communist activities. On 7 August 1951, the American embassy sent a despatch to the Dhaka consulate containing a coordinated program for combating communism in East Pakistan' with the purpose 'to destroy communist influence and develop a positive (counter) program based on the new national ideals of Pakistan'. To achieve this goal, media, including the press, radio, motion pictures, film strips, publications (books and pamphlets, and graphic arts (posters, cartoons, and posts), were to be employed. Organizations and individuals to be used for media disposal were to include cultural organizations (literary, musical, etc.), reading rooms (publicly-and privately-sponsored), religious groups, speaker's bureau (to be established and so organized that there will be a continuing schedule of speeches throughout the province by the government and civic leaders). Lecture programs were to be organized with the objective 'to utilize native and important talent to come from areas that have been victimized by Soviet aggression'. Target groups included education (mainly students and faculty of Dhaka University, and its sixty-seven affiliated colleges), labour (leaders, groups, and publications), armed forces, and the general populace (agrarian groups, women's clubs, youth groups, etc.)'.[173] One of the major aims of this program was to develop 'an understanding with religious leaders...so that an anti-communist drive...[could] be launched from the pulpit'. It was advised that the 'campaign should use the theme that communists being anti-religion... were therefore anti-Muslim'. To achieve this objective the strategy was to use 'material showing persecution of religious groups and in particular persecution of Muslims should be provided for this campaign'.[174] The governor of East Pakistan was more than willing to support this program and gave special instructions to the bureaucracy of the government of East Pakistan 'that cooperation with US information forces should be undertaken'.[175] Under this program, Information officers in the government of East Pakistan were sent to Washington for training and the State Department was requested 'to furnish materials requested by Dhaka upon urgent basis.[176] Collaboration between the USIS and the Government of East Bengal [Pakistan]...[was] to be kept secret'.

With this background, it should not be difficult to understand why the principle of parity was not acceptable to the province of Punjab, which represented the base of real power, the army, the landed elite and the bureaucracy using religion as its vehicle. To make its voice even more forceful, the pro-Shariat lobby in the province was activated by the power brokers to protest against the non-implementation of the recommendations of the Board of Talimat-i-Islamia. To satisfy the religious factions, the Basic Principles Committee had proposed a number of provisions, including that the head of the state should be a male and the government should be guided by the principles set out in the Objectives Resolution. In addition, there were such provisions like urging the teaching of the Quran, abstention from alcohol consumption, prohibition of gambling and prostitution, greater propagation of Islam among the people, and measures to bring existing law into conformity with the Quran and the Sunnah. There were many more provisions, including a proposal for an Ulema board, to serve as an expert agency to prevent the implementation of any legislation of the assembly repugnant to the principles of Islam, which raised a strong reaction among those who had hoped for a constitution reflecting modern and secular concepts. To satisfy the religious factions, the Basic Principles Committee Report went beyond the intent of the Objectives Resolution by including Islam in the constitutional framework.[177] The majority of the religious factions were content with this, having gained many of their objectives in the draft of the constitution.

However, the religious factions in Punjab joined hands with the Punjab Muslim League members in opposition of the Basic Principles Committee report.[178] Under the instructions of Daultana and Mamdot, two strong leaders of the Punjab Muslim League, major newspapers of the province, such as the *Nawa-i-Waqt* and the *Pakistan Times*, carried on a vigorous opposition campaign. At the All Parties Conference held in Lahore on 28 December 1952, great pressure was exerted to force Nazimuddin to withdraw the report. Those tactics proved successful. Nazimuddin withdrew the report and adjourned the assembly *sine die* on 21 January 1953. To negotiate with Punjab, Nazimuddin visited Lahore along with eight members of his cabinet. Negotiations to find solutions to the disagreements in the constitution were underway, but before anything could be finalized the nation was plunged into the Ahmadi disturbances.

The religious factions in Punjab, who were not happy with the Basic Principles Committee report, found a way to pressurize Nazimuddin by demanding that the government should declare the Ahmadis a non-Muslim minority, and Zafrullah Khan and all other Ahmadis holding government posts should be dismissed. A Council of Action was formed by the Ulema to campaign for their demands. On 21 January 1953, the Council met Prime Minister Nazimuddin and delivered an ultimatum, threatening to resort to direct action if the government did not accept their demands.[179] The anti-Ahmadi forces enjoyed the backing of the chief minister of Punjab, Daultana, who was the strongest Muslim League leader in West Pakistan.

> The Punjab Muslim League had accepted the demands and many Muslim Leaguers whose government was in office had joined the agitation. While accepting their demands, the Chief Minister of Punjab had informed the deputationists that the matter was for the Centre to decide.[180]

Daultana had signed a proclamation which,

> stated that the Provincial Government was also to negotiate with the centre, and that Daultana was to present the demands of the people to the Prime Minister. The demands were the "unanimous demands of the nation" and called for the immediate resignation of Zafrullah from the cabinet.[181]

What the centre was thinking is reflective in Mirza's conversation with the charge d' affairs of the American embassy on 16 January 1953, who 'emphasized need for stronger Government' in Pakistan, considering 'foolish to talk of democracy in US or British sense with only 10 per cent population literate'. Mirza 'called BPC report worse than useless and basically an "irreligious document"', describing 'Mullahs as dangerous element in Pakistan after communists although without significant power'.[182] Though Prime Minister Nazimuddin had sympathies with the Ulema, 'he was confronted with the situation that either he should accept the demands or as Prime Minister treat the ultimatum as a challenge to law and order'.[183] On 7 March, Nazimuddin ordered the arrest of the anti-Ahmadi leaders. As a result, the whole province, particularly Lahore, became engulfed in violent religious riots.

To maintain law and order, the army was called in and martial law was imposed 'in spite of PRIMIN objections'.[184] The anti-Ahmadi disturbances were initiated to create pressure on Nazimuddin's administration:

> This situation was brought about by people who wanted to get into power in the centre. They thought that by creating unrest, the men at the helm of affairs in the centre would have to go. The old and tried method of attacking the religious minority sect called Ahmadis was used to inflame the minds of otherwise peaceful people.[185]

Using Section 92 A, the prime minister dismissed Daultana as the Punjab premier and appointed Firoze Khan Noon in his place. This action proved to be disastrous for him. In a surprise move, on 17 April 1953, the governor-general in alliance with his domestic and international partners, called Nazimuddin and his cabinet members to his residence and demanded their resignations. Nazimuddin refused to obey and was dismissed by Ghulam Mohammad. Nazimuddin termed the action 'illegal and unconstitutional course...against the basic principles of democracy'.[186] Justifying the governor-general's undemocratic action, the American embassy considered it a 'method of effecting change', which could 'be criticised as undemocratic' but the 'only other way to remove CAB [cabinet] would.... [had] been by military coup'. There is strong evidence that Ghulam Mohammad acted on the advice of his defence secretary, Iskandar Mirza, and army chief, General Ayub. John K. Emmerson, charge d' affairs of the American embassy reported that:

> It becomes clear that Nazimuddin dismissal was planned and accomplished through combined efforts of Army leadership (Specially Def Secy Iskandar Mirza and C-in-C Gen Ayub) and Gov Gen himself. Frustrations which EBMB has reported over past few months grew to exasperation at weakness and vacillation of Nazimuddin.[187] Conclusions must have been reached that only remedy for situation was departure PRIMIN from scene.[188]

Considering it as 'one of the most popular coups in history,'[189] the American charge d' affairs appreciated Nazimuddin's 'departure from scene' and wrote that, 'No doubt that change....[had] accomplishment removal those individuals least friendly to United States'.[190] Nazimuddin was replaced with Mohammad Ali Bogra—Pakistani ambassador in Washington. Nazimuddin's government was accused of providing strength to Pakistani communists who 'had recovered sufficient confidence in their own strength and in the weakness of the government to challenge the later with a display of open violence'. This was reported in a CIA secret report dated 10 July 1953, concluding that 'Installation of new Pakistani government on 17 April 1953, fully supported by high civil and military officials, however, effectively blocked the communists'.[191]

With the unconstitutional dismissal of Nazimuddin, a shift in the power base took place. The institutional balance tilted towards the non-democratic institutions, and representative institutions lost their say. In the process, the army emerged as the most powerful institution of the post-colonial state, which developed a dependant relationship with the American power system by entering into military and economic alliances, and Pakistan took the shape of a 'client' state of the US American charge d' affairs observes on 25 September 1954:

> Pakistan's policy of alignment with the west was set in motion by the change in Government of April 1953.[192]

NOTES

1. Judith Justice, 1987, 'The Bureaucratic Context of International Health: A Social Scientist's View', *Social Science and Medicine*, 25: 1301-1306.
2. Arthuro Escober, 1985, 'Discourse and Power in Development: Michael Foucault and the Relevance of His Work to the Third World', *Alternatives* 10: 227-400.
3. See Gabriel Almond and J. Coleman (eds.), 1960, *The Politics of the Developing Areas* (Princeton); Joseph La Palombara, (ed.), 1961, *Bureaucracy and Political Development*; Leonard Binder, *Religion and Politics in Pakistan* (Berkeley); and Samuel P. Huntington, 1968, *Political Orders in Changing Societies* (New Haven).
4. K.S. Singh, 'Colonial Transformation of Tribal Society in Middle India', *Economic and Political Weekly*, 29 July 1978:1221. B. Chandra described colonialism as an 'unsuccessful effort at modernization', Bipan Chandra, 'Colonialism, Stages of Colonialism and the Colonial State', *Journal of Contemporary Asia*, 10 (1980), p. 272.
5. W. Rostow, 1962, *The Stages of Growth: a Non communist Manifesto*, Cambridge: Cambridge University Press.
6. J. Tendler, 1975, *Inside Foreign Aid*, Baltimore: Johns Hopkins Press.
7. Anthony Smith, 1978, 'The Case of Dependency Theory', in W. Scott Thomson (ed.), *The Third World: Premises of U.S. Policy*, California: Institute of Contemporary Studies, San Francisco.
8. G. Hancock, 1989, *Lords of Poverty: The Power, Prestige, and Corruption of the International Aid Business*, New York: The Atlantic Monthly Review, 1989.
9. Nigel Harris, 'States, Economic Development, and the Asian Pacific Rim,' in Richard Appelbaum and Jefferey Henderson (eds.), 1992, *States and Development in the Asian Pacific Rim*, Newbury Park: Sage Publications, p. 76.
10. Hamza Alavi, 1972, 'Class and State in Pakistan', in Hassan Gardezi and Jamil Rashid (eds.), *Pakistan: The Unstable State*, op. cit., p. 65. The term 'military-bureaucratic oligarchy' was used by Hamza Alavi in his discourse on the state-formation process in post-colonial states. See for example 'The State in Post-Colonial Societies' in *New Left Review*, 74.
11. See Khalid Bib Sayeed, *Pakistan: The Formative Phase 1857-1948*, London: Oxford University Press, 1968; and Allen McGrath, *The Destruction of Pakistan's Democracy*, op. cit.
12. See Zahid Chaudhry, 1990, *Pakistan Ki Siyasi Tareekh* [Urdu], Vol. 4, Lahore: Idara Mutalia Tareekh.
13. See Hector Bolitho, 1964, *Jinnah, the Creator of Pakistan*, London: John Murray, pp. 208-16.

14. Shahid Javed Burki and Robert Laporte, Jr. (eds.), 1984, *Pakistan's Development Priorities-Choices for the Future*, Karachi: Oxford University Press, p. 239.
15. Allen McGrath, *The Destruction of Pakistan's Democracy*, op. cit., p. 32.
16. Ibid.
17. Mohammad Ali Jinnah, *Speeches as Governor-General of Pakistan 1947-48*, Karachi: Government of Pakistan, n.d.
18. Shahid Javed Burki and Robert Laporte, Jr. (eds.), *Pakistan's Development Priorities-Choices for the Future*, op. cit., p. 239.
19. Ibid., p. 242.
20. Ralph Braibanti, 1959, 'The Civil Service of Pakistan—A Theoretical Analysis', *South Atlantic Quarterly* (Spring), Vol. VIII, No. 2: 266-7.
21. Ibid.
22. Shahid Javed Burki and Robert Laporte, Jr. (eds.), *Pakistan's Development Priorities-Choices for the Future*, op. cit., p. 242.
23. Hamza Alavi, 'Class and State in Pakistan', in Hassan Gardezi and Jamil Rashid (eds.), op. cit., p. 74.
24. Ibid.
25. Ibid., p. 75.
26. See Jinnah's address to the Gazetted Officers at Chittagong, 25 March 1948. Mohammad Ali Jinnah, *Speeches as Governor-General of Pakistan 1947-48*, op. cit.
27. Jinnah's address to a gathering of the Civil Officers of Balochistan of the rank of Naib-Tehsildars and above at Sibi, February 1948, op. cit.
28. Jinnah's address to the Gazetted Officers at Chittagong, 25 March 1948, Mohammad Ali Jinnah, *Speeches as Governor-General of Pakistan 1947-48*, op. cit.
29. Hamza Alavi, 'Class and State in Pakistan', in Hassan Gardezi and Jamil Rashid (eds.), op. cit., p. 66.
30. Ayesha Jalal, *The State of Martial Rule*, op. cit., p. 119.
31. American Embassy, Karachi to Secretary State, Washington, 5 November 1951, T-523, 350 Pak-political (combat communism), NND 842430, RG 84, NA.
32. Ayesha Jalal, *The State of Martial Rule*, op. cit., p. 113.
33. Ibid.
34. 'US Strategic Interests in Area', submitted by the US embassy at Karachi, op. cit.
35. Dennis Kux, *The United States and Pakistan, 1947-2000: Disenchanted Allies*, op. cit., p. 38.
36. From American Embassy, Karachi to the Secretary of State, Washington, 5 October 1951, No. 439, NND 775078, RG 59, NA.
37. Copy of the Third Progress Report on NSC 98/1, 23 April 1952, submitted by Dean Acheson to James S. Lay, Executive Secretary, National Security Council, NND 959417, RG 59, NA.
38. Hasan Zaheer, 1998, *The Times and Trial of the Rawalpindi Conspiracy 1951*, Karachi: Oxford University Press, p. xvi.
39. Ibid., p. xviii.
40. Ibid.
41. Secretary, Rawalpindi case trial committee to Louis Saillart (general secretary) and Serge Rostovsky (secretary), World Federation of Trade Unions-Vienna, 7 September 1951; intercepted by the American Legation in Vienna, 2 October 1951, op. cit.
42. Memorandum of the Record, 10 March 1951 by D.W. Hickey, Col GSC, Army Attaché, 350 Pak-political, NND 842430, RG 84, NA.

43. Cold War Policies. Retrieved 21 December 2002, http://history.sandiego.edu./gen/20th/korea.htm.
44. Francis J. Gavin, 'Politics, Power, and US Policy in Iran, 1950-53', *Journal of Cold War Studies* 1:1. Retrieved 9 March 2003, http://muse.jhu.edu/demo/cws/1.1gavin.html.
45. Third Progress Report on NSC 98/1, 23 April 1952, submitted by Dean Acheson to James S. Lay, Executive Secretary, National Security Council, NND 959417, RG 59, NA.
46. M.S. Venkartamani, 1987, *The American Role in Pakistan*, Lahore: Vanguard Books, 1987, pp. 137-9.
47. Ayesha Jalal, 1989, 'Towards the Baghdad Pact', *International History Review*, pp. 409-612.
48. Confidential Security Information, A-251, 11 February 1952 sent to the American Embassy, Karachi from the State Department, Washington, NND 842430, RG 84, NA.
49. American Ambassador, Karachi to Secretary State, Washington, Telegram No. 825, 10 March 1951, 350 Pak-political, NND 842430, RG 84, NA.
50. Ayub Khan wrote in his autobiography, 'I think General Raza and a few others were among the senior-most officers and they were frequently spoken of. There was also a great deal of talk about General Iftikhar, a good officer...Unfortunately he and General Sher Khan were killed in an air crash at Jungshahi'. Ayub Khan, *Friends Not Masters*, Karachi: Oxford University Press, 1967, pp. 34-35. According to the British High Commissioner in Pakistan, 'Major-General Raza...a born intriguer, has been lobbying for [C-in-C] a very long time. Raza has neither the ability nor the personality or the part...He is disliked by the majority of the British Officers and, with one of two exceptions, is unpopular with his fellow major generals. His two favourites are Iftikhar-ud-Din, 10 Div. Cdr. and Nazir Ahmed, 9 Div. Cdr'. L/WS/1/1188, IOR.
51. Ayub Khan, *Friends Not Masters*, op. cit., p. 39.
52. Hasan Zaheer, *The Times and Trial of the Rawalpindi Conspiracy 1951*, op. cit., p. xxii.
53. Ibid., p. 1.
54. Ibid.
55. Memorandum of the Record, 10 March 1951, by D.W. Hickey, Col GSC, Army Attaché, NND 842430, RG 84; and Telegram No. 825, 10 March 1951, American Ambassador, Karachi to Secretary State, Washington, 350 Pak-political, NND 842430, RG 84, NA.
56. American Ambassador, Karachi to Secretary State, Washington, Telegram No. 825 10 March 1951, 350 Pak-political, NND 842430, RG. 84, NA.
57. Ibid.
58. Ayub Khan, *Friends Not Masters*, op. cit., pp. 35-36.
59. Ibid., p. 37.
60. Hasan Zaheer, *The Times and Trial of the Rawalpindi Conspiracy 1951*, op. cit., pp. xxiii-xxiv.
61. Ibid., p. 234ff.
62. Ibid.
63. Ayesha Jalal, *The State of Martial Rule*, op. cit., p. 123.
64. Ibid., p. 121.
65. Hasan Zaheer, *The Times and Trial of the Rawalpindi Conspiracy 1951*, op. cit., p. xxiii.

66. British High Commissioner's Opdom No. 15, Part II, 10-23 July 1950, FO371/84201, TNA: PRO.
67. Ibid.
68. Acting High Commissioner to Atlee, Review of Events, April-June 1950, ibid.
69. Office of the High Commissioner, Lahore, 26 March 1949, L/WS/1188, IOR.
70. Ibid.
71. Hasan Zaheer, *The Times and Trial of the Rawalpindi Conspiracy 1951*, op. cit., p. xxiii.
72. John C. Craig, Dispatch no. 28. 7/26/51, NND 842430, RG 84, NA.
73. 'Current Intelligence Weekly', Central Intelligence Agency, OCI No. 5012, 10 July 1953, approved for release 2003/03/04; CIA-RDP79-00927A000100060001-6
74. Hasan Zaheer, *The Times and Trial of the Rawalpindi Conspiracy 1951*, op. cit.
75. Secret Memorandum, 29 September 1949, NND 959417, RG 59, NA.
76. CRO Fortnightly Summaries of communist Developments in Commonwealth Countries, L/WS/1/1200, IOR.
77. Ibid.
78. CRO Fortnightly Summaries of communist Developments in Commonwealth Countries, 8 November 1948, L/WS/1/1207, IOR.
79. Ibid.
80. CRO Fortnightly Summaries of communist Developments in Commonwealth Countries, May 1949, L/WS/1/1207, IOR.
81. Ibid.
82. Stephen P. Cohen, 1999, 'The United States, India and Pakistan: Retrospect and Prospect', in Selig S. Harrison, Paul H. Kreisberg, and Dennis Kux (eds.), *India and Pakistan: The First Fifty Years*, Cambridge: University of Cambridge Press, p. 191.
83. 'McCarthyism'-Wikipedia-the Free Encyclopedia. Retrieved 21 December 2002, http://en.wikipedia.org/wiki/Kirkpatrick_Doctrine.
84. Lahore D-135, Top Secret No. 29, Conversation with Pakistan C-in-C, 3/13/53, NND 959417, RG 59, NA.
85. Memorandum of Conversation: General Mohammad Ayub Khan, C-in-C, Pakistan Army and Raleigh A. Gibson, American Consul General, 23 December 1952, American Embassy, Karachi to the Department of State, Washington, D-105, 350 Pakistan-Pak. Army, NND 842430, RG 84, NA.
86. Lahore D-135, Top Secret No. 29, Conversation with Pakistan C-in-C, 3/13/53, NND 959417, RG 59, NA.
87. Memorandum of Conversation: General Mohammad Ayub Khan, C-in-C, Pakistan Army, Charles D. Withers, First Secretary. From Karachi, D-851, 28 February 1953, NND 959417, RG 59, NA.
88. Hildreth to Emmerson, 14 October 1954, 360/constitutional coup/123, 10-14-54, NND 842430, RG 84, NA.
89. Hugh Tinker, 1967, *India and Pakistan: A Political Analysis*, London: Pall Mall Press, p. 9.
90. I. Talbot, *Pakistan: A Modern History*, op. cit., p. 11.
91. J. Brown, 1995, *Modern India: The Origins of an Asian Democracy*, Oxford: Oxford University Press, pp. 123ff.
92. I. Talbot, *Pakistan: A Modern History*, op. cit., p. 55.
93. C. Dewy, 'The Rural Roots of Pakistan Militarism' in D.A. Low (ed.), *The Political Inheritance of Pakistan*, op. cit., p. 261.
94. Ibid., p. 14.
95. Ayesha Jalal, *The State of Martial Rule*, op. cit., pp. 144-45.

96. According to the First Census of Pakistan, 1951, Karachi: Government of Pakistan, 1951.
97. Walker to Redman, 24 September 1948, L/WS/1/1187, IOR.
98. Enclosure to Despatch No. 13 of 7 August 1951, from American Embassy, Karachi to Dhaka Consulate. NND 842430, RG 84, NA.
99. Ayesha Jalal, *Democracy and Authoritarianism in South Asia*, op. cit., p. 37.
100. Hugh Tinker, *India and Pakistan: A Political Analysis*, op. cit., pp. 75-76.
101. Despatch No. 407 sent to Sec. State, 16 October 1951, NND 842430, RG 84, NA.
102. Hugh Tinker, *India and Pakistan: A Political Analysis*, op. cit., p. 76.
103. Ibid., p. 75.
104. Allen McGrath, *The Destruction of Pakistan's Democracy*, op. cit., p. 82.
105. Ibid.
106. American Embassy Karachi to Secretary State Department, T-251, 7 September 1951, 350 Pak-Political (Ghulam Mohd-McGhee), NND 842430, RG 84, NA.
107. American Embassy, Karachi to Secretary State, Washington, T-418, 18 October 1951, 350 Pak-Political (Ghulam Mohd-McGhee), NND 842430, RG 84, NA.
108. Zafrullah was Foreign Minister of Pakistan.
109. American Embassy Karachi to Secretary State Department, T-251, 7 September 1951, 350 Pak-Political (Ghulam Mohd-McGhee), NND 842430, RG 84, NA.
110. Intelligence Report No. 5662, Department of State, 17 October 1951. Approved for Release 2000/08/29: CIA-RDP79S01011A000500060001-8.
111. Department of State to Karachi Embassy, No. A-251, 11 February 1952, 320 Pak-US-relations, NND 842430, RG 84, NA.
112. Intelligence Report No. 5662, Department of State, 17 October 1951. Approved for Release 2000/08/29: CIA-RDP79S01011A000500060001-8.
113. Ibid.
114. Summary Developments September-October 1951' Report from American Embassy, Karachi, No. 963, 30 January 1951, 350 Pak. Political, NND 842430, RG 84, NA.
115. Hugh Tinker, *India and Pakistan: A Political Analysis*, op. cit., p. 40.
116. Mirza was a direct descendant of the 'traitor' of the Battle of Plassy, Mir Jafar, see Humayun Mirza, 2002, *From Plassey to Pakistan*, Washington, D.C.: University Press of America.
117. American Embassy, Karachi to Secretary of State, Washington, D. 463, 361.2-cabinet-Mirza, 1-25-55, NND 842430, RG 84, NA.
118. Ibid.
119. Hildreth to Emmrson, Top Secret, Eyes Only, 27 September 1954, NND 959417, RG 59, NA.
120. American Embassy, Karachi to the Secretary of State, Washington, 20 September 1956. Approved for release 2003/04/02/: CIA-RDP80B01676R002600100035-7, RG 59, NA.
121. Chaudhry Mohammad Ali, 1967, *The Emergence of Pakistan*, New York: Columbia University Press, 1967, p. 243.
122. Hamza Alavi, 'Class and State in Pakistan', in Hassan Gardezi and Jamil Rashid (eds.), op. cit., p. 43.
123. Hassan Gardezi, 'Feudal and Capitalist Relations in Pakistan', in Hassan Gardezi and Jamil Rashid (eds.), op. cit., pp. 36-37.
124. It has been suggested that Ghulam Mohammad persuaded Nazimuddin to vacate the post of governor-general because, he, Ghulam Mohammad, realized it was an office which could be made powerful again. It has been reported that Mushtaq Ahmed Gurmani, cabinet minister for Kashmir who was stationed in Rawalpindi,

EMERGENCE OF THE INSTITUTIONAL IMBALANCE 135

accompanied the dying Liaquat to the hospital and summoned Ghulam Mohammad to Liaquat's bedside. They notified the Governor-General Nazimuddin who was on vacation in Murree. Nazimuddin joined them in Rawalpindi and they decided among themselves the new composition of the government without consulting the Muslim League Parliamentary party and the Legislative Assembly. Nazimuddin stepped down to become the prime minister and Ghulam Mohammad opted to be the governor-general. See I. Hussain, 1967, *The Failure of Parliamentary Politics in Pakistan*. PhD Dissertation, Oxford University, p. 57.

125. Ayesha Jalal, *The State of Martial Rule*, op. cit., p. 119.
126. Ibid.
127. Ziaul Haque, 'Pakistan and Islamic Ideology', in Hassan Gardezi and Jamil Rashid (eds.), op. cit., p. 314.
128. Strategic Implications of the Situation in China, Report by the Joint Planning Staff, 12 January 1949, op. cit.
129. Ibid.
130. Inward Telegram to CRO from UK High Commissioner in Pakistan [henceforth UKHC], 25 December 1948, L/WS/1/1198, IOR.
131. Ibid.
132. Ibid.
133. Inward Telegram to CRO from UKHC, 8 March 1949, L/WS/1/1198, IOR.
134. Ibid.
135. Inward Telegram to CRO from UKHC, 14 March 1949, L/WS/1/1198, IOR.
136. Inward Telegram to CRO from UKHC, 16 March 1949, L/WS/1/1198, IOR.
137. Outward telegram from Commonwealth Relations Office to UKC, 17 March 1949, L/WS/1/1198, IOR.
138. Dispatch sent to the State Department by Frank W. Wolf. Counsellor for Economic Affairs, US Embassy in Karachi, who accompanied McGhee on his visit to Ghulam Mohammad on 9 December 1949, cited in M.S. Venkataramani, *The American Role in Pakistan, 1947-1958*, op. cit., p. 106.
139. Ibid., p. 105.
140. Ghulam Mohammad's meeting with the US Assistant Secretary George McGhee on 9 December 1949 in Karachi, cited in M.S. Venkataramani, *The American Role in Pakistan, 1947-1958*, op. cit., p. 104.
141. Ironically, Foreign Minister Zafrullah Khan himself became the target of the religious parties who demanded his expulsion on the grounds that he belonged to Ahmadiya sect, a sect which was declared non-Muslim in 1974.
142. Inward Telegram to CRO from UK HC, 14 March 1949, op. cit.
143. CRO Fortnightly Summaries of communist Developments in Commonwealth Countries, first half of June 1949, L/WS/1/1207, IOR.
144. Ayesha Jalal, *The State of Martial Rule*, op. cit., p. 16.
145. Cited in Farooq Naseem Bajwa, *Pakistan and the West*, op. cit., p. 34.
146. Ibid.
147. Enclosure to Despatch N. 13 of 7 August 1951, from American Embassy, Karachi to Dhaka Consulate. NND 842430, RG 84, NA.
148. Quoted in Hector Bolitho, *Jinnah: Creator of Pakistan*, op. cit., p. 197.
149. Lawrence Ziring, *Pakistan in the Twentieth Century—A Political History*, op. cit., p. 98.
150. Ibid.
151. Ayesha Jalal, *The State of Martial Rule*, op. cit., p. 16.
152. Ibid.

153. Mohammad Munir, *From Jinnah to Zia*, Lahore: Vanguard Books, 1980, p. xv.
154. Ibid.
155. Ibid.
156. Allen McGrath, *The Destruction of Pakistan's Democracy*, op. cit., p. 82.
157. David Gilmartin, *Empire and Islam*, op. cit., p. 62.
158. S.S. Thandi, 'The Unidentical Punjab Twins: Some Explanations of Comparative Agricultural Performances since Partition', *International Journal of Punjab Studies*, (Jan-June 1997) 4, 1: 72.
159. See *Eastern Times* (Lahore), 29 September 1947.
160. See *Report of the Agrarian Committee appointed by the Working Committee of the Pakistan Muslim League*, published by S. Shamus Hasan, 1949.
161. Ayesha Jalal, *The State of Martial Rule*, op. cit., p. 102.
162. A.R. Peterson [American Consul General, Lahore], Dispatch No. 137, 1 June 1950, NND 842909, RG 59, NA.
163. Ibid.
164. Allen McGrath, *The Destruction of Pakistan's Democracy*, op. cit., p. 75.
165. *Pakistan Observer*, 13 October 1950.
166. See Constitutional Assembly Debates [henceforth CAD] VIII.
167. *Nawa-i-Waqt*, 5 December 1951.
168. See CAD XII, pp. 80-160.
169. *Dawn*, 22 November 1952.
170. *Dawn*, 24 and 25 December 1952.
171. Four hundred members were to be evenly divided in the Lower House between the eastern and the western wings. There were to be nine units of West Pakistan in the upper house. These units included: Punjab, Sindh, NWFP, Tribal Areas, Bahawalpur, Balochistan, Balochistan State, Khairpur State, and Karachi.
172. See *Pakistan Times*, 24-26 December 1952.
173. Enclosure to Despatch N. 13 of 7 August 1951, American Embassy, Karachi to Dhaka Consulate. NND 842430, RG 84, NA.
174. Ibid.
175. American Embassy to Sec. State, T-523, 15 November 1951, NND 842430, 350 Pak-Political (combat communism), RG 84, NA.
176. Ibid.
177. *Dawn*, 31 December 1952.
178. Leonard Binder, 1963, *Religion and Politics in Pakistan*, Berkeley, California: University of California Press, p. 258.
179. Muhammad Munir, *From Jinnah to Zia*, op. cit., p. 39.
180. Ibid.
181. Office Memo. From W.B. Miller to Withers, 10 March 1953, NND 842430, 350 Riots-Lahore-Anti-Ahmadiya, RG 84, NA.
182. John K. Emmerson [American Embassy, Karachi] to the Secretary of State, 16 Jan. 1953, D-1056, 350-Riots Karachi Students, NND 842430, RG 84, NA.
183. Ibid.
184. Jalal writes that General Azam, the area commander had 'taken over...[apparently] entirely on his own, imposing Martial Law in Lahore and ensuring the dismissal of Daultana's ministry'. Ayesha Jalal, *The State of Martial Rule*, op. cit., p. 177. Giving the reference of personal interview Khalid Bin Sayeed conducted in Pakistan, McGrath wrote that 'K.B. Sayeed informed the author that it was Mirza who ordered the army to take action in the Punjab when he believed Nazimuddin was vacillating'. According to McGrath, Sayeed was unable to get affirmation or denial when he

interviewed Nazimuddin, who was so sensitive on this point that he terminated the interview when Sayeed broached the subject'. Allen McGrath, *The Destruction of Pakistan's Democracy*, op. cit., p. 254, reference notes. Sayeed 's information is confirmed by Emmerson (First Secretary, American Embassy), who wrote in a secret telegram sent to Secretary of State, Washington, 20 April 1953, that, 'Without doubt action by Iskandar Mirza to declare martial law in Lahore Mar 6 in spite of PRIMIN objections saved country from what might have become national disaster'. T-1582 to Dept, 350 Gen. Pakistan, 4/20/530, RG 84, NA.
185. Firoze Khan Noon, 1966, *Test of Time* (Lahore), p. 234.
186. *Pakistan Times*, 19 April 1953.
187. John K. Emmerson [American Embassy, Karachi] to the Secretary of State, T-1582 to DEPT 350 Gen._Pakistan, 4/20/53, NND 842430, RG 84, NA.
188. T-1573, 361.2 Cabinet-Dismissal Nazimuddin Cabinet, 4/18/53, NND 842430, RG 84, NA.
189. Emmerson to the Secretary of State, Karachi, 4/23/53, 350-Pak. Pol. NND 842430, RG 84, NA.
190. Ibid.
191. Current Intelligence Weekly, OCI No. 5012, 10 July 1953, approved for release 2003/03/04: CIA-RDP79-00927A000100060001-6, NA.
192. American Embassy Karachi to the Department of State, D-166 to DEPT, 360 Gen, 9-25-54. RG 84, NA.

4

The Destruction of Democracy and Consolidation of an Authoritarian State

EMERGENCE OF A 'CLIENT STATE'

The first major blow to democracy came when Governor-General Ghulam Mohammad, assisted by the army, and with the approval of the US, dismissed Prime Minister Nazimuddin, and appointed Mohammad Ali Bogra as the new prime minister for his pro-American stance. This unconstitutional act of the governor-general was soon followed by the dismissal of the first constituent assembly, in October 1954,

> There have indeed been times-such as the October Night in 1954—when with a General to the right and a General to the left of him, a half-mad Governor-General imposed upon a captured Prime Minister the dissolution of the Constituent Assembly and the virtual setting up of semi-dictatorial Executive.[1]

These unconstitutional acts of a 'half mad' governor-general were actively supported by the US government and, therefore, demonstrated its involvement in Pakistan's internal affairs to an extent that no government in Pakistan could survive without toeing the line dictated by US interests—a trend that continues till today. These unconstitutional acts became legitimized by the tame judiciary and initiated a 'game of 'musical chairs' of appointments and removals of prime ministers. In a short span of four years, following the dismissal of the first constituent assembly in 1954 and the imposition of the first martial law in 1958, five prime ministers were appointed and removed. Instability of democratic institutions ultimately cleared the path for direct military rule, which has since characterized much of Pakistan's history since then.[2]

THE DESTRUCTION OF DEMOCRACY

In this chapter, the circumstances which led to the destruction of democratic institutions in Pakistan, beginning with the unconstitutional dismissal of Prime Minister Nazimuddin in 1953, and which concluded with the dissolution of the first constituent assembly of Pakistan in October 1954, and which eventually led to the first martial law, in 1958, will be further investigated. By dismissing Prime Minister Nazimuddin, 'the governor-general had taken an action that was clearly political and beyond the normal scope of a constitutional head of state'.[3] Apparently, there was no indication of any political difficulty prior to Ghulam Mohammad's actions against Nazimuddin. Only a week before the dismissal, the governor-general had defended the policies of the government in a speech given to the Karachi Rotary Club. The important question to answer is why then was Nazimuddin dismissed. As discussed earlier, the answer does not lie in domestic politics, rather it involves global politics and needs to be examined beyond the internal dynamics of the political process. Religious fanaticism was used to remove a prime minister whose power kept expanding through legislative measures and who was able to provide a draft constitution after a lengthy and extensive exercise of five years, 'In April Nazimuddin was in command of the Muslim League both nationally and in Parliament'.[4] A strong democratic government, with a power seat in East Pakistan, could pose a threat to American interests in this region, 'What better explains Ghulam Mohammad's action was the fact that the new budget proposed by Nazimuddin called for a cut in the defence expenditure by one-third. This was an unprecedented move, and was bound to alarm Ayub and the army'.[5] The governor-general, stepping out of his constitutional limits, paved the way for an authoritarian government in Pakistan, concentrating power into the hands of the bureaucratic-army elite, who were committed to bolstering the defence establishment in alliance with the global American power system. The governor-general's unconstitutional action 'destroyed or gravely weakened' three major conventions of cabinet government:

> First, the tradition of impartiality of the governor-general had been demolished. Second, the convention of cabinet and party solidarity had been disregarded. Third, the role of the legislature as the maker of and sustainer of governments had been impugned.[6]

By destroying these three major conventions of the cabinet government, the governor-general had helped strengthen the role of the non-democratic institutions, like the army, for further interference in the political arena, and thereby, dominating the policy-making process in Pakistan. General Ayub had declared in 1953, that the 'Army was a stabilizing force in Pakistan and that he would take no nonsense from the politicians'.[7] In the period between April 1953 and October 1954, Pakistan took the shape of a 'client state' of the US. In this process, the defence establishment emerged as the most powerful institution of the state. The interplay of domestic and international actors in demolishing democratic institutions, is the most intriguing chapter of Pakistan's history.

The 1952 elections in the US brought Dwight D. Eisenhower to the White House, who chose John Foster Dulles as his secretary of state. Together, Eisenhower and Dulles further modified the Containment Doctrine as articulated in NSC-68. With Eisenhower in office, the US defence policy took a more offensive 'New Look'. Secretary of State John Foster Dulles, 'a patrician, visceral anti-communist closely tied to the nation's financial establishment, was obsessed with communism's challenge to the US corporate power in the Third World'.[8] Dulles criticized Truman's foreign policy and argued that the policy of 'containment' should be replaced by a policy of 'liberation'. Dulles considered neutrality as an obsolete, immoral, and short-sighted concept. Alliances such as NATO, SEATO, and the Baghdad Pact (later re-named as CENTO) were, in addition to 'McCarthyism', part of his 'liberation strategy'. Pakistan's civil and military elite, under Ghulam Mohammad, were more than willing to join hands with Dulles in his war against communism. Dulles conceived the concept of the Northern Tier of states running along the southern rim of Soviet Asia, and including Turkey, Pakistan, Iraq, and Iran.

To secure Pakistan's assistance, some domestic changes were required. Those changes included the removal of Prime Minister Nazimuddin in April 1953, under the pretext of religious riots, which were linked with 'Pakistani communists', and selection of Mohammad Ali Bogra as the new prime minister. Bogra was described as a 'pathologically pro-American', non-political entity, chosen for 'his popularity in Washington'.[9] Later, Army Chief Ayub Khan's inclusion in the cabinet as defence minister along with Iskandar Mirza as the interior minister, ensured Pakistan's smooth entry into Dulles's strategic plans. Bogra was installed as a civilian prime minister of a country where the military was made to take 'indirect control' of government affairs. General public opinion was not in favour of any military alliance with the US, and it was felt necessary to make any military pact under the auspices of a 'civilian government'.[10] Bogra's presence was an assurance of such an alliance.

After the Free Officers' coup in Egypt, and military takeovers led by young officers in Syria and Lebanon, General Ayub had reasons to worry about 'talk of the Pakistan Army taking over the Government'. Ayub could not afford to allow 'nationalist feelings' to grow in the ranks of young officers on the same pattern as Egypt or Syria. In the killing of such feelings, Ayub had demonstrated his skills in the case of the Rawalpindi conspiracy. Under his watchful eyes, no such move could be initiated.[11] It was not an appropriate time for assuming 'direct control'; for that the Pakistan army had to wait, though the army was in a position to take control of the government if 'the situation was critical', as claimed by Pakistan's commander-in-chief, who was more than eager to join the Middle East Defence Organization (MEDO) versus the careful approach of Nazimuddin's government.[12] Nazimuddin was considered 'non-committal' on Middle Eastern defence.[13] Pakistan's participation in a Middle Eastern defence pact had become a bone of contention between American and British policymakers. Britain was reluctant to involve Pakistan on the grounds that it might invite a strong reaction from India. On the other hand, the US was keen to persuade Pakistan into accepting some form of the military alliance since 1951. The American ambassador in Pakistan had asked Liaquat before his fatal trip to Rawalpindi about such a possibility. After Liaquat's assassination, the issue was raised with Ghulam Mohammad and the new foreign secretary.[14] In November 1951, the State Department formally requested the British government to re-evaluate their attitude regarding India and demanded an 'immediate approach to Pakistan to ask them to join the Middle East Command and to provide forces for the defence of the Middle East in the event of War'.[15]

Under American pressure and due to political upheaval in Iran and Egypt, Britain was forced to review its position on Pakistan's participation in the MEDO. In August 1952, the foreign office invited Pakistan to participate in the MEDO, recognizing her unique position in the Commonwealth as one of the world's leading Muslim states, which had strategic interests in the proposed plan.[16] Pakistan's membership in the organization was considered useful because of its strategic position with its military bases and airfields. The 'Value of Pakistan as a Main Base' was the argument military strategists in the ministry of defence in London had been insisting upon since 1949.[17] To persuade Pakistan to participate in the organization, it was assured increased security on its western border and an opportunity to play a leading role in the region with British and American support.

In 1952, a barter agreement between Russia and Pakistan was very disturbing for the US embassy in Karachi, which viewed this agreement as a reorientation of Pakistan's foreign policy.[18] Concerned with this development, the American embassy in Karachi reviewed the possible reaction of Pakistan's participation in the MEDO. Officials in the foreign and defence ministries were seen in favour of such a participation, but the cabinet's reaction was found uncertain.[19] In an early analysis, Nazimuddin was described as an 'unimaginative man' doing a job that was 'too big for him' and under his leadership, Pakistan had 'no prospect to be drawn into closer formal relationships with the Western powers'.[20] Pakistan's request for a one million ton wheat grant could not be considered unless a more reliable pro-West government was guaranteed, though, a grain loan of $190 million had been provided to India under the Emergency Food Aid Act of 1951, which had enabled India to purchase 2,231,000 tons of grain.[21] Generals and bureaucrats were anxious to guarantee such a government. General Ayub Khan who was being groomed as an insurance to protect the American and British strategic interests in this region, in a meeting with the US Consul General in Lahore on 23 December 1952, assured that 'the Pakistan Army...[would] not allow the political leaders to get out of hand and same...[was] true regarding the people of Pakistan'. He informed the consul general that he had told 'leading politicians to make up their minds to go whole-heartedly with the West', stating that last year when Pakistan was in a strong financial position, the political leaders were not interested in making a decision, and wanted to stay neutral'.[22] Ayub was referring to Liaquat's government and he confirmed that Pakistan was a friend of the US, and reminded the consul general that the US had a strategic interest in Pakistan.[23] In February 1953, Ayub Khan met the American first secretary, Charles D. Withers, in a party at Lahore where Mirza was also present. Ayub told the first secretary that 'the Pakistan cabinet did not have enough international minded people,'[24] and demanded that 'the United States should invite Pakistan to participate in a regional defence organization immediately and that if there were no such organization at present we should have a bi-lateral agreement'. Ayub asked Withers to 'by-pass the British in this matter' because he considered them as 'the primary obstacle to Pakistan's immediate participation' and thought of it as 'a result of their fear of

THE DESTRUCTION OF DEMOCRACY

Indian reaction'. Ayub accused the British 'to act as the broker in this defence planning' who 'were trying to collect their brokerage fees at... [Pakistan's] expense'. He urged that the United States 'should take the initiative in the matter and not wait for British acquiescence'. Ayub affirmed that the Pakistan army was 'a first class fighting force despite its size and equipment deficiencies' and ready to play its role in Middle Eastern defence against communism with American assistance. When the first secretary asked him about the reaction of certain politicians 'if Pakistan were invited to join a MEDO,' Ayub assured him 'that they would do what he told them to do and he repeated the phrase that he would stand no nonsense from the politicians'. In his concluding remarks, Withers wrote that Ayub was in complete control of the Pakistan army and it would do what Ayub told it to. Withers wrote: 'During my discussion with Ayub, whom I have been known for several years, I found him much more self-assured and much more self-confident than in the past...During the conversation, Ayub never used the editorial we, it was always first person pronoun'.[25]

A survey report prepared by the State Department on 6 April 1953, revealed 'a keen positive interest in MEDO shared by the public and many top civil and military authorities in Pakistan'.[26] The document 'Re-examination of United States Programs for National Security', submitted by the secretaries of state and defence, and the director for mutual security on the last day of the Truman's administration, stated:

> it...[was] believed that Pakistan's active cooperation in defence of the Middle East might be obtained...The strengthening of Pakistan on the Eastern flank of Iran, in conjunction with Turkish strength on the Northwest, might add to Iranian self-confidence and would exercise a stabilizing influence in the area.[27]

Pakistan's army and bureaucracy were quite enthusiastic in providing active cooperation. According to Akhtar Hussain, the acting foreign secretary, 'the leaders of Pakistan were on the verge of openly aligning themselves with the West'. He held the view that Pakistan would 'jump at...[the] chance of joining the Middle East Defence Organization. However, he was not sure if Nazimuddin 'kn[ew] the score'. But he assured that the influence of the foreign office and ministry of defence 'would be decisive'.[28] In this situation, a change at the centre was unavoidable. In March 1953, the eruption of anti-Ahmadis riots provided an opportunity to the nexus of the army and the bureaucracy to remove Nazimuddin from the scene, and bring in a reliable prime minister who was willing to cooperate with Washington. 'Nazimuddin's dismissal was planned and accomplished through [the] combined efforts of [the] Army leadership...particularly...Iskandar Mirza and... General Ayub...and [the] Governor-General himself'.[29] General Ayub admitted that 'he had worked hard to have something along this line accomplished'.[30] The governor-general, with the aid of army establishment, had 'brought about one of the most popular coups in history'.[31] 'It was, however, a coup that was not recognized as a coup at that time'.[32]

It is interesting to note that:

> on 4 April 1953, the US Central Intelligence Director, Allen W. Dulles approved $1 million to be used "in any way that would bring about the fall of Mossadegh", the Prime Minister of Iran whose socialist reforms and increasingly close partnership with the Iranian communist party...prompted fears that Iran might develop close ties with the Soviet Union.

Aided by the CIA and British MI5, Mohammad Mossadegh was arrested on 19 August 1953. The extent of the US role in Mossadegh's overthrow was never formally acknowledged for many years. 'In March 2000, then Secretary of State Madeleine Albright stated her regret that Mossadegh was ousted'. In the same year, *The New York Times* published a detailed report about the coup based on CIA documents.[33] Although, there is no available documentary evidence to suggest the CIA's involvement in the overthrow of Nazimuddin's government in Pakistan, his weak government was considered to 'stir up anti-imperialistic sentiment which in different ways and degrees, consciously or unconsciously... strongly influence[ed] the thinking of most Pakistanis'.[34] The change of governments in Iran and Pakistan, during the same period of time, suggests a relationship between these two events at a time when 'friendly' governments were required in Iran and Pakistan for moving towards Dulles's strategic defence plans. Anti-West governments in Iran and Pakistan could endanger the strategic interests of the US and her allies in the region.

Therefore, the change in government was seen as 'great opportunities' and it was believed that 'tactful guidance' and a 'firm example' would 'do much to develop the stability of this area so important to the foreign policy of the United States'.[35] Installing a prime minister with no base in Pakistani politics ensured that the generals and bureaucrats were in firm control to lead Pakistan on the path marked by neo-colonial forces,

'Mohammad Ali Bogra was not chosen by the people nor did he represent any political party, but was the personal choice of the Governor-General'.[36] What made him attractive to Ghulam Mohammad and his allies was that he had strong links with Washington and lacked any independent constituency. 'Moreover, he was a Bengali, and the government desperately needed evidence that it represented Bengal [East Pakistan],'[37] particularly in a situation when the whole cabinet was from West Pakistan, 'Without...[any]...base it was thought that he could not be other than a tool of Ghulam Mohammad'.[38] 'This made him the right man to redirect the foreign policy of Pakistan into close military and economic alliance with that country'.[39] The American embassy described Mohammad Ali Bogra as a 'vigorous, youthful, enthusiastic, and boyishly pro-American...ready to steer Pakistan into full cooperation with the United States'.[40] John Foster Dulles, wasted no time in declaring that Pakistan 'was most friendly to us [and] needed immediate assurance of our aid'.[41] As a gesture of goodwill, a wheat grant was sent to Karachi. Bogra reciprocated the feelings by showing his gratitude in a most 'embarrassing' manner. Camels carrying 'Thank You America' placards strolled on the beaches of Karachi.

This reception was the mirror image of Pakistan's new face in the coming years of a 'client state' economically, politically, and militarily dependent on the United States. A popular democratic government had no role in this emerging scenario. Bogra was made a leader of the Muslim League that was fast losing its grip over the control of affairs and had become a hostage to the ambitions of generals and bureaucrats. He was given a very specific objective: to ensure Pakistan's participation in defence pacts against communism. It was not an easy task, as a majority of the Pakistani people were not in favour of any pro-West alliance. Anti-imperialistic feelings were high, particularly in East Pakistan where the army and the bureaucracy were viewed as partners of 'imperialism'. Americans were fully aware of these facts. Dulles's advice to the US embassy in Karachi for 'continuing evaluation [of the] Prime Minister's position,' not only reveals Bogra's delicate position, it also suggests the extent of US involvement in the political affairs of Pakistan.[43] Bogra appeared to be a more tragic figure than Nazimuddin:

> Many decisions of government were effectively taken by a group that included the Governor-General and [some] influential ministers...There is nothing about new or important about an "inner cabinet". What was unusual

was that it appeared to centre on the Governor-General rather than the Prime Minister.[43]

Dulles arrived in Karachi on 22 May 1953, as part of an exceptional tour of the Middle East and South Asia, with the aim of familiarizing himself with the people and leaders of this strategically important region. The armed guard arranged for his reception greatly impressed Dulles. Reporting to the senate committee of foreign relations, he remarked that 'they had an armed guard for my visit which...[was] one of the finest I...[had] ever seen in the world'.[44] He was full of praise for the 'carriage and demeanour of...[the] people and...[the] army'.[45] Dulles's meetings with Ghulam Mohammad and Bogra were very encouraging, however, the most important talks were held with General Ayub, recognizing him as the real power broker in the emerging framework. Dulles met Ayub at the residence of the American ambassador. The record of this meeting reveals very interesting facts; most significant is Dulles's inquiry about the state of Pakistan's army, air force, the air bases in Pakistan, and the state of the navy.[46] Relations between India and Pakistan were discussed and General Ayub assured Dulles that if any military aid were given to Pakistan, it would not be used against India, rather, Pakistan was willing to help India if it was attacked by another country.[47] Ayub affirmed that the government in Pakistan was 'extremely anxious' to cooperate with the US.

Dulles returned home from this trip convinced that Pakistan and Turkey were the potential guardians of US interests in the region. The 'Northern Tier' concept seemed to be the result of this trip when Dulles realized the Soviet threat was more imminent near its borders. Dulles's message to the prime minister of Pakistan, at the end of his tour, set the stage for the role assigned to Pakistan in case of a possible war against the Soviet Union. Pakistan was seen 'as one of the great bulwarks in that area against communism'. Dulles confessed that he had 'strong feelings that the combination of strength of religious feeling and martial spirit of...[Pakistani] people...[would make] Pakistan a country that...[could] be relied upon as one of the great bulwarks in that area against communism'. In this message it is important to note Dulles's reference to the combined strength of religious feelings and martial spirit of the Pakistani people. It was the re-claimant of the old imperial policy. He assured the prime minister of Pakistan that, 'I shall continue to follow this matter, urging quick action, as I completely share your view that it is in our common interests to assist your country in this regard'.[48]

Dulles felt it necessary to send such a message to Pakistan, because Nehru 'made it plain [in his meeting with Dulles] that any military block violating the fundamentals of India's policy of non-alignment' was not acceptable to India. It was made clear to Dulles that 'India would not be carried along with Dulles's enthusiasm for fighting the "menace" of international communism and abandon its cherished policy, a policy endorsed in Moscow, accepted in Peking, and embraced in the new countries of Asia'.[49]

The quick action, Dulles had promised, came in the form of invitation for General Ayub to visit Washington to discuss regional defence problems since he was viewed as the 'strongest individual in Pakistan'. It was confirmed that 'if the U.S. believed in any closer arrangements with Pakistan then the right person to talk to was Ayub'.[50] Ayub arrived in Washington in September 1953 and held crucial discussions with Dulles who reported the details of the discussions to President Eisenhower. General Ayub was more interested in a bilateral agreement with the United States for receiving military aid than participating in a large defence pact. For Americans, military aid to Pakistan was an integral part of a larger defence strategy with immediate focus on the 'Northern Tier' organization. The idea was to link countries of the northern tier including Iran, Turkey, and Pakistan with each other and with the US, creating a 'barrier against Soviet encroachment'.[51] Negotiations were not completed and Ayub was invited to a return visit in mid-October.

During Ayub's second visit, Dulles recommended a meeting between General Ayub and President Eisenhower to be arranged during this visit.[52] This visit started with Ayub meeting the assistant secretary of state on 21 October 1953, in which US officials from the Defence Department, South Asia Desk, and the Mutual Security Program, also participated. In this meeting, a possible contract of Mutual Assistance Agreement was discussed, that ensured the strengthening of Pakistan's defence capabilities, its association with the West, and acceptance of the political assurances contained in the agreement.[53] Soon, Governor-General Ghulam Mohammad, who had gone to Washington for 'medical treatment', joined the negotiations that were being carried out without the knowledge of the Pakistan's parliament and the cabinet, though Bogra and Zafrullah 'actively participated'.[54] On 7 December 1953, Vice-President Richard Nixon arrived in Karachi for a three-day visit to Pakistan. The aim was to evaluate the situation in Pakistan before attaining the approval of the National Security Council regarding the

Mutual Defence Agreement between Pakistan and the US.[55] Nixon made it clear in his meeting with Bogra that, 'according to him a military aid arrangement would have two…main users: (i) Pakistan's defence forces could be adequately built up; and (ii) Pakistan would then be able to face any communist threat'.[56] Nixon proved to be most instrumental in bringing Pakistan into a close alliance with the US. His biographer wrote that Nixon not only supported Pakistan's position in the defence against the Soviet Union, he also strengthened Pakistan 'as a counter force to the confirmed neutralism of Jawaharlal Nehru's India'.[57]

Surprisingly, the political decision to grant military aid to Pakistan was formally approved by President Eisenhower on 31 September 1953, before the start of Ayub's second visit; however, it was not made public.[58] The probable reasons, it seems, were the difference of opinion between Britain and the United States over the question of military aid to Pakistan and the lack of Pakistan's firm commitment to participate in defence pacts. Britain argued that it would also like to see the Pakistan military strengthened, but the fear of India's strong reaction was a major concern. The UK government observed that 'broadly speaking, London did not like the U.S. proposal' on the grounds that India would regard the military aid to Pakistan as spreading the Cold War to the subcontinent.[59] Although, no public announcement was made about President Eisenhower's decision to provide military aid to Pakistan, the news had travelled to Moscow, who expressed profound anger and concern over the possibility of military assistance, and some kind of a defence pact between Pakistan and the US:[60]

> On 19 December 1953, the Government of Pakistan presented a note to the Soviet Embassy in Karachi replying to the Soviet Note of 30 November, which demanded "clarification" of the press reports on the subject of "American military air bases" in Pakistan.

In this note, assurances were given to the USSR that Pakistan 'did not intend to take any hostile step toward the USSR or any other state with which it had friendly relations'.[62] On 25 February 1954, Eisenhower declared that his government was ready to give military aid to Pakistan on the condition that Pakistan and Turkey should agree on a defence strategy. On 27 February 1954, without consulting the cabinet, Ghulam Mohammad sent a letter to Dulles, congratulating him on the declaration of arms aid to Pakistan, which was considered 'an outstanding document'. A copy of this letter was sent to the American ambassador in Pakistan with the request to show it to Bogra with these remarks:

> We believe that Ghulam Mohammad's communication makes it necessary for us to explain quite clearly to him and other members of the Government of Pakistan as appropriate that United States military assistance to Pakistan does not involve any commitment on our part to support Pakistan vis-à-vis India.[63]

These remarks were made in response to Ghulam Mohammad's plea for the United States' help in persuading Nehru who was 'trying to use the American Aid....as an excuse for going back on international stipulations and obligations' regarding Kashmir. Ghulam Mohammad reminded the secretary of state that 'we took a calculated risk....depending on....[their] word and promise'.[63]

Pakistan's policy of aligning with the US was a decision taken by the generals and bureaucrats at the cost of sacrificing national interests, ignoring the popular mood in the streets, especially in East Pakistan. The people of East Pakistan expressed their disapproval of the alliance of the central bureaucracy, army and the feudal politicians of Punjab with the US, during the elections held in March 1954, for the provincial assembly. The defeat of the ruling party, the Muslim League, led by Bogra, indicated that the central government's policies did not enjoy the support of the majority of the Pakistani people. The United Front, composed of more than half a dozen political parties, fought the election on a twenty-one point agenda. The union of these political parties was a threatening call for the brokers of state power. The United Front included pro-Beijing Pakistan Awami League, the East Pakistan communist party, the left-leaning Ganatantri Dal, Krishak Sramik party, and a fragment of left-wing student groups. The most critical demands of the twenty-one point agenda were the call for the nationalization of jute and the demand for provincial autonomy, restricting the central government's authority to three subjects only: defence, foreign affairs, and currency. The United Front polled 64 per cent of the popular vote and secured 223 seats out of a total of 309.[64] The Muslim League was not able to secure more than 10 seats.[65] This was a hammer blow to the policies of the central government led by the Muslim League, which was reduced to a puppet party manipulated solely by the governor-general. After stripping the Muslim League of its political power, and selecting a cabinet of his own choice, mostly from West Pakistan, the governor-general desired to control the constituent assembly as well, which was dominated by members from East Pakistan, by proposing his own constitutional formula. At a time when the bureaucratic-army alliance, under the leadership of the governor-general, was engaged in negotiations with the US government for a possible mutual defence agreement, any sign of opposition from East Pakistan could not be tolerated.

The governor-general's constitutional formula envisaged the unification of all the provinces and states of West Pakistan into 'One Unit', with the aim of balancing the domination of East Pakistan in the assembly, and an 'election of a new Constituent Assembly which would not be a sovereign body and over which the Governor-General would have a right of veto'.[66] Prime Minister Mohammad Ali Bogra very faithfully presented the governor-general's constitutional formula in the constituent assembly, which was rejected by the majority of the assembly. The constituent assembly was now under great pressure to formulate a constitution as soon as possible to prove its writ. The Basic Principles Committee report submitted by Nazimuddin along with the amendments suggested by Prime Minister Mohammad Ali Bogra, was now taken up by the assembly to finalize a constitution for Pakistan. On 7 October 1953, Bogra reintroduced the Basic Principles Committee report. The report was the same as had been presented by Nazimuddin, except two amendments, which included a compromise on assembly representation, popularly known as the Mohammad Ali Formula, 'to which the politicians of the east and west wings had succeeded in reaching agreement'.[67] The Mohammad Ali Formula provided that the lower house was to consist of 300 members elected on the basis of population, and the upper house would consist of 50 members equally divided among the five units, who would be elected by the legislatures of the units, each unit having equal voting weight. East Pakistan, as one of the five units, would have a minority in the upper house, but, would continue to have a majority in the lower house on the basis of population. By 14 November 1953, the assembly had approved 130 paragraphs of the new constitution after sitting for fifty-five days, when it was adjourned.[68]

The Bengali members had to return home to campaign for the provincial elections scheduled in March 1954. The politicians from East Pakistan were now convinced that the governor-general, with the assistance of the defence establishment, was determined to prevent East Pakistan from participating in the formulation of major policy decisions.

To assert their voice, all political parties united on one platform under the banner of the United Front, which won with a thundering majority. This was a vote of no-confidence given by the majority population against the central government's policies. On 3 April 1954, Fazlul Huq as leader of the United Front, formed the ministry in East Pakistan.[69] After the formation of the ministry, the United Front unanimously demanded the immediate dissolution of the constituent assembly on the grounds that it was no longer representative of the people of East Pakistan and called for an immediate national election on the basis of adult franchise. An appeal was made to organize a 'peoples' movement' against the central government of the Muslim League.[70] The demand for the national election was obviously a blow to US interests in the region. Bogra's government was committed to a mutual defence agreement with America and at this stage the dissolution of the constituent assembly in accordance with the United Front's demand would have certainly shackled the progress on the agreement. Then, there was no guarantee that any newly-elected popular government would continue the policy of alignment with the US. However, the governor-general and his aides were not yet given the directions to dissolve the assembly.

The situation became alarming when 162 members of the newly-elected Bengal provincial assembly, reacting to the signing of the United States-Pakistan military aid pact on 19 April 1954, showed their 'grave concern' over the undermining of Pakistan's freedom and sovereignty'.[71] This was followed by a call given by almost all political parties in East Pakistan to observe 'Anti-United States-Pakistan Military Pact Day'.[72] Soon, they were joined by some voices from West Pakistan as well. This resulted in a wave of arrests of the government's political opponents in Punjab and Karachi by use of the Public Safety Acts, in order to strengthen the central government's grip on West Pakistan.[73] To check the growing resentment among the masses, the ministry of the United Front had to be sent home at the 'pretext of the Red scare'.[74] On 29 May 1954, the United Front ministry was dismissed and the governor-general using Section 92A of the Government of India Act assumed the provincial administration and put the province under the control of Governor Iskandar Mirza, who was known for his espousal of 'controlled democracy'. Mirza alleged that the parliamentary government had failed in East Pakistan, and announced that it would be restored only when he determined that the province was ready for it. The East Pakistan Assembly was not allowed to meet again until 22 May 1956. Iskandar

Mirza, in his first press conference, declared that Pakistan was faced with the danger of 'communism in East Pakistan' and called for a permanent ban on the communist party.[75] The air force was utilized to drop leaflets and 10,000 troops and a navy frigate were reportedly sent to East Pakistan.[77] Mirza threatened to impose martial law and warned that there were enough troops plus 40,000 police available to meet any 'protest'.[77] Censorship was imposed on the press and a hunt for the arrest of political activists under the Public Safety Act was launched. Under his instructions, 'screening committees' were formed in all the industrial units 'to weed out' all communist elements.[78] Approximately 200,000 industrial workers were to be screened. On 6 July 1954, the communist party in West Pakistan was also banned. The suppression of the United Front removed the pressure for changes in the constituent assembly.

This was all being done in the wake of Pakistan signing the mutual defence agreement with the United States in Karachi on 19 May 1954. The main terms of the agreement included that 'the Government of Pakistan...[would] use the assistance exclusively to maintain its internal security, its legitimate self-defence, or to permit it to participate in the defence of the area,' would 'not take any act of aggression against any other nation' and 'join in promoting international understanding and goodwill, and maintaining world peace' and also 'take such actions as may be mutually agreed upon to eliminate causes of international tension'. Pakistan was also expected to develop and maintain 'its own defensive strength and the defensive strength of the world'. Pakistan was not permitted to trade 'with nations which threaten[ed] the maintenance of world peace'.

This agreement 'besides establishing a close military, political and economic alliance with the United States also allowed her military bases in Northern Pakistan to spy on the Soviet Union'.[79] By signing the mutual defence agreement, Pakistan had not only made the Soviet Union and China hostile, it also sealed all hopes for resolving the conflict of Kashmir. In August 1953, after bilateral talks lasted some months, Nehru and Bogra had agreed to issue a joint communiqué on Kashmir, declaring that 'it was their firm opinion that [Kashmir dispute] should be settled in accordance with the wishes of the people of that State...The most feasible way of ascertaining the wishes of the people was by fair and impartial plebiscite'. Further, 'it was decided that the plebiscite Administrator should be appointed by the end of April 1954...He...[would] then make such proposals as he...[thought] proper for preparations to be made for the holding of a fair and impartial plebiscite in the entire State and take such other steps as may be considered necessary'.[80] At that time Nehru had no knowledge of the negotiations going on between Pakistan and the United States for a mutual defence agreement. After receiving news that Pakistan was likely to enter into an alliance with the United States, in his meeting with Nixon in December 1953, Nehru 'raised the question of military aid to Pakistan'. Nehru told Nixon:

> that any military pact between USA and Pakistan would (i) delay the settlement of the Kashmir and other disputes and (ii) might be used for aggression against India, adding that even though there might not be any actual danger of aggression, people in India would nevertheless think that there was.[82]

Nixon conveyed Nehru's apprehensions to Bogra who considered them as 'Nehru's bluff'. However, Nehru protested strongly in his letter written to Bogra on 21 December 1953, stating that:

> We, in India, have endeavoured to follow a foreign policy which we feel is not only in the interests of world peace but is particularly indicated for the countries of Asia. That policy is an independent one and of nonalignment with any power block. It is clear that the policy which Pakistan intends to pursue is different...It means that Pakistan is tied up with in a military sense with the U.S.A. and is aligned to that particular group of powers of imperialism. This produces a qualitative change in the existing situation and therefore, it affects Indo-Pakistan relations, and more especially the Kashmir problem.[82]

Again, speaking in the Indian parliament, Nehru observed that 'the whole context in which these agreements were made...[would] change if military aid...[came] from America'.[83] Reacting to Nehru's remarks, General Ayub was anxious to convince India that 'Pakistan could not possibly pose any threat to India' by assuring its leadership that the military aid provided under the agreement was not to be used against her.[84] He argued that it should be in the interest of the world peace, 'particularly of India's security that Pakistan remain[ed] strong and stable'. The question that needs to be explored is why Pakistan needed any military assistance if it was not to be used against India which was perceived as its only enemy. The people of Pakistan never felt threatened by any potential communist threat—an assumed threat that was the creation of a few individuals made to sit in the 'control room' to steer Pakistan towards aligning with the neo-colonial forces. If, in accordance with the communiqué, the plebiscite was carried out, as agreed upon for resolving the Kashmir conflict, there was no need for any defence establishment in Pakistan. But, that was not in line with the strategic designs planned for Pakistan in the Cold War era. Pakistan's defence establishment had to serve as the 'bulwark' against communism, and therefore, had to be strengthened. The mutual defence agreement was the guarantee for ensuring Pakistan's entrance into the defence alliances conceived by Dulles in his efforts to contain communism.

There has already been an earlier discussion on how under the 'Red Scare', political parties, progressive groups, liberal forums, trade unions, and all 'peoples' movements' were destroyed, and central and provincial governments were dismissed without any lawful authority, thus consolidating the power in non-democratic institutions. In the following discussion, we will examine how Pakistan was persuaded to join defence pacts against communism besides leading to a towards consolidation of authoritarianism within.

DEFENCE PACTS AND AUTHORITARIANISM IN PAKISTAN

As planned, the mutual defence agreement resulted in Pakistan signing the SEATO (South East Asia Treaty Organization), and the Baghdad Pact, also referred to as the Middle East Treaty Organization (METO). SEATO was established by the South East Asia Collective Defence Treaty (Manila Pact), which was signed in Manila in September 1954. The South East Asia Organization (SEATO) became effective on 19 February 1955, and was signed by Pakistan, Australia, France, Great Britain, New Zealand, the Philippines, Thailand, and the United States. Pakistan was included in the alliance, though it was not part of South East Asia.

The Baghdad Pact was formed by Iraq, Turkey, Pakistan, Iran, and Great Britain, in 1955, and was a Western effort to build a Middle Eastern organization linking NATO with SEATO. It failed in that purpose and turned instead, as John Foster Dulles put it, 'into a forum for Arab politics and intrigues'.[85] Its name was changed to CENTO (Central Treaty Organization) in 1959, when Iraq left the pact, 'it continued to comprise Turkey, Iran, and Pakistan as its regional members. Early in 1959, Pakistan signed (as did Turkey and Iran) a bilateral agreement of cooperation with the United States, which was designed further to reinforce the defensive purposes of CENTO'.[86]

Reinforcing Pakistan's alliance with the United States, General Ayub Khan very proudly claimed that:

> Pakistan...[was] associated with the United States through not one, but four mutual security arrangements. In this sense, it...[had] been sometimes termed "American most allied ally in Asia". It...[was] the only Asian country which...[was] a member both of SEATO and CENTO'.[87]

By signing these defence pacts, Pakistan became one of the first few allies of the American power system in its war against communism in an environment when most of the Third World countries were campaigning for nationalism, social reformism, and anti-imperialism, and refused to be a part of any one side in the Cold War era. In the previous discussion, it was seen how any such movement was not allowed to grow in Pakistan, and in the process, democratic institutions were destroyed to facilitate the alliance of the army and bureaucracy dominating the state's policies in favour of Dulles's system of mutual defence pacts. A popular democratic government, with its power seat in East Pakistan, and following a policy of non-alignment or tilting towards the Soviet Union, did not fit into Dulles's strategic design, who is known in history for his efforts to 'integrate the entire non-communist Third World into a system of mutual defence pacts, travelling almost 500,000 miles in order to cement new alliances that were modelled after (NATO)'.[88] The emphasis on pacts was a logical culmination of the Truman-Acheson containment doctrine, which called for strong alliance systems directed by the US, and collective security pacts. Dulles, along with most US foreign policymakers of the era, failed to distinguish between the indigenous Third World social revolutionaries and nationalists, from those who were under the Soviet influence. Neutrality for Dulles was 'an obsolete, immoral, and short-sighted conception'.[89]

As already discussed, the key event in the South Asian arena of Cold War competition, was the signing of the Mutual Defence Agreement between Pakistan and the United States. Its major objective was to build a defence establishment in Pakistan to be used for blocking any Soviet thrust into the crucial Middle East, and provide the United States with valuable military bases against the Soviet Union. In its war against communism, Dulles found cooperative partners—generals and bureaucrats, who were trained by the British colonial strategist to believe in the concept of a security state, and who were groomed in the colonial tradition of 'controlled democracy'. They were put in control of affairs, at the expense of the democratic institutions, to steer Pakistan towards Dulles's collective security pacts. It has already been discussed how the governor-general, destroying the notion of a cabinet government, dismissed Prime Minister Nazimuddin in April 1953 in order to pave the way for negotiating the Mutual Defence Agreement under an 'authoritarian regime'. This new 'authoritarian regime' was going to be unaccountable to the people of Pakistan and had the backing of the army. This authoritarian regime, led by Governor-General Ghulam Mohammad, was again successful in dismissing the provincial government of East Pakistan when it raised its voice against the signing of the Mutual Defence Agreement. An authoritarian regime under the guise of a democratic set-up was felt necessary to influence Pakistan into joining the defence pacts, SEATO and the Baghdad Pact, since a majority of the parliamentarians, as well as the people of Pakistan, were not in favour of joining them. The fear of widespread public protests, over the question of Pakistan joining these defence pacts and the Soviet Union's support for such a movement, kept Pakistan's authoritarian regime in a dilemma, regarding public announcements of its intentions of joining these defence pacts against communism.

In the following discussion, an examination will be made on how Pakistan was persuaded to join these defence pacts, thereby, facilitating the non-representative bureaucracy-army alliance and consequent strengthening of authoritarianism, resulting, eventually, in the supremacy of the defence establishment to the extent that the country was put under a direct army rule by the October 1958 *coup d'état*.

Pakistan and SEATO

Dulles initiated the South East Asia Treaty Organization (SEATO) as a security arrangement for the region. The idea was publicly discussed at the Geneva Peace Conference in May 1954, in the aftermath of the Indo-China conflict. On 24 July 1954, presenting his 'Five Point Program on South-East Asia and Europe,' Dulles, the US secretary of state highlighted the following points:

> First, as an interim protection, to fill what is clearly a dangerous vacuum in Southeast Asia, there should be a prompt declaration of intention on the part of all the free nations, including the so-called neutralist block, against further aggression by means of external invasion or internal penetration. Second...Simultaneously, every effort should be made to move ahead on the

longer range of hard and fast military commitments under a Southeast Asia defence pact. While all the many Asiatic powers we would like to see join such a pact may not be willing to enter it that should not serve as a veto on all the others.[90]

During the Geneva Peace Conference, the Foreign Office in London was informed that Dulles had already invited the Colombo powers to join in a pact for the defence of South East Asia and that Burma had refused.[91] Following the conference, the joint United Kingdom-United States Study Group on South East Asia, agreed upon 'collective security pact and declaration of intention'.[92] It was recorded that the United States had agreed that 'invitations should be issued by 7 August for a meeting at the beginning of September to draw up a treaty'. It was further recorded that 'an approach should now be made to the Colombo Powers to urge their participation in talks on the treaty'. Earlier, on 24 July 1954, the State Department had informed all the US embassies in Asia that an agreement had been reached between America and Britain to hold a conference on South East Asian defence as a first step. The diplomatic missions were also told that the British government was assigned the responsibility to invite the governments of Australia, New Zealand, Ceylon, India, Indonesia, and Pakistan, on the possibility of participating in establishing a collective security agreement in South East Asia.[93] On 30 July 1954, the Commonwealth Relations Office in London, sent a telegram to its high commissioners in India, Pakistan, Ceylon, Australia, New Zealand, Canada, and South Africa, which stated that, 'the Foreign Secretary...[had] undertaken that invitation should be issued not later than 7th August to Conference to be held not later than 1st September to prepare recommendations on the conclusion of a Collective Defence Agreement'.[94] To make an immediate approach to the Colombo powers, a telegram, containing the text of a message, from the foreign secretary to the prime ministers of India, Pakistan, and Ceylon, was sent by the Commonwealth Relations Office in London, on the same day. A similar message was sent to the prime ministers of Burma and Indonesia. In the telegram a fear was expressed that the Indian reaction to the approach was bound to be negative, therefore, it was considered important 'to ensure that Nehru's reaction should be as favourable as possible'. It was hoped that positive reactions from Pakistan, Ceylon, and Burma, would 'exercise a moderating influence on Nehru'. The Commonwealth Relations Office was 'cognizant of the difficulties vis-à-vis India, if Pakistan were to go it alone without the support of any other Colombo Power, but there...[could] be no question of our dissuading either Pakistan or Ceylon from joining'. The Commonwealth Relations Office conveyed to high commissioners that they were 'indeed most anxious to have the support of any Asian country or countries, other than Siam and the Philippines that...[could] be persuaded to join or to be associated with the organization'. In his message, the UK foreign secretary invited the prime ministers of the Colombo powers by informing them that:

> We have long been in favour of creating a broadly based defensive organization in South East Asia and the South West Pacific. After careful study of this problem, our ideas have now crystallized sufficiently for me to seek your views on them, and I hope you will give them very serious consideration.[95]

In his message, the foreign secretary expressed the hope 'to see the Asian powers play a leading role in the defence of South East Asia'. Emphasizing the importance of the area, he was of the view that 'its peace...[was] as yet so insecure, that...[they felt it] vital to safeguard its peaceful development and ensure its stability'. The purpose of the meeting was 'to consider possible measures of collective defence for South East Asia and the South West Pacific in the hope of producing agreed recommendations for consideration by the participating governments and a draft collective defence agreement'. Three specific subjects to be considered at the meeting were:

> (a) measure of military, economic or technical assistance to countries wishing to strengthen their resistance to external interference of any kind; (b) consultation with a view to common action, should the territorial integrity, political independence or security of one of the parties, or the peace of the area, be endangered; (c) action in the event of overt aggression.[97]

The treaty was said to have already been discussed with Chou En-lai in Geneva and the Chinese were reported to be 'well aware that [Anglo-American bloc] intende[d] to press forward on these lines'. It was evident that 'during these discussions Chou En-lai was mainly concerned to obtain assurances about the neutrality of Laos, Cambodia and Vietnam'. It was made clear that these countries were not going to 'be the members of the proposed organization'.[97]

THE DESTRUCTION OF DEMOCRACY

The news that Pakistan had decided to participate in the conference on South East Asian defence was received with great pleasure and considered 'an excellent development'.[98] Although, Pakistan had decided to participate in the Manila treaty conference, it was not yet ready to become a member of the South East Asian organization. The message of Mohammad Ali Bogra stated:

> My colleagues and I have carefully considered your secret personal message of 30th July. I am glad to be able to inform you that Pakistan will be represented at the proposed meeting, which is planned for the beginning of September to consider possible measures of collective defence for South East Asia and South West Asia. Our participation in the meeting does not imply prior acceptance of any scheme that might emerge from the discussions in the meeting. Any recommendations made by the meeting will be considered on their merits.[99]

On the other hand, Nehru's reaction to the Manila treaty conference as expected, was very critical. Refusing to be associated with any such proposed organization, Nehru argued that 'an organization of the kind proposed was more likely to promote mistrust and suspicion than security'.[100] He observed that, 'though it was called a defensive arrangement it was by inference directed against China and was motivated by fear about Chinese intentions'. He opined that any such organization 'would only serve to divide South and South East Asia into rival groups and would therefore, in his opinion largely undo much of the great achievement of Geneva'. Nehru was convinced that 'China harboured no aggressive intentions' and there was no need for its neighbours to feel threatened. This was not the view upheld by the Anglo-American block, which professed that 'China was the exponent of a militant political philosophy to which [they] were unalterably opposed and which by its very nature could scarcely allow weak neighbours to develop freely along lines of their own choosing'.[101] Criticizing both the South East Asian and the South West Pacific organizations, Nehru asserted that 'it was far from being a collective peace system...rather a military alliance'.[102] Nehru warned that it would 'possibly result in the formation of a counter-military alliance'. He further argued that 'the majority of Asian countries...[would] not be participating in the organization. Some would even be strongly opposed to it, thus rendering South East Asia a potentially explosive theatre of the cold war'.[103]

Nehru's stand made it more essential that either Ceylon or Pakistan should be persuaded to participate in the organization. It was more convenient to press the authoritarian regime in Pakistan to bow before the wishes of Dulles and his partners. In view of India's criticism and anticipated strong reactions from Moscow and Peking, it was not easy for Pakistan's pro-West leadership to offer unconditional support to the proposed organization, a fact reflected in Bogra's message, while accepting the invitation to participate in the Manila conference. However, the governments of both the UK and US were 'anxious to secure Pakistan's participation or association with...a South East Asia Organization even if she were the only Colombo Power'.[104] It appears that there were some serious Anglo-American differences over the strategy and control of a South East Asian organization. It is interesting to note how both the parties exploited Pakistan's association for gaining their specific interests. After knowing that Dulles had already invited the Colombo powers to join in a pact for South East Asian defence, the Foreign Office in London, and the secretary of state for Commonwealth Relations, were keen to show that they were more 'anxious' than the US for Pakistan's association, hoping that 'there would be at least one Asian country...to act as a counter-weight to the American protégées—Siam and the Philippines'.[105] It was argued that 'Pakistan could make a more useful military contribution than either Siam [Thailand] or the Philippines'. The Foreign Office felt 'if Pakistan were excluded, it would be widely believed that [the British], rather than the Americans, were responsible, and there would be a repetition of the resentment towards the United Kingdom felt at the time of the conclusion of the Agreement with Turkey'. The fear was expressed that the United States might prefer to dominate SEATO by excluding the Colombo powers, therefore, Pakistan's association was considered essential. To make their case more convincing, the Foreign Office in London, argued, 'if Pakistan were to come in now it would make it easier for other Colombo Powers to come in later, e.g. Ceylon, Burma, and if there [was] a victory of the Masjumi (Moslem Party) in the elections next February—Indonesia'.[106] To convince Pakistan to participate, it was argued that 'Pakistan's interests in East Bengal [Pakistan] give her a direct interest in South-East Asian security'.[107] According to American analysis, the closeness of East Pakistan to the vulnerable areas in South East Asia could serve as a justification for Pakistani participation. It was emphasized that it would be more difficult to justify the introduction of American military equipment in East Pakistan, if Pakistan's security interests were primarily directed towards the Middle East.[108]

It was widely believed that:

> Foreign Minister [of Pakistan] by signing the instrument in Manila had gone rather further than his Government had intended, and that there had been genuine embarrassment between the Prime Minister and the Foreign Minister about something which the latter had done in order to be as cooperative as possible with Mr Dulles.[110]

The Pakistani ambassador sought to maintain the 'balance between tacit approval of South Asia Treaty Organization and strict neutrality supported by fear of possible Chinese reaction'.[110] As expected, the South East Asia Collective Defence Treaty provoked great criticism in Moscow and Peking. Defending the Manila treaty, the British ambassador in Bangkok, observed in a press conference on 24 September 1954, that:

> The propaganda attack against the treaty made by Moscow and Peking and echoed by other communist agencies have been very violent. All have denounced the Manila Treaty as 'aggressive'. The falseness of this charge and the fury with which it had been levelled show how effective it must appear in communist eyes for the purpose for which it was designed, namely the defence of South East Asia against aggression. It should not be forgotten that Chinese have their own treaty with the Soviet Union and hence have no right to question whatever arrangement we may make with our friends for our mutual defence.[111]

Despite the difficulties Pakistan could face over the ratification of SEATO, Prime Minister Mohammad Ali Bogra was not given a sympathetic hearing whenever he tried to explain Pakistan's difficult position. Bogra was on his way to Washington after successfully completing the task of constitution-making by the constituent assembly of Pakistan. The minutes of a meeting with the secretary of state and the minister of defence, held on 30 September 1954, in the Foreign Office in London, reveal how the prime minister was humiliated rather than shown an understanding attitude for the difficult position in which he had been placed in by Pakistan promising to sign on to SEATO.[112] It was reported that Bogra 'haggled a lot and adopted a stupid and rather blackmailing attitude on the lines of what "do we get out of it if we did become members, what about India etc?"' The minutes recorded that 'the Secretary of State and Minister of Defence...pressed Mohammad

Ali [Bogra] strongly on loss of prestige and other good reasons why it would be very short-sighted of Pakistan to back down now'.[113] The record further reveals that, 'later the Foreign Secretary and Lord Alexander had a further discussion with Mohammad Ali [Bogra] when later said that he would like to think more about this and have another meeting after he returned from Washington'.[114]

Bogra's reluctance to join the SEATO was due to the reaction he felt he would face from the legislators of East Pakistan, who had strengthened his authority as the prime minister by passing a law clipping the abusive executive powers of the governor-general to dismiss the prime minister and his cabinet at his will, and were also opposing Pakistan's participation in any defence pact. The constituent assembly that was reconvened on 14 March 1954, after a long break of four months, had resumed the work on the finalization of the remaining clauses of the Basic Principles Committee report. The governor-general, who was in control of the central executive but was unable to extend its authority over the constituent assembly, was not pleased with these developments. Once the constitution was framed, the governor-general's position would change and the focus of the power had to shift to the representative forces. In July, Sir Ivor Jennings arrived in Pakistan to assist in the drafting of the constitution at the invitation of the assembly's constitutional drafting committee. On 15 September, Bogra announced in the Assembly that, 'he [was] grateful to God that at long last [they had]...crossed the last hurdle in Pakistan'.[115] On 20 September, the assembly abolished the Public and Representative Offices (Disqualification) Act (PRODA), the most powerful executive weapon, since it was passed during Liaquat's ministry. The next day, the constituent assembly amended the Government of India Act, thereby preventing the governor-general from dismissing the cabinet, who, now was made responsible to the National Assembly through this amendment, 'This was the move to make the government completely dependent upon the Assembly and to prevent the repetition of the exercise of the Governor-General's power of intervention'.[116] According to the Fifth Amendment, only members of the assembly were to be selected as cabinet ministers and could continue to hold office only as long as they retained the confidence of the legislature, and similarly, the prime minister was required to be a member of the assembly at the time of his appointment.[117] Furthermore, the cabinet was to be collectively responsible to the assembly and would be required to resign if any one of its members lost the confidence of the assembly. By making these amendments, the assembly declared its supremacy and its objective to ensure that the 'formation and working of government' should be in accordance with the 'accepted principles and conventions' of a parliamentary system of government'.[118] Under the headlines, 'Parliament Made Supreme Body', *Dawn* stated that 'the Constituent Assembly of Pakistan yesterday laid down in clear and unambiguous terms that from that day the supreme authority in the country shall be the Parliament'.[119]

On 21 September, the assembly voted its approval of the constitution in the form of the Basic Principles Committee report as amended.[120] Out of forty votes polled, twenty-seven votes were in favour, eleven Hindu members voted against, while none of the members from the Punjab voted on the constitution. The assembly then was adjourned until 27 October, concluding what was called a 'historical session'.[121] In contrast, this was seen as 'veritable coup' carried out by Bengali members of the assembly, backed by some have-nots of the Muslim League.[122] These views of the British high commissioner were shared by the American embassy which reported:

> Nevertheless clear that action was in nature "constitutional coup" brought about suddenly and apparently as complete surprise to Governor-General... Whatever other motives...[might] be action achieve[d] for Nazimuddin group for latter's dismissal last year and appeared[d] as temporary setback Punjabi clique.[124]

The British high commissioner observed that 'one result [of the constitutional changes was] to bring a step nearer the possibility that the Army and the higher Civil Services...[might] one day come to the conclusion that the politicians have made such a mess that it is necessary for non-political forces to take over'.[124] This observation was a mirror image of the thinking of the 'neo-colonial powers', who claimed to be the champions of democracy and protectors of the 'free world' but to secure their strategic interests, found justification in promoting non-political and non-democratic forces instead of strengthening the democratic process in Pakistan. 'Pakistan's international supporters were ambivalent about democracy too. The American Agenda was clear: a pro-Western Pakistan, a stable Pakistan, prosperous Pakistan, and a democratic Pakistan were all desirable, but in that order. When democracy threatened to remove a leadership that was less than pro-America, the US Embassy conveyed this priority to Pakistanis,'[125] a fact clearly demonstrated in a despatch sent by the American embassy on 25 September 1954, stating that:

> To most of the outer world the passage of this act will appear as a victory for democratic, parliamentary government; the enactment into law of the normal procedures which govern the administration of a responsible cabinet system of government. Actually, however, what has happened is a long step toward seizure of power on the part of a group of ambitious politicians determined to oust those whom they regard as enemies.[126]

This 'group of "ambitious politicians" who "stripped powers from the Governor-General, gave the Prime Minister powers over his cabinet Ministry, and made the Prime Minister dependent upon the confidence of the Assembly" was speculated to promote Miss Fatima Jinnah both for President of the League and for the first President of the Islamic Republic of Pakistan'.[127] It was feared that Fatima Jinnah might be elected as the Muslim League's president in a convention scheduled on 29 October 1954.[128] Talks of 'reforming and revitalizing' the League 'for some time' were being reported. The convention was announced after Prime Minister Bogra's proposal to separate the offices of the prime minister and that of the president of the Muslim League.

After the passing of the constitution, a national election had to be arranged. Under the leadership of Fatima Jinnah, the Muslim League, in alliance with the leaders of the United Front parties, could have emerged as a real political force by challenging the executive's control over authority and establishing a democratic government instead. This scenario was most frightening for the American policymakers who had pinned their hopes on Mirza and Ayub for giving their 'full support' to the governor-general, 'since both General Mirza and General Ayub, commander-in-chief of the Army...[had] stated categorically on various occasions that they would never allow the stability of the country to be broken up in political squabbles'.[129] Supported by domestic and external protectors of the 'free world', the governor-general ordered the police to bar the members of the constituent assembly, of a 'politically immature country', from attending the assembly session on 27 October 1954, which was called specifically to vote on the draft constitution approved in the assembly's previous session.[130] The next day, the governor-general dissolved the constituent assembly, and appointed a 'semi-dictatorial executive' praised as a 'cabinet of talents', in which the army chief, General Ayub, was included as the defence minister.

THE DESTRUCTION OF DEMOCRACY   165

> From all accounts available, it seems clear that Ghulam Mohammad's plan to dismiss the Constituent Assembly once and for all and to start again was worked out with General Ayub's prior knowledge. It is, moreover, probable that without the assurance of the Army's support, Ghulam Mohammad might have hesitated.[132]

General Ayub's inclusion in the cabinet was the indication to suggest that 'this was no time for nonsense'[132] and that there was no doubt left that the army was the negotiating power in the state construction and the real partner in Dulles's strategic defence plans.

'On 28 October 1954, the Assembly, which until then had been an operating political body and had produced a new constitution, became a "failure". But it was the success not the failure, which brought about its demise'.[133] The termination of parliamentary democracy was not the result of 'failure' within the assembly, or due to any defects in the new constitutional changes, as pointed out by the British high commissioner and campaigned for by the governor-general and his associates; on the contrary, it was the strategic partnership with neo-colonialism that promoted authoritarianism which was the real culprit. The justification of wrongful dismissal of the constituent assembly was that the electorate was bound to act foolishly, as they had done in the East Pakistan election, and this was clearly so because the masses were illiterate and needed further training in democratic institutions. The assertion was that until this was accomplished there would be a need of 'controlled democracy'. Mirza, in a public statement, issued on 10 February 1955, declared that 'the government...[would] pay no attention to...[the Sindh High Court's] ruling of 9 February that Governor-General's action on 24 October seizing overt control and dismissing the Constituent Assembly was illegal'. Mirza added that 'if the federal court upheld the 9 February decision, it too would be ignored'.[134] However, the governor-general's action of dissolving the constituent assembly attained judicial legitimacy by the federal court's theory of 'Law of Necessity', declaring 'that which otherwise is not lawful, necessity makes lawful'.[135] The effect of this theory was that those in command of the coercive powers of the state had the right to suspend a constitutional government when and for however long they deemed necessary. The subsequent courts in Pakistan have retroactively cited the theory of Law of Necessity 'to justify coups against civilian governments by generals Ayub, Yahya, Zia and Musharraf'.[136]

The bureaucrat-military alliance, with the support of their strategic partners, was successful in eroding the democratic institutions and establishing a 'constitutional dictatorship' in Pakistan which was appreciated by their strategic partners in these words:

> With the concurrence also of Defence Minister Ayub and senior military and civil service officials, therefore either Ghulam Mohammad or Mirza would probably adopt blunter tactics than heretofore, to keep Pakistan politically and economically alive. This presumably would entail abandonment of present constitutional plans in favour of more frankly authoritarian government...and more open reliance on the army as the ultimate political arbiter if necessary.[137]

This constitutional dictatorship was the vehicle to be used for ensuring Pakistan's membership in the SEATO and the Baghdad pacts. 'The interplay of domestic, regional and international factors had brought about a decisive shift in the institutional balance of power; bureaucrats and generals had triumphed over politicians'.[139]

Pakistan and the Baghdad Pact

After joining SEATO, Pakistan had to enter into another defence pact, the Baghdad Pact. Dulles had modelled the Baghdad Pact after the North Atlantic Treaty Organization (NATO), with the 'aim of strengthening regional defence and preventing the influence of the Soviet Union into the Middle East'.[139] The formation of the Baghdad Pact resulted primarily from post-war British and American fears of Soviet expansion into the Middle East. In Anglo-American conception, the Middle East was a crucial area because of its extensive oil deposits and its strategic geographic location, harbouring communication links for the navy and aviation lines. Further, several military bases made the area important as a staging post for military attacks against the Soviet Union.[140] The Baghdad Pact was the manifestation of Dulles's concept of a Northern Tier. As a first step, Turkey signed a pact of mutual cooperation with Pakistan in February 1954. This was soon expanded to Iraq, followed by Iran and Britain.[141] It was hoped that 'Syria and Jordan would complete the arc of countries sweeping across the region'. But the Baghdad Pact:

> faced strong popular Arab opposition encouraged by Egyptian President Gemal Abdel Nasser...Syria refused to join, while the young anglophile King

THE DESTRUCTION OF DEMOCRACY

Hussain of Jordan wavered...In the end, he bowed to the will of his people who took to the streets in large numbers to denounce the pact.[142]

The Baghdad Pact appeared to be the 'accidental, rather than the natural successor to the ill-fated Middle East Defence Organization (MEDO), which had never got past the planning state'.[143]

Pakistan's joining of the Baghdad Pact is an interesting episode. It shows how international and domestic partners in the Cold War era played a skilful game to exploit Pakistan's strategic location in achieving their individual goals. It has already been shown how democratic institutions were destroyed by this partnership to ensure Pakistan's membership in SEATO, and a constitutional dictatorship was established. As we have seen, this process began with Pakistan's participation in the planning talks over the proposed Middle East Defence Organization (MEDO). During these talks General Ayub Khan emerged as the 'major negotiator' and the Pakistan army as the 'strategic partner' which had to be built-up before being given any assignment in the Middle East defence. The Mutual Defence Agreement between Pakistan and the United States was meant for attainment of this objective. The State Department believed that an alliance of Northern Tier states of the Middle East, i.e., Iran, Iraq, Pakistan, and Turkey, was the best bet for a secure defence of the Middle East against any communist aggression. The military agreement between Pakistan and Turkey, signed in February 1954, was the first step leading in this direction. Dulles was pushing the other countries to follow, but due to Britain's strategy, there were delays. Britain was concerned about the possible hostile reaction of Egypt under the leadership of Nasser, who was advocating a policy of 'popular Arab Nationalism'. The other concern was America's consideration for the possibility of including Israel in the proposed pact. That showed Dulles's lack of understanding of Arab feelings towards Israel. Turkey and Iraq signed the Baghdad Pact on 24 February 1955. It was observed that 'the government [of Iraq] had gone beyond public opinion in signing the pact with Turkey'.[144]

The government of Turkey was asked to invite Pakistan to join the pact. The Commonwealth Relations Office was of the view that Pakistan should be invited by the British government as a Commonwealth country.[146] The officials in the foreign office of Pakistan were of the view that one or two of the Middle Eastern states should join the pact before Pakistan could adhere to it. This was because of the unpopular reaction the pact was expected to face in Pakistan. Britain joined the Pact on 30 March. It was expected that Pakistan should announce its adherence before participating in the Bandung conference scheduled in April 1955.[146] Pakistan's military leadership hoped to secure a full military commitment before joining the pact.[147] They wanted an alliance with America and without America's participation they were sceptical about the value and prospects of a Middle Eastern pact. General Ayub declared in the cabinet that 'this pact can only be saved if the Americans join in. We shall join as soon as the Americans do. Our joining in it earlier will be premature and do no good to us or them'.[148] However, Pakistan had to join under the pressure of the United States, Britain, Turkey, and Iraq. Pakistan became a member on 30 June 1955, and soon Iran entered the pact as well. The status of the United States was 'ambiguous; it was a member of most of the committees without having signed the Pact'.[149]

The Soviet Union considered the pact as 'aggressive' and that there was a 'false pretext that this…[was] in the interests of the defence of the countries of this area'.[150] Similar opinions were expressed by Mao Zedong who observed:

> The second question is what is the nature of the international military alliances organized by the Americans and the other imperialists, such as the North Atlantic, Baghdad and the Manila? We say that they are of an aggressive nature. However, against which side do these organizations direct their spearhead? Are they attacking socialism, or nationalism? It seems to me that they are currently attacking the nationalist countries, such as Egypt, Lebanon, and the other weak countries in the Middle East.[151]

Very soon the question about the benefits of Pakistan's participation in the defence pacts was being raised in the country. A conversation between the Commonwealth secretary and the speaker of the National Assembly of Pakistan highlights this point. Responding to a question by the speaker, 'what value there was in the pacts for Pakistan,' the Commonwealth secretary said, 'the value of the pacts to Pakistan was that they brought her firmly under the Western defence umbrella'. The speaker was assured that 'quite apart from any consideration, it was in the direct national interest of Britain and America to defend all pact members against communist attack'.[152] Knowing that the people of Pakistan were more concerned with the threat of India rather than the communist attack, the Commonwealth secretary wanted to know 'what the reaction would be in Pakistan if Britain and America offered jointly to guarantee Pakistan against any attack by India, India against any attack by Pakistan'. The speaker was of the opinion that any such guarantee would be 'welcome in Pakistan only after the Kashmir problem had been settled'. He further clarified his point by emphasizing that 'if such a guarantee were given before [the settlement of the Kashmir problem], then it would be tantamount to guaranteeing India in her illegal possession of Kashmir'.[153]

The question of plebiscite in Kashmir was the burning issue. The Soviet Union had maintained a neutral stand on the Kashmir dispute until Pakistan's signing of the Mutual Defence Agreement with the United States, and its joining of SEATO and the Baghdad pact. The Soviet Union held the view that the Kashmir dispute was being exploited by the Western powers for their own ends and that it would prefer to see it decided through direct negotiations between India and Pakistan, without the intervention of those powers. The Soviet Union felt that by joining the Baghdad Pact, Pakistan had become a member of 'an aggressive Western alliance', and responded by radically altering its stand on Kashmir. Thenceforth, the Soviet Union began to support India's claim that no plebiscite was possible or necessary in Kashmir and vetoed every resolution of the Security Council on Kashmir which India had objected to. Pakistan had to pay a very high price for its alliance with the West. The fact that Pakistan was losing ground on the Kashmir issue was the cause of growing disapproval of Pakistan's foreign policy in the public arena.

The broadcast speech of the American ambassador in Dhaka on 24 January 1956 was an effort to pacify the increasing unpopularity of these defence pacts and the program of substantial military aid to be provided by the United States. The speech sparked strong criticism in Moscow. In an article entitled, 'A Legitimate Question', published in *Pravda* on 30 January 1956, expressing the official thinking of Moscow, the article speculated, if Pakistan was feeling that 'the meshes of the military blocks set up by colonizers' had made her isolated in her neighbourhood, where the Soviet Union, India, Afghanistan, and Burma were strengthening the ties of friendship and business cooperation.[154] It was claimed that the public in Pakistan was 'demanding a definite revision of the country's foreign political course, justly noting that Pakistan's participation in the Baghdad Pact and SEATO...[had] placed it in a position of isolation on the international arena'. The article claimed that 'these demands...[were] put forth most vigorously in East Pakistan', where 'the political situation...[had] always caused constant uneasiness in Britain and the USA—Pakistan's senior partners in the military blocks'. Reacting to the speech the article termed it of 'provocative nature' and against the diplomatic norms 'to go over the head of the Government of Pakistan and appeal to the pro-American leaders to support the alliances with the West'. It was considered a 'direct interference in Pakistan's internal affairs and pressure on certain circles'. It was reported that 'these days the public of Pakistan...[was] expressing legitimate alarm over the future fate of its country...The public welcomed Pakistan's participation in the Bandung Conference of Asian and African countries'. The article further reported that, 'the press of Asian countries...[was writing] unanimously that Pakistan's participation in the Baghdad Pact and SEATO testifie[d] to Pakistan's deviation from the 'spirit of Bandung'. Resentment was also expressed over Pakistan's proposal to host the meeting of the Council of the 'aggressive' SEATO in Karachi on 6 March 1956. It was observed that 'the public circles of Pakistan...[were] say[ing] openly that the blind policy of close alliance with the colonial powers...[had] already caused inestimable harm to the country in all respects'. Reference to the editorial article, published in the *Evening Star*, of Karachi, was highlighted. Commenting on the planned meeting of the Council of SEATO, it wrote that 'this organization...[had] not been able to make any impression on the minds of the Pakistanis, who...[might] now ask the legitimate question: just what...[was] the benefit of such alliances? Highlighting these observations, the article concluded that the question raised by the Pakistani public awaite[d] an answer from the ruling circles of Pakistan'.[155]

The 'ruling circles of Pakistan', at that time, were the army and the bureaucracy, who knew exactly what benefits they were getting out of these alliances. In the SEATO council meeting, Pakistan demanded for 'the recognition of urgency of providing Pakistan with the necessary military resources to enable her to meet threat from subversion and aggression and affectively discharge her Treaty obligations'.[156] They reportedly 'pressed for a specific resolution instructing military advisors to work out a program immediately for strengthening of indigenous military forces'.[158] In his letter, that was forwarded to the prime minister of UK through the Pakistan high commissioner in London on 16 April 1956, Chaudhry Mohammad Ali, the 'cosmetic' prime minister of Pakistan, made a show about the 'quick Soviet military supplies to Afghanistan'.[158] He believed that 'at least forty million dollars out of the total loan of one hundred million dollars [was] being devoted to the purchase of arms and ammunition'. Chaudhry Mohammad Ali's plea was that in the context of Soviet aid to Afghanistan:

> it...[was] therefore, necessary that the political support extended to... [Pakistan] by the SEATO powers should be endorsed at Tehran [in the forthcoming meeting of Baghdad Pact] and followed without any loss of time, by increased military and economic assistance...[Pakistan] need[ed] to hold our northern frontiers effectively.

The 'increased military assistance' was what was required by General Ayub, 'the final arbiter of the destiny of Cabinets'[159] and his associate, President Major General Iskandar Mirza, who were now the unchallenged authority in Pakistan under the shadow of a 'cosmetic form of democracy'. The increased military assistance was not going to help Pakistan in any conflict with India, a fact, that was made clear by Dulles at Colombo in a press conference, when he declared that 'if Pakistan committed aggression against India, it would be a breach of the SEATO Pact, of the Military Aid Agreement between the USA and Pakistan, and of the Charter of the United Nations, and that the United States would support India under its United Nations obligations'.[160] Pakistan was told that 'the material was intended solely to [her] in a position to resist communism'.[161]

Chaudhry Mohammad Ali, once the 'Lord of Bureaucracy' in Pakistan, was selected as the new prime minister when Bogra was removed from office and sent back to Washington as Pakistan's ambassador, a post he was holding when he was picked to the prime minister in April 1953. Bogra was removed because he tried to block Iskandar Mirza from becoming the governor-general when Ghulam Mohammad had to be retired due to his sagging health and age.[162] 'Mirza needed the unqualified support of all his old associates' at a time when Pakistan 'very boldly...[had developed] intimate contacts with the United States'.[163]

With this group in power, all the key positions in the central government went to those from West Pakistan, which was now being merged into 'one unit' combining all four federal units and states.[164] One Unit was created to check the threat of East Pakistan's majority in any future constitutional formula. East Pakistan, which had been kept under the governor's rule since April 1954, following the dismissal of the United Front ministry, could not be allowed to disrupt the 'power game' of the domestic and international partners of the Defence Pacts.

Therefore, the need was to design a constitutional formula that would safeguard the interests of this alliance. In this framework of things, politicians, political parties and the political process were the 'necessary evil' to be tolerated at a time when those in the 'control seat' felt able to exercise their authority, without leaning on any crutches of the democratic institutions. Instead of holding elections for the new legislature, the second constituent assembly was formed indirectly by the vote of the members of the provincial legislatures. The risk of holding a national election, on the basis of adult franchise, could not be afforded by the bureaucratic-army alliance, anticipating the popular mood of the majority of Pakistani people who were not in favour of any military defence pacts aligning their country with the imperialist powers. This was clearly demonstrated by the provincial elections held in 1954 for the provincial assembly of East Pakistan. The mood in smaller provinces was also very similar.

To give legitimacy to their policies, the authoritarian regime in command of the central authority, required some kind of constitutional understanding between the constituent units of Pakistan. The creation of One Unit was an attempt to control the power of East Pakistan, which was being used to obstruct the construction of the state, according to the dictates of the defence needs of the neo-colonial forces. On 4 October 1954, General Ayub wrote a memorandum entitled, 'A Short Apprehension of Present and Future Problems of Pakistan'.[165] This memorandum reflected the thinking of the commander-in-chief of the Pakistan army who was selected for a specific purpose and remained in this position for almost two decades. He played the most prominent role in shaping Pakistan's destiny and making it a 'client state' of the United States. In his view, people of East Pakistan had been and still were:

> under considerable cultural and linguistic influences. As such, they [had] all the inhibitions of downtrodden races and [had] not...found it possible psychologically to adjust to the requirements of their newborn freedom. Their peculiar complexes, exclusiveness, suspicion and a sort of defensive aggressiveness probably emerge[d] from this historical background.[167]

Ayub suggested that 'they may be helped so as to feel equal partners and prove an asset'. On the other hand, Ayub believed that West Pakistan 'strategically and economically...[was] destined to stand or fall as a whole' and 'in order to develop properly and prove a bulwark of defence from the north to south, must be welded into one unit'.[167]

The West Pakistan Bill was the first bill, the second constituent assembly passed on 30 September 1955. Under the watchful eyes of General Ayub and Iskandar Mirza, the constituent assembly completed the task of framing the 1956 Constitution, which reflected their aspirations. 'Intimidations, outright coercion and extension of patronage had been critical in the central leadership's success in forcing the constitutional bill through the Constituent Assembly'.[168] The 1956 Constitution was an exercise in flirtation with parliamentary democracy and federalism, with executive authority to appoint and dismiss the cabinet, vested in the president instead of the prime minister, thereby undermining its collective responsibility to the National Assembly.[169] The president was also given the powers to summon, prorogue and dismiss the National Assembly, which was to consisted of 310 members divided equally between East and West Pakistan. The most striking clause was that the annual budget had to be approved by the president before placing it in the National Assembly.[170] This provision was especially made to protect the defence expenditure and the military assistance provided by the United States. During talks with Nehru in New Delhi, Dulles had confirmed that the military supplies program to Pakistan 'was well in arrears. It was the American intention therefore to increase the delivery pace during the next year so as to catch up with their commitments'.[171] Americans felt that 'they were behind in their commitments to Pakistan'.[172] There was therefore, 'an obligation to speed up deliveries and they would do their best to honour their obligation. At the moment, they had only sent a quarter of what they had promised'. On 9 July 1956, US Vice-President Richard Nixon and his wife, accompanied by various military and civilian aides, made a four-hour break at Karachi, while returning to the United States following a tour of the Far East. 'Nixon went straight to the President's House where he had brief talks with President Mirza and his cabinet ministers'.[173] Mirza told the British high commissioner that 'he pressed Nixon for some further clarification on recent statements regarding neutralism'. Nixon assured Mirza that 'there was no change in American Policy towards Pakistan'. To reassure their friends in Pakistan, Nixon spoke to the press just before leaving for Turkey, and expressed his full support for 'Mohammad Ali's statement in London that peace could be maintained "only by measures of collective security"'. The British high commissioner was told that 'there had been a good deal of talks about further American aid to Pakistan'.[174]

In these circumstances, a powerful president who was not responsible to the parliament, was the guarantee to maintain Pakistan's dependence upon the United States and prevent any 'political adventure', that the politicians might decide to take. 'Pakistan had become a party in the Cold War, had chosen the United States as its most important ally, and had openly challenged the Soviet Union'.[175] Therefore, all those elements, which could upset this relationship, had to be under the constant check of controlled democracy, 'The seeds of the crisis that enveloped the state during the remaining two and half years' of constitutional dictatorship before the final takeover of the state by the army were sown in the 1956 constitution.[176] During this period, four prime ministers were appointed and dismissed by the all-powerful President Iskandar Mirza, in alliance with General Ayub. Both were unwilling to work within the bounds of any constitution. They were fond of making and breaking political alliances and choosing their political partners till they got tired of this game and decided to get rid of the politicians and political parties in toto and declared their direct rule.

On 7 October 1958, Iskandar Mirza, first president of the Islamic Republic of Pakistan, holding office under the constitution, issued the proclamation that the central and provincial governments had been dismissed and that the central and provincial assemblies stood dissolved. Political parties were abolished, and General Ayub Khan was appointed supreme commander of the armed forces of Pakistan and the chief martial law administrator. On 24 October 1958, President Mirza announced his new cabinet with General Ayub as prime minister. The new cabinet was sworn in on 27 October 1958. This was the end of Mirza's shameful defeat of all democratic forces of Pakistan. The next morning, Ayub 'completed military take-over of 7 October by assuming full presidential powers, and forced President Mirza to tender a formal resignation.[177] Mirza was given a few hours to pack his belongings and board a plane which took him to England. Ayub declared, 'My authority is revolution; I have no sanction in law or constitution'.[178]

General Ayub Khan executed his coup of 1958 with the approval of the US. This coup was the indicator that the time had come when the pretence of any kind of democracy or political process was no more necessary. The army had attained the ability and strength to run the government without any further interference from politicians and constitutional legitimacy. Therefore, the new law introduced was 'martial law'. General Ayub Khan wrote in his political autobiography:

> The hour had struck. The moment so long delayed had finally arrived. The responsibility could no longer be put off. It was the 4th of October 1958, and as I settled down in my railway saloon I knew that an era was coming to an end. I was going to Karachi where an agonizingly prolonged political farce was drawing to close.[179]

28 October 1958 was the formal burial-day of parliamentary democracy in Pakistan that had died four years ago, when Ghulam Mohammad had dissolved the first constituent assembly. From now onward, the democratic institutions had to take a subordinate position in the new power structure established by neo-colonialism in the post-colonial state of Pakistan, a trend which continues to date.

NOTES

1. *Dawn*, 11 August 1957.
2. The tenure of the various prime ministers was as follows: Liaquat Ali Khan, August 1947 to October 1951 (4¼ years); Nazimuddin October 1951-April 1953 (1½ years); Mohammad Ali Bogra, April 1953-August 1955 (2¼ years); Chaudhry Mohammad Ali, August 1955-September 1956 (13 months); Huseyn Shaheed Suhrawardy, September 1956-October 1957 (13 months); I.I. Chundrigar, October-December 1957 (2 months); and Firoze Khan Noon, December 1957-October 1958 (10 months).
3. Keith Callard, 1957, *Pakistan—A Political Study*, London: George Allen and Unwin, p. 135.
4. Ibid., p. 137.
5. Allen McGrath, op. cit., p. 97.
6. Ibid.
7. Memorandum of Conversation: General Mohammad Ayub Khan, C-in-C, Pakistan Army, Charles D. Withers, First Secretary. From Karachi, Desp. No. 851, 28 February 1953. NND 959417, RG 59, NA.
8. 'Cold War (1953-1962)'. Wikipedia, The Free Encyclopedia. Retrieved 26 June 2004. http://en.wikipedia.org/wiki/cold_war.
9. Allen McGrath, op. cit., p. 108.
10. Emmerson to the Secretary of State, T-55, 15 July 1953, 360-Govt. General, NND 842430, RG 84, NA.
11. Ayub instructed his divisional commanders to put a stop to such speculations in army messes. See Gibson to the Department of State, Lahore, D-150, 23 December 1952, 350-Pakistan-Pak. Army, 12/23/52, NND 842430, RG 84, NA.
12. Memorandum of Conversation between General Ayub and Raleigh A. Gibson, 13 February 1953, Lahore D-135, Top Secret No. 29-Conversation w/Pak C-in-C, 3/13/53, NND 959417, RG 59, NA.

13. Karachi to CRO, 23 October 1951, FL 1027/17/G, FO 371/92876, TNA: PRO.
14. Warren to Kennedy, 30 October 1951, 790D.5 MSP/3151, NDD 842909, RG 59, NA.
15. Karachi to CRO, FL 1027/17/G, FO 371/92876, TNA: PRO.
16. Foreign Office London [henceforth FO], Memo, 16 August 1952, FY 1023/14, FO 371/101198, TNA: PRO.
17. See note by the Secretary, 'Value of Pakistan as A Main Base', prepared for Chiefs of Staff Committee, Joint Planning Staff, 3 May 1949, L/WS/1/1236, IOR.
18. American Embassy to the Department of State, 13 November 1952, 350-Pak. Pol., NND 842430, RG 84, NA.
19. Ibid.
20. Perkins to the Department of State, 27 September 1952, 350-Pak. Pol., NND 842430, RG 84, NA.
21. Berry to Warren, 20 May 1952, NND 959417, RG 59, NA.
22. Memorandum of Conversation between General Ayub and Raleigh A. Gibson, 23 December 1952, 350 Pakistan-Pak Army 12/23/52, NND 842430, RG 84, NA.
23. Ibid.
24. Memorandum of Conversation: General Mohammad Ayub Khan, C-in-C, Pakistan Army, Charles D. Withers, First Secretary. From Karachi, D-851, 28 February 1953, NND 959417, RG 59, NA.
25. Ibid.
26. Kennedy to Byroade, 6/4/53 cited in M.S. Venkartamani, *The American Role in Pakistan*, op. cit., p. 56.
27. 'A Report to the NSC by the Secretaries of State and Defence and the Director of Mutual Security on Re-examination of United States Programs for National Security', 19 January 1953, cited in M.S. Venkartamani, *The American Role in Pakistan*, op. cit., pp. 200-1.
28. Emmerson to the Secretary of State, T-941, 22 December 1952, 320-Pak-Egypt, NND 842430, RG 84, NA.
29. Emmerson to the Secretary of State, 20 April 1953, 350-Pak-Pol. NND 842430, RG 84, NA.
30. Memorandum of conversation between General Ayub and Gibson in Lahore, 28 April 1953, 350 Pakistan-Pak Army 4/28/53, NND 842430, RG 84, NA.
31. Emmerson to the Department of State, 23 April 1953, 350-Pak-Pol. NND 842430, RG 84, NA.
32. Allen McGrath, op. cit., p. 97.
33. 'Mohammed Mossadegh'. Wikipedia, The Free Encyclopedia. Retrieved 26 June 2004, op. cit.
34. Perkins to the Department of State, 27 September 1952, 350-Pak. Pol., NND 842430, RG 84, NA.
35. Emmerson to the Department of State, 23 April 1953, 350-Pak. Pol., NND 842430, RG 84, NA.
36. Allen McGrath, op. cit., p. 108.
37. Keith Callard, op. cit., p. 138.
38. Allen McGrath, op. cit., p. 108.
39. Keith Callard, op. cit., p. 138.
40. American Embassy, Karachi to the State Department, Washington, D-1666 to Dept, 360-Gen, 9-25-54. NND 842430, RG 84, NA.
41. John Foster comments on the 'The Food situation in Pakistan', 890D.03/4-2853, NDD 842909, RG 59, NA.

42. Dulles to Karachi, 1 September 1953, 320-Pak, India, NDD 842430, RG 84, NA.
43. Keith Callard, op. cit., p. 139.
44. M.S. Venkartamani, *The American Role in Pakistan*, op. cit., p. 203.
45. Ibid.
46. Memo of Conversation, State Department, 23 May 1953, 37D-MUHP-1953, NND 842909, RG 59, NA.
47. Ibid.
48. Ibid.
49. G.W. Choudhury, *India, Pakistan, Bangladesh, and the Major Powers*, op. cit., p. 82.
50. Hildreth to Dulles, 15 August 1953, 350-Pak. Pol., NND 842430, RG 84, NA.
51. G.W. Choudhury, *India, Pakistan, Bangladesh, and the Major Powers*, op. cit., p. 84.
52. Dulles to Under Secretary, 1 October 1953, A-67-28, NND 842909, RG 59, NA.
53. Memo of Conversation, 21 October 1953, 790D.5 MSP/10-2153, NND 842909, RG 59, NA.
54. G.W. Choudhury, op. cit., p. 84.
55. Dulles was requested by Nixon to delay the decision of the National Security Council till the report of his visit was made available. Nixon was assured that no decision would be taken until his report. See State Department Memo, 9 December 1953, 790D.5 MSP/12-953, NND 842909, RG 59, NA.
56. Aid Memoire, brief resume of talks between the Prime Minister and the Vice-President of USA held on 7 December 1953, NND 959417, RG 59, NA.
57. Cited in G.W. Choudhury, op. cit., p. 86.
58. Memo of Conversation, State Department, 16 October 1953, 790D.5 MSP/10-1653, NND 842909, RG 59, NA.
59. Ibid.
60. Prime Minister Bogra showed a note to the American ambassador, sent by the Soviets expressing their anger and warning. See Hildreth to Dulles, 2 December 1953, T-399, 350-Pak. Pol., NND 842430, RG 84, NA.
61. American Embassy, Karachi to the Department of State, Washington, D-393, 350 Karachi Weekly Despatch, 12/24/53, NND 842430, RG 84, NA.
62. Byroade to Hildreth, 23 March 1954, 350-Pak-Pol., NND 842430, RG 84, NA.
63. Ibid.
64. Rafique Afzal, *Political Parties in Pakistan*, Vol. 1, Islamabad: National Institute of Historical and Cultural Research, 1998, pp. 197-8.
65. Ibid.
66. Allen McGrath, op. cit., p. 112.
67. Ibid.
68. Ibid., p. 115.
69. *Dawn*, 3 April 1954.
70. *Dawn*, 12 April 1954.
71. Rafique Afzal, *Political Parties in Pakistan*, Vol. 1, op. cit., p. 203.
72. Ibid.
73. See *Pakistan Times*, 20, 21, 23, 24, and 29 April, 8 May, 1, 2, and 6 June 1954.
74. *Dawn*, 2 June 1954.
75. *Dawn*, 11 June 1954.
76. *The New York Times*, 31 May 1954.
77. *Dawn*, 30 June 1954, and *Pakistan Times*, 7 June 1954.
78. *Dawn*, 2, 19 and 21 June 1954, and *Pakistan Times*, 27 May, 1, 2 and 6 June 1954.

79. 'Cold War Policies'. Wikipedia-The Free Encyclopedia. Retrieved 26 June 2004.
80. Mohammad Ayub Khan, *Pakistan Perspective*, a collection of important articles and excerpts from major addresses, Washington: The Embassy of Pakistan, n.d., p. 19.
81. Aid Memoire, Brief resume of talks between the Prime Minister and the Vice-President of USA held on 7-12-53, NND 959417, RG 59, NA.
82. Mohammad Ayub Khan, *Pakistan Perspective*, op. cit., p. 19.
83. Ibid.
84. Ibid., p. 20.
85. Elie Podeh, 1995, *The Quest for Hegemony in the Arab World: The Struggle over the Baghdad Pact*, Leiden: E.J. Brill.
86. Ibid.
87. Mohammad Ayub Khan, *Pakistan Perspective*, op. cit., p. 17.
88. 'Dulles'. Wikipedia-The Free Encyclopedia. Retrieved 26 June 2004.
89. Ibid.
90. Extract from pages 11288-9 of Congressional Record, 24 July 1954, FO 371/111875, TNA: PRO.
91. Geneva to FO, 17 May 1954, D 1074/10, FO 371/111862, TNA: PRO.
92. FO Minute, 30 July 1954, D 1074/302, FO 371/111875, TNA: PRO.
93. Laithwaite to CRO, 23 July 1954, D 1074/271, FO 371/111873, TNA: PRO.
94. Telegram no. 334, 30 July 1954, D 1074/302, FO 371/111875, TNA: PRO.
95. Telegram no. 335, 30 July 1954, D 1074/302, FO 371/111875, TNA: PRO.
96. Ibid.
97. Ibid.
98. FO Minute, 5 August 1954, D 1074/300, FO 371/111875, TNA: PRO.
99. Laithwaite to CRO, 4 August 1954, D 1074/323, FO 371/111876, TNA: PRO.
100. Telegram no. 734, D 1074/303, FO 371/111875, TNA: PRO.
101. Ibid.
102. Telegram no. 739, D 1074/303 (A), FO 371/111875, TNA: PRO.
103. Ibid.
104. Pakistan and SEATO, D 1074/300 (A), 29 July 1954, FO 371/111875, TNA: PRO.
105. Ibid.
106. Ibid.
107. Ibid.
108. Allen to State Department, 28 July 1954, Telegram no. 118, 310 SEATO, NDD 842430, RG 84, File 350-Pak.Pol., NA.
109. The Pakistan ambassador told the British high commissioner in Sri Lanka, A letter by the British High Commissioner in Sri Lanka [Ceylon] to (Peterson) South East Asia Department Foreign Office, D 1074/693, FO 371/116933, TNA: PRO.
110. Ibid.
111. Bangkok to CRO, FO 371/111890, TNA: PRO.
112. FO Minute, 30 September 1954, FO 371/111890, TNA: PRO.
113. Ibid.
114. Ibid.
115. XVI CAD (Con.), pp. 353-65
116. Keith Callard, op. cit., p. 105.
117. XVI CAD (Con.), p. 251, Government of India (5th Amendment) Act, 1954, amending Sections 9, 10, 10A, 10 B, and 17. *Pakistan Times*, 22 September 1954; *Dawn*, 21 September 1954.
118. Keith Callard, op. cit., p. 107.
119. *Dawn*, 22 September 1954.

120. XVI CAD (Con.), pp. 499-510, 570-72.
121. *Dawn,* 22 September 1954.
122. Karachi to CRO, 30 September 1954, DO35/5135, TNA: PRO.
123. American Embassy, Karachi to Secretary State, Washington, T-392 to DEPT, 360 Gen., 9-22-54, NND 842430, RG 84, NA.
124. Ibid.
125. Stephen P. Cohen, 2005, *The Idea of Pakistan,* Lahore: Vanguard Books, p. 56.
126. American Embassy, Karachi to Secretary State, Washington, D-166 to DEPT, 360- General, 9-25-54, NND 842430, RG 84, NA.
127. American Embassy, Karachi to Secretary State, Washington, D-171 to DEPT, 360- Constitutional Coup, 10-2-54, NND 842430, RG 84, NA.
128. American Embassy, Karachi to Secretary State, Washington, D-166 to DEPT, 360- General, 9-25-54, NND 842430, RG 84, NA.
129. Ibid.
130. Stephen P. Cohen, *The Idea of Pakistan,* op. cit., p. 60.
131. Herbert Feldman, 1967, *Revolution in Pakistan,* London: Oxford University Press, p. 41.
132. Ibid.
133. Allen McGrath, op. cit., p. 218.
134. Current Intelligence Bulletin, Office of Current Intelligence, CIA, Copy no. 88, 12 February 1955, RG 59, NA.
135. Stephen P. Cohen, op. cit., p. 58.
136. Ibid.
137. Current Intelligence Weekly, CIA, OCI no. 1052/55, 4 February 1955, RG 59, NA.
138. Ayesha Jalal, *The State of Martial Rule,* op. cit., p. 193.
139. Gerald Butt, 'Lesson from History: 1955 Baghdad Pact', BBC News World Edition. Up 26 February 2003. Retrieved 10 May 2004. httm:/news.bbc.co.uk/2/hi/middle_ east/2801487.stm.
140. Magnus Persson, *Great Britain, the United States and the Security of the Middle East,* Lund: Almqvist & Wiksell.
141. 'Baghdad Pact', Lexicorient. Retrieved 10 May 2004. httm://i-cias.com/e.o/Baghdad_ pact.html.
142. Gerald Butt, 'Lesson from history: 1955 Baghdad Pact', op. cit.
143. Farooq Naseem Bajwa, *Pakistan and the West,* op. cit., p. 134.
144. *The Economist,* 27 February 1955.
145. FO Minute, 18 March 1955, V 1073/549, FO 371/115497, TNA: PRO.
146. FO Minute, 4 April 1955, V 1073/700, FO 371/115506, TNA: PRO.
147. Karachi to CRO, 14 June 1955, V 1073/869, FO 371/115513, TNA: PRO.
148. G.W. Choudhury, op. cit., p. 90.
149. Ibid.
150. Baghdad Pact, Lexicorient, op. cit.
151. 'Speech, Mao Zedong at the Fifteenth Meeting of the Supreme State Council, 5 September 1958 (Excerpt)', Cold War International History Project, Virtual Archive. Retrieved 25 June 2004. <http://wwics.si.edu/index.cmf?topic_id=1409&fuseaction =library.Collection>
152. Note of a Conversation in Rawalpindi on Wednesday, 28 November 1955, between the Commonwealth Secretary and the Speaker of the National Assembly, DO/96/71, TNA: PRO.
153. Ibid.
154. Moscow to FO, 1 February 1956, FO/371/123672, TNA: PRO.

155. Ibid.
156. FO to Tehran, Telegram no. 446, 14 April 1956, FO 371/123674, TNA: PRO.
157. Ibid.
158. High Commissioner for Pakistan London to FO, 17 April 1956, DY. 1071/2, FO 371/123674, TNA: PRO.
159. Hildreth to the Secretary of State, 26 August 1955, *Foreign Relations*, VIII, South Asia, Washington DC, 1987, p. 436.
160. New Delhi to CRO, 16 March 1956, FO 371/123677, TNA: PRO.
161. Telegram no. 1086, 1 May 1956, DY. 1192/13, FO 371/123677, TNA: PRO.
162. Symon to Laithwaite, 31 July 1955, DO35/5378, TNA: PRO.
163. Lawrence Ziring, *Pakistan in the Twentieth Century*, op. cit., p. 176.
164. These units included Sindh, Punjab, NWFP, British Balochistan, Balochistan States Union, Bahawalpur, Khairpur State, and Frontier State. Karachi was the federal area.
165. Hassan Askari Rizvi, *The Military and Politics in Pakistan*, op. cit., Appendix A, pp. 282-7.
166. Ibid., p. 282.
167. Ibid., p. 283.
168. Ayesha Jalal, *The State of Martial Rule*, op. cit., p. 214.
169. See *Constitution of the Islamic Republic of Pakistan* (Passed by the Constituent Assembly of Pakistan on 29 February 1956, and assented to by the Governor-General), Articles 32-57.
170. Ibid.
171. Telegram no. 1086, 1 May 1956, DY. 1192/13, FO 371/123677, TNA: PRO.
172. Ibid.
173. Karachi to CRO, 13 July 1956, FO 371/123672, TNA: PRO.
174. Ibid.
175. Lawrence Ziring, *Pakistan in the Twentieth Century*, op. cit., p. 171.
176. Ayesha Jalal, *The State of Martial Rule*, op. cit., p. 215.
177. NSC Briefing, 'Pakistan', submitted by the Department of State, 29 October 1958. Approved for Release 2002/08/06: CIA-RDP79R00890A001000060026-2.
178. H. Tinker, *India and Pakistan*, op. cit., p. 85.
179. Mohammad Ayub Khan, *Friends Not Masters*, op. cit., p. 70.

5

Authoritarianism and Underdevelopment

In this chapter, forms of authoritarianism and theories of development, focusing on divergence in development, will be examined. The 'Dependency Paradigm' can explain the existing underdevelopment in Pakistan and many other Third World countries. A 'Dependency Model' that can be applicable to Pakistan has been suggested. A comparative analysis of India and Pakistan in the context of neo-colonial states and economic development reveals the similarities and differences in the two inheritors of British colonialism. However, 'the base from which each started and significant differences in political, economic, and social circumstances make direct comparisons difficult.'[1]

FORMS OF AUTHORITARIANISM AND THEORIES OF DEVELOPMENT

Divergence in the development of East Asian and Latin America NICs (Newly Industrialized Countries) has triggered a debate over the theory between advocates of modernization, and dependency approaches, in accounting for the regional divergences. Influenced by the new American development theory, based on American pragmatism and empiricism, a large section of the research using the modernization approach on divergent development focuses on 'economic development'[2] that has become 'equated *de facto* if not *de jure* with economic growth. It in turn was measured by the growth of GNP per capita.'[3] While, the writers of dependency approach insist on a broader 'concept of development' having three aspects: growth (the economic aspect), equality (the social aspect), and liberty (the political aspect).[4] The broad definition then includes those societal conditions that promote personal growth, economic growth, equality in the distribution of wealth, and political liberty, 'The degree of equality in the distribution of wealth may be analyzed along a number of national dimensions: urban-rural, labour-capital, and along intra-class dimensions: large-small industries, large-small farms, skilled-unskilled labour'.[5] Liberty is an essential element of democracy, along with a state executive accountable to an elected parliament, and regular, fair elections.[6] More specifically, liberty includes both political rights, and civil liberties.[7] From this perspective, 'determinant factors in economic development were really social' and 'social change', therefore, seemed the key to both social and economic development.[8] This perspective argues for introducing equity and efficiency in economic development.[9]

Modernization Theories and Neo-modernization

The current democratization theory is indebted to a greater degree to the modernization theory of the 1950s and 1960s that evaluated the requisites of democratization in developing countries. It contended that beyond certain thresholds of economic development, societies become too complex and socially mobilized, to be governed by authoritarian means.[10] The major argument the modernization theory presented was that high income countries were most likely to be democratic and that increasing literacy, urbanization, and non-agricultural employment, were linked with growing tendency to political participation, by inferring that authoritarianism need not be unviable at lower levels of modernization, and may even be quite harmonious with the features of many pre-modern societies. There are two major flaws with the modernization theory. First, it does not identify the threshold beyond which authoritarianism is no more viable.[11] The high levels of income and social mobilization in many communist countries in Europe and authoritarian regimes in East Asia indicate that a quite high level is required for the disappearance of authoritarianism. However, the experience of democracy in India, at a very low level of income, and low levels of modernization, poses a problem to this proposition and makes it apparent that modernization levels are not determinate and merely constitute an environment that may be more or less facultative of certain kinds of regime, ruling out democracy only at the very lowest levels, and authoritarianism, only at the very highest levels.

Furthermore, modernization theories were variants of the original 'stages of growth' idea proposed by Rostow.[12] This approach of development employs a major problem: how to encourage traditional economies to reach the stages of 'takeoff' into sustained economic growth. The advice for increasing growth required new investments in industry: either import substituting, as was the mode in Pakistan, and in a majority of Latin American countries, or export-oriented as in East Asia with the purpose of generating employment and improving labour productivity. This development model presumes that as growth occurs, the positive effects of increased production will 'trickle-down', to those sections of people who are not directly involved in the dynamic sectors. This model leads towards a linear development path ending in 'Western-style', market-oriented societies. The underlying belief is that the cultural diffusion of Western economic/technological processes and the compatibility of social structures, will force developing countries, in the long run, to adopt the characteristics of the developed ones. In this linear progress, the prediction is that traditional societies will eventually advance through the stages that have been achieved by developed societies. It is assumed that the lack of human skills and investment capital are the major problems, therefore, the system of banks and development assistance agencies, such as the IMF and the World Bank, are designed to provide capital for investment to developing countries who are trailing in these policies.

Despite the fact that modernization theories have met with increasing criticism, they remain at the cornerstone of development policies, religiously promoted by the bilateral and multilateral aid organizations under global capitalist accumulation.[13] Wolf observed that the modernization theory has 'become an instrument for bestowing praise on societies deemed to be modern and creating a critical eye on those that had yet to attain that achievement'.[14] Attacking the modernization theorists, he claimed that 'the political leaders of the United States had pronounced themselves in favour of aiding the development of the Third World, and modernization theorists seconded that pronouncement. Yet modernization theory effectively foreclosed any but the most ideologically charged understanding of the world'.[15] Wolf accused that the modern theory 'used the term modern, but meant by that term the United States, or rather an ideal of a democratic, pluralistic, rational, and secular United States. It said traditional, but meant all those others that would have to adopt the ideal to qualify for assistance'. Wolf concluded that as a theory, the modern theory was 'misleading' and 'imparted a false view of American history, substituting self-satisfaction for analysis'.[16]

The failure of the early modernization theory's expectations for democratization in the developing countries of the Third World, demanded reconsideration of the theory, exemplified by Huntington's political order in changing Societies.[17] His contention was to show that social mobilization in developing countries might lead, not to democratization but to what he called 'praetorianism'. He asserted that it would happen because mobilization exceeded the economic development and political institution-building needed to satisfy and accommodate it. His argument was that an expected outcome of resulting frustration of demands would be disorder and chaos, in turn, giving rise to military intervention.[18] Huntington's argument on order-building is criticized for advocating dictatorship as a solution to praetorianism, though he was actually quite explicit that military dictatorships only replicated praetorianism, and stability required that participation demands be satisfied through institution-building. Redefining early modern theory, Huntington argued that through enough participation and organizing a constituency for the regime, particularly among previously non-participant masses, single party systems can be a viable and modern form of authoritarianism, and stabilize states in the transition to modernity. He believed that since armies and bureaucracies are capable of imposing order 'from the outside', and clientalist networks do not have the legitimacy to buy the loyalty of large masses of people, they lack such institution building that was essential if regimes were to 'penetrate' society and incorporate constituencies.

Another barrier to democratization, proposed by the writers of modern theories, is that capitalist accumulation in modernizing countries demanded high profits for investors, while squeezing workers and peasants, resulting in increased inequality in the development process.[19] They thought that democratic institutions were unable to contain this stimulated class-conflict which invited authoritarian solutions. The other argument presented is that the disparity between state and identity, generated from the disorganized imposition by imperialism of territorial boundaries, meant that majority of the Third World neo-colonial states lacked fundamental consensus on political community-shared nationhood. Enlarged economic inequality generated by unconsolidated political identity promotes a democratic-unfriendly socio-economic environment.

Within the modernization paradigm, the school of 'new institutionalism' argues that authoritarian regimes cannot be put together in one category.[20] The level of institutionalization gives them the particular shape, which is decided by the social forces that they include and exclude. This school distinguishes between fairly primitive forms, such as personal dictatorships and military juntas and more 'institutionalized' authoritarian regimes, with single party/corporatist systems and bureaucratic/technocratic institutions. It argues that authoritarian forms of personal dictatorships and military juntas lack institutional ability to include supportive social forces and implement policy, and are only likely to be viable at lower levels of development. On the contrary, more 'institutionalized' authoritarian regimes, with single party/corporatist systems and bureaucratic/technocratic institutions, are considered relatively more 'modern', having the possibility to be more inclusive and enhance the capacity to pursue development goals and the ability to be durable at considerably higher levels of development. This school suggests that there is a need to separate 'populist authoritarian' regimes from 'bureaucratic authoritarian' regimes, although both represent the developed form of authoritarianism. From this point of view, Japan is considered as representative of 'bureaucratic authoritarianism' and China as an example of 'populist authoritarianism'. According to this view, populist authoritarian regimes are initiated during early-middle periods of development, as a result of middle class rebellions against old oligarchies, and they intend to activate and include larger sections of the population in the name of redistributive reform. On the other hand, bureaucratic authoritarian regimes are described as a phenomenon of the transition to mass politics, in which authoritarian power is used by the military, acting on behalf of the bourgeoisie and foreign capital, to exclude the mobilizing working class in the name of capital accumulation. Some writers claim that populist authoritarianism is a successful form because it constitutes a formula for constructing quite durable regimes that managed to overcome 'praetorianism'.[21] They suggest that the durability of populist authoritarianism depends on several factors which are interlocking.[22]

It should not be surprising when hard-liners suggest that the East Asian model, 'economic growth first, democracy later', holds more attraction. Within the modernization paradigm, it has been argued that countries ruled by authoritarianism, especially in East and South-east Asia, are more likely to be economically successful than democratic countries. Examples quoted in favour of this thesis are South Korea, Singapore, Malaysia, and Taiwan, which were under authoritarian regimes during their period of growth. This thesis is based on the concept of Asian values, which maintains that authoritarian government is ultimately superior to democracy, although it suffered a great blow after the Asian financial crisis of 1998. It suggests that the common Confucian heritage provides the explanation for the developmental success of Japan, and the East Asian NICs.[23] The neo-modernization literature views that the tenets of Confucianism, including respect for education, discipline, hard work, and cooperation, were at the heart of traditional social practices in Chinese societies; Japan and South Korea, and contributed towards constituting the basis of a new economic culture.[24] However, there have been shifting positions on the benefits of Confucian heritage. The most significant is Huntington's influential study on democracy, which posits a fundamental incompatibility between the Confucian heritage and modern democratic practices. At the same time, Huntington is forced to acknowledge that the Confucian heritage may have 'some elements that are compatible with democracy'.[25] Existing typologies classify most East Asian countries as authoritarian.[26] Japan, the Philippines, Taiwan, Thailand, and South Korea, are considered democracies; Indonesia is considered ambiguous; all other East Asian states (Brunei, Cambodia, China, Laos, Malaysia, Myanmar, North Korea, Singapore, and Vietnam), are considered authoritarian.[27] It is observed that every region in the world, except Asia, has been able to establish some cultural commonality upon which to base a regional system of human rights.[28]

However, problems with this classification system and its assumptions emerge as soon as they are placed under close scrutiny. Within East Asia, the thesis has met with contradictory evidence. If examples of states in North East Asia support it, the states in South East Asia pose a serious problem for its validation. Economic development in North East Asian countries including Taiwan, Japan, and South Korea, seems to have accelerated a transition to democracy, while its absence in Mongolia and North Korea, is prescribed as an obstacle in the 'path to democracy'. The South East Asian countries illustrate a reverse case as shown in Tables 5-7.

Table 5: Indicators of Political Freedom and Economic Growth (Un-free countries: Rating 5.5-7)

Southeast Asian countries	Freedom House rating (2000)	Average annual GDP per capita (1975-2000) (%)
Myanmar	7.7	1.3
Vietnam	7.7	4.8
Laos	7.6	3.2
Brunei	7.5	Unavailable
Cambodia	6.6	1.9

Table 6: Indicators of Political Freedom and Economic Growth (Partly-free countries: Rating 3-5.5)

Southeast Asian countries	Freedom House rating (2000)	Average annual GDP per capita (1975-2000) (%)
Malaysia	5.5	4.1
Singapore	5.5	5.2
Indonesia	4.4	4.4

Table 7: Indicators of Political Freedom and Economic Growth (Free countries: Rating 1-2.5)

Southeast Asian countries	Freedom House rating (2000)	Average annual GDP per capita (1975-2000) (%)
The Philippines	2.3	0.1
Thailand	2.3	5.5

Source: 'Comparative Survey of Freedom, Freedom in the World: Political Rights and Civil Rights', Year 2000, Freedom House, Retrieved 10 May 2004. <http://www.freedomhouse.org/research/index.htm>

Empirically, the reality of political regimes in East Asia provides contradictory evidence to the economic determinism of modernization theories. As discussed above, modernization theorists are, themselves, aware of these weaknesses and have indulged in an effort to repair the theory without relinquishing the essential paradigm or categories.

Confronted with miraculous economic progress in East Asia, during the 1980s and early 1990s, the theory was reviewed to suggest that authoritarianism benefited newly-industrializing countries as they kick-started their economies, and that after the initial phase of growth, contradictions between authoritarianism and capitalism would trigger the revolution to democracy. What is significant to note is that revised modernization theorists do not deviate significantly from the modernization paradigm; they merely redefine authoritarianism as a stepping-stone towards the end-point of democracy.[29] Frank observes that

> the likes of Rostow, Pye, Pool and Huntington wrote and acted to impose "democracy" under the military boot. Even the Quaker Benoit claimed to have statistically demonstrated that more military equals more development. Political modernizers like Apter, Almond and Coleman condoned the Third World right wing authoritarian regimes in the name of political "democracy" and economic "development".[30]

Another attempt to revise the modernization theory is the 'modern authoritarianism' thesis. Prior to this revision, authoritarianism had been thought of as a pre-modern phase, and it was believed that with modernization, societies develop either into totalitarian or democratic polities. Rejecting this typology, Linz's observation of Spain led him to argue that regimes could be authoritarian and modern.[31] His definition of authoritarianism has become classic:

> Authoritarian regimes are political systems with limited, not responsible, political pluralism; without elaborate and guiding ideology (but with distinctive mentalities); without intensive or extensive political mobilization (except some points in their developments); and in which a leader (or occasionally a small group) exercises power within formally ill-defined limits but actually quite predictable ones.[32]

The concept of Asian values, which argued for a unique set of Asian institutions and political ideologies, involving an authoritarian government, was challenged by Sen's work that helped define the emerging field of social choice. The theory of social choice was proposed first by the American economist Ken Arrow, who argued that all voting rules, be they majority voting or two-thirds majority or status quo, must inevitably conflict some basic democratic norm. Sen's work showed under what conditions Arrow's Impossibility of Theorem would come to pass.[33] His contribution not only extended and enriched the field of social choice but it also influenced the area of economic measurement of poverty and inequality. Sen's concept of 'capability' is the most revolutionary contribution to development economics and social indicators, which argues that governments should be measured against the concrete capabilities of their citizens. It is up to the individual society to make the list of minimum capabilities guaranteed by that society. In his insistence on asking questions of value, long removed from serious economic consideration, Sen posed a major challenge to the economic model that portrayed self-interest as the prime motivating factor of human activity.[34] Similarly, Frank argues that

> development must include more democracy. (More) democracy must include (more) respect for human rights. These rights must include (more) political freedom of speech, organization and choice. However, these human rights must also include access to the economic and social basic human needs necessary to exercise such political choice.[35]

THE DEPENDENCY THEORY AND NEO-COLONIALISM

The dependency theory provides a better understanding for divergence in the development in East Asia, Latin America and many Third World countries, including Pakistan, focusing on the regional variations of US policy during the construction of US hegemony, or the American system of power after the Second World War. It argues that the development paradigm was the child of neo-imperialism and neo-colonialism, 'It developed as part and parcel instrument of the new post-war American hegemony. American ambitions extended over the ex-colonial world in the South and against both the real old Western colonialism and the perceived threat of new Eastern colonialism and imperialism'.[36] At the end of the Second World War, the United States ascended to 'neo-imperial hegemony'.[37] During this period of neo-colonialism, the United States assumed responsibility to reconstruct the world capitalist economy, aiming for integration of different regions—Europe, Asia, Latin America, the Middle East, and Africa within the emerging American system of power. The dependency perspective attempts to explore how the different trajectories of development, in various regions, were influenced by the US hegemony. This perspective argues that East Asian societies should not be viewed as successful products of the 'modernization process', as proponents of that theory suggest. Rather, the 'success' of these societies should be viewed as rooted in their historical inclusion of the American system of power and the strategic importance of the region, in which they were housed, and is not necessarily repeatable by other Third World societies.

This phenomenon can be examined in the perspective of the dependency paradigm, which explains the interdependent nature of the world capitalist system in its historical dimension, focusing on the total network of social relations as they evolved in different contexts over time. The Dependency Theory heavily borrows from the World-System Theory,[38] which proposes a mutually reinforcing system of nation-states and a market system of capitalism emerged in Europe between 1450 and 1620. The system, through processes of broadening and deepening, has developed over time and now encompasses virtually all areas of the world. It is divided, in an international division of labour, into zones of economic activity in which the core states, through unequal exchange, exploit peripheral areas and states. The underlying principle, upon which exploitation is based, is an effort by the capitalist class in the world-system to profit from this relationship, by deriving surplus capital and expanding markets. Between the zones of core and periphery is the semi-periphery. A similar relationship exists between core and semi-periphery. In this case, capital derived by the core from the semi-periphery comes from commodities that require more advanced technologies—industrial rather than agricultural. First incorporation and then integration occurs. The semi-peripheral states work to ascend towards the core by engaging in core-like activities.[39] The core itself attempts to maintain its position relative to the other zones. The process involves a series of economic cycles, in which there are alternating periods of global economic growth and of economic stagnation/contraction/hegemonic.

What makes the dependency paradigm so powerful is its holistic and historical approach. It views social reality as an integrated whole. From its perspective, political and economic processes in a society have no independent existence; they integrate into a single web of structural relations. The dependency paradigm stresses the importance of the way internal and external structural components are connected in elaborating the structural context of underdevelopment. As such, underdevelopment is not just the outcome of 'external constraints' over peripheral societies like Pakistan. Nor can dependency be 'operationalized' exclusively with reference to external variables.

Valenzuela and Valenzuela described that 'Dependency in a given society is a complex set of associations in which the external dimensions are determinative in varying degrees, and indeed, internal variations may very well reinforce the pattern of external linkages'.[40] They claim that historically, it has been difficult for 'the local interests to develop on the periphery, which are capable of charging a successful policy of self-sustained development'. The nature of class arrangements, emerging from the characteristics of peripheral economies, produced such dominant local interests, which preferred to favour the preservation of re-articulation of patterns of dependency in their interests.[41]

The Cold War and the American system of power brought deep-rooted economic and political changes in East Asia. In alliance with conservative elites of East Asia, it was ensured that the enclaves of capitalism in China, Korea, and Indochina, were well-preserved. As a consequence of American intervention, all these countries were to be partitioned. To maintain its hegemonic hold, it was essential for the United States that it preserve a capitalistic economic sphere in Asia, for that it fought major wars in East Asia after failing in attempts to do so by non-military and political means. The great strength of indigenous communism in East Asia forced the US to opt for war in Korea and Vietnam. Countries like the Philippines and Indonesia 'were contained' without recourse to full-scale US military intervention.[42]

The protection of capitalism in East Asia, by political-military means, was the integral part of the larger process of accommodating a restructured Japanese core into the global capitalist core. Japan was the key in American designs to maintain stability in Asia and to preserve as much of the region as possible for participation in world capitalism and block any communist influence. It was felt that the defeat of Japan in the summer of 1945 created a vacuum, which encouraged the spread of communism in East Asia and subsequent military conflicts sponsored by the US.[43] Therefore, US interests found it necessary to preserve Japanese capitalism, which subsequently required an Asian periphery, primarily kept under American political protection, but later taken over by Japanese capital.[44] Accordingly, Japanese core capital and industry was revived for the reconstruction of Japan as the regional workshop of Asia.[45] It was easy to do so because 'Japan was never *underdeveloped*, precisely because it was never economically or politically colonialized'.[46] In addition, the US assumed the responsibility of meeting the security requirements of Japan. It was essentially considered for two purposes: firstly, to guarantee political control, and secondly, to use military aid for safeguarding the strategic interests of US policymakers. This period witnessed Japan's dependence on the US markets and technology for the production of its exports and 'upgrading' these goods with infusions of advanced technology.[47] The capitalist elites in South Korea, Taiwan, and South Vietnam, were part of the post-war 'guided capitalism', and its neo-mercantilist state-capital alliance. Therefore, they were committed to the Free World, despite their anti-democratic character. As noted earlier, this model of authoritarian development was not repeated in other regions of the World, including Latin America, which did not enjoy the same strategic position in the American system of power.

The relative success of East Asia was based on a complex interweaving of variables such as global historical and geo-political factors, temporal factors like booming world trade in the 1950s and 1960s, the role of international corporations and institutions, particularly the IMF, the US military, and military funding, especially during the Korean and Vietnam wars, the role of relative state autonomy and effective state intervention in the economy, and spill-over effects such as the trans-border expansion of the Japanese sub-contracting system.

Here, the idea is to draw parallels between the South East Asian development model and the Pakistani development model. Like South East Asian countries, Pakistan was also located on the 'front line' of post-Second World War global politics, adjacent to communist Asia. Being a member of SEATO and CENTO, Pakistan was the key partner in US strategic designs in its war against communism. There appeared many similarities between Pakistan, South Korea, and Taiwan. In all the three cases, the role of the state, in creating classes and capital groups, becomes very apparent. The left was effectively wiped out in all these countries. The state military elite, supported by the US, was the dominant domestic actor in South Korea following the US occupation; in Taiwan, after the KMT fled there, following the Chinese Revolution in 1949, and in Pakistan, following the Rawalpindi conspiracy case in 1951. In East Asia, both Korea and Taiwan received high levels of US aid and benefited later from the rebuilding of Japan as the regional workshop of East Asia, a process helped immensely by the Korean and Vietnam wars and by the Japanese FDI, trade, technology transfer and the trans-border expansion of Japan's sub-contracting firms.[48] Like East Asia, Pakistan also received massive US aid in the 1950s and 1960s. In spite of the fact that Pakistan was turned into a 'client state' of the US, it did not experience the 'miracle' in its economic performance.

Explanation for this divergence in development can be found by comparing the economic strategies followed in these countries. If we take the example of four 'Tigers' or 'Dragons' in East Asia where 'export led growth has been efficient..., it is also thanks to the prior increase in the equity of the distribution of income and the domestic market. These improvements were due to the land reforms forcibly imposed there [in Taiwan, South Korea and Japan] by the United States after the war'.[49] There is a need to 'take account of these exceptional political and strategic factors'. It is argued that these factors 'make these NIC more of a unique experience than a copy-able model and "their hardly equitable political repression" cannot be recommended as a model'.[50] Unlike in South Korea and Taiwan, the authoritarian elite in Pakistan only used its power to pursue the goals of military strength at the cost of national economic wealth. No land reforms were carried out in Pakistan, and the landed elite, in alliance with the civil and military bureaucracy, dominated the national policies resulting in an unequal distribution of resources. Contrarily, in South Korea and Taiwan, because of the security threat from North Korea and China, respectively land reforms were carried out, thereby, effectively destroying the power of the landlord class.

Furthermore, the emphasis on the education sector played a key role in economic development of East Asian countries. 'Of all the elements that created the East Asian miracle, basic education for all and relevant technical skills were by far the most important factors. Recent World Bank studies have estimated that over 75 per cent of the real wealth of East Asian countries is their human and social capital'.[51] On the contrary, the education sector was not given due priority in Pakistan, thereby, contributing to a growth of unskilled, untrained, and uneducated manpower. In addition, the agriculture sector was ignored while pursuing the establishment of an industrial base, which in turn backfired because of non-availability of trained and skilled labour. Two major sets of resources, population and labour, and land and water, play an important role in the economic development of any country. 'Population and labour force, however, are resources only in a potential way—their utilization and effectiveness depend on the availability of complementary inputs as well as suitable technology and organization'.[52] Low levels of investment in education and agriculture resulted in very low levels of literacy and this was accompanied by a high fertility rate, and a high level of unemployment in Pakistan.

Pakistan not only failed to manage the economies of scale experienced by South Korea and Taiwan, which had resulted from acting in a wide economic space, and the innovations induced by competitions, but also the advantages of protection and selective industrial promotion. Although, Pakistan had opted to ride the wave of trans-nationalizing capitalism, however, unlike South Korea and Taiwan, it was unable, at the same time, to impose strong control over resource allocation within its national territory for constraining the controllers of capital, to operate within an unconstrained logic of global profit maximization. The lack of some buffers between the national and the international economies, not only resulted in the slow pace of integrating and transforming the production structure, but also failed to protect people from the disruptions of market volatility. This in turn, helped generate the harsh social and political instability, that tends to characterize societies struggling for national integration without a unified culture, and marked with regional inequalities. Pakistan 'accumulated an enormously large foreign debt, without having developed the socio-economic infrastructure necessary to sustain a growth process'.[53]

A Neo-colonial Capitalist Model and Pakistan

Using the dependency theory, a neo-colonial capitalist model that can be termed as a dependency model based on the following definition of dependency, can explain underdevelopment in Third World countries. This model can also be applied to Pakistan's first decade of development; it was further consolidated in the second decade under the direct military rule, and which has been maintained till today except during Zulfikar Ali Bhutto's rule (1971-77).

Dependence is a situation in which an asymmetrical exchange between nations reinforces the power of one, (the dominant) nation, and inhibits the self-reliance of the other, (dependent) nation.[54] In this model,[55] each of the many kinds of exchange, including trade, technology, capital, food, and debt, may be characterized by more, or less, dependence. The model suggests six groups of dependencies:

(1) Trade Dependence: Trade dependence is high when, due to deteriorating terms of trade the volume of raw material exports must continually increase in order to import a constant volume of manufactured goods.

(2) Technology Dependence: The increase in technological dependence is related to the increase in the royalty payments on imported technology that reduces resources available for local research and development, constraining technological self-reliance.
(3) Capital Dependence: Capital dependence is high when new inflows of foreign investment are needed to compensate for the outflows of profit repatriation and the asymmetrical transfer payments between subsidiaries and the head office of multinational firms.
(4) Food Dependence: Food dependence is high when the payment for food imports to meet minimum caloric standards derives from the exports of agricultural cash crops, further shifting land use away from subsistence crops.
(5) Debt Dependence: Debt dependence will be high when in order to continue debt-service payments on the past loans new international loans are required because of the increasing interest rates and appreciation of the dollar.
(6) Security Dependence: Security dependence is high, because, for a establishing large military apparatus, military assistance is required.

This model focuses on the mode of production, patterns of international trade, political and economic linkages between elites in peripheral, central countries, and group and class alliances, and gives the following explanation for the failure of development.

'Development' is a multinational capitalist scheme to enslave the world, saddling many Third World countries with international debts, thereby, crippling economic growth, accompanied by the 'top-down' approach proposed by international aid and advice-giving agencies. This explanation questions the assumption that experts, such as notable economists, can diagnose problems and devise plans for implementation by governments to improve the people's lives.

The first decade of Pakistan's history is the beginning of her pursuance of a neo-colonial capitalist, model—based on capitalist exploitation—essentially a cycle of developmental dependency. In an environment of 'containment', the alliance of the bureaucracy, army and the feudal elite, was able to centralize the authority in their hands by cooperating with the forces of the capitalist world system under the hegemony of the US.

> Soon after independence the rulers of Pakistan began to yield to all types of inducements to enter into neo-colonial economic and military alliances in order to preserve the internal systems of privilege and power, and the external control of the cheap labour and raw material of the country.[56]

The first decade is characterized with the institutional imbalance, that in the following years shifted in favour of non-democratic institutions, thus, keeping the representative institutions at their doorsteps. This resulted in concentration of authority in the hands of the representatives of non-representative institutions and pursuance of economic policies, in line with the neo-colonial capitalistic mode of production, ignoring the needs of a majority of the population.

> Once…rulers accepted dependence on the world capitalist market economy and its prime movers, especially the transnational corporations and aid agencies either based in or sponsored by the United States of America, the impact of Western Economic doctrines and development models proved to be decisive in shaping ensuing events of both national and geopolitical significance.[57]

During the first five-year plan (1955-60) period, Pakistan received over $1 billion in foreign assistance, that rose to $3 billion during the second five-year plan (1960-65) period.[58] Pakistan grew increasingly dependent on US aid and was consequently drawn into a dependency relationship with the United States and the principal representatives of internationalized capital in the world today, the World Bank and the IMF. The first international credit agreement was signed between Pakistan and the United States on 25 May 1948, when the ministry of finance accepted a $10 million loan. The credit was provided under the US war assets administration for purchasing stores and equipment from its surpluses. The finance minister on his way to Washington in July 1950, announced that 'during…[his] stay in United States he would certainly take the opportunity of meeting Directors of the International Monetary Fund, many of whom…[were] very personal friends'.[59] On 11 July 1950, the United States approved a sum of $600,000 for technical assistance to Pakistan under President Truman's Four-Point Program. Along with the technical assistance, grants, and credits were offered by many other US-sponsored financial agencies, including a $1.6 million Ford Foundation grant and a $60 million loan from the World Bank in 1951.[60] In order to manage these trade, aid, and military relationships, the US government and private foundations stepped up the training of

Pakistani administrators, social scientists, and military officers. The Ford Foundation pictured its role in 1951 as creating and strengthening institutions needed to train manpower and develop the knowledge and approaches required for economic and social progress.[61] Table 8 gives a picture of balance of trade and foreign assistance in the 1950s (1947-8 to 1959-60), and the 1960s:

Table 8: Export, Imports, and Foreign Assistance in the 1950s and 1960s (Yearly averages, US$ million)

	1950s (1947-8 to 1959-60)	1960s
Exports	69	118
Imports	111	302
Trade Balance	-42	-184
Foreign Assistance	118	585

Source: *Pakistan Economic Survey*, 1977-8, Finance Division, Government of Pakistan, Islamabad, 1978, Table 9, p. 117 and Table 28, p. 77, Statistical Annexure.

The 'economic and social progress', in line with this neo-colonial model, meant an increased dependence on US technical, military and commodity aid. In an environment of weak political culture, bureaucrats and generals were more interested in building a defence establishment rather than investing in social sectors. Heavy industries linked with military needs had become the priority of the central government, resulting in a serious neglect of the agricultural sector, in addition to the lack of will on part of the central government to implement any land reforms. The progressive, or left-minded elements in the Muslim League (the ruling party), favouring land reforms and abolition of *zamindari*, were forced to vacate their positions in favour of the conservative landed class belonging, particularly, to the Punjab. The very first casualty was Mian Iftikharuddin, the minister for refugees and rehabilitation, in the Punjab cabinet, who was forced to resign due to non-implementation of agrarian reforms, including the tenancy reforms and redistribution of land, which were to be pursued in the resettlement program in Punjab.

These proposals were part of the 1945 draft plan of the All-India Muslim League planning committee and later included in the Muslim League's agrarian reform report in July 1949, which was never allowed to be implemented in West Pakistan by the powerful landed lobby.[62]

However, in East Pakistan, the social landscape was different, where a majority of the landlords were Hindu who fled to West Bengal in 1947, and the remaining ones were 'weakened by the East Bengal State Acquisition and Tenancy Act of 1950. Under this act, all rent-receiving interest between the cultivating tenant and the state was abolished and a ceiling of 33 acres was placed on individual ownership of land'.[63] The bill was passed by the provincial assembly in February 1950, but its implementation was blocked for over a year by the central government, on the assumption that it could jeopardize Pakistan's chances of attracting foreign investment.[64] Firoze Khan Noon representing the landed elite of the larger province of West Pakistan, the Punjab, used this argument because he feared its implementation in the Punjab also.

The landed lobby in West Pakistan, particularly in the Punjab, was fully supported by the financial managers of the new state, who were trained in the colonial tradition of safeguarding the interests of the landed class. Archibald Rowlands, the first financial advisor to the government of Pakistan, was against the abolition of *zamindari*, since this might lead to a reduction in state revenue.[65] In an agrarian society, where the majority of the people were dependent upon agrarian economy, this policy mirrored the shifting balance of power within the state apparatus. Aided by the US economic experts, in 1951, the central government launched an ambitious six-year development plan, which was supplemented by an even more loud-mouthed, two-year priority programs. The six-year development program, proposed and implemented crash development of industry, that resulted in a rapid increase in industrial output (three-fold in four years), but agriculture had to suffer. The food grain output declined from six million tons in 1950-1 to five million tons in 1954-5. Due to the drought of 1952, food-grain production reduced to four million tons, necessitating the need to import about one million tons of wheat.

The economic planners were forced to face the hard realities of realizing the weaknesses in their overambitious economic programs, and reacted by imposing strict import controls. This further aggravated the situation by draining inventories of essential consumer goods, creating an inflation spiral, a serious food shortage, and a speedy decline in foreign exchange reserves. The difficult economic situation was reflected in the analysis of the appraisal committee, specially constituted in 1953 by the central government to review the economic situation.[66] Showing the distribution of resources, the committee pointed of that between the period 1947-48 and 1952-53, a large portion of the central government's total revenue was spent on defence, ranging between 51 to 71 per cent of the total revenue. The other major expenditure was the share of the civil administration, which rose from 16 to 20 per cent of the total revenue expenditure of the central government. The imbalance between expenditure on defence and civil administrative structures, and development, was the main cause of economic difficulties faced by the majority of the Pakistani people. The report recommended that to achieve a 'correct balance, minimum expenditure on defence consistent with security and the maximum expenditure on development consistent with resources' was essential. It was emphasized that 'development alone [could] sustain the expenditure on defence'. Proposing a cut in the expenditure on the civil administration, it was observed that 'no organization [could] afford to spend such a large proportion of its income on administration...at a time when income [was] declining'.[67] These recommendations could not be given serious consideration by the decision-making elite in the country, at a time when Pakistan was being geared up for inclusion in the Western-led defence alliances against the spreading wave of communism; a large military establishment was the prerequisite of these defence alliances.

As a consequence of the report of the appraisal committee, in May 1953, the central government announced the abandonment of the six-year plan along with the two-year priority program, launched with loud cheers of applause, and much publicity. Another economic plan, 'a more realistic economic development program', for the next five years was to be conceived by the newly-established planning board, assisted by a brigade of US experts and advisers, working under the umbrella of the technical assistance program. During the year 1953-54, there were more than one hundred US experts and advisers in Pakistan, who were in control of the financial mechanism. Pakistan's economy became tied-up with US aid and the economic policies designed by these experts and advisers. Aid was being used to 'exercise a major influence on... [Pakistan's] financial development'.[68] By strengthening the public administration and defence services of Pakistan, the US government was helping to 'buttress political and economic stability during the immediate period of crises.[69] The United States was aiming to 'assume responsibility for the successful administration, external financing and technical effectiveness of some 35-40 per cent of Pakistan's total development program'.[70]

In December 1953, the government of Pakistan signed an agreement with the Ford Foundation to send an international team of experts to assist the planning board in preparing the first five-year plan.[71] Under this agreement, the Harvard Advisory Group (HAG) started working on the preparation of the first five-year plan in April 1954, which was made public in May 1956, revised in April 1957, and eventually finalized in May 1958. Known as the 'masterstroke of economic planning', David Bell, a key advisor of the HAG, revealed that it was based on 'best guesses, idle speculation and wishful thinking', a trademark of capitalism.[72] While ignoring the real problems of mass poverty, 'the priesthood of development planners' were more concerned with 'econometric models' and less with 'economic policy formulation or decent project appraisal'.[73] The people of Pakistan had to pay a heavy price for their alignment with the neo-colonial world and its economic model. Slowly and gradually but surely, the major political party, the Muslim League, started losing its grip over state's policies and became hostage to the conservative forces of neo-colonialism.

Despite the severe food-grains shortage, as a result of the six-year development program launched in 1951 and abandoned in 1953, the government's policies did not change in favour of agriculture during the first five-year plan, which was prepared with such enthusiasm. The draft of the first five-year plan proposed land reforms including ceilings of 150 acres, 300 acres and 450 acres, respectively, for irrigated, semi-irrigated, and non-irrigated lands it, however, left its final approval subject to further study.[74] In this plan period, the food-grain output increased at an annual average rate of 0.3 per cent, while the population increased by 1.5 per cent. The annual food grain imports, during the second-half of the 1950s, averaged about 640,000 tons. To manage scarce food supplies, the government had to introduce 'rationing' and 'compulsory procurement'.[75] This compulsory procurement was at below market prices that produced a strong disincentive, thus, reinforcing the existing constraints of a feudal land tenure system, unsatisfactory credit facilities and poor availability of important agricultural inputs, inadequate irrigation supplies, and non-remunerative technology. These facts were reflected in the fourth five-year plan that stated:

> there was a considerable transfer of savings from the agriculture to the industrial sector...as terms of trade were deliberately turned against agriculture through such policies as licensing of scarce foreign exchange earned primarily by agriculture to the industrial sector, compulsory

Government procurement of food-grains at low prices to subsidize the cost of living in the cities, industrial incentives for commercial agricultural investment.[76]

It was rightly observed that the five-year development plans tended to ignore problems of unemployment, rural poverty, urban unrest, and poor social services, since there was so little quantitative information available in these areas.[77]

Equipped with the theoretical concepts of capitalist development, these advisers of HAG left the masses of Pakistan 'more acutely aware of the inadequacies of the rewards of growth and of the socially disruptive nature of the entire process of development'.[78] The interwoven relationship of the landed class, army, civil bureaucracy, and the indigenous bourgeoisie, in the capitalistic world economy, forced the neo-colonial state to acquire an authoritarian character. In this authoritarian culture, there was little room for democratic forces to operate. Unfortunately, the political institutions were not strong enough to shed away the colonial past and were made vulnerable to the control of the bureaucratic elite trained in a colonial administrative tradition of autocracy, which preferred to enter into all types of neo-colonial economic and military alliances, and opted for an economic model, which could not alienate those groups in society whose support was vital for the smooth functioning of the neo-colonial state.

This development model was not what Jinnah had thought was suitable for Pakistan. He had made it very explicit that Pakistan should be a progressive democracy based on the concepts of brotherhood, fraternity and equality. Announcing the economic policies of Pakistan, Jinnah in his inaugural speech at the opening of the State Bank in Karachi, stated:

> The economic system of the west has created almost insoluble problems for humanity, and to many it appears that only a miracle can save it from the disaster that is now facing the world. It has failed to do justice between man and man and eradicate friction from the international field. On the contrary, it was largely responsible for the two world wars in the last half-century. The Western world, in spite of its advantages, of mechanization and industrial efficiency, is today in a worse mess than ever before in history. The adoption of Western economic theory and practice will not help us in achieving our goal of creating a happy and contented people. There is need to work destiny in our own way, and present to the world an economic system based on the true Islamic concept of equality of mankind and social justice.[79]

Jinnah's rejection of the Western economic model, and his emphasis on the concept of equality of mankind and social justice on the occasion of the opening ceremony of the State Bank of Pakistan, was the restatement of his faith in creating a new state for the Muslims of India for their economic and social betterment and his assurance for all federating units of Pakistan of their equal participation in the State's resources in accordance with the principle of equity, liberty and social justice. Earlier, in his inaugural address to the Constituent Assembly of Pakistan, Jinnah had declared, 'If we want to make this great state of Pakistan happy and prosperous we should wholly and solely concentrate on the well being of the people, and especially of the masses and the poor'.[80]

Centre vs. the Provinces—Unequal Distribution of Resources and Unequal Development

The neo-colonial capitalist model pursued by the early policymakers of Pakistan, posed serious challenges for equal distribution of state's resources and establishing an equal economic infrastructure for every federating unit of the country. As earlier discussed, the continuation of the colonial legacy of a 'Security State', in the context of the Cold War, had forced the concentration of authority into an alliance of the bureaucracy, army, and the feudal class, which was working in close collaboration with the forces of neo-colonialism. This alliance, which was non-representative and authoritarian in character, was in control of the state's resources and their distribution, representing, mainly, the interests of West Pakistan only. All three partners of this alliance, had their roots in West Pakistan, particularly in one province, the Punjab. The army headquarters was in Rawalpindi; the Civil Service Academy, established in 1949, for the training of civil bureaucracy, was in Lahore; the Administrative Staff College, established in 1957, with the help of American assistance, was again located in Lahore. The first National Institute of Public Administration was established in Dhaka in 1961, when two similar institutes were also established in Karachi and Lahore. 'East Bengal [Pakistan] lacked effective representation in the new state apparatus'.[81] As late as 1956, no officer above the rank of joint secretary in the central secretariat, was from East Pakistan. Out of the 741 top jobs in the federal government, 93 per cent were held by the West Pakistanis, with the Punjabis and the Urdu-speaking migrants, claiming the plums.[82]

The focus here is on the uneven pattern of development and unequal distribution of resources between East and West Pakistan. This may cloud the real issue of distribution between all provinces of Pakistan on the basis of equity, but this framework of analysis is essential because of the artificial unity and homogeneity of interests enforced by the ruling elite in West Pakistan, in its bargaining position vis-à-vis East Pakistan. The question of parity was raised by the pressure group created, both, inside and outside of the constituent assembly, as the basis of any constitutional formula to fight the majority status of East Pakistan. The formation of One Unit in 1955, imposed the artificial unity and homogeneity of interests between the four provinces of West Pakistan. As discussed earlier, the fact that East Pakistan had the majority of the population, and thus, had the right to govern, was not acceptable to the Punjab. If Punjab could raise the principle of political parity in the constituent assembly, then the question arises, why was the principle of parity in economic development was so threatening? It appeared obvious that the new state started its working with a biased attitude that was inherent in its creation and its colonial legacy.

Despite the majority of the Pakistani population residing in East Pakistan, the central government was seated in Karachi. It was not just an issue of geographical location of the central government, the distance between the central government and the eastern province of the country was also reflective in allocation of resources and the state's economic policies. Announcing the industrial policy of the new state, Rowlands declared, 'what their state needed was an industrial base built around cotton, jute and hides, not social welfare schemes requiring large capital outlays'.[83] The trade and industrial polices introduced by Rowlands, which were very faithfully followed by the managers of finance who followed him, under the advice of the HAG, generated an accumulation of profit in few hands, thus, promoting an indigenous bourgeoisie. Between September 1949 and June 1950 alone, M.A.H. Ispahani, 'the largest jute dealer', earned a profit amounting to Rs 20 million. Ispahani was the member of the jute board, which was established by the central government to support the growers' prices.[84] Instead of providing relief to small jute traders, the jute board became a tool for exploitation, benefiting large trade dealers like Ispahani, who, while sitting in Karachi, controlled the jute trade of East Pakistan. The board was under the supervision of Ghulam Farooq—a non-Bengali secretary of industry, who later became the chairman of the Pakistan Industrial Development Corporation, and soon emerged as a major industrialist in the country by misusing his high offices. He represented the class of senior civil and military bureaucrats of West Pakistan who 'soon turned out to be owners of some of the largest business enterprises in the country'. With elaborate bureaucratic controls, a colonial practice, the development of industrial capitalism favoured only big businessmen against the small ones and resulted in extreme concentrations of wealth. A high rate of growth was the main economic objective, with a cavalier disregard for distributional questions. The question of disparity was raised mainly in the context of the regional distribution. Table 9 shows the budgetary allocations between the centre and the provinces of the first five-year plan:

Table 9: Budgetary Allocations between the Centre and the Provinces in the First Five-Year Plan

	In millions of Rupees	%
Centre (including Karachi)	2731	30
West Pakistan	3503	38
East Pakistan	3002	32
Total	9236	

Source: *The First Five Year Plan (1955-60)*, outline of the plan (draft) Karachi, May 1956, Table 4, 13-4.

In addition to this allocation of resources, the emphasis was again on the industrial development to be planned in West Pakistan ignoring more than 80 per cent of the population that was dependant on agriculture and living in rural areas. It was done despite the fact that between 1949-50 and 1954-5, the agricultural sector was stagnant, recording a dismal average annual growth rate of 1.3.

As discussed earlier, neglect of the agriculture sector had resulted in severe shortage of food-grains, which caused public unrest and demonstrations. It has also been observed how this situation was exploited and public unrest against non-implementation of tenancy laws and land reforms was turned into religious riots and violence against a minority sect in Punjab in March 1953; this further provided the rationale to 'power brokers' sitting in Karachi and Rawalpindi[85] to dismiss the Bengali Prime Minister Khwaja Nazimuddin, and thus, facilitate Pakistan's entrance into the defence pacts. Pakistan's emergence as a 'client' state of the USA and its status as 'bulwark' against communism demanded a defence establishment which was beyond its scarce means and absorbed most of its foreign exchange earned mostly through its jute exports.

A strong central administration and a defence establishment were two major requirements to deliver the goods in accordance with the expectations of these defence pacts. This responsibility could not be met by US assistance alone. Pakistan was expected to enlarge its economic base and raise domestic resources for military expenditure. American advice was present in the form of HAG. That was the primary reason for a large army of American economic experts working on finding solutions for introducing development in Pakistan. Industrial development of West Pakistan, at the expense of East Pakistan, was part and parcel of this thinking. This further aggravated the grievances of the people in East Pakistan who were denied their due share of state resources. As a result of the central government's policies, there was virtually no development in East Pakistan, a fact recorded while setting the objectives for the first five-year plan.[86] There were five main objectives of the plan period including, 'to quickly increasing the rate of development in East Pakistan and other less developed regions in the country'.[87] However, the plan could not meet this target as was reflected in the average annual growth rate of the gross domestic product in East Pakistan, which was a mere 0.2 per cent, compared with 3.6 per cent in West Pakistan. 'The East Pakistan industrialization never really took off, as private investment tended to concentrate almost exclusively in West Pakistan'.[88]

The manner in which the interests of East Pakistan were given a secondary priority was also exemplified in the policy that kept the rupee overvalued in order to lower the import bill for military items. Through this policy, small exporters of jute, East Pakistan, became the principal victims, who could earn more through their jute exports at a time when food was selling at astronomical prices. In addition, the importers in East Pakistan were only able to secure 35 per cent of the total import licenses issued by the central government in the period between 1950-8. As a result, East Pakistan had to purchase consumer items from the manufacturers of West Pakistan, at a price 40 per cent higher than in the world market.[89]

> The deleterious effects of the pro-industrial policies on agriculture...hit East Pakistan harder as its dependence on agriculture was greater and as it consisted largely of small farmers producing cash crops with low bargaining

power *vis-à-vis* the intermediaries many of whom were engaged in smuggling jute across the border.[90]

The inequality in distribution of resources was not a major concern of the HAG for two fundamental reasons: first, East Pakistan did not have its share in either the bureaucracy or the defence establishment; second, equity in distribution was not the goal of the advocates of the modernization theory. Voicing concern over unequal distribution of the state resources and West Pakistan's hegemony, the East Pakistan Muslim League, as early as December 1949, demanded full autonomy in all matters except defence and foreign affairs, as well as increased representation in the constitutional assembly. The East Pakistan Muslim League also proposed nationalization of the jute industry, a proposal rejected out of hand by the central government. This demand was soon followed by the famous thesis of 'two economies', which argued that East and West Pakistan should be treated as entirely separate economies.[91]

Neo-colonial States and Economic Development—A Comparative Analysis of Underdevelopment in Pakistan and India

The two inheritors of British colonialism, India and Pakistan, who got independence in the aftermath of the Second World War, inherited poverty and underdevelopment at the end of colonial rule. Colonial rule succeeded in destroying the traditional and indigenous institutions and left behind a legacy of colonial capitalism. Each of the two newly-independent nations, Pakistan and India, followed a different approach to its development. India chose the path of self-reliance, predicated upon an ideology of nationalism associated with political democracy, while Pakistan was enforced into pursuance of a neo-colonial capitalist model, in which authoritarianism and economic growth were blended together. However, after six decades of development, the observers find 'striking parallels in the achievements and the failings of India and Pakistan', despite their different models of development.

This section presents a comparative analysis of the underdevelopment found in Pakistan and India and argues that human security is linked to human development and human rights. The two 'nuclear countries' of South Asia who maintain two larges armies and spend a large share of their resources on military account are both predominantly poor and underdeveloped. The state of human development and human rights in both the countries demands that military expenditure should be reduced and the resources, thus saved, be used for social development. Political democracy, without including the principle of economic equality, cannot address the issue of underdevelopment. Table 10 demonstrates the status of underdevelopment in the first few years of their national growth:

Table 10: Status of Underdevelopment in India and Pakistan in the First Decade

Countries	Literates %	Rural Population %	Urban Population %	Average per capita income, 1952-4 (US$)	Annual Rate of Population increase (1953-6) %
India	16.6	82.7	17.3	60	1.3
Pakistan	18.9	89.6	10.4	70	1.5

Source: Gabriel A. Almond and James S. Coleman (ed.), 1960, *The Politics of the Developing Areas*, Princeton: Princeton University Press, p. 171.

A comparative analysis of underdevelopment in India and Pakistan, in the context of neo-colonial states, reveals the similarities and differences in those two inheritors of British colonialism; however, 'the base from which each started, and significant differences in political, economic, and social circumstances, make direct comparisons difficult'.[92] As stated above, Pakistan and India followed two different approaches to their respective economic development. Pakistan was forced into pursuance of a neo-colonial capitalist model, in which authoritarianism and economic growth were blended together, a trend which continues even today. Pakistan could not build a strong constitutional base and has been threatened by challenges from the military and is still striving to find a stable and effective form of political government.[93] Due to the frequency and longevity of military rule in Pakistan, observers label its approach to development as the 'economy of defence',[94] which led to a civil war and division of the country in 1971, and whose continuation poses a serious threat to the security of the remaining parts of the country. On the other hand, India chose the path of self-reliance, predicated upon an ideology of nationalism associated with political democracy, dominated by the Nehru family, with Congress as the leading political party for a long time. Though India chose an ideology blend of nationalism and socialist economic policies, its heritage of colonial administrative rule was not destroyed and it became a major obstacle to bringing radical economic change.

As discussed earlier, the concept of 'liberating' the governments in economically backward countries and then forcing them to take part in a competitive world system, in order to develop economically, was the landmark of the post-Second World War period. This idea of economic development imposed a set of new and special changes in social and administrative centralization, in addition to introducing exploitative work disciplines, social turmoil, and revolutions, in these societies. These new disciplines proved to be equally bad when compared with those forced upon them by former colonial rulers, certainly for most of the newly liberated countries of the Third World, because national liberation was equated with competition in the capitalist world economy.[95] In this capitalist world economy, the balance of trade is determined by the relationship of a nation-state with the forces of the world markets. The world markets determine the capacity of a nation-state to compete in this capitalist world economy and decide the size of its exports and imports. Development has been marked by a struggle between two opposing forces: one, that was commensurate with self-reliance, predicated upon an ideology of nationalism; and another that positions the Third World countries within global capitalism.

After the collapse of the Soviet Union, the ideology of nationalism was replaced with 'economic reforms', suggested by the World Bank—with its focus on economic growth. Third World countries are left with no choice except to operate within the system of global capitalism and choose an agenda of economic reforms, as suggested by the World Bank. The last two decades have witnessed a shift in economic policies which have resulted in an accelerated growth, and has been accompanied with a rise in inequality. In both countries, there continues to be wide disparities in social indicators between different states (or provinces), and between urban and rural areas. Despite differences in approach, centralized political and economic authority, inherited from the colonial era, continue in both the post-colonial states that resulted in deep divides—among regions, sectors, and people—many of which are still growing. 'Inequality has risen because of increases in inequality between regions. India's rapidly-growing states in the South and West are leaving behind others in the North and North-east, leading to the phrase "two India"; a similar situation had happened in Pakistan when the phrase of 'two economies' was heard in the context of East and West Pakistan and which ended in the creation of Bangladesh. Still no lesson has been learnt in Pakistan, where interregional disparities are increasing with the Punjab at the high end and Balochistan and the North West Frontier Province, on the lower one.[96]

Societal changes in India and Pakistan do not match the aspirations of the people, who fought long against British colonialism to get their independence.

> The goals of ending or even reducing poverty, providing adequate health care, offering educational opportunities for all, and reducing regional, urban/rural, and gender inequality remain targets for the future at the end of the first half century of independence.[97]

Educational quality, access to schools at all levels, nutrition, sanitation, health, and women's rights, in all respects have lagged behind. With inadequate financial resources, the absence of consistent and viable national and provincial policy formation, and implementation at all levels, becomes more critical.[98] There are increasing disparities of wealth and living conditions in both countries. Although, a rapidly growing middle class in India shares the benefits of the economic growth but hundreds of millions of Indians are still deeply impoverished, having no access to the better life offered by economic growth.[99] A very similar situation exists in Pakistan, where the majority of people are denied their share in the economic growth. Growing evidence not only underlines a delink between economic growth and human development but also indicates that economic policies in both the countries have also made people more vulnerable to shocks and insecurities in their lives.[100]

The state of underdevelopment, which these two South Asian countries inherited at the end of British colonialism, has not fundamentally changed after sixty years of their existence as post-colonial states. At the first half-century of their independence, both Pakistan and India were rated among the most-deprived regions of the world,[101] a status not much improved by the year 2007. Though, over the last decade these two countries have witnessed some growth, both of them have also witnessed a rise in inequality. The profile of human deprivation in Pakistan and India demonstrates a sombre picture. Table 11 shows the profile of spending on health, education, defence, and percentage of population living in poverty. It reveals that 28 per cent of total population in India and 33 per cent of total population in Pakistan is living below the poverty line. Public expenditure on education in the years 2000-2 was only 4.1 per cent of GDP in India, and 1.8 per cent in Pakistan. Public expenditure on health in the year 2002 was only 1.3 per cent of GDP in India, and 1.1 per cent in Pakistan. In contrast, the defence expenditure, as percentage of the total central government expenditure, was 14.2 per cent in the year 2003 in India, and 23.9 per cent in Pakistan.

Table 11: Profile of Spending in India and Pakistan

	India	Pakistan
Total estimated population (millions) 2003	1,071	152
GDP per capita (US$) 1960	617.0	820.0
1994	1348.0	2154.0
2003	2892.0	2097.0
GNI per capita (US$) 1995	340	460
2003	540	520
Population below income poverty line (%)		
US$1 a day 1990-2003	34.7	13.4
National poverty line 1990-2002		
(%) of total population	28.6	32.6
Public expenditure on education (as % of GDP) 2000-2002		
Public expenditure on health (as % of GDP)	4.1	1.8
2002	1.3	1.1
Debt service ratio (debt service as % of exports of goods and services) 2003	18.1	16.8
Defence expenditure (as % of central government expenditure)		
1980	19.8	30.6
2003	14.2	23.9
Defence expenditure (as % of GNP)		
(as % of GNP) 1980	2.5	5.1
(as % of GDP) 2003	2.3	4.1
Defence expenditure (as % education and health)		

| 1960 | 68 | 393 |
| 1995 | 65 | 125 |

Source: Based on Tables 8 and 9 in *Human Development in South Asia 2003*, Karachi: Oxford University Press, pp. 184-5; and Tables 2.7 and 2.8 in *Human Development in South Asia 2003*, op. cit., p. 25; and Tables 1, 2, 3, 4, 5 and 8, *Human Development in South Asia 2005*, Karachi: Oxford University Press, pp. 206-13.

Table 11 demonstrates that 'territorial security' is more important than 'human security' in these two poverty-ridden, nuclear possessing South Asian states, who have been engaged in territorial conflicts with each other since their independence and have not succeeded in settling them despite many major and minor direct and proxy wars. Major chunks of their resources are being spent on marinating the two largest armies in the region with huge purchases of arms at the cost of human development. Large armies and nuclear weapons cannot guarantee security. Human security can only be guaranteed by addressing the root causes of conflicts. More than border conflicts, India and Pakistan both are confronted with increasing forms of conflicts within their states/regions/provinces due to social, religious or communal issues. Increasing political, economic, and social inequality, is the real threat to the security of the South Asian region.

Pakistan began its journey with a resource disadvantage in comparison with the physical and human capital available to India. But, soon after its birth, being the 'buffer state' between the Soviet Union and the 'free world', it was cajoled into entering into a dependent relationship with the US, and therefore, was forced into accepting its neo-colonial capitalist model of development. The first decade of Pakistan's history is the beginning of her pursuit of a neo-colonist capitalist model—based on capitalist exploitation—a cycle of developmental dependency. In an environment of 'containment', the alliance of bureaucracy, army, and the feudal elite, was able to centralize the authority in their hands by cooperating with the forces of capitalist world system under the hegemony of the US.

> Soon after independence the rulers of Pakistan began to yield to all types of inducements to enter into neo-colonial economic and military alliances in order to preserve the internal systems of privilege and power, and the external control of the cheap labour and raw material of the country.[102]

The first decade is characterized with the institutional imbalance, which in the following years, shifted in favour of non-democratic institutions keeping the representative institutions at their doorsteps. This resulted in the concentration of authority in non-representative institutions and pursuance of economic policies in line with the neo-colonial capitalistic mode of production, ignoring the needs of the majority of population.

> Once...rulers accepted dependence on the world capitalist market economy and its prime movers, especially the transnational corporations and aid agencies either based in or sponsored by the United States of America, the impact of Western Economic doctrines and development models proved to be decisive in shaping ensuing events of both national and geopolitical significance.[103]

Economic planning in Pakistan was initiated under the influence of the HAG, that promoted the notion of economic growth, focusing on industrial development and encouraging capital accumulation, disregarding the economic and social needs of the people. This growth model was accompanied by an authoritarian elite of the bureaucracy, army, and the feudal class, that was bolstered by the custodian of the 'free world', the United States, to ensure Pakistan's association with Defence Pacts against communism. Against the wave of nationalism, spreading in its neighbouring counties like India, Iran, Indonesia, and many Arab states, the ruling elite in Pakistan chose to be the 'client' state of the US by ignoring the aspirations of the people. Authoritarianism and economic growth were blended together and prescribed as the best economic model for Pakistan. By 1959, the first stage of Pakistan's industrialization, based on import substitution, was over. The following period saw the unfolding of the second phase of Pakistan's industrialization, based primarily on export-oriented growth, and financed through large doses of foreign aid. In the early 1960s, under the military rule of General Ayub, Pakistan was being projected as 'a better bet to succeed economically than Korea, Indonesia or Malaysia', and 'to cross over into the ranks of 'middle-income' countries'.[104] But, this did not happen. The decade of development, as proposed by many writers of the modernization theory, ended in an anti-development movement against the concentration of wealth in a few hands, which forced General Ayub to resign and which proved to be just a 'prelude to the events of the civil war and the de-linking of the Eastern Province'.

As a result of the authoritarianism initiated in its first decade, Pakistan has witnessed three martial laws, one civilian martial law and four military rules. Because of these repeated disruptions of the political process, 'Pakistan is still in the making, still striving to find a stable and effective form of government'.[105] On the other hand, India is considered 'the world's largest democracy' and is praised for its success in building a solid constitutional structure where civil authorities have never been threatened by challenges from the military. India, unlike Pakistan, has never experienced military rule or even a serious attempt by the military to intervene in the political process, and senior military officers have never held any ministerial office or challenged the authority of the civilian minister of defence.[106] Regular transfers of power have taken place through free and generally fair elections, in which public participation has been strong. And new political forces have been able to emerge, representing previously weak and underrepresented groups in society, despite opposition from traditional power elites. But political democracy, without including the principle of economic equality, cannot address the issue of underdevelopment. The gap between economic and political capabilities undermines Indian democracy.[107] Although the achievement of economic equality was declared to be the target of the long-term economic development policies, based on socialist ideology and the mechanism of centralized planning, 'in practice, in reality, and even in the admission of those who developed these early economic plans, the actual goals were different'.[108] Comparing India and Pakistan, it can be argued that authoritarianism and democracy should be seen as a case of a continuum rather than opposites in the subcontinent's politics.[109]

After independence, India declared that it will follow the socialist pattern of society incorporating the doctrine, 'that India would rely on pervasive government ownership and strong-handed public direction of the industrial, financial, communications, and transport sectors'.[110] A National Planning Commission of India, under the chairmanship of Prime Minister Jawaharlal Nehru, was established in March 1950, and was 'defined as "the Economic Cabinet", not merely for the Union but also for the States'.[111] The commission was empowered to investigate and recommend policies for almost every aspect of national life. The commission had control over the distribution of economic resources among the states and was in a position to dictate the form of development, it felt, was suitable for individual states'.[112] Indian economic goals 'entailed altering the structure of economy from predominantly agricultural to conspicuously industrial, attacking poverty and inequality, and achieving an acceptable rate of economic growth. Commitments were made to provide the country's 5,550,000 villages with basic amenities such as primary schools, clinics, potable water, sanitary facilities, and electricity'.[113] The continuity in Indian economic planning (1950-1964) is known as Nehruvian Planning. This mode of planning was different from Gandhian Socialism. The constitution of India, passed in 1950, borrowed heavily from the 1935 Act; it was committed to parliamentary democracy and contained no mention of Gandhian constitution, 'A Gandhian constitution seems not to have been given a moment's thought'.[114] The constitution of India reflected Nehru's line of thinking; he believed that India needed a centralized constitution to establish the stability and the unity necessary for the social revolution. Under the influence of socialism, Nehru believed that, centralized authority and centralized planning were two essential factors for economic progress.[115] In contrast to Pakistan, which underwent economic modernization through haphazard reliance upon private enterprise and the market system, Indian economic planners intended to rely purposely on governmental initiative to create an integrated industrial sector. However, opting for an industry-first development program, as in Pakistan, was associated with the idea of the interwoven relationship of industrialization with urbanization and modernization, in most of the post-colonial states. This development model was in line with the paradigm of development that assumed that state power should supersede markets. The major theme of this paradigm was control or suppression of market forces. Thus, the intellectual inheritance of the developing countries in the post-colonial period became an overwhelming emphasis on the role of the state.

In this context it is hardly surprising that extreme forms of economic nationalism became almost universal among post-colonial states. These forms emphasized import controls, overvalued exchange rates, large-scale public ownership, and investment incentives, direct investment with managed interest rates, prices, and wages, etc.[116] At the end of the colonial period, economic nationalism was embraced, regardless of political ideology in the competitive world context, and was driven by the perceived importance of external competition rather than domestic social priorities. In the Indian context, growth of a centralized state and political economy, generated ethnic, linguistic, religious, and regional conflicts in later periods, which were not allowed to grow under Nehru, when compromises were made for recognition of multiplicity of claims made by distinct language groups.[117] Giving warning signals against the development paradigm, Gandhi wrote in *Harijan* in July 1946:

Congressmen themselves are not of one mind even on the contents of independence. I don not know how many swear by non-violence or the *charkha* (the spinning wheel) or, believing in decentralization, regard the village as the nucleus. I know on the contrary that many would have India become a first-class military power and wish for India to have a strong centre and build the whole structure round it.[118]

India, like Pakistan, ignored its agricultural sector and opted for industrialization, but in contrast to Pakistan, the exploitative colonial farming system, dominated by big landlords and princes, was abolished immediately after independence to give a lip-service to the Gandhian ideal. A countrywide system of peasant proprietorship was established, in which the title to land or its effective control was transferred to the farmer—cultivating tenants. This became the basis of long-term socialist schemes for reorganizing Indian agriculture through land reforms, land re-distribution, and cooperative farming. In the first five-year plan 'to appease Gandhian strand of thought, cottage, village, and small scale industries were promised support and preferences'.[119] Although, the primary goal for all these efforts was to grow enough food for the nation to feed itself, the rural sector was not given its proper share in the resources.

> India's elite leadership believed that the rural masses could not be enlisted in the development effort until centuries-old habits and institutions were transformed. Hence, land reform, community development, and village self-rule, or *punchayati* raj, were needed to break down inequality, passivism, and castism.[120]

It was believed that cooperatives would bring a revolutionary change in the village economy by releasing it from the exploitative dependence on the middlemen and moneylenders, along with provision of credit facility and access to the market. It was expected that with spread of irrigation, these coordinated institutional changes would result in an increase in the agricultural product.[121] The drought in the mid-1960s, however, made the planners realize that the neglect of the agricultural sector at the cost of industrialization in the early years, along with centralized planning, had resulted in an increase in poverty rather than alleviating it. The percentage of the urban and rural poor increased somewhat in the early 1950s and then remained nearly constant for the next twenty years.[122]

Many writers observe that India might have achieved the goals of social revolution envisioned in the Gandhian constitution if it had followed a path of decentralization with a focus of the village economy instead of opting for centralized planning and industrialization. This centrally planned economic development strategy continued until the 1980s, when a policy change occurred in the form of economic reforms, which resulted in an acceleration of economic growth. However, like Pakistan, this accelerated economic growth and the ongoing privatization process, has contributed to increased inequality and economic insecurity in India also. Against the backdrop of greater global economic integration, poverty, widening income inequality, food insecurity, the changing nature of employment and unemployment, all underline the economic vulnerability of the two nuclear states of South Asia.

There is a need to focus on the broader 'concept of development' having three aspects: growth (the economic aspect), equality (the social aspect), and liberty (the political aspect), and its linkage with human security. The broad definition then includes those societal conditions that promote personal growth, economic growth, equality in the distribution of wealth, and political liberty. This perspective argues for introducing equity and efficiency in economic development, by creating a link between growth and human development, through investment in education and health, skill development, job creation, and women's empowerment, and a reduction in military expenditure. In this conceptual framework, equitable distribution of assets, provision of social safety nets, and political and cultural freedom, provide the critical connection between human development and human security.

NOTES

1. Selig S. Harrison, Paul H. Kreisberg and Dennis Kux, *India and Pakistan: The First Fifty Years*, op. cit., p. 1.
2. Gabriel Almond and G. Bingham Powell, 1966. *Comparative Politics: A Developmental Approach*, Boston: Little, Brown; Daniel Lerner, 1958. *The Passing of Traditional Society*, New York: Free Press.
3. Andre Gunder Frank, 'The Development of Underdevelopment: An Autobiographical Essay'. Retrieved 26 June 2004, http://rrojasdatabank.info/agfrank.
4. Lawrence R. Alschuler, 'Divergent Development: The Pursuit of Liberty, Equality and Growth in Argentina and the Republic of Korea', *Journal of World Systems Research*, 3 (1997): 115-207; Peter Evans, 1979, *Dependent Development: The Alliance of Multinational, State and Local Capital in Brazil*, Princeton: Princeton University Press.
5. Lawrence R. Alschuler, op. cit., p. 121.

6. Dietrich Rueschemeyer and Peter Evans, 'The State and Economic Transformation: Toward an Analysis of the Conditions Underlying Effective Intervention', in Peter Evans, Dietrich Rueschemeyer and Theda Skocpol (eds.), 1985, *Bringing the State Back In*, New York: Cambridge University Press, pp. 44-77.
7. Raymond Gastil, 'The Comparative Study of Freedom: Expressions and Suggestions', *Studies in Comparative International Development* 25, 1 (1990): 25-50.
8. Andre Gunder Frank, 'The Development of Underdevelopment: An Autobiographical Essay', op. cit.
9. Ibid.
10. Gabriel Almond and G. Bingham Powell, *Comparative Politics: A Developmental Approach*, op. cit., pp. 255-332. Also see Daniel Lerner, *The Passing of Traditional Society*, op. cit.
11. For threshold see Ghassan Salame (ed.), 1994, *Democracy without Democrats: the Renewal of Politics in the Muslim World*, London: I.B. Tauris.
12. Economic theory of modernization is based on five stages of development from Rostow's model. These five stages are; traditional society, precondition for takeoff, the takeoff process, the drive to maturity, and high mass consumption. According to this exposition, Rostow has found a possible solution for the promotion of Third World modernization. If the problem facing the Third World countries resides in their lack of productive investments, then the solution lies in the provision of aid to these countries in the form of capital, technology, and expertise. W. Rostow, 1962, *The Stages of Growth: A Non-communist Manifesto*, Cambridge: Cambridge University Press.
13. Walden Bello and Stephanie Rosenfeld, 1990, *Dragons in Distress—Asia's Miracle Economies in Crisis*, San Francisco: The Institute for Food and Development.
14. Eric Wolf, 1982, *Europe and the People without History*, Berkeley: University of California Press, p. 13.
15. Ibid.
16. Ibid.
17. Samuel P. Huntington, 1998, *Political Order in Changing Societies*, op. cit. For the distinction between early and revised modernization theory, see Vicky Randall and Robin Theobald, *Political Change and Underdevelopment*, Basingstoke: Macmillan, pp. 45-85.
18. Samuel P. Huntington, *Political Order in Changing Societies*, op. cit.
19. Simon Kuznets, 'Economic Growth and Income Inequality', *American Economic Review*, V. 45 (March 1955): 1-26.
20. For the argument about institutions, see J.C. March and J.P. Olsen, 'The New Institutionalism: Organizational Factors in Political Life', *American Political Science Review*, 78 (1984): 734-49. Jan-Erik Lane and Svante Ersson, 2000, *The New Institutional Politics: Performance and Outcomes*, London and New York: Routledge. For the 'modernity' of authoritarianism, see Amos Perlmutter, 1981, *Modern Authoritarianism: A Comparative Institutional Analysis*, New Haven: Yale University Press. For the distinctive features of populist authoritarianism, see Nazih Ayubi, 1995, *Overstating the Arab State: Politics and Society in the Middle East*, London: I.B. Tauris, pp. 196-223.
21. Steven Heydemann, 1999, *Authoritarianism in Syria: Institutions and Social Conflict*, Ithaca and London: Cornell University Press, pp. 1-29.
22. Raymond Hinnebusch, 2003, *International Politics of the Middle East*, Manchester: Manchester University Press, pp. 80-85.

23. See, P. Berger, 1986, *The Capitalist Revolution: Fifty Propositions about Prosperity, Equality and Liberty*, New York: Basic Books. P. Berger and M.H. Hsiao (ed.), 1988, *In Search of An East Asian Development Model*, New Brunswick, N.J.: Transaction Books. S.G. Redding, 1990, *The Spirit of Chinese Capitalism*, Berlin: De Gruyter.
24. Alan Ted Wood, 2004, *Asian Democracy in World History*, New York & London: Routledge, p. 52.
25. Samuel P. Huntington, 1996, 'Democracy's Third Wave', in Larry Diamond and Marc F. Plattner (eds.), *The Global Resurgence of Democracy*, Baltimore: Johns Hopkins University Press, p. 21.
26. These are 'liberal democracy', 'electoral democracy', 'ambiguous regimes', competitive authoritarian', 'hegemonic electoral authoritarian', and 'politically closed authoritarian'. See L. Diamond, 'Thinking about Hybrid Regimes', *Journal of Democracy*, 2000, 13(2): 5-21.
27. Ibid.
28. V. Leary, 1990, 'The Asia Region and the International Human Rights Movement', in C. Welch and V. Leary (eds.), *Asian Perspectives on Human Rights*, San Francisco: Westview Press, pp. 13-15.
29. G. Rodan, 1993, *Political Oppositions in Industrializing Asia*, London: Routledge.
30. Andre Gunder Frank, op. cit.
31. J. Linz, 1970, 'An Authoritarian Regime: The Case of Spain', in E. Allard and S. Rokkan (eds.), *Mass Politics: Studies in Political Sociology*, New York: Free Press.
32. Ibid., p. 255.
33. See Amartya Sen, 1982, *Choice, Welfare and Measurement*, Oxford: Oxford University Press.
34. See Amartya Sen, 1987, *On Ethics and Economics*, Oxford: Oxford University Press.
35. Andre Gunder Frank, op. cit.
36. Ibid., p. 6.
37. Ibid.
38. Immanuel Wallerstein, 1979, 'The Present State of the Debate on World Inequality', in Mitchell A. Seligson (ed.), op. cit. I. Wallerstein, *The Modern World System*, op. cit. I. Wallerstein, *The Capitalist World Economy*, Cambridge: Cambridge University Press. I. Wallerstein, 'Development or Illusion?' *Economic and Political Weekly*, Vol. 23, No. 39 (September) 1988: 2017-23. I. Wallerstein, 'The Collapse of Liberalism', *The Socialist Register 1992*, 1992b: 96-110. I. Wallerstein, 1991, *Geopolitics and Geoculture: Essays on the Changing World-System*, Cambridge.
39. Christopher Chase-Dunn, 1989, *Global Formation: Structures of the World Economy*, New York: Basil Blackwell.
40. Samuel Valenzuela and Arturo Valenzuela, 'Modernization and Democracy: Alternative Perspectives in the Study of Latin American Underdevelopment', in Mitchell A. Seligson (ed.), *The Gap Between Rich and Poor: Contending Perspectives on the Political Economy of Development*, op. cit., p. 109.
41. Ibid.
42. Barry Gills, 1993, 'The Hegemonic Transition in East Asia: A Historical Perspective', in Stephen Gill (ed.), *Gramsci, Historical Materialism and International Relations*, London: Cambridge University Press, p. 205.
43. Ibid., p. 204.
44. Bruce Cumings, 1990, 'Archaeology, Decent, Emergence: Japan in British/American Hegemony, 1900-1950', in Masao Miyoshi and H.D. Harootunian (eds.),1990, *Japan in the World*, Durham: Duke University Press, pp. 79-114.

45. Ronald McGlothen, 1993, *Controlling the Waves: Dean Acheson and U.S. Foreign Policy in Asia*, W.W. Norton & Company, pp. 191-92.
46. Andre Gunder Frank, op. cit., p. 22.
47. Laura E. Hein, 'Growth versus Success: Japan's Economic Policy in Historical Perspective', in Andrew Gordon (ed.), 1993, *Post-war Japan as History*, Berkeley: University of California Press, p. 108.
48. Giovanni Arrighi, S. Ikeda, and A. Irwin, 'The Rise of East Asia—One Miracle or Many?' in Ravi Arvind Palat (ed.), 1992, *Pacific-Asia and the Future of the World Economy*, Westport: Greenwood Press, pp. 41-66.
49. Andre Gunder Frank, op. cit.
50. Ibid.
51. Mahbub ul Haq and Khadija Haq, *Human Development in South Asia, 1998*, op. cit., p. 31.
52. S.M. Naseem, *Underdevelopment, Poverty and Inequality in Pakistan*, op. cit., p. 24.
53. Viqar Ahmed and Rashid Amjad, 1984, *The Management of Pakistan's Economy: 1947-82*, Karachi: Oxford University Press, p. 288.
54. Lawrence R. Alschuler, op. cit., p. 122.
55. This model is based on the 'Dependency sub-model' used by Lawrence R. Alschuler, in 'Divergent Development: The Pursuit of Liberty, Equality, and Growth in Argentina and The Republic of Korea', op. cit. The original model suggests five groups of dependence 2-6; Group 1 'Security dependence' is added.
56. Hassan Gardezi and Jamil Rashid, *Pakistan: The Unstable State*, op. cit., p. 5.
57. Ibid.
58. *Pakistan Economic Survey, 1977-8*, 1978, Finance Division, Government of Pakistan, Islamabad, Table 9, p. 117, and Table 28, p. 77, Statistical Annexure.
59. L/E/9/363, IOR.
60. Hassan Gardezi and Jamil Rashid, 'Pakistan Independent: Theory and Practice of Political Economy', in Hassan Gardezi and Jamil Rashid (eds.), op. cit., p. 7.
61. Ibid.
62. Ian Talbot, *Pakistan: A Modern History*, op. cit., p. 122.
63. Khalid B. Sayeed, *Politics in Pakistan: The Nature and Direction of Change*, op. cit., p. 39.
64. Memorandum of Whiters' conversation with Firoz Khan Noon, Dacca, D-73, 8 November 1950, NDD 842430, RG 84, 350-Pak. Pol. 1950, NA.
65. Summary of Archibald Rowland's report to the Government of Pakistan, DO/35/2746, TNA: PRO.
66. *Report of the Economic Appraisal Committee*, 1953, Karachi: Finance Division, Government of Pakistan.
67. Ibid.
68. American Embassy to the Department of State, 12 August 1953, NDD 842909, Box 5542, 890D.00/8-1253, NA.
69. Ibid.
70. Ibid.
71. See George Rosen, 1985, *Western Economies and Eastern Societies: Agents of Change in South Asia, 1950-1970*, Oxford: Oxford University Press.
72. Ibid., p. 154.
73. Mahbub ul Haq, *The Poverty Curtain, Choices for the Third World*, op. cit., pp. 12-13.

74. West Pakistan, 1959, *Report of the Land Reform Commission*, Lahore: Government Printing Press, p. 27.
75. *The Fourth Five-Year Plan: 1970-75*, 1970, Islamabad: Planning Commission, Government of Pakistan, pp. 1-18.
76. Ibid. *The Fourth Five-Year Plan: 1970-75*, 1970, Islamabad: Planning Commission, Government of Pakistan, pp. 1-18.
77. Ibid., p. 13.
78. Ibid., p. 12.
79. Quoted in Hector Bolitho, *Jinnah, the Creator of Pakistan*, op. cit., pp. 217-8.
80. Ibid.
81. Muhammad Waseem, 1989, *Politics and the State in Pakistan*, Lahore: Progressive, p. 243.
82. CAD No. 52, 1 January 1956, 1843-4.
83. Summary of Archibald Rowland's report to the Government of Pakistan, DO/35/2746, TNA: PRO.
84. Ayesha Jalal, *The State of Martial Rule*, op. cit., p. 105.
85. Rawalpindi was the army headquarters, where General Ayub, C-in-C of the Pakistan army, had his seat.
86. See *The First Five-Year Plan, 1955-60*, op. cit.
87. Ibid.
88. S.M. Naseem, *Underdevelopment, Poverty and Inequality in Pakistan*, op. cit., p. 293.
89. Ibid., pp. 126-27.
90. Ibid., p. 293.
91. American Consulate to the Department of State, D-45, 13 December 1951, NND 842909, RG 59, NA.
92. Selig S. Harrison, Paul H. Kreisberg, and Dennis Kux (eds.), 1999, *India and Pakistan: The First Fifty Years*, Cambridge: University of Cambridge Press) p. 1.
93. Robert LaPorte, Jr., in Selig S. Harrison, Paul H. Kreisberg and Dennis Kux (eds.), *India and Pakistan: The First Fifty Years*, op. cit., p. 60.
94. Ayesha Jalal, *Democracy and Authoritarianism in South Asia*, Cambridge: University of Cambridge Press.
95. Nigel Harris, 1992, 'States, Economic Development, and the Asian Pacific Rim', in Richard Appelbaum and Jefferey Henderson (eds.), *States and Development in the Asian Pacific Rim*, Newbury Park: Sage Publishers, p. 76.
96. World Bank Report 2006.
97. Selig S. Harrison, Paul H. Kreisberg and Dennis Kux (eds.), *India and Pakistan: The First Fifty Years*, op. cit., p. 1.
98. See *Human Development in South Asia, 1998, 2003* and *2005*, Karachi: Oxford University Press.
99. Ibid., p. 11.
100. *Human Development in South Asia 2005*, Karachi: Oxford University Press.
101. Mahbub ul Haq and Khadija Haq, *Human Development in South Asia 1998*, Karachi: Oxford University Press, p. 4.
102. Hassan Gardezi and Jamil Rashid, *Pakistan: The Unstable State*, op. cit., p. 5.
103. Ibid.
104. Ibid., p. 174.
105. Robert LaPorte Jr., 'Pakistan: A Nation Still in Making', in Selig S. Harrison, Paul H. Kreisberg, and Dennis Kux (eds.), op. cit., p. 45.

106. Paul R. Brass, 'India: Democratic Progress and Problems', in Selig S. Harrison, Paul H. Kreisberg, and Dennis Kux (eds.), op. cit., p. 23.
107. Atul Kohli, 1990, *Democracy and Discontent: India's Growing Crisis of Governability*, New York: Cambridge University Press.
108. Paul R. Brass, op. cit., p. 35.
109. Ayesha Jalal, 1995, *Democracy and Authoritarianism in South Asia*, Cambridge: Cambridge University Press.
110. John Adams, 'India: Much Achieved, Much to Achieve', in Selig S. Harrison, Paul H. Kreisberg, and Dennis Kux (eds.), op. cit., p. 65.
111. Hugh Tinker, 1967, *India and Pakistan: A Political Analysis*, London: Pall Mall Press, p. 45.
112. Ibid. See A.H. Hanson, 1966, *The Process of Planning: A Study of India's Five-Year Plans, 1950-1964*, London: Oxford University Press. George Rosen, 1966, *Democracy and Economic Change in India*, Berkeley: University of California Press. Francine R. Frankel, 1978, *India's Political Economy, 1947-1977: The Gradual Revolution*, Princeton: Princeton University Press.
113. John Adams, op. cit., p. 65.
114. Granville Austin, 1996, *The Indian Constitution: Cornerstone of A Nation*, London, p. 34.
115. Ibid., p. 45.
116. Nigel Harris, 'States, Economic Development, and the Asian Pacific Rim', in Richard Appelbaum and Jefferey Henderson (eds.), op. cit., p. 77.
117. Paul R. Brass, op. cit., p. 37.
118. Granville Austin, p. 40.
119. John Adams, op. cit., p. 68.
120. Ibid., p. 69.
121. Ibid.
122. S. Mohendra Dev and Ajit Ranade, 'Poverty and Public Policy: A Mixed Record', in K. Parikh (ed.), 1998, *Indian Development Report 1997*, Delhi: Oxford University Press.

Conclusion

Pakistan inherited the legacy of a 'security state', a colonial legacy that had dominated its colonial past and has continued to shadow the process of nation-building in the post-colonial state. Strategic and economic consequences of the partition placed the rulers of the new state in a challenging situation, where they were forced to make some vital decisions; either, to declare their independent policy thinking without the historical baggage of the colonial past, or to continue with the colonial legacy of the obsession with the Soviet invasion and be included in the 'free world of capitalism', protected and safeguarded by the 'American system of power'. Since, the democratic structure on which the new state was to be built was very fragile, it crumbled under the heavy burden of the Cold War even before its proper birth.

The colonial legacy of 'a security state' in the region was reinforced by the thinking of a select group of members of the civil and military bureaucracy, who were trained by the colonial strategists. This elite group became the influential force of the nation-building process in the formative years of the new state's life, at the expense of the representative institutions. As a result, the security of the new state was tied-up with the US, the new custodian of the 'free world' in its 'Cold War' against Communism. Defence establishments in the Third World, dependent on the economic and military assistance of the US, were the vital strategy of the Cold War.

Many writers concerned with the issue of development, view the 'American system of power' as a new form of colonialism, which ensures America's political and economic control over the 'free world'.[1] The 'free world' was persuaded to opt for the capitalist model of development, which favours growth over distribution. The elite governments were less concerned with the poverty of the people and more willing to spend on large defence establishments. The capitalist model of economic growth along with large defence establishments has not only drowned the majority of people of these nation-states into an ocean of absolute poverty but also trapped their future generations into a web of 'dependency'. Pakistan is an example of this model.

CONCLUSION

From 1947-51, the first four years of the new state, established against so many odds, was a struggle of survival and all its institutions were in the process of being built up. It was unfortunate for the new state to lose its mentor and leader just a year after its birth on 11 September 1948. Though Liaquat Ali Khan could not fill the gap fully, he was still able to run the affairs of the government very smoothly and assert his position as the prime minister, in accordance with the parliamentary traditions. Khwaja Nazimuddin, successor to Jinnah, as the governor-general, never overstepped his constitutional bounds and facilitated Liaquat in asserting his authority as the prime minister. From 1948 to 1951, the centre of power was the prime minister and his cabinet. The imbalance between the office of the governor-general and the prime minister, which emerged in the following years, cannot be attributed to the extraordinary powers vested in Jinnah as the first governor-general of Pakistan, as viewed by some historians. On the contrary, there is convincing evidence to suggest that the international forces should be seen as the determining factor for strengthening the civil bureaucracy and the military in Pakistan for safeguarding their own strategic interests during the Cold War era.

This book argues that the development of the institutional imbalances, which have plagued Pakistan's history, was due to the crafty approach of international managers of the Cold War, who allied with the domestic actors in order to continue the colonial legacy of 'controlling the democratic institutions' through an authoritarian administrative structure. Going through the secret documents stored in the National Archives of the USA and the UK presented in the previous pages, provides enough evidence to confirm Alavi's observation that 'effective power within the state apparatus lay in the hands of a [feudal-] military bureaucratic oligarchy from the inception of the state, rather than with the political leadership'.[2] This oligarchy—a select group of civil and military bureaucracy, trained by the colonial strategists in alliance with their international connections—pursued the colonial policy of a 'security state' in the region, which could guarantee the 'Containment of Communist Revolution', and protect the neo-colonial interests. With this mindset, there was only a remote chance of building democratic institutions. East Bengal was perceived as a potential land for the germination of communist seeds and had no share in the defence establishment.[3] Due to these 'sins', there were deliberate efforts on part of the Punjab, which emerged as the major partner of the neo-colonialism, to check East Pakistan claim in the state-formation process. Punjab monopolized the central authority through a group of powerful men, all trained in the autocratic bureaucracy of British India, who disliked democracy and politicians alike. These representatives of civil bureaucracy, the 'guardians of the British Empire', were trained in colonial authoritarian culture and were used to work in the environment of 'controlled democracy'. They had a special dislike for any feelings of nationalism and politicians. The chaotic circumstances of the partition, in the international context of the Cold War, had put them in charge of the affairs of the new state. 'Officers at the top echelons of the non-elective institutions—the military and the bureaucracy—began to skilfully manipulate their international connections with London and Washington', in order to maintain their control over the state authority.[4] The top three members of this oligarchy, Ghulam Mohammad, Iskandar Mirza, and Ayub Khan, were obsessed with the notion of being 'custodians' of the nation and while cooperating with forces of the American power system, determined the fate of millions of Pakistanis, throwing them in the web of developmental dependency, and making Pakistan a client state of the US.

This oligarchy was not concerned with the legitimacy of their actions. 'The failure to empower the mass of its population has lain at the heart of successive regimes' legitimacy problems'.[5] The problem of legitimacy first confronted the state of Pakistan just after four years of its birth, when in 1951, after Liaquat's assassination, Nazimuddin the then governor-general, stepped down to become the prime minister and Ghulam Mohammad, the finance minister in Liaquat's cabinet, elevated himself to the office of the governor-general without following any convention of a parliamentary form of the cabinet government. It was followed by a chain of illegitimate actions such as Prime Minister Nazimuddin's dismissal in April 1953, the appointment of a handpicked and 'imported' Prime Minister Mohammad Ali Bogra, and finally the dissolution of the first constituent assembly in October 1954. The final blow to democracy in Pakistan was delivered on 28 October 1954, when 'the police who barred the entrances of the constituent assembly's meeting place in Karachi prevented the members from casting their votes to formalize the new constitution which they had adopted in their previous meetings'.[6]

This was not the 'failure' of the assembly, or the politicians, who have been blamed for the demise of democracy in Pakistan, rather 'it was the success, not the failure, of the Assembly which brought its demise'.[7] A democratic constitution and a democratic government, with its power seat in East Pakistan, which it claimed was 'having swift growing communist influence,'[8] could pose a threat to American interests in this region at a time when Pakistan was geared to enter into the SEATO and the Baghdad Pact. An authoritarian government, with concentration of power in the hands of the bureaucratic-army elite, which was committed to bolstering the defence establishment in alliance with the American power system, was a requirement neither of a democratic government nor of a democratic constitution,

> Demeaning politicians was easy game to play. While politicians are essential in any free and democratic society, they are vulnerable. Democracy itself is a messy form of government, made up in large part of talk and clashes among competing interests.[9]

Blaming politicians for causing political instability in Pakistan was a trend set in the context of the 'containment doctrine' that preferred 'controlled or guided democracy' rather than a truly people's one.

Which form of democracy is best suited to Pakistan, is a question not yet resolved along with the legitimacy problem that confronts every successive regime. 'Assessment of Pakistan's political development since 1947, paints an uneasy and troubled picture. Pakistan is a state...still in the making, still striving to find a stable and effective form of government'.[10] During the period of two-and-a-half decades from 1947 to 1971, 'ordinary citizens were denied a role in public policy making, regular military intervention in politics began, and efforts to reconcile the political and economic interests of Pakistan's two wings collapsed and led to civil war and division of the country'.[11] Politicians and political parties cannot be blamed for this scenario. Rather, international actors, working within the broad parameters of neo-colonialism, are responsible for promoting authoritarianism in Pakistan.

The failure of democracy and emergence of authoritarianism, accompanied by underdevelopment, in a peripheral post-colonial society like Pakistan, can only be understood in the theoretical framework of the 'dependency paradigm', which argues that authoritarianism and underdevelopment is an interrelated and interdependent phenomenon and it needs to be examined in the historical evolution of colonial and neo-colonial capitalism. Divergence in the development of East Asian and Latin America NICs (Newly Industrialized Countries) has triggered debate over the theory between advocates of modernization and dependency approaches in accounting for the regional divergence. Influenced by the new American development of development theory based on American pragmatism and empiricism, a large section of the research using the modernization approach on divergent development focuses on 'economic development'[12] that has become 'equated *de facto* of not *de jure* with economic growth. It, in turn, was measured by the growth of GNP per capita'.[13] The writers of dependency approach insist on a broader 'concept of development' having three aspects: growth (the economic aspect), equality (the social aspect), and liberty (the political aspect).[14] The broad definition then includes those societal conditions that promote personal growth, economic growth, equality in the distribution of wealth, and political liberty. Frank argues that:

> development must include more democracy. (More) democracy must include (more) respect for human rights. These rights must include (more) political freedom of speech, organization and choice. However, these human rights must also include access to the economic and social basic human needs necessary to exercise such political choice.[15]

The dependency paradigm suggests that, 'the degree of equality in the distribution of wealth may be analyzed along a number of national dimensions: urban-rural, labour-capital, and along intra-class dimensions: large-small industries, large-small farms, skilled-unskilled labour'.[16] Liberty is an essential element of democracy, along with a state executive accountable to an elected parliament and regular, fair elections.[17] More specifically, liberty includes both political rights and civil liberties.[18] From this perspective, 'determinant factors in economic development were really social' and social change, therefore, seemed the key to both social and economic development.[19] This perspective argues for introducing equity and efficiency in economic development.[20] The dependency theory provides a better understanding for divergence in the development in East Asia, Latin America, and many Third World countries including Pakistan and India by focusing on the regional variations of US policy during the construction of US hegemony or the American system of power after the Second World War. It argues that the development paradigm was the child of neo-imperialism and neo-colonialism, 'It developed as part and parcel instrument of the new post-war American hegemony. American ambitions extended over the ex-colonial world in the South and against both the real old Western colonialism and the perceived threat of new Eastern colonialism and imperialism'.[21] At the end of the Second World War, the United States ascended to 'neo-imperial hegemony'.[22] During this period of neo-colonialism, the United States assumed the responsibility to reconstruct the world capitalist economy aiming for integration of different regions—Europe, Asia, Latin America, the Middle East, and Africa, within the emerging American system of power.

The dependency perspective attempts to explore how the different trajectories of development in various regions were influenced by the US hegemony. This perspective argues that East Asian societies should not be viewed successful products of the 'modernization process', as proponents of that theory suggest. Rather, the 'success' of these societies should be viewed as rooted in their historical inclusion in the American system of power, and the strategic importance of the region in which they were housed, and is not necessarily repeatable by other Third World societies.

The end of the Second World War brought the end of the colonial era and colonial rulers of India were left with no other choice but to grant independence to India. The Cold War:

> brought the United States back to South Asia in search of allies (or at least friends) in a struggle against another global threat. The "loss" of China in 1949 accelerated the search, as did the discovery that the Soviet Union was catching up in the nuclear arms race and had consolidated its power in Central and Eastern Europe.[23] •

Because of Pakistan's proximity to the Soviet Union and China, the emerging communist block as well as, the Middle East and Iran, the centre of oil resources or 'wells of power', it was forced to join the 'security map of the free world'. Pakistan as an ally of the United States, and a non-aligned India, both served the objectives of the containment policy. It should not be surprising to find out that 'America's Cold War strategic engagement with India and Pakistan was varied and complex'.[24] Pakistan was secured as a 'bulwark' having the shield of Islamic ideology against the communist threat and locked into a 'client-patron' relationship with the United States, while a non-aligned India was seen to do little damage to 'substantive American interests'.[25]

To counter any revolutionary movements in South Asia, the US initiated 'a variety of developmental, intellectual and information programs in South Asia'.[26] In addition, local communist parties in India and Pakistan were countered with the help of intelligence and information networks supported and aided by the CIA and the British intelligence agencies.[27] Under the pretext of a communist threat, the state of Pakistan took the shape of a 'garrison state', where any activity concerning the people's participation, ranging from students' associations to trade unions and the opposition political parties, was considered anti-state. All administrative measures of political coercion inherited from the colonial state, were made an integral part of the administrative structure of a neo-colonial state. These included preventive detention (originated in Bengal State Prisoners Regulation III of 1818), prohibition of political actions seen by magistrates as prejudicial to public order (Section 144 of the Criminal Code of Procedure), and control of the Press (1931, Indian Press Emergency Powers Act).[28] The colonial legacy of a 'security state in the north-west [of] India', that was meant to discourage political participation of the people resulting in far less-developed political institutions and its survival dependent upon the support of certain tribal and landowning interests, was reinforced in the post-colonial state in line with 'containment' policies. Pakistan's 'overdeveloped' administrative and military institutions have their roots in this colonial legacy. 'Despite incessantly changing political regimes, constitutions and institutions, the inherited democratic deficit of semi-feudalism, strategic insecurity and the vice-regal tradition of British Raj has remained influential'.[29]

The Kashmir conflict between Pakistan and India helped the United States and its allies to build a defence establishment in Pakistan, in the name of defending against the Soviet and Chinese threats. Through the Kashmir conflict, the fear of India's hegemony was created and reinforced by cultivating the alliance of the bureaucracy, army, and the feudal elite, for securing Pakistan's position as a 'bulwark' against communism. Pakistan's entrance into the SEATO and the Baghdad Pact–Cold War alliances, built along the Soviet Union's southern rim, was smoothed by destroying the democratic institutions and consolidating an authoritarian central government in Karachi. In this process, Pakistan's status as the 'security state' was consolidated, which facilitated the emergence of the army as the major beneficiary institution. The domestic argument for spending on the defence establishment, beyond the nation's resources, was the 'security' against India in the context of the Kashmir conflict. This conflict has been the cause of fighting between the two countries that began almost immediately after India and Pakistan gained their independence, and it has proceeded intermittently ever since.

India and Pakistan have adopted opposing strategies for dealing with their security problems...In its first fifteen years of independence, India under Nehru tried to put together a non-aligned movement that would stand above and outside the Cold War. Pakistan attached itself to the United States through Cold War alliances—the Baghdad Pact, SEATO, and CENTO—that were building along the Soviet Union's southern rim.[30]

The large defence establishment, built with the assistance of the United States and her allies, has been swallowing the larger portions of the national exchequer, leaving very little in the kitty for investment in human and social resources, thus, resulting in underdevelopment and poverty. In the initial stages of the state construction, the decision to give priority to the defence establishment that was only concentrated in one province, Punjab, and a few settled districts of the North West Frontier Province, initiated a feeling of neglect in East Pakistan and the remaining provinces of West Pakistan. The Economic Appraisal Committee's observations, made in 1953, were the first warning signals concerning the trend of heavy annual expenditures on top-heavy and extremely expensive defence and civil administration beyond the available national resources. As expected, this exploded in tension between the central authority and those who were looking for provincial autonomy. Subsequently, the bureaucracy and the army, in search of additional resources, became increasingly locked into a dependent relationship with the United States that provided them with both the motives—the exclusion of domestic political objectors on foreign policy issues and increasing resources—to tilt the balance of power away from representative parties and politicians. Political parties, politicians and mass public opinion were seen as negative factors in achieving the strategic interests of the American power system.

Liaquat's decision to accept the Soviet government's invitation to visit Moscow in May 1949, and the enthusiasm shown by the Pakistani people regarding it, was the first indicator that public mood in Pakistan was not in favour of the United States and its allies. The spreading wave of nationalism, and the increasing popularity of the communist party in Pakistan and its associations and groups, were areas of concern in the then prevailing Cold War environment of 'containment'. Anti-West feelings were again expressed at the time of Pakistan's signing of the Mutual Defence Agreement with the US in April 1954, when an anti-Pact Day was observed in East Pakistan and major cities of West Pakistan. The Rawalpindi conspiracy case of 1951, and governor's rule in East

Pakistan (1954-56) following the dismissal of the elected, government United Front's provincial a coalition of all opposition parties that was resisting pro-West policies of the central government, under the pretext of 'security' of the state, are two such events. These actions by the central government clearly demonstrated that any anti-West feeling, be it among the ranks and files of the Pakistan army or among the people of Pakistan, could not be allowed to grow in the era of 'containment'.

With the onset of the Cold War, European colonialism was replaced with the American power system or a neo-colonialism, and the political and economic interests of colonialism became the interests of the emerging US hegemony. The concept of economic development, based on Rostow's model of stages of growth, was the landmark of this period to control the economic resources of ex-colonies and bring them into the economic and political influence of capitalism, at a time when Marxism and nationalism were sweeping the world. The Marshall Plan, the World Bank, and the International Monetary Fund (IMF), were all designed to achieve these targets. The immediate concern was the wave of nationalism supported by Moscow, that was sweeping the newly-established nation-states of Africa and Asia, and was termed the non-aligned 'Third World'. Leading members of this original 'Third World' movement were Yugoslavia, Indonesia, and Egypt.[31] Frustrated by the non-aligned movement and obsessed with the idea of 'liberating' the Third World countries, John Foster Dulles, the US secretary of state, stated in 1955 that 'neutrality...[had] increasingly become an obsolete and except under very exceptional circumstances, it...[was] an immoral and short-sighted conception'.[32] The concept of economic development was meant to 'liberate' Third World countries from the ills of underdevelopment, and protect them from falling in to the Marxist camp of development, or the 'Nationalist-non-aligned' camp.

The first decade of Pakistan's history is the beginning of her pursuance of a neo-colonial capitalist model—based on capitalist exploitation—a cycle of developmental dependency instead of following the policies of nationalism, like India, Indonesia, and Egypt. In an environment of 'containment', an alliance of the bureaucracy, army, and the feudal elite, three basic institutions of colonial capitalism, continued to operate in the post-colonial state as before and by cooperating with the forces of the capitalist world system, under the hegemony of the US, resulted in the centralizing of authority in the province of Punjab. The 'economic and social progress', in line with this neo-colonial model, meant an increased dependence on the US technical, military, and commodity aid. In an environment of a weak political culture, bureaucrats and generals were more interested in building a defence establishment rather than investing in social sectors. Heavy industries linked with military needs became the priority of the central government, thus, seriously neglecting the agricultural sector. The lack of will on part of the central government, to implement any land reforms in West Pakistan and to transform the previously existing, exploitative colonial capitalist structure of the agrarian economy, also harmed this important sector at the national level.

> The mobilization of limited domestic resources for defence' and 'the failure to introduce effective land reform...perpetuated the social inequalities inherited from the colonial era. The over-development of the military institution has encouraged authoritarianism in an environment of political opportunism and weak institutionalization.[33]

In the absence of any general national elections, on the basis of adult franchise, the non-representative elite of the landed class, which was elected on a restricted franchise in pre-independence nationals election held in 1945-46, continued to cooperate with the anti-democratic forces and any dissuading voice was silenced by unconstitutional and non-parliamentary means. Pakistan's struggle with constitution-making was also over shadowed by these anti-democratic forces which were not in favour of a democratic, constitutional structure providing an equitable distribution of resources, and social and economic justice, on the basis of equality. Religion was used as a vehicle to promote conservative and anti-democratic segments of the population, by projecting an 'Islamic Ideology' to confront the challenges of communism. 'Islam was assumed to confer a natural immunity to communism; Pakistan was at once both explicitly Muslim and near the world's two great communist powers'.[34]

The use of religion in politics produced a complex set of consequences, which are still unresolved today. It caused the very first religious riots in Pakistan, which resulted in the dismissal of Prime Minister Nazimuddin in April 1953, thus, strengthening the bureaucratic-army-feudal alliance. It also affected the process of constitution-making, which was delayed due to the initiation of a debate for defining the relationship of Islam and the nation-state, a debate not yet concluded. Land reform proposals were opposed by proclaiming that Islam allows the concentration of land and forced evacuation of land, for the purpose of redistribution, was not permitted by Islam. This religious proclamation was to support the landed elite of West Pakistan who were resisting the implementation of any land reforms. After three land reforms, Pakistan is still dominated by the colonial capitalist feudalism, and the feudal, landed class continues to dominate all the elected, or non elected, legislatures.

Emphasis on Islamic ideology with the fear of 'Indian hegemony' helped in the building of a defence establishment out of line with the available resources, and proposing a strong centre with such slogans as 'one religion, one centre, one economy', ignored the divergence in social, cultural, and economic needs of the different provinces of Pakistan. Difference of opinion on major policy making issues, expressed by the 'smaller' provinces, was called 'provincialism', and considered a dangerous trend for the unity and security of the state, and was dealt with an iron hand, a tendency still fully practiced. This thinking was adopted to protect the negotiating role of the Punjab in any constitutional framework and its ability to influence the policy making, be it political or economic, or on the domestic or the foreign front. In this process, Punjab became the upholder of the strategic interests of neo-colonialism in a manner similar to its colonial legacy.

> The fact that the Pakistan Army has remained a predominantly Punjabi force has intensified the feelings of the smaller provinces [after the loss of East Pakistan] that they are colonized by a Punjabi province which both benefits from this policy and has a stake in its continuation'.[35]

Punjab's hegemony has created an imbalance of power in favour of the army, bureaucracy, and the landed aristocracy, thus, adversely affecting the democratic institutions and the interests of smaller provinces, thereby threatening the identity of the state. A predominantly Punjabi army is incapable 'to fabricate an identity compatible with Pakistan's multiethnic and multi-sectarian realities...yet because of its dominant position, the army can block attempts to change the consensus concerning Pakistan's identity'.[36] Spending on a large defence establishment by authoritarian regimes has made Pakistan a politically, socially, and economically vulnerable state, with unprecedented demographic pressures, aggravated by the poor performance of the economy, an inadequate educational system and an astoundingly rate of urbanization.[37]

It is certain that without curtailing the large defence budget and reorienting state priorities, 'Pakistan will fall further and further behind as a "modern" state when compared with most of its peers'.[38] The culture of authoritarianism, cultivated in the first decade of Pakistan's life, is likely to continue shadowing the democratic struggle unless the army fully divorces itself from politics[39] and allows the political system to work.

The two 'nuclear countries' of South Asia, who maintain two large armies and spend a heavy share of their resources on huge military establishments, are predominantly poor and underdeveloped. The state of human development and human rights in both countries demands that military expenditures should be reduced and the amount thus saved be used for social development. In both Pakistan and India, where one-third of the population is living below the poverty line and the large majority is denied basic facilities like health, education, sanitation, safe water, and a safe environment, the real threats are poverty, disease, environmental degradation, and regional and ethnic conflicts. Human deprivation is the major threat to human security. Without human security, territorial security becomes ineffective and ultimately, self-defeating.

NOTES

1. Perry Anderson, 'Force and Consent', *New Left Review* (September-October 2002) 17: 5-30.
2. Hamza Alavi, 'Class and State in Pakistan', in Hassan Gardezi and Jamil Rashid (eds.), *Pakistan: The Unstable State*, op. cit., p. 65.
3. Enclosure to Despatch No. 13 of 7 August 1951, from American Embassy, Karachi to Dacca Consulate, NND 842430, RG 84, NA.
4. Ayesha Jalal, *Democracy and Authoritarianism in South Asia*, op. cit., p. 37.
5. Ian Talbot, *Pakistan: A Modern History*, op. cit., p. 368.
6. Allen McGrath, *The Destruction of Pakistan's Democracy*, op. cit., p. 218.
7. Ibid.
8. American Embassy to Secretary of State Department, Washington T-961 to Dept., 350 Riots-East Pakistan, 5/29/54, NND 842430, RG 84, NA.
9. Allen McGrath, op. cit., p. 218.
10. Selig S. Harrison, Paul H. Kreisberg, and Dennis Kux (eds.), *India and Pakistan: The First Fifty Years*, op. cit., p. 4.
11. Ibid.
12. Gabriel Almond and G. Bingham Powell, *Comparative Politics: A Developmental Approach*, op. cit., and Daniel Lerner, *The Passing of Traditional Society*, op. cit.
13. Andre Gunder Frank, 'The Development of Underdevelopment: An Autobiographical Essay', op. cit.
14. Lawrence R. Alschuler, 'Divergent Development; The Pursuit of Liberty, Equality and Growth in Argentina and the Republic of Korea', op. cit., and Peter Evans, *Dependent*

Development: The Alliance of Multinational, State and Local Capital in Brazil, op. cit.
15. Andre Gunder Frank, op. cit.
16. Lawrence R. Alschuler, op. cit., p. 121.
17. Dietrich Rueschemeyer and Peter Evans, 'The State and Economic Transformation: Toward an Analysis of the Conditions Underlying Effective Intervention', in Peter Evans, Dietrich Rueschemeyer and Theda Skocpol (eds.) *Bringing the State Back In*, op. cit.
18. Raymond Gastil, 'The Comparative Study of Freedom: Expressions and Suggestions', op. cit.
19. Andre Gunder Frank, op. cit.
20. Ibid., p. 4.
21. Ibid., p. 6.
22. Ibid.
23. Stephen P. Cohen, 'The United States, India, and Pakistan: Retrospect and Prospect', in Selig S. Harrison, Paul H. Kreisberg, and Dennis Kux (eds.), op. cit., p. 190.
24. Ibid., p. 192.
25. Ibid.
26. Ibid., p. 191.
27. Ibid.
28. Ian Talbot, *Pakistan: A Modern History*, op. cit., p. 54.
29. Ibid., p. 368.
30. Thomas W. Simons, Jr., 'India and Pakistan: Mutually Assured Destruction, South Asian Style', *Hoover Digest*, (2000) 4. Retrieved 10 May 2004, http://www.hooverdigest.org/.
31. 'Third World'. Wikipedia, the free encyclopedia. Retrieved 26 June 2004, http://en.wikipedia.org/wiki/third world.
32. 'John Foster Dulles'. Wikipedia, the free encyclopedia. Retrieved 26 June 2004, http://en.wikipedia.org/wiki/Dulles.
33. Ian Talbot, *Pakistan: A Modern History*, op. cit., p. 371.
34. Stephen Philip Cohen, *The Idea of Pakistan*, op. cit., p. 302.
35. Ian Talbot, *Pakistan: A Modern History*, op. cit., p. 371.
36. Stephen Philip Cohen, *The Idea of Pakistan*, op. cit., p. 274.
37. Ibid., p. 271.
38. Ibid., p. 272.

Select Bibliography

Manuscript Sources

British Library, India Office Record, London.
The US National Archives and Record Administration, Washington, D. C.
National Archives, Islamabad.
National Documentation Centre, Cabinet Division, Islamabad.
Punjab Archives, Lahore.
Punjab Board of Revenue, Lahore.
The National Archives, Public Record Office, London.

Published Sources

Official

Budget of the Central Government of Pakistan, 1947-48 [15 August to 31 March] (Karachi: Government of Pakistan).
Budget of the Central Government of Pakistan, 1948-49 (Karachi: Government of Pakistan).
Budget of the Central Government of Pakistan, 1950-51 (Karachi: Government of Pakistan).
Butler, M.S.D., *Record of War Services in the Attock District 1914-1919* (Lahore: Government Printing Punjab, 1921).
Government of India, *Census of India, 1911* (Calcutta: Government Central Printing, 1913).
Government of India, *Census of India, 1921* (Calcutta: Government Central Printing, 1923).
Government of the Punjab, *Census of the Punjab, 1921* (Lahore: Government Printing Punjab, 1923).
Population Census, 1951 (Karachi: Government of Pakistan, 1953).
Census of Pakistan, 1961 (Karachi: Government of Pakistan, 1962).
Constituent Assembly Debates, 1947-1958 (Karachi: Government of Pakistan).
Government of Pakistan, *Constitution of Islamic Republic of Pakistan, 1956*.
Speeches of Muhammad Ali Jinnah as Governor-General of Pakistan 1947-48 (Karachi: Government of Pakistan, n. d.).
Court of Wards, Account Code (Lahore: Government Printing Punjab, 1935).
Dwyer, Michael O', 1923, *India's contribution to the Great War* (Calcutta, Government Central Press).
Griffin, L.H. and C.F. Massy, 1940, *Chiefs and Families of Note in the Punjab*, 2 vols. [1906] (Lahore: Government Printing Punjab,).
Punjab Census 1868 (Lahore: Government Printing Punjab, 1870).
Leigh, M.S., 1922, *The Punjab and the War* (Lahore, Government Printing, Punjab).

Ouselev, G. and W.G. Davies, 1886, *Report on the Revised Settlement of the Shahpoor District in the Rawlpindee Division, 1886* (Lahore: Government Printing, Punjab).
Pakistan Economic Survey, 1977-8 (Finance Division, Government of Pakistan, Islamabad, 1978).
Punjab Administrative Reports 1922-23 (Lahore: Government Printing Punjab).
Report of the Administration of Estates under the Charge of the Court of Wards for the year ending 30 September 1895 (Lahore: Government Printing, Punjab, 1896).
Reports of Indian Statutory Commission, Vol. X (London: His Majesty's Stationary Office, 1930).
Report of the Economic Appraisal Committee (Karachi: Finance Division, Government of Pakistan, 1953).
Saunders, Leslie S., 1873, *Report on the Revised Land Revenue Settlement of the Lahore District in the Lahore Division of the Punjab, 1865-69* (Lahore, Government Printing, Punjab).
Selected Circular Orders of the Board of Administration in the General and Political Departments (Lahore: Government Printing, Punjab, 1871).
Shahpur District Gazetteer (Lahore: Government Printing, Punjab, 1917).
The Fourth Five-Year Plan: 1970-75 (Islamabad: Planning Commission, Government of Pakistan, 1970).
Tupper, C.L. 1880, *Punjab's Customary Law: Statements of Customary Law in Different Districts, Vol. II* (Simla: Government Central Branch Press).
War Services of the Shahpur District (Lahore: Government Printing Punjab, n. d.).
War Speeches of Sir Michael O' Dwyer, Lieutenant Governor of the Punjab (Lahore: Government Printing, Punjab 1918).

Unofficial

Newspapers

Dawn (Karachi)
Nawa-i-Waqt (Lahore)
The Pakistan Times (Lahore)
The Pakistan Observer (Dacca)
Eastern Times (Lahore)
The New York Times (New York)

Reports

Cohen, Stephen P., *Security Decision-Making in Pakistan*, a report prepared for the Office of External Research, Department of State, September 1980, Contract # 1722-020167, University of Illinois, Urbana, Unclassified monograph, Copy # 45.
Mahbub ul Haq Human Development Centre, 2004, *Human Development in South Asia 2003: The Employment Challenge* (Karachi: Oxford University Press).
Haq, Mahbub ul and K. Haq, 1998, *Human Development in South Asia* (Karachi: Oxford University Press).
Report of the Agrarian Committee appointed by the Working Committee of the Pakistan Muslim League (Karachi: S. Shamusul Hasan, 1949).
The World Bank, 1997, *World Development Report* (New York: Oxford University Press).
UNDP, 2003, *Human Development Report* (New York: Oxford University Press).

UNDP, 1997, *Human Development Report* (New York: Oxford University Press).

Articles

Alavi, Hamza, 'India: Transition from Feudalism to Colonial Capitalism', *Journal of Contemporary Asia* 10 (1980): 359-99.
Alavi, Hamza, 'The State in Post-Colonial Societies: Pakistan and Bangladesh,' *New Left Review* 74 (July-August 1972): 59-81.
Aldrich, Richard and Michael Coleman, 'Britain and the Strategic Air Offensive against the Soviet Union: The Question of South Asian Air Bases- 1945/9', *History* (October 1989).
Alschuler, Lawrence R., 'Divergent Development: The Pursuit of Liberty, Equality and Growth in Argentina and the Republic of Korea', *Journal of World Systems Research* 3 (1997): 115-207.
Anderson, Perry, 'Force and Consent', *New Left Review* 17 (September-October 2002): 5-30.
Blyn, G., 'Revenue Administration of Calcutta in the first half of the 18th century', *The Indian Economic and Social History Review*, New Delhi 1, 4 (1964): 120-9.
Braibanti, Ralph, 'The Civil Service of Pakistan—A Theoretical Analysis', *South Atlantic Quarterly* VIII, 2 (Spring 1959): 260-72.
Chandra, Bipan, 'Colonialism, Stages of Colonialism and the Colonial State', *Journal of Contemporary Asia* 10 (1980): 272-85.
Diamond, L., 'Thinking about Hybrid Regimes', *Journal of Democracy* 13, 2 (2000): 5-21.
Escober, Arthuro, Discourse and Power in Development: Michael Foucault and the Relevance of His Work to the Third World', *Alternatives* 10 (1985): 227-400.
Frank, Andre G. 'The Development of Underdevelopment', *Monthly Review* (September 1966)18: 17-31.
Gastil, Raymond, 'The Comparative Study of Freedom: Expressions and Suggestions', *Studies in Comparative International Development* 25, 1 (1990): 25-50.
Gurr, Ted Robert, Jaggers, Keith and Will Moore, 'The Transformation of the Western State: The Growth of Democracy, Autocracy, and State Power since 1800', *Studies in Comparative International Development* 25, 1 (Spring 1990): 78-85.
Habib, Irfan, 'Potentialities of Capitalistic Development in the Economy of Mughal India', *The Journal of Economic History* XXIX (March 1969): 32-78.
Jalal, Ayesha, 'Towards the Baghdad Pact', *International History Review* (1989): 409-612.
Kuznets, Simon, 'Economic Growth and Income Inequality,' *American Economic Review* 45 (March 1955): 1-26.
March, J.C. and J.P. Olsen, 'The New Institutionalism: Organizational Factors in Political Life', *American Political Science Review* 78 (1984): 734-49.
Moore, Raymond A., 'The Army as a Vehicle for Social Change in Pakistan', *The Journal of Developing Areas* 2 (October 1967): 55-74.
Rehnema, Majid, 'Under the Banner of Development', *Development* 3 (1986): 47-67.
Singh, K.S. 'Colonial Transformation of Tribal Society in Middle India', *Economic and Political Weekly* (Bombay), 29 July 1978.
Sovani, N.V. 'British Impact on India after 1850-57', *Journal of World History* II (April 1954): 77-105.
Thandi, S.S. 'The Un-identical Punjab Twins: Some Explanations of Comparative Agricultural Performances since Partition', *International Journal of Punjab Studies* 4, 1 (Jan-June 1997): 68-81.

Valenzuela, Samuel and Arturo Valenzuela, 'The Rise and Future Demise of the World Capitalist System: Concepts of Comparative Analysis', *Comparative Studies in Society and History*, XVI, 4 (October 1974): 387-415.

Wallerstein, I., 'Development or Illusion?' *Economic and Political Weekly* 23, 39 (September 1988): 2017-23.

Wallerstein, I., 'The Collapse of Liberalism', *The Socialist Register 1992*, (1992b): 96-110.

Printed Books

Adelmann, I. and Morris, C.T., 1973, *Economic Growth and Social Equality in Evolving Countries* (Stanford: Stanford University Press).

Afzal, Rafique, 1998, *Political Parties in Pakistan, Vol. 1* (Islamabad: National Institute of Historical and Cultural Research).

Ahmed, Viqar and Amjad, Rashid, 1984, *The Management of Pakistan's Economy: 1947-82* (Karachi: Oxford University Press).

Ali, Imran, 1988, *The Punjab Under Imperialism, 1885-1947* (Princeton: Princeton University Press).

Almond, Gabriel and Powell, G. Bingham, 1966, *Comparative Politics: A Developmental Approach* (Boston: Little, Brown).

Amin, S., 1976, *Unequal Development: An Essay on the Social Formation of Peripheral Capitalism* (New York: Monthly Review Press).

Amin, S., 1973, *Neo-Colonialism in West Africa* (New York: Monthly Review Press).

Almond, Gabriel and Coleman, J. (eds.), *The Politics of the Developing Areas* (Princeton: Princeton University Press, 1960).

Arrighi, Giovanni, Ikeda, S., and Irwin, A., 1992, 'The Rise of East Asia—One Miracle or Many?', in Ravi Arvind Palat (ed.), *Pacific-Asia and the Future of the World Economy* (Westport: Greenwood Press).

Austin, Granville, 1996, *Indian Constitution: Cornerstone of a Nation* (London).

Ayubi, Nazih, 1995, *Overstating the Arab State: Politics and Society in the Middle East* (London: I.B. Tauris).

Baden-Powell, Sir Henry, 1892, *Land Systems of British India* Vol. II (Oxford: Clarendon Press).

Barrier, N.G., 1966, *The Punjab Alienation of Land Bill of 1900* (Durham: Duke University Press).

Bello, Walden and Rosenfeld, Stephanie, 1990, *Dragons in Distress—Asia's Miracle Economies in Crisis* (San Francisco: The Institute for Food and Development).

Berger, M., 1960, *Military Elite and Social Change* (Princeton: Center for International Studies, Princeton University).

Berger, P., 1986, *The Capitalist Revolution: Fifty Propositions about Prosperity, Equality and Liberty* (New York: Basic Books).

Berger, P., and Hsiao, M.H. (ed.), 1988, *In Search of an East Asian Development Model* (New Brunswick, N.J.: Transaction Books).

Blunt, Sir Edward, 1937, *The ICS: The Indian Civil Service* (London: Faber).

Binder, Leonard, 1963, *Religion and Politics in Pakistan* (Berkeley, California: University of California Press).

Bolitho, Hector, 1964, *Jinnah, the Creator of Pakistan* (London: John Murray).

Brown, J., 1995, *Modern India: The Origins of an Asian Democracy* (Oxford: Oxford University Press).

Bauer, Peter T., and Basil S. Yamey, 1983, 'The Third World and the West: An Economic Perspective', in W. Scott Thomson (ed.), *The Third World: Premises of U.S. Policy* (California: Institute of Contemporary Studies San Francisco).

Burki, Shahid Javed and Robert Laporte, Jr. (eds.), 1984, *Pakistan's Development Priorities—Choices for the Future* (Karachi: Oxford University Press).

Callard, Keith, 1957, *Pakistan—A Political Study*, (London: George Allen and Unwin).

Cardoso, Fernando Henrique and Falettu, Enzo, 1978, *Dependency and Development in Latin America* (Berkeley and Los Angeles: University of California Press).

Casper, Gretchen, 1995, *Fragile Democracies: The Legacies of Authoritarian Rule* (Pittsburgh: University of Pittsburgh Press).

Chase-Dunn, Christopher, 1989, *Global Formation: Structures of the World Economy* (New York: Basil Blackwell).

Chaudhry, Zahid, 1990, *Pakistan Ki Siyasi Tareekh, Vol. 4* (Lahore: Idara Mutalia Tareekh). [Urdu].

Choudhury, G.W., 1975, *India, Pakistan, Bangladesh, and the Major Powers* (New York: Free Press).

Cohen, Stephen P., 1984, *The Indian Army: Its Contribution to the Development of a Nation* (Berkeley: University of California Press).

Cohen, Stephen P., 1983, *The Pakistan Army* (Berkeley: University of California Press).

Cohen, Stephen P., 2005, *The Idea of Pakistan* (Lahore: Vanguard Books).

Cumings, Bruce, 1990, 'Archaeology, Descent, Emergence: Japan in British/American Hegemony, 1900-1950', in Masao Miyoshi and H.D. Harootunian (eds.), *Japan in the World* (Durham: Duke University Press).

Dev, S. Mohendra, and Ranade, Ajit, 1998, 'Poverty and Public Policy: A Mixed Record', in K. Parikh (ed.), *Indian Development Report 1997* (Delhi: Oxford University Press).

Dwyer, Michael O', 1925, *India As I Knew It, 1885-1925* (London: Constable & Company Ltd.).

Evans, Peter, 1979, *Dependent Development: The Alliance of Multinational, State and Local Capital in Brazil* (Princeton: Princeton University Press).

Fagan, Sir Patrick, 1932, 'District Administration in the United Provinces, Central Provinces and the Punjab, 1818-1857', in H.H. Dodwell (ed.), *The Cambridge History of India Volume VI: The Indian Empire 1858-1918* (Cambridge: Cambridge University Press).

Feldman, Herbert, 1967, *Revolution in Pakistan* (London: Oxford University Press).

Frank, Andre G., 1981, *Crisis In the Third World* (New York: Homes and Meier).

Frank, Andre G., 1979, *Dependent Accumulation and Underdevelopment* (New York: Monthly Review Press).

Frank, Andre G., 1972, 'The Development of Underdevelopment', in James D. Cockroft et al. (eds.), *Dependence and Underdevelopment: Latin America's Political Economy* (New York: Anchor Books).

Frank, Andre G., 1968, *Capitalism and Underdevelopment in Latin America* (Harmondsworth: Penguin).

Franke, R.W. and B.H. Chasin, 1980, *Seeds of Famine* (New York: Seabury Press).

Frankel, Francine R., 1978, *India's Political Economy 1947-1977: The Gradual Revolution* (Princeton: Princeton University Press).

Gaddis, John, 1982, *Strategies of Containment: A Critical Appraisal of Post-war American National Security* (New York: Oxford University Press)

Gallagher, I., Gordon, J. and A. Seal, 1973, *Locality, Province and Nation: Essays on Indian Politics 1879-1940* (Cambridge: Cambridge University Press).

SELECT BIBLIOGRAPHY

Gardezi, Hassan and Jamil Rashid (eds.), 1983, *Pakistan: The Unstable State* (Lahore: Vanguard Books).

Gardezi, Hassan and Jamil Rashid (eds.), 1983, *Roots of Dictatorship—The Political Economy of a Praetorian State* (London: Zed Press).

Gilmartin, David, 1988, *Empire and Islam: Punjab and the Making of Pakistan* (London: I.B. & Tauris Co. Ltd.).

Gilmartin, David, 'Kinship, Women and Politics in Twentieth Century Punjab', in Gail Minault (ed.), 1981, *The Extended Family: Women and Political Participation in India and Pakistan* (Columbia: Columbia University Press).

Gills, Barry, 1993, 'The Hegemonic Transition in East Asia: A Historical Perspective,' in Stephen Gill (ed.), *Gramsci, Historical Materialism and International Relations* (London: Cambridge University Press).

Gough, Kathleen and Sharma, Hari P. (eds.), 1973, *Imperialism and Revolution in South Asia* (New York: Monthly Review Press).

Griffin, K., 1978, *International Inequality and National Poverty* (London: Macmillan).

Habib, Irfan, 1963, *The Agrarian System of Mughal India: 1556-1707* (Bombay: Asia Publishing House).

Hancock, G., 1989, *Lords of Poverty: The Power, Prestige, and Corruption of the International Aid Business* (New York: The Atlantic Monthly Review).

Hanson, H., 1966, *The Process of Planning: A Study of India's Five Year Plans, 1950-1964* (London: Oxford University Press).

Haq, Mahbub ul, 1976, *The Poverty Curtain: Choices for the Third World* (New York, Columbia University Press).

Harris, Nigel, 1992, 'States, Economic Development, and the Asian Pacific Rim', in Richard Appelbaum and Jefferey Henderson (eds.), *States and Development in the Asian Pacific Rim* (Newbury Park: Sage Publications).

Harrison, Selig S. et al. (eds.), 1999, *India and Pakistan: The First Fifty Years* (Cambridge: University of Cambridge Press).

Hassan, Ibn, 1967, *The Central Structure of the Mughal Empire* (London: Oxford University Press).

Hassan, Nurul, 'Zamindars under the Mughals', in Richard E. Frykenberg (ed.), 1969, *Land Control and Social Structure in Indian History* (Madison: University of Wisconsin).

Hein, Laura E., 1993, 'Growth Versus Success: Japan's Economic Policy in Historical Perspective,' in Andrew Gordon (ed.), *Post-war Japan as History* (Berkeley: University of California Press).

Heydemann, Steven, 1999, *Authoritarianism in Syria: Institutions and Social Conflict* (Ithaca and London: Cornell University Press).

Hinnebusch, Raymond, 2003, *International Politics of the Middle East* (Manchester: Manchester University Press).

Huntington, Samuel P., 2000, The Third Wave: Democratization in the Late Twentieth Century (Norman: University of Oklahoma Press).

Huntington, Samuel P., 1996, 'Democracy's Third Wave,' in Larry Diamond and Marc F. Plattner (eds.), *The Global Resurgence of Democracy* (Baltimore: John Hopkins University Press).

Huntington, Samuel P., 1968, *Political Orders in Changing Societies* (New Haven: Yale University Press).

Hyder, Sajjad, 1987, *Foreign Policy of Pakistan: Reflections of an Ambassador* (Lahore: Vanguard Books).

SELECT BIBLIOGRAPHY

Jalal, Ayesha, 1995, *Democracy and Authoritarianism in South Asia: A Comparative and Historical Perspective* (New York: Cambridge University Press).

Jalal, Ayesha, 1990, *The State of Martial Rule: The Origins of Pakistan's Political Economy of Defence* (Cambridge: Cambridge University Press).

Janowitz, M., 1960, *The Professional Soldier: A Social and Political Portrait* (Glencoe, Ill: The Free Press).

Janowitz, M., 1964, *The Military in the Political Development of New Nations* (Chicago: University of Chicago Press).

Jordan, Amos A. Jr., 1962, *Foreign Aid and Defence of South Asia* (New York: Praeger).

Jordan, Amos A. Jr., 1962, *The Role of the Military in Underdeveloped Countries* (Princeton: Princeton University Press).

Josh, B., 1979, *communist movement in the Punjab 1926-1947* (New Delhi: Peoples Publishing House).

Kavic, Lawrence J., 1967, *India's Quest for Security: Defence Policies, 1947-1965* (Berkeley & Los Angeles: University of California Press).

Khan, Mohammad Ayub, 1967, *Friends Not Masters: A Political Autobiography* (Karachi: Oxford University Press).

Khan, Mohammad Ayub, President of Pakistan. *Pakistan Perspective: A Collection of Important Articles and Excerpts from Major Addresses* (Washington: The Embassy of Pakistan, n.d.).

Lane, Jan-Erik and Ersson, Svante, 2000, *The New Institutional Politics: Performance and Outcomes* (London & N.Y: Routledge).

LaPalombara, Joseph (ed.), 1963, *Bureaucracy and Political Development* (Princeton: Princeton University Press).

Leary, V., 1990, 'The Asia Region and the International Human Rights Movement', in C. Welch and V. Leary (eds.), *Asian Perspectives on Human Rights* (San Francisco: Westview Press).

Leffler, Melvyn P., 1992, *A Preponderance of Power: National Security, The Truman Administration and Cold War* (Stanford: Stanford University Press).

Lerner, Daniel, 1958, *The Passing of Traditional Society* (New York: Free Press).

Levy, Marion J., 1966, *Modernization and the Structures of Societies: A Setting for International Affairs* (Princeton: Princeton University Press).

Linz, J., 1970, 'An Authoritarian Regime: The Case of Spain', in E. Allard and S. Rokkan (eds.), *Mass Politics: Studies in Political Sociology* (New York: Free Press).

MacMunn, George F., 1979, *The Martial Races of India* [1930] (Delhi: Mittal Publications).

Major, Andrew J., 1996, *Return to Empire: Punjab Under the Sikhs and British in The Mid-Nineteenth Century* (Karachi: Oxford University Press).

Major, Andrew J., 1991, 'The Punjab Chieftains and the Transition from Sikh to British Rule', in D.A. Low (ed.), *The Political Inheritance of Pakistan* (London: Macmillan).

Malik, Iftikhar H., 1997, *State and Civil Society in Pakistan* (New York: St. Martin's Press).

McGrath, Allen, 1996, *The Destruction of Pakistan's Democracy* (Karachi: Oxford University Press).

McGlothen, Ronald, 1993, *Controlling the Waves: Dean Acheson and U.S. Foreign Policy in Asia* (W.W. Norton & Company).

Menon, V.P., 1957, *Transfer of Power in India*. (Princeton: Princeton University Press).

Moore, Barrington, 1966, *Social Origins of Dictatorship and Democracy: Lord and Peasants in the Making of the Modern World* (Boston: Beacon Press).

Muhammad Ali, Chaudri, 1967, *The Emergence of Pakistan* (New York: Columbia University Press).
Munir, Muhammad, 1980, *From Jinnah to Zia* (Lahore: Vanguard Books).
Murdoch, William W., 1980, *The Poverty of Nations* (Baltimore: Johns Hopkins University Press).
Naseem, S.M., 1980, *Underdevelopment, Poverty and Inequality in Pakistan* (Lahore: Vanguard Books,).
Noon, Firoze Khan, 1966, *Test of Time* (Lahore).
Page, David, 1987, *Prelude to Partition: The Indian Muslims and the Imperial System of Control 1920-1932* (Karachi: Oxford University Press).
Pasha, Mustafa Kamal, 1998, *Colonial Political Economy: Recruitment and Underdevelopment in the Punjab* (Karachi: Oxford University Press).
Paterson, Thomas, 1988, *Meeting the communist threat* (New York).
Perlmutter, Amos, 1981, *Modern Authoritarianism: A Comparative Institutional Analysis* (New Haven: Yale University Press).
Persson, Magnus, 1998, *Great Britain, the United States and the Security of the Middle East: The Formation of the Baghdad Pact* (Lund: Lund University Press).
Podeh, Elie, 1995, *The Quest for Hegemony in the Arab World: The Struggle over the Baghdad Pact* (Leiden: E. J. Brill).
Randall, Vicky and Theobald, Robin, 1998, *Political Change and Underdevelopment* (Basingstoke: Macmillan).
Raychaudhuri, Tapan and Habib, Irfan, (eds.), 1984, *The Cambridge Economic History of India, Volume 1, c.1200-c.1750* (Hyderabad: Orient Longman in association with Cambridge University Press).
Redding, S.G., 1990, *The Spirit of Chinese Capitalism* (Berlin: De Gruyter).
Rizvi, Hasan-Askari, 2000, *The Military and Politics in Pakistan, 1947-1997* (Lahore: Sang-e-Meel Publications).
Roberts, Andrew, 1994, *Eminent Churchillians* (London: Oxford University Press).
Roberts, Lord, 1898, *Forty-one Years in India: From Subaltern to Commander-in-Chief* (London: Macmillan).
Rodan, G., 1993, *Political Oppositions in Industrializing Asia* (London: Routledge).
Rosen, George, 1985, *Western Economies and Eastern Societies: Agents of Change in South Asia, 1950-1970* (Oxford: Oxford University Press).
Rosen, George, 1966, *Democracy and Economic Change in India* (Berkeley: University of California Press).
Rostow, W., 1962, *The Stages of Growth: A Non-communist manifesto* (Cambridge: Cambridge University Press).
Rueschemeyer, D., Stephens, E. and Stephens, J., 1992, *Capitalist Development and Democracy* (Cambridge: Polity Press).
Rueschemeyer, Dietrich and Evans, Peter, 1985, 'The State and Economic Transformation: Toward an Analysis of the Conditions Underlying Effective Intervention', in Peter Evans, Dietrich Rueschemeyer and Theda Skocpol (eds.), *Bringing the State Back In* (New York: Cambridge University Press).
Sayeed, Khalid Bin, 1980, *Politics in Pakistan: The Nature and Direction of Change* (New York: Praeger Press).
Sayeed, Khalid Bin, 1968, *Pakistan: The Formative Phase 1857-1948* (London: Oxford University Press, 1968).
Salame, Ghassan (ed.), 1994, *Democracy without Democrats: The Renewal of Politics in the Muslim World* (London: I.B. Tauris).

Seligson, Mitchell A. (ed.), 1984, *The Gap Between Rich and Poor: Contending Perspectives on the Political Economy of Development* (Boulder and London: Westview Press).

Sen, Amartya, 2003, 'Democracy As a Universal Value', in Lubna Saif and Javed Iqbal Syed (eds.), *Pakistani Society and Culture, Vol. II* (Islamabad: Allama Iqbal Open University).

Sen, Amartya, 1987, *On Ethics and Economics* (Oxford: Oxford University Press).

Sen, Amartya, 1982, *Choice, Welfare and Measurement* (Oxford: Oxford University Press).

Siddiqui, N.A., 1970, *Land Revenue Administration under the Mughals* (Bombay: Asia Publishing House).

Singh, S. Gurcharn, *The Punjab Alienation of Land Act XIII of 1900* (Lahore: n.p. 1901).

Singh, Khushwant, 1963, *History of the Sikhs, Vol. 2, 1839-1964* (Princeton: Princeton University Press).

Smith, Anthony, 1978, 'The Case of Dependency Theory', in W. Scott Thomson (ed.), *The Third World: Premises of U.S. Policy* (California: Institute of Contemporary Studies, San Francisco).

Spear, Percival, 1965, *A History of India, Vol. 2* (Harmondsworth, Middlesex: Penguin Books).

Spier, Hans, 1962, 'Preface', in John. L. Johnson (ed.), *The Role of Military in Underdeveloped Countries* (Princeton: Princeton University Press).

Stokes, Erick, 1959, *The English Utilitarians and India* (Oxford: Oxford University Press).

Talbot, Ian, 1996, *Khizr Hayat, The Punjab Unionist Party and the Partition of India* (Richmond, Surrey: Curzon Press).

Talbot, Ian, 1990, *Pakistan: A Modern History* (Lahore: Vanguard Books).

Talbot, Ian, 1988, *Punjab and the Raj: 1847-1947* (New Delhi: Manohar Publications).

Tendler, J., 1975, *Inside Foreign Aid* (Baltimore: Johns Hopkins Press).

Theoharis, Athan G., 1970, *The Yalta Myths: An Issue in U.S. Politics, 1945-1955* (New York: University of Missouri Press).

Thorburn, S.S., 1971, *The Punjab in Peace and War* (New York: AMS Press).

Tinker, Hugh, 1967, *India and Pakistan: A Political Analysis* (London: Pall Mall Press).

Tunzelmann, Alex Von, 2007, *Indian Summer: The Secret History of the End of an Empire* (London: Simon & Schuster).

Valenzuela, Samuel and Valenzuela, Arturo, 1974, *The Modern World-System: Capitalist Agriculture and the Origins of the European World Economy* (New York and London: Academic Press).

Venkartamani, M.S., 1987, *The American Role in Pakistan* (Lahore: Vanguard Books).

Wallerstein, Immanuel, 1991, *Geopolitics and Geoculture: Essays on the Changing World-System* (Cambridge: Cambridge University Press).

Wallerstein, Immanuel, 1979, *The Capitalist World Economy* (Cambridge: Cambridge University Press).

Wallerstein, Immanuel, 1974, *The Modern World System: Capitalist Agriculture and the Origins of the European World Economy* (New York and London: Academic Press).

Waseem, Muhammad, 1989, *Politics and the State in Pakistan* (Lahore: Progressive).

Wolf, Eric, 1982, *Europe and the People Without History* (Berkeley: University of California Press).

Wood, Alan Ted, 2004, *Asian Democracy in World History* (New York & London: Routledge).

Zaheer, Hasan, 1998, *The Times and Trial of the Rawalpindi Conspiracy 1951* (Karachi: Oxford University Press).

Ziring, Lawrence, 2003, *Pakistan in the Twentieth Century: A Political History* (Karachi: Oxford University Press).

Unpublished Dissertations

Hashmi, Bilal, 'US Role in Pakistan's Army', PhD dissertation (Washington State University, 1972).
Hussain, I., *The Failure of Parliamentary Politics in Pakistan*, PhD dissertation (Oxford University, 1967).

Web Sources

'Baghdad Pact', Lexicorient. Retrieved 10 May 2004. httm://i-cias.com/e.o/Baghdad_pact.html.
Butt, Gerald, 'Lesson from history: 1955 Baghdad Pact', BBC News World Edition. Updated 26 February 2003. Retrieved 10 May 2004. httm:/news.bbc.co.uk/2/hi/middle_east/2801487.stm.
'Cold War (1953-1962)'. Wikipedia, The Free Encyclopedia. Retrieved 26 June 2004. http://en.wikipedia.org/wiki/cold_war.
'Cold War'. Cold War Policies. Retrieved 9 December 2002. http://history.sandiego.edu/gen/20th/coldwar0.html.
'Cold War'. Cold War Policies. Retrieved 17 September 2003. http://history.sandiego.edu/gen/20th/coldwar0.html.
'Comparative Survey of Freedom', Freedom in the World: Political Rights and Civil Rights, various years. Freedom House. Retrieved 10 May 2004. http://www.freedomhouse.org/research/index.htm.
Frank, Andre Gunder, 'The Development of Underdevelopment: An Autobiographical Essay'. Retrieved 26 June 2004. http://rrojasdatabank.info/agfrank.
Gavin, Francis J. 'Politics, Power, and U.S. Policy in Iran, 1950-53', *Journal of Cold War Studies* 1:1. Retrieved 9 March 03. http://muse.jhu.edu/demo/cws/1.1gavin.html.
'Harry Truman's letter to James Byrnes, 5 June 1946'. Cold War Policies. Retrieved 21 December 2002. http://history.sandiego.edu./truman46.html.
'John Foster Dulles'. Wikipedia, The Free Encyclopedia. Retrieved 26 June 2004. http://en.wikipedia.org/wiki/Dulles.
'Kirkpatrick Doctrine'. Wikipedia-The Encyclopedia. Retrieved 21 December 02. http://en.wikipedia.org/wiki/Kirkpatrick_Doctrine.
'Korea'. Cold War Policies. Retrieved 21 December 2002. http://history.sandiego.edu/gen/20th/korea.htm.
'Mohammed Mossadegh'. Wikipedia, The Free Encyclopedia. Retrieved 26 June 2004. http://en.wikipedia.org/wiki/cold_war.
Nabudere, Dani, W. 'The Role of the United States in the Global System after September 11th' Social Science Research Council, Retrieved 25 June 2004 http://conflicts.ssrc.org/.
'NSC 68'. Cold War Policies. Retrieved 19 December 2002. http://history.sandiego.edu/gen/1950s/nsc68.html.
Simons, Thomas W., Jr., 'India and Pakistan: Mutually Assured Destruction, South Asian Style', *Hoover Digest*, (2000) 4. Retrieved 10 May 2004. http://www.hooverdigest.org/

'Speech, Mao Zedong at the Fifteenth Meeting of the Supreme State Council, 5 September 1958 (Excerpt)', Cold War International History Project, Virtual Archive. Retrieved 25 June 2004. http://wwics.si.edu/index.cmf?topic_id=1409&fuseaction=library.Collection.

'Third World'. Wikipedia, The Free Encyclopedia. Retrieved 26 June 2004. http://en.wikipedia.org/wiki/third world.

'Truman'. Cold War Policies. Retrieved 21 December 2002. http://history.sandiego.edu./gen/20th/truman46.html.

Index

A

Abbottabad, 63
Abdullah, Sheikh, 52
Administrative Staff College, 202
Adult franchise, 151, 172, 231
Afghan(s), 73; invasion, 13; question, 73
Afghanistan, 11, 18, 55, 61, 64, 73, 105, 169, 170
Africa, 87, 189, 227, 230
African countries, 170
Afridis (tribe), 62
Agra, 10-1
Agrarian Committee (of Muslim League), 122-3
Agrarian reform report (1949), 197
Agrarian society, 1, 6, 28, 123, 198; reforms, 115, 123, 197; economy, 231
Agricultural colonization, 5, 15, 17
Agricultural tribes, 122 *see also* Sajjada nashins; Pirs
Agriculture sector, 1-2, 4, 11, 193, 197-8, 200, 204-5, 215, 230; reforms, 1, 16, 123
Ahmadis, 127; declared as non-Muslims, 127
Aitchison College (1886), 22
Aitchisonian, 22
Akbar (Mughal emperor), 6, 10
Alavi, Hamza, 1, 4, 6, 28, 111, 223
Albright, Madeleine, 144
Alexander, Lord, 162
Ali, Chaudhry Mohammad, 74, 92, 108, 113-4, 122, 170-1, 173; member of the military 'oligarchy' or the 'executive group', 113; induction in the cabinet, 114; as the 'Lord of Bureaucracy', 171
Ali, DIG-CID Anwar, 102
Ali, Imran, 1, 4-6, 31
All Parties Conference (Lahore, 1952), 127
Almond, Gabriel, 87, 188

Amb, 104
Ambala division, 22
American empiricism, 226
American intelligence agencies, 96, 99, 103, 116, 118
American Power System, 43-5, 49, 67, 72-3, 78, 85, 101, 130, 139, 155, 189, 190-2, 222, 224-7, 229, 230
American pragmatism, 181, 226
Americans, 48-9, 51, 55-6, 70, 77, 94-5, 97, 99, 101, 109, 111, 114, 141-3, 145, 147, 155, 160, 164, 166, 168, 173, 189, 191, 205; interests, 110, 139, 142, 225, 227; ambassador, 112, 141, 146, 149, 169; policy maker, 96, 164, 192; economic experts, 198-9; Agenda, 163; development theory, 181; forces, 94; history, 183; military air bases, 49, 148, 152
Amritsar, 22
Anderson, Perry, 45
Anglo-American Imperialism, 97
Anglo-American opposition, 46, 69, 72-3, 76, 101, 159, 160
Anglo-Iranian oil companies, 56, 95
Anti-Ahmadiya riots (1953), 116, 127-8, 143
Anti-communism, 103, 118-9, 126
Anti-development movement, 212
Anti-imperialist feeling, 95, 144-5
Anti-Moscow policies, 96, 114
Anti-United States-Pakistan Military Pact Day, 151, 229
Anti-West feelings, 229, 230
Anti-*zamindari* legislation, 25, 115
Apter, 188
Arab Nationalism, 167
Arab(s), 73, 166; politics, 154; states, 73, 212
Arabian Sea, 55
Arrow, Ken, 188
Asia financial crisis (1998), 186

Asia, 87, 97, 147, 153, 158, 186, 189, 191-2, 230
Asian countries, 170
Asian institution, 188
Assam, 59
Attock, 14, 22, 62
Auchinleck, Field Marshal, 49, 63, 68
Aurangabad, 10
Aurangzeb (Mughal emperor), 13
Australia, 154, 157; government of, 157
Authoritarianism, 44, 88, 105, 111, 154, 156, 165, 181-2, 184-6, 188, 192, 202, 206-7, 212-3, 225, 231, 233
Authority, Personalization of, 105
Autocracy, 105, 201, 224
Awadh, 7, 13
Azad Pakistan Party, 100
Azad Pakistan Students Federation, 100

B

Baghdad Pact, 140, 154, 156, 166-9, 170-1, 225, 228-9
Baghdad, 168
Bahadur, Guru Tegh, 13
Bahawalpur, 104
Balochistan, 3, 18, 56, 59, 93, 104, 209
Bandung conference (1955), 168, 170
Bangkok, 161
Bangladesh, 209
Barani areas (of Punjab), 3, 23
Barter agreement (1952), 142
Basic Principles Committee (BPC), 127, 150
Basic Principles Committee Report, 127-8, 162-3
Bay of Bengal, 55
Beas river, 61
Begar system (labour rent or corvee), 25
Bell, David, 200
Bengal State Prisoners Regulation III of 1818, 228
Bengal, 7, 13, 16, 52, 59, 104-5,121, 145, 151; not part British security state, 105
Bengalis, 59, 107, 124, 145, 150, 163; Muslims, 105
Benoit, Quaker, 188
Berlin, 46
Bhera, Pir Badshah of, 20

Bhittanis (tribe), 62
Bhopal, 60
Bhutto, Zulfikar Ali, 25; rule 1971-77, 194
Binder, Leonard, 87
Biradries, 28-9
Black Sea, 46
Board of Administration (colonial system), 26-7
Board of Talimat-i-Islamia, 126
Bogra, Mohammad Ali, 129, 138, 140-1, 145, 147-9, 150, 152-3, 159, 160-2, 171, 224; a Pakistani Ambassador in Washington, 129, 171; as pro-American, 140, 145
Bombay, 16
British administrators, 12, 15, 18, 28-9, 30, 91-2; considered as 'guardians of the Empire', 91, 224
British Balochistan, 110
British Colonial rule, 1-2, 5, 15, 17-9, 21, 28, 32, 115, 206, 208, 222, 227; power in Punjab, 105
British colonialism, 2, 10, 43, 105, 122, 155, 181, 206-7, 209
British Commonwealth Empire, 46, 51, 68-9, 70, 73, 76, 141, 167; Ministers, 117; secretary of, 168
British Empire, 4, 31, 105, 107, 224
British Foreign Office, 52, 117, 157, 160-1
British government (London), 53-5, 58-9, 67, 73-4, 118, 141, 148, 160, 167
British India Civil Service (ICS), 51, 90-1; training of, 91
British India, 1-4, 27, 31, 59, 89, 104-5, 107, 224
British Information Office, 117
British intelligence agencies, 96, 99, 101, 103, 116, 228; network, 101-2, 118, 121
British MI5, 144, 228
British Punjab, 14, 105; population of, 14
British raj/rule, 4, 11-2, 16-9, 20, 22-3, 25, 28, 30-1, 57, 77, 105, 110, 122, 228
British security state, 43-4, 49, 69, 75-6, 85, 88, 105
British, 1-5, 14, 16-7, 19, 21, 26, 29, 30, 48-9, 50-2, 55-7, 59, 62-3, 67-8, 74, 77, 91, 95-6, 111, 128, 141-3, 155, 160-1, 165-6; debts, 45; army trucks, 62; high commissioner in Pakistan, 66, 70, 74,

100, 102, 117, 162, 173; policies, 69; racism of the, 91; administration, 17-8, 30-1; created the tribal social organization, 18, 28-9, 122; land revenue, 6, 26-8; imperialism, 3, 16
Brunei, 186
Buddhism, 11
Bureaucratic-military alliance, 44, 150, 155, 166, 172, 225 *see also* elite's government
Burma, 157, 160, 169
Buxar (1764), 104
Byrnes, James, 49

C

Cambodia, 158, 186
Canada, 157
Canal colonies, 4, 16, 30-1; which became 'landed gentry's grants', 20-1, 31
Capital Dependence, 195 *see also* Dependency Model
Capitalism, 45, 188, 190-1, 208, 222, 230; 'guided', 192
Capitalist economy, 44, 88, 201, 208, 222, 227
Capitalist world system, 53, 190, 195, 211, 230; elites, 192; exploitation, 195, 230
Capitalistic system (of Pakistan), 1, 201
Caroe, Sir Olaf, 51
Cawthorn, General, 54
Ceasefire agreement of 1965, 99
Census 1921 (of British India), 15
CENTO (Central Treaty Organization), 140, 154-5, 192, 229
Central Asia, 11, 18, 105; nomadic tribes, 11; empires, 11
Central Europe, 227
Central government, 66-7, 77, 123, 128, 149, 151, 154, 174, 197-9, 203, 206, 210, 230-1
Central Intelligence Department (CID), 101-2
Central Office of Information, London, 117-8
Ceylon, 56, 157-8, 160; government of, 157
Chan, Pir, 20
Charkha (the spinning wheel), 215
Chaudary, 12

Chenab river, 61
Chief of staff (COS), 54
Chiefs of Staff Committee, 53-4
China, 48, 52, 61, 96, 117, 152, 159, 185-6, 191, 193, 227; as representative of 'populist authoritarianism', 185
Chinese Revolution, 52, 115-6, 192
Chinese, 48, 158-9, 161, 186, 228; Forces, 96
Chitral, 104
Chittagong, 93
Choudhury, G.W., 71
Churchill, 46
CIA, 101, 144, 228; report, 129; documents, 144
Civil administration, 199, 205, 229
Civil bureaucracy, 2, 26, 32, 43-4, 66, 69, 85, 87, 89, 90, 92-3, 97, 105, 107, 109, 113-4, 118-9, 124, 126, 129, 140, 143, 145, 149, 155, 163, 170, 195, 201-2, 205, 212, 222-4, 228-9, 232; pro-west, 75, 109, 110, 122
Civil Government, 104
Civil Liberties Union, 100
Civil Procedure, Section 144 of the Rules of, 125, 228
Civil Service Academy, 202
Civil war (1971), 207, 212, 225
Clientelism, 19
Close Border Policy (of British administration system), 3
Cold War, 26, 43-5, 48-9, 50, 52, 56, 69, 75, 87-8, 90, 93, 95, 97, 100, 103, 107, 124, 148, 154-5, 167, 174, 191, 202, 222-4, 227, 229, 230
Coleman, 188
Collective Defence Agreement, 157
Colombo conference (1951), 95-7
Colombo Powers, 157-8, 160
Colombo, 171
Colonial administrative policies, 6, 17-9, 24, 26-9, 93, 105, 201; of 1860, 17; of 1870, 17; principle of appointing limited judicial powers to Punjabis, 21
Colonial authoritarian culture, 107, 201, 203, 224
Colonial capitalism, 1, 5-6, 15-6, 23, 28, 43, 45, 85, 115, 122, 230-1
Colonial development, 15
Colonial economy, 2, 115

Colonial farming system, 215
Colonial legacy, 43-4, 49, 69, 85, 88, 104, 106, 122, 202-3, 222-3, 227-8, 231
Colonial rule, 214
Colonialism, 1, 17, 86-7, 93, 222, 230; Western, 189, 226; new Eastern, 189, 226
Comintern's 1949 call, 103
Committee on Comparative Politics (1954), 87
Commonwealth Consultation (paper), 54
Commonwealth countries, 71, 167; communist developments in, 102
Commonwealth Defence, 54-5
Commonwealth Prime Ministers' Conference (London, April 1949), 69, 72
Commonwealth Prime Ministers' Conference (London, October 1948), 54
Commonwealth Relations Office, 53, 55, 71-2, 74, 76, 102, 117, 157-8, 160, 167
Communism, 44-5, 47, 70, 72, 78, 88, 100-1, 115-9, 121, 126, 140, 143, 145, 152, 154-6, 191-2, 199, 204, 212, 222, 228, 231; depiction as a 'malignant parasite', 47
Communist bloc, 48, 52-3, 72, 227
Communist governments, 46
Communist ideology, 116
Communist party (Pakistan), 98-9, 100-1, 123, 149, 152, 229; propaganda of, 101-2, 118
Communist party (USA), 103
Communist Revolution, 116, 223
Communists, 52, 70, 95, 97, 103, 107, 110, 115, 117-9, 125-6, 148, 167, 223, 225, 227-8
Confucianism, 186
Congress, Indian National, 31, 57-9, 60, 73, 207
Constituent Assembly (of India), 89
Constituent Assembly (of Pakistan), 89, 90, 106, 119, 121, 124, 150-2, 161-5, 172, 202-3; dissolution of, 111, 138-9, 224; Second, 172-3
Constitution of India, 214
Constitution of Pakistan, 110, 150, 162; of 1956, 112-3, 173, 224; making process,
125, 172, 231; for Islamic, 125; Section 92 A, 129, 151
Containment Doctrine (US policy), 46-7, 49, 52, 94, 140, 155, 195, 211, 223, 225, 228-9, 230 see also Kennan, George
Cooperative farming, 215
Coup d'etat, 156, 165; of 1958, 174
Court of Wards Administration, 21-2
Crimean, 46
CSP (Civil Service of Pakistan), 90; trained under colonial rule, 90
Curzon line, 46
Czarist, 14

D

Dacca (now Dhaka), 10
Dalhousie, Lord, 26-8
Daultana, 127-8; as Chief minister of Punjab, 128; dismissal of, 129
Daurs (tribe), 62
Dawn, 102, 163
Debt Dependence, 195 see also Dependency Model
Decentralization, 214, 216
Defence establishments, 44-5, 50, 57-8, 63-5, 75-7, 85, 97, 106-7, 116, 119, 144, 150, 154-6, 205-6, 222-3, 225, 228-9, 232-3
Defence expenditure, 65-6, 139, 207, 210, 216, 229, 232-3; in the year 1947-51, 66, 199
Defence Pacts, 171-2, 204, 212
Delhi, 10, 14, 59, 61-2
Democratic Students Federation, 100
Democratic Women's Association, 100
Democratization theory, 182, 184
Dependency Model, 181, 189, 190-1, 194, 196-7, 222, 224-6; six groups of, 194
Dependency paradigm, 45, 181, 190, 226-7
Deputy Commissioner, 27 see also British administrators
Dera Ghazi Khan, 23, 31
Development paradigm, 226
Development, concept of, 216, 226; growth (the economic aspect), 216, 226; equality (the social aspect), 216, 226; liberty (the political aspect), 216, 226
Dhaka American consulate, 125

Dhaka University, 126
Dhaka, 115, 122, 124, 126, 169, 202
Diarchy, 91
Diffusionism thesis, 86
Dir, 104
Divisional Artillery, 68
Dodie (Mrs Humayun Mirza), 112
Domel, 62
Downing Street, 49
Draft plan of 1945, 197
Drought (India, 1960s), 215
Dulles, Allen W., 144
Dulles, John Foster, 112, 140, 145-8, 154-7, 160-1, 166-7, 171, 173, 230; conceived the concept of Northern Tier of States, 140, 146

E

East Asia, 181-3, 185-9, 191-3, 225, 226; societies, 189, 227; 'Tigers' of, 193; 'Dragons' of, 193
East Bengal State Acquisition and Tenancy Act of 1950, 198
East Bengal, 57, 104, 107, 110, 112, 118, 125, 160, 202, 223; population of, 106
East India Company, 20, 104
East Pakistan Muslim League, 124, 206; Mirza abolish the, 113
East Pakistan, 113, 123-6, 139, 145, 149, 150-2, 155, 161-2, 165, 169, 171-3, 198, 203, 205-6, 209, 224-5, 229, 232; industrialization of, 205
East Pakistan, Governor' rule in (1954-56), 151, 229, 230
East Pakistani, 124
Eastern (Indian) Punjab, 25, 61, 123
Eastern Europe, 45, 227
Eastern Province, 212 *see also* East Pakistan; Bangladesh
Economic Appraisal Committee, 66, 229
Economic Commission (for Asia and Far East), 110
Economic Commission (for Middle East), 109
Egypt, 54, 94-7, 141, 167-8, 230; refusal to renegotiate treaty of 1936, 95
Egyptian-Iranian-Pakistan bloc, 94
Eisenhower, Dwight, 46, 140, 147-8
Elections of 1946, 25, 32

Elections of 1954, 113, 149, 150-1
Elite's government, 44-5, 88, 115, 170, 204, 222
Emergency Food Aid Act of 1951, 142
Emmerson, John K., 129
Empire and Islam: Punjab and the Making of Pakistan, 4
England, 71, 174
En-Lai, Chou, 158
Escobar, 86; 'underdeveloped world', 86
Europe, 4, 46, 86, 182, 189, 190, 227
European colonialism, 4, 230
European Recovery Program, 47
Europeans, 4
Evening Star, 170
Evolutionism thesis, 86
Executive Council (of British administration system), 26
Exercise Stalin (war game), 56
Ex-*sepoy*, 24

F

Fagan, Sir Patrick, 27
Faiz, Faiz Ahmed, 100-3
Far East, 46, 173
Farooq, Ghulam, 203
Fatehpur Sikri, 10
Fathepur, 7
Faujdars (provincial officials), 8
Federalism, 173
Feudal economy, 6
Feudal(s), 19, 100, 105, 115, 195, 212, 228, 232; exploitation, 28
Feudalism, 1, 4, 16-7, 228
Feudal-military-bureaucratic oligarchy, 90, 223
Fifth Amendment, 162
First Five-year plan (1955-60), 196, 200
First Sikh Battalion, 62
Fission bomb, 47
Five Point Program on South-East Asia and Europe (document), 156
Food Dependence, 195 *see also* Dependency Model
Food shortage (summer 1952), 67, 198, 200, 204
Ford Foundation, 196-7, 200
Foreign assistance/aid, 196-7, 212

INDEX

Forward Policy ((of British administration system)), 3
France, 154
Franchise Committee Report, 24
Franchise, 23; distribution of seats, 23-4; urban seat, 23; rural seat, 23; restricted franchise in Punjab, 28
Frank, 2, 188-9, 226
Free Officers' coup, 141
Free World, 44-5, 47-8, 53, 72, 74, 93, 163-4, 192, 211-2, 222

G

Ganatantri Dal party, 149
Gandharan civilization, 11
Gandhi, 214
Gandhian constitution, 214-5
Gandhian Socialism, 214-5
Gardezi, 6, 12
Gazette of Pakistan, 112
Geneva Peace Conference (1954), 156-7
Geneva, 156-9
Germany, 45-6
Ghala batai (crop sharing), 6
Ghaznavid Muslim Empire, 11
GHQ, 96, 103, 202
Gilmartin, David, 4
GNP per capita, 181, 226
Government of East Pakistan, 126; Assembly, 151
Government of India (British raj), 24, 89
Government of India Act of 1919, 91
Government of India Act of 1935, 25, 89, 124
Government of India Act, 162
Government of India, 58, 73, 103, 157; reaction to Mutual Defence Agreement, 142-3, 160
Government of Pakistan (GOP), 54, 69, 72, 74, 77, 92-4, 98, 102-3, 109, 117, 128-9, 144, 146, 148-9, 152, 157, 170, 198, 200-1, 223 *see also* pro-west policies
Government, Colonial system of, 92
Gracey, General Douglas, 56, 58, 63, 67-8, 97, 99, 107, 114
Great Britain, 49, 50, 64, 74-5, 95, 121, 148, 154, 157, 166-8, 170
Gross domestic product (GDP), 205, 210
Gujrat, 22
Gurdaspur, 61-2
Gurmani, Mushtaq A., 108

H

Habib, 5-9, 10
Habibullah, Brigadier, 96
Haq, Mahbub ul, 1
Harijan, 214
Harrapan civilization, 11
Harriam, 109
Harvard Advisory Group (HAG), 200-1, 203, 205-6, 212
Harvard Business School, 113
Haryana, 14
Henderson, 77
Hickey, D.W., 98
High Court, 26
Hildreth, H.A., 112
Himachal Pradesh, 14
Himalayas, 77
Hindu Jats, 22
Hindu Muslim unity, 121
Hinduism, 11
Hindus, 14-5, 23, 25, 59, 60, 120, 122, 124, 163, 198; domination, 52
Hindustan, 49, 50, 59, 120
Honorary magistrates, 20-1
House of Commons, 24
Human development, 206-7, 209, 211, 216, 226, 233
Human security, 206, 211, 216, 233
Huntington, Samuel P., 87, 184, 186, 188
Huq, Fazlul, 151
Hussain, Akhtar, 143
Hussain, Brigadier, 98
Hyder, Sajjad, 70
Hyderabad, 13, 59, 60

I

ICS, 90
Iftikharuddin, Mian, 197
Ikramullah, 117
Imperial Council (1917), 19, 26
Imperial defence policy, 51
Imperial experiment (between 1848-1856), 26, 28
Imperialism, 45, 145, 155, 168, 184, 189, 227

INDEX

Imperialist powers, 172
Impossibility of Theorem (Arrow's), 188
Inams, 21, 30
India, 1-2, 5, 10-2, 14, 16, 18-9, 23, 43, 50-8, 60-5, 67, 70-2, 75-7, 87, 89, 92, 94-5, 97, 99, 103-5, 119, 121, 141-2, 147-9, 153, 157, 161, 168-9, 171, 202, 206-9, 210, 212-6, 226-9, 230, 233; base, 49; 'two India', 208; border conflicts, 211; commitment to parliamentary democracy, 214; Land reforms of, 215; as a Nuclear state, 206, 216, 233; hegemony, 228, 232;
Indian army (British), 2, 4, 11, 15-9, 20, 22, 24, 30, 49, 67-8, 105; recruitments from Punjab, 16-8, 22, 25, 30; military vote, 24; land grant for ex-servicemen, 30; division of the, 49, 51
Indian army (post-partition), 58, 60-1, 63, 68, 95; army aggressions, 96
Indian Councils Act of 1861, 27, 104
Indian Councils Act of 1892, 27
Indian Councils Act of 1909, 27
Indian economic planning (1950-1964), 214 *see also* Nehruvian Planning
Indian Empire, 49
Indian Hill States, 61
Indian Independence Act, 89, 124
Indian Muslims, 93, 120-1, 202
Indian Ocean, 4, 55
Indian Press Emergency Powers Act of 1931, 228
Indian Press, 73, 77
Indian Village Community, 8, 29
Indian(s), 63, 72, 77, 91; economic planners, 214; defence, 49; democracy, 213; demography, 61; revenue, 2-3; society, 2, 8-9; political parties, 91; ministers, 91-2
Individualization, 6
Indo-China conflict (1954), 156
Indochina, 191
Indo-Islamic, 10; empires, 11
Indonesia, 157, 160, 186, 212, 230
Indo-Pakistan relations, 153
Industrial capitalism, 204
Industrial sector, 198, 200, 214; development, 205
Industrialization, 205, 212, 215-6
Institutionalization, 105, 185, 214, 231

Inter Services Intelligence Directorate, 56, 98-9
Interim Report, The (draft), 124-5
International Bank for Reconstruction and Development, 86, 109
International Monetary Fund (IMF), 87, 109, 183, 192, 196, 230
Iran, 46, 48, 56, 94-7, 140-1, 143, 147, 154, 166-8, 212, 227
Iranian Communists Party, 144
Iranian Oil Fields, 56; nationalizing of, 95
Iraq, 49, 97, 140, 154, 167-8; government of, 167
Islam, 11, 118, 122, 124, 127, 231
Islamic bloc, 73, 109, 110
Islamic economic conference, 119
Islamic Ideology, 116, 118-9, 121, 227, 231-2
Islamic religious leaders, 122, 127
Islamic University, 119
Ispahani, M.A.H., 203; member of Jute board, 203
Israel, 73

J

Jagirdari Magistrates, 21
Jagirs (estate), 6-7, 13, 17, 21, 25, 123
Jahangir (Mughal emperor), 9, 11
Jahanian Shah, 20
Jahanian Shah, Pir Sultan Ali Shah of, 20; received a First Class *Khillat* in 1917, 20; received a Sword of Honour in 1919, 20
Jalal, 4, 67, 94, 100, 114, 120, 123
Jamaat-i-Islami, 125
Jammu and Kashmir, 59, 60-2
Japan, 45, 56, 185-6, 191-3; as representative of 'bureaucratic authoritarianism', 185; rebuilding of, 192
Japanese, 191-2; capitalism, 191; FDI, 192
Jat Sikhs, 22, 25
Jenkins, 101; as DIG of Central Intelligence Department, 101
Jenkins, Evan, 58
Jennings, Sir Ivor, 162
Jhang, 20
Jhelum, 20, 22, 25, 61
Jinnah, 58-9, 60, 62-3, 88-9, 91, 93, 108, 119, 120-1, 124, 201; his death, 90, 223;

his address to the civil bureaucracy, 93; his inaugural speech at the opening of State Bank, 201; rejected the western economic model, 202
Jinnah, Miss Fatima, 164
Joint Planning Staff, 53; draft report of 12 January 1949, 53; draft report of 27 April 1949, 54
Joint Select Committee, 24
Jordan, 166-7
Jordan, King Hussain of, 166-7
Journalist, Punjab Union of, 100
Jumna-Ganges Doab, 10
Junagadh, 59, 60
Jute, 149, 203, 205-6

K

Kalat, 104
Kalra estate, 21
Karachi Rotary Club, 139
Karachi, 55-6, 74, 98, 117-9, 124-5, 142, 145-8, 151-2, 170, 173, 175, 201-4, 224
Kashmir Affairs, minister of, 70, 108
Kashmir dispute/ war, 57-8, 63, 67, 69, 76, 94, 99, 110, 152, 154, 169, 228
Kashmir, 51-2, 57-8, 60-2, 72-3, 95-8, 149, 152, 169; policy, 97
Kennan, George, 46-7; became the father of containment, 46-7
Khairpur, 104
Khalisa, 7
Khan Bahadur (title), 21
Khan, Ayub, 25, 67-8, 97-9, 103-4, 112-4, 129, 139, 140-4, 146-8, 152, 155, 164-8, 171-5, 212, 224; as first Commander-in-chief, 67, 114, 141; coup of, 99; as America's most trusted 'man', 99; willing to form a military government, 103; groomed to protect the American and British strategic interests, 142; wrote a memorandum on 4 October 1954, 172; as Chief marital law administrator, 174-5; became Prime minister on 24 October 1954, 174
Khan, Liaquat Ali, 54, 68-9, 72-4, 76-7, 89, 90, 92, 94-5, 101, 107-8, 110, 114, 119, 121-2, 124, 141, 223, 229; government, 67, 162; as pro-American, 69; acceptance of Russian invitation to visit Moscow, 70-4, 76, 92, 95; his visit to United States, 74-5, 77; his pro-west cabinet, 75; his idea of 'territorial guarantee', 75, 77, 95; his assassination, 94, 107, 109, 114, 124, 141, 224; decision not to send Pakistani troops, 94
Khan, Major General Akbar, 96, 98-9
Khan, Sardar Mohammad Nawaz, 20
Khan, Sikandar Hayat, 20, 25
Khan, Sir Umar Hayat, 24
Khan, Zafrullah, 127, 128, 147; declared as an Ahmadiya, 127
Kharan, 104
Khattaks (tribe), 62
Khilafat movement, 108
Khillat, 20 *see also* Jahanian Shah, Pir Sultan Ali Shah of
Khojak Pass, 56
Khushalgarh, 62
Kisan Committee, 100
Kisan party, 122
KMT, 192
Korea, 94-6, 191, 212
Korean War, 96, 192
Kotwal, 8
Kremlin, 44, 47-8, 50, 71, 73, 75-6, 93
Krishak Sramik party, 149
Kuriles, 46

L

La Palombara, Joseph, 87
Lahore, 10-1, 13, 22, 63, 101, 102, 109, 117-8, 127-8, 142, 202; as capital of Mughal empire, 11
Lambardar, 12, 23-4, 27, 29
Land Administrative Manual ((of British administration system)), 12
Land distribution, 2, 30-1, 122-3, 197, 215
Land grants, 20-1, 30; Yeoman grants, 31; Capitalist grants, 31; Horse-breeding grants, 31; stud farm grants, 31
Land reforms, 193, 197, 200, 204, 215, 231-2
Land Settlement and Land Alienation Act of 1900, 3, 19, 20, 30; Landowners regards it as their Magna Carta, 30

INDEX

Land settlement policy, 4, 16, 19, 28-9, 30
Land tenure, 1-2, 200, 215
Landowners/landlords, 2-3, 5, 17-9, 20, 22-4, 28, 30, 43, 105, 107, 118-9, 197-8, 201, 215, 231; as rural elites, 24, 31, 126, 193, 197-8, 232; creation of tribal rural elites, 29, 122; aristocracy, 232
Landownership, 123
Laos, 158, 186
Las Bela, 104
Latin America, 181, 183, 189, 192, 225-7
Lebanon, 141, 168
Linz, 188
Lockhart, General, 68
London Press, 69
London, 49, 52, 59, 64, 69, 71-2, 74, 88, 107, 113, 117, 141, 148, 157, 160-1, 170, 173, 224
Lower Bari Doab Colony, 23, 31
Loyal families, 20-3, 29, 31 *see also* Tiwana family; Noons, 30
Ludhiana, 22

M

Madras, 16
Mahal, 8 *see also* wards
Mahaladars, 8
Mahalla, 8-9 *see also* wards
Mahsuds, 62
Major, A.J., 13
Makhad, Pir Ghulam Abbas of, 20
Mal, 6 *see also* Mughal land revenue; *Ghala bata*
Malaysia, 185-6, 212
Mamdot, Nawab, 122, 127
Manila, 154, 168
Mansabdari system, 6
Mansabs, 6-7
Marginalization, 3, 16
Marital Law (1958), 99, 113, 138-9, 156, 174-5
Marital Law, 152, 175, 212
Marshall Plan and Recovery Programs, 86
Marshall Plan, 47, 230
Marshall, George, 46
Martial law (in Punjab), 116, 128
Martial races, 4, 19, 115
Marxism, 230
Marxist camp of development, 230

Marxist regime, 77
Masjumi (Moslem Party), 160
Maududi, Maulana, 125
McCarthy, Joseph, 103
McCarthyism, 103, 140
McGhee, Assistant Secretary (US), 74, 109
Mechanization, 201
Mekran, 104
Menon, V.P., 58-9, 62
Mesopotamia, 20, 49
Messervy, General Frank, 58, 68
Middle East Command, 141
Middle East Defence Group, 119, 141
Middle East Defence Organization (MEDO), 141-3, 167
Middle East Treaty Organization (METO), 154
Middle East, 9, 48-9, 51, 53-6, 68-9, 73, 94-6, 101, 109, 110, 143, 146, 154-5, 160, 166-8, 189, 227
Military bureaucracy, 43-4, 66, 69, 85, 87-8, 92, 114, 119, 129, 140, 143, 195, 204, 222-4, 228
Military rule, 212-3 *see also* Martial Law
Military-civil bureaucracy-feudal alliance, 90, 94, 115, 139, 149, 193, 202, 211, 230-1
Minister of refugee and rehabilitation, 122, 197
Ministry of Defence, London, 52-3, 55, 141
Mirasidars, 3
Mirza, Humayun, 112-3
Mirza, Iskandar, 68, 96-8, 111-3, 122, 128-9, 140, 144, 151-2, 164, 165-6, 171, 173-4, 224; became Governor-General of Pakistan, 112; his pro-free world and pro-US foreign policy, 113; his loyalty towards US, 113; abrogation of the 1956 constitution by, 113; became all powerful first President of Pakistan, 174; shameful end of, 174
Misls (armed band), 13, 17
Missouri, 46
Modern History of Pakistan, 4
Modernization, 4, 17, 86, 181-5, 187-8, 190, 212, 214, 225
Mohammad Ali Formula, 150

256 INDEX

Mohammad, Malik Ghulam (1895-1956), 65, 94, 107-9, 110-2, 122, 125, 129, 141, 145-9, 156, 165-6, 171, 175, 224; as governor-general (1951), 107, 110, 138-9; US consider him pro-western, 109, 110; his dissolution of constituent assembly in 1954, 110, 175
Mongolia, 186
Montague-Chelmsford Reforms (1919), 23-4, 26, 28, 91
Morley-Minto Reforms, 27
Morocco, 96
Moscow, 69, 70, 72-5, 77, 92, 95, 99, 101, 147-8, 160-1, 169, 229, 230
Moslems, 73 see also Muslims
Mossadeq, Mohammad, 95, 144
Mountbatten, 49, 57-9, 60-3; as India Governor General, 60
Mountbatten, Lady Edwina, 57-8, 62
Mughal Empire, 10, 12; land revenue (*mal*), 6-7, 13; administration, 6, 10; collapse of, 12
Mughal India, 6, 8-9, 10-1, 104
Mughal Punjab, 11-2
Mughals, 6-7, 10-1, 13
Muhtasib, 8
Multan, 13, 20
Munir, Chief Justice, 111
Muqaddams (the village headmen), 12
Musharraf, General, 165
Muslim Empire, 11
Muslim League Paper, 102
Muslim League (All-India), 25, 31-2, 58-9, 60; formation of, 105, 120-2
Muslim state, 93, 104, 120-1, 141 see also Pakistan
Muslim World, 51, 94, 96-7, 101, 109, 110, 116, 118
Muslims, 14-5, 17-8, 20, 22-5, 28, 59, 60, 67, 119, 120-1, 126, 202, 231; class of landowners, 31; ICS Officers, 91; majority provinces, 121; politics, 4, 105
Mutual Assistance Agreement, 147
Mutual Defence Agreement, 110-1, 142-3, 147-8, 150, 152-6, 167, 169, 171, 229
Mutual Security Act (1951), 95, 141
Muzaffarabad, 62
Muzdoor-Kisan, 100
Muzzafargarh, 20

Myanmar, 186

N

Nasser, Gemal Abdel, 166-7
National Archives, 223
National Assembly, 162, 168, 173
National Institute of Public Administration, 202
National Planning Commission of India, 213; defined as 'Economic Cabinet', 213
National Security Act of 1947 (US), 47
National Security Council (NSC), 48, 97, 147
Nationalism, 24, 31, 107, 155, 168, 206-8, 212, 214, 224, 229, 230
Nationalist movement, 96
Nationalist –non-aligned camp, 230 see also Marxist camp of development
Nationalization policy, 67-8, 149, 206
Nation-states, 45, 88, 93, 190, 208, 222, 230-1
NATO, 140, 154-5, 166
Nawa-i-Waqt, 118, 127; launched a campaign to prove 'incompetence of the Assembly', 125
Nazim, 13
Nazimuddin, Khawaja, 90, 92, 107 109, 110-1, 125, 127-9, 138, 140-5, 150, 163, 223-4; dismissal of, 129, 139, 144, 156, 204, 224, 231
Necessity, Law of, 111, 165
Nehru family, 207
Nehru, Jawaharlal, 57-8, 69, 70-3, 75-6, 147-9, 152-3, 157, 160, 173, 213-4, 229; his visit to USA, 71, 74; reaction to defence treaty, 159, 160
Nehru's Bluff, 153
Nehruvian Planning, 214
Neo-colonial capitalism, 43, 194, 195, 196-7, 202, 206, 211-2, 225, 230
Neo-colonial state/world, 50, 85, 99, 115, 125, 163, 181, 184, 200-1, 207, 228; forces, 154, 172
Neo-Colonialism, 43, 49, 93, 107, 114-5, 144, 165, 175, 189, 200, 202, 223-6, 230, 232
Neo-imperialism, 189, 226
Neutralism, 148, 173

INDEX

New Delhi, 173
New institutionalism, 184
New York Times, The, 75, 144
New Zealand, 154, 157; government of, 157
Nicolas, Czar, 46
NICs (Newly Industrialized Countries), 181, 186, 193, 225
Nishtar, Abdur Rab, 108
Nixon, Richard, 147-8, 153, 173
Non-aligned movement, 229
Non-Europeans, 4
Non-Muslims, 59, 61, 67, 127
Noon family, 30-1
Noon, Firoze Khan, 113, 129, 198
North America, 71
North Atlantic, 47, 168
North East Asia, 186
North Korea, 186
North Korean, 94
North West Frontier Province (NWFP), 3, 14, 18, 49, 51, 53, 56, 59, 104-5, 107, 209, 229; air bases in, 49
Northern Tier organization, 140, 146-7, 166-7
NSC 68, 47, 140 *see also* National Security Council

O

O'Dwyer, Sir Michael, 19, 22, 30-1
Objectives Resolution, 121-4, 127
Oder River, 46
Oil resources, 44, 48, 51, 54-5, 73, 96, 116, 166, 227; or 'wells of power', 48, 227
Oligarchy, 88, 90, 111, 113-4, 185, 223, 224 *see also* Feudal-military-bureaucratic oligarchy
One Unit, 150, 171-2, 203
Order of British India (military honour), 21
Order of Merit (military honour), 21
Ottoman armies, 20
Outer Mongolia, 46

P

Page, David, 17-8
Pak-China Cultural Association, 100
Pakistan army, 56, 58, 63, 67-9, 94, 96-8, 103-4, 111, 115, 124, 129, 140-3, 145-6, 155, 163, 165, 167, 170, 172, 174, 201-2, 212, 229, 230, 232; as US strategic partner, 167
Pakistan Awami League, 149
Pakistan cabinet, 75, 108, 110-2, 114, 122, 129, 139, 140, 142, 147-9, 156, 164, 171, 173-4, 223
Pakistan Independence (1947), 1, 89, 90, 120
Pakistan Industrial Development Corporation, 203
Pakistan Muslim League, 70, 110, 115, 123, 139, 145, 149, 151, 163-4, 197, 200; officially finished in West Pakistan by Mirza in 1954, 113
Pakistan Observer, 124
Pakistan Press, 69, 76, 117; Urdu, 102, 117-8; English language; 102, 117; Pushto, 117; Gujrati, 117
Pakistan Times, 101-2, 125, 127
Pakistan Trades Union Federation, 100, 102, 118
Pakistan, 1-2, 17, 19, 43, 48-9, 50-9, 62-7, 69, 70-8, 85, 88, 91-5, 97-8, 100-2, 104-5, 110-4, 116-8, 120-2, 124, 126, 130, 138-9, 140-3, 147-9, 152-9, 160-2, 165-9, 170, 172, 174-5, 181, 183, 189, 192-4, 196, 199, 201, 203-9, 210-3, 215-6, 222-9, 230-3; as a 'security state', 43-4, 49, 69, 75-6, 85, 88, 106-7, 155, 202, 222-3, 228, 230; USA military aid to, 53, 147-9, 153, 173-4; defence of, 53, 64; share of assets, 64; first budget (1948) of, 65, 123; annual expenditure, 66; foreign policy, 72, 97, 113, 130, 142, 145, 169; institutional imbalances of, 88; parliamentary democratic system of, 89, 93, 108-9, 114, 138, 163-5, 173-5, 224-5; viceregal system, 89; 'authoritarian rule' in, 90, 139, 156, 160, 166, 172, 193, 223, 225, 228, 233; inherited the colonial ICS system, 91; colonial-feudal political culture of, 101; establishment of intelligence system in, 103; relations with countries, 110; as a 'client' state of the USA, 130, 140, 145-6, 151, 172, 192, 204, 212, 224, 227; as Pro-western, 160, 163; constitutional

dictatorship, 166-7, 174; military agreement with Turkey, 167; ruling circles of, 170, 204; 'two economies', 209; buffer state between Russia and free world, 211; as a Nuclear state, 206, 216, 233; took the shape of 'garrison state', 228; is still dominated by colonial capitalist feudalism, 232
Pakistan, Armed Forces of, 65, 148
Pakistani development model, 192, 198-9
Pakistani military establishment, 68, 99, 199, 213 see also Defence establishment
Pakistanis, 71, 74, 77, 96, 99, 118, 144-6, 149, 163, 170, 172, 200, 224, 229; ambassador, 112; communists, 129, 140; US provides training to, 196-7; politics, 144, 149, 164; languages, 102
Pak-Soviet Cultural Association, 100
Palestine, 76
Pargana, 7
Partition (of colonial India), 43, 49, 50-1, 57, 60-1, 64; communal war, 49
Partition Plan (3 June 1947), 58-9
Patel, Vallabhbhai, 60
Paternalism, 105
Pathankot, 61
Pathans, 62
Pax Americana, 49
Peace Committee, 100
Peasant proprietorship system, 215
Peking, 147, 160-1
Peoples Publishing House, 100
Peoples' movement, 151, 154
Persia, 49
Persian Gulf, 76, 101
Persian, 6, 97
Philippines, 154, 158, 160, 186
Pirs, 19, 20, 22; became 'landed gentry' 20
Planning board, 199, 200; aided by US team of experts, 199
Plassey (1757), 104
Pluralism, 188
Point Four Program (Truman's), 196
Poland, 46
Pool, 188
Population, 104, 106, 124, 203-4, 210, 212, 224, 233
Position of the United States with respect to South Asia, The (US policy), 48-9, 69

see also US government policy NSC 98/1
Praetorianism, 184-5
Pravda, 169
Primogeniture, Law of, 21
Pro-American, 138, 145, 149, 163, 170
Pro-Beijing, 149
Production, Mughal mode of, 5-6; no 'private ownership', 6
Progressive Movement, 100
Progressive Writer's Association, 100
Property ownership/rights, 2-3, 6, 28
Pro-Shariat lobby, 121, 123, 126
Provincial assembly, 172
Provincial autonomy, 85, 149, 206
Provincial government, 66, 77, 128, 154, 174
Provincialism, 232
Pro-west policies, 96, 114, 118-9, 130, 145, 149, 160, 230
Public administration, 199
Public and Representative Offices (Disqualification) Act (PRODA), 162
Public expenditure, 210
Public Safety Acts, 151-2
Punchayat, 8-9, 12
Punchayati raj, 215
Punjab Administration, 27 see also Board of Administration; Colonial administrative policies
Punjab and the Raj 1847-1947, 5
Punjab cabinet, 122, 197
Punjab Council, 24
Punjab government, 19, 20-1, 23-4, 29
Punjab Laws Act of 1872, 21
Punjab Legislative Council (1897), 24, 27; division of seats, 24; formation of, 27; twenty six meeting held between 1897 and 1909, 27; Indian members in the, 28
Punjab Muslim Association, 24-5
Punjab Muslim League, 108, 125, 127-8
Punjab National Unionist Party, 20, 25, 32
Punjab Protection and Restoration of Tenancy Rights Act, 123, 197
Punjab School of Administration, 26
Punjab Zamindar Central Association, 25
Punjab, 1-2, 4-5, 7, 10-1, 13, 15-9, 20, 22, 24-8, 30-2, 43, 57-9, 60, 98, 101, 104-5,

107, 114-6, 119, 120-3, 126-7, 149, 151, 163, 197-8, 202-4, 209, 223, 229, 230, 232; as the most 'loyal province', 2, 20, 105; means 'the land of five rivers', 11; Sikh-ruled, 13-4; three hydraulic zones, 14; creation of tribal social organization, 18, 28-9; was a 'security province', 23; 'flower bed for the Indian army, 17, 25; no constitutional government till 1919, 26; as non-regulation province, 26-7; introduction of commercial agriculture in, 30; 'military machine', 31-2; as the 'corner stone of Pakistan', 120; hegemony, 122, 124, 232

Punjabi army/force, 232 see also Pakistan Army

Punjabi chieftains/ tribal leaders, 17, 21-2, 28-9, 30, 122 see also Pirs; Sajjada nashins

Punjabi electorate, 23, 25; rural electorate, 24; military vote, 24

Punjabi(s), 59, 107, 111, 118, 202, 232; political structure, 31, 122; rural structure, 18-9, 22, 28-9; society, 3, 16; soldiers, 19, 22, 24, 28

Pye, 188

Q

Qasbas (town), 10
Qazi, 8
Quran, 127

R

Racial deterioration (thesis), 4
Radcliffe Award, 61
Radcliffe, Sir Cyril, 61-2
Raiyati villages (peasant-held), 7, 11-2
Rajasthan, 10
Ravi river, 61
Rawalpindi Case Trial Committee, 96
Rawalpindi Conspiracy, 94, 96, 98-9, 100-1, 103, 114, 116, 141, 192, 229; as a 'communist plot', 98-9
Rawalpindi division, 107
Rawalpindi, 22, 25, 98, 141, 202, 204
Recruitment policy (colonial), 3-4, 19, 91, 107, 115
Red Scare, 151, 154

Red Shirts, 56
Re-examination of United states Programs for National Security (document), 143
Religious controversy, 122-4
Republican Party, 113
Reserve Bank, 64
Revolt of 1857, 5, 11, 17, 20-1, 104
Rhine river, 46
River Indus, 14, 61-2
Roberts, Lords, 4, 19; chief architect of theory of martial races, 4, 19
Roosevelt, 45-6; administration, 45
Rostosvsky, Serge, 96
Rostow, 87, 182, 188, 230; stages of growth model of, 230
Rowlands, Archibald, 198, 203; trade and industrial policies of, 203
Rural manufacturing sector, 9, 10
Russia, 46, 51-2, 55, 61, 64, 70-3, 76, 96, 142, 211
Russian Empire, 14, 18
Russian(s), 4, 45, 51-2, 73, 76; invitation to Liaquat, 70-1, 95; charge d' Affaires, 71; foreign policy, 73; expansion, 105; ambassador, 118; annexation, 73

S

Sahiwal, 20
Saillart, Louis, 96
Sajjada nashins, 122
Sanads (deeds), 21
Sansikritic (traditions), 10
Sardar Bahadur (title), 21
Sarkar (government), 8, 23
Sayeed, Khalid Bin, 29, 30
Searchlight, 73
SEATO (South East Asia Treaty Organization), 140, 154-6, 159, 160-1, 166-7, 169, 170-1, 192, 225, 228-9
Second Five-year plan (1960-65), 196
Security Council, 169
Security Dependence, 195 see also Dependency Model
Self-rule/government, 91-2
Semi-feudal landowners, 19, 228
Sen, 188-9
Shah, Syed Ghulam Mohammad, 20; given a seat on the Bench of Honorary Magistrate, 20

Shahjahan (Mughal emperor), 9, 11
Shahjahanbad, 10
Shahpur, 20-2, 30-1
Sharia (Islamic law), 8, 122
Sheikh Abdullah's government, 52
Short Apprehension of Present and Future Problems of Pakistan, A (memorandum), 172
Siam, 158, 160 *see also* Thailand
Sibi, 93
Sikh army, 14
Sikhism, 11
Sikhs, 11, 13-5, 17, 20, 23, 25, 122; rule, 12-4, 17; revolt against the Mughals, 13
Sindh Hari Committee, 100
Sindh High Court, 111, 165
Sindh, 3, 18, 59, 104-5
Sinews of Peace (speech), 46
Singapore, 185-6
Singh, Guru Gobind, 13
Singh, K.S., 87
Singh, Maharaja Ranjit, 13-4
Sinkiang, 52
Sirhind, 13
Six-year development programme (1951), 198-9, 200, 212
Smith, Lt.-Gen. Arthur F., 50
Social reformism, 155
Social revolution, 214-5
Socialism, 168, 208, 214
South Africa, 157
South Asia, 55, 95, 97, 103, 146, 159, 206, 209, 215, 227
South Asian, 48, 75, 155; states, 209, 211
South East Asia Collective Defence Treaty (Manila Pact), 154, 159, 160-1
South East Asia, 9, 52, 154, 156-9, 160, 185-6, 192
South East Asian defence (conference), 157-9
South Korea, 185-6, 192-4
South Sakhalin Island, 46
South Vietnam, 192
South West Pacific, 158
South Western Asia, 51, 159
Soviet Asia, 140
Soviet bloc, 77
Soviet invasion, 26, 44, 46, 49, 50, 53, 65, 147, 155, 222

Soviet power (1945), 46, 53-4
Soviet Revolution, 45, 88
Soviet Union, 47-8, 56, 72, 74-7, 96, 98-9, 100-1, 144, 146, 148, 152, 155-6, 161, 166, 168-9, 174, 208, 227-9; influence, 52, 191, 228; expansionist design, 57; propaganda, 100; military supplies, 170; aid to Afghanistan, 171; army, 46; atomic capabilities, 47; government, 76, 229; press, 71
Soviet/Russian Embassy, 98, 100, 148
Soviet-Pakistani relations, 71
Spain, 188
Special Durbar (18 February 1918), 223
Sri Prakasha, 57
Srinagar, 60, 62-3
Stalin, 46, 69, 73, 95
State Bank of Pakistan, 201-2
State Department (USA), 55, 69, 74, 95, 111, 118-9, 126, 141, 143, 157, 167; relation with Ghulam Mohammad, 109
Statesman, 62
Stephens, Ian, 62-3
Suba (province), 8, 12
Subcontinent, 10-1, 16, 50, 52, 54, 56, 74, 90, 104, 148
Subedars (provincial officials), 8
Suez canal, 95
Suhrawardy, 113
Sunnah, 127
Sutlej river, 61
Swat, 104
Sword Arm of the British Raj, 2-4, 15-7, 19, 24 *see also* Punjab
Sylhet, 104
Symonds, 77
Syria, 141, 166

T

Ta'luqqdari, 7
Taiwan, 185-6, 192-4
Talbot, Ian, 4-5, 16, 18-9, 20, 30, 105
Talukdars, 3, 13
Tamizuddin, Maulvi, 112
Technology Dependence, 195 *see also* Dependency Model
Tehran, 71, 171
Territorial guarantee, 75-7, 95

INDEX

Territorial security, 211
Thailand, 154, 160, 186
Theocracy, 121
Third World, 44-5, 85-6, 88, 94, 140, 155, 181, 184, 189, 190, 194-5, 208, 226-7, 230
Thorburn, 26-7
Tibet, 61
Tiwana family, 21, 31
Tiwana Maliks, 21, 30
Tiwana, Sir Khizr Hayat, 21, 25
Tottenham, Major General, 56, 96
Trade Dependence, 194 *see also* Dependency Model
Travancore, 60
Treaty of 1936 (Egypt), 95
Tribal movement, 62-3
Truman Doctrine, 47, 52 *see also* European Recovery Program; North Atlantic
Truman, Harry, 46, 48, 71, 74-5, 95, 97, 140, 155, 196; administration, 96, 143
Truman-Acheson containment doctrine, 155
Tumendars, 23, 31
Tunzelmann, Alex von, 58
Turis (tribe), 62
Turkey, 46, 56, 140, 147-8, 154, 160, 166-8, 173; government of, 167
Turkish, 143
Two Boundary Commission, 59, 61
Two-nation theory, 119
Two-year priority programmes 1951, 198-9

U

Ulema board, 127-8
Ulema Council of Action, 127
Underdeveloped world, 86, 191 *see also* Escobar
Underdevelopment, 1-2, 15-6, 23, 31, 44-5, 85, 181, 190, 194, 206-7, 209, 213, 225, 230, 232
Unionists Punjab, 120
United Front, 110, 112, 149, 151-2, 164, 171, 230; dismissal of ministry of, 151
United Kingdom (UK), 54-5, 64, 70, 72, 102, 118, 158, 160, 170, 223

United Kingdom-United States Study Group on South East Asia conference, 157
United Nations (UN), 46-7, 171
United Nations Commission for India and Pakistan, 72
United States Military Assistance Program (MAP Training), 44
United States of America (USA), 45-8, 51, 55, 64, 66, 69, 70-2, 74-8, 93-6, 99, 103, 109, 110, 113-4, 128-9, 140-2, 144-6, 148, 152-5, 157, 167-9, 170-4, 183, 191-3, 196, 205, 211-2, 222-4, 227, 229; ascended to 'neo-imperial hegemony', 189, 227; ; hegemony, 189, 191, 195, 211, 226, 230; military aid, 191-2
United States-Pakistan military aid pact, 1954, 151, 153, 155
Urban *rais*, 3
Urbanization, 232
Urdu literature, 100
Urdu-speaking immigrants, 202
US aid, 196, 199
US Defence Department, South Asia Desk, 147
US elections 1952, 140
US embassy, 56, 96, 98, 104, 108, 118, 125, 128-9, 142, 145, 157, 163-4; charge d' affairs of the, 128-9
US government policy NSC 98/1 (1951), 48, 69, 97
US government, 74, 103, 138, 150, 160, 196; policy toward Palestine issue, 76; policy towards Pakistan, 173; defence policy, 140; policy, 226
US Strategic Interest in Area (report), 56
US Technical assistance programme, 199, 230
US, 44-5, 48, 51 *see also* United States of America
User Conference, 113
USIS (United States Information Services), 118-9, 126
USSR, 44, 49, 56, 70, 148 *see also* Soviet Union; Russia

V

Valenzuela, 191
Vienna, 96

Vietnam war, 192
Vietnam, 158, 186, 191

W

Wards (*Mahalla, Mahal*), 8-9
Washington, 45, 65, 67, 70, 72, 74-5, 88, 92, 94-5, 103, 107-9, 111-2, 126, 129, 140, 144-5, 147, 160, 162, 171, 196, 224
Waziristan, 62
Wazirs (tribe), 62
Wealth distribution, 181-2, 216, 226
Weiner, Myron, 87
West Bengal, 198
West Pakistan Bill, 172
West Pakistan, 56, 61, 66, 95, 102, 105-7, 113, 118, 125, 128, 145, 149, 151-2, 171-3, 197-8, 202-5, 209, 229, 230, 232; hegemony of, 206
West Pakistanis, 202
Western (Pakistani) Punjab, 25, 29, 30-1, 61, 107-8, 123
Western Allies/forces, 50, 55, 77
Western Democracies, 72
Western *doabs*, 30
Western Economic doctrines, 212
Western economic theory, 201
Western economic/technological processes, 87
Western Europe, 9
Western powers, 98, 142, 169
Westminster College, Fulton, 46
Wheat grant, 142, 145
White House, 140
Whitehall, 49

Wisconsin, 103
Withers, Charles D., 142-3
Wolf, 183
Wolpert, 62
World Bank, 87, 183, 193, 196, 208, 230
World Federation of Trade Unions, 96
World Order, 88
World Wars, 3, 201; First, 16, 19, 22, 24, 49; Second, 43, 45, 49, 51, 56, 64, 85-6, 189, 206, 208, 226-7
World-System Theory, 190

Y

Yahya, General, 165
Yalta Conference, 46; the 'Big Three', 46
Yalu, 96
Young Turk party, 99
Yugoslavia, 230

Z

Zafrullah, Chaudhry, 109, 118
Zaheer, Sajjad, 100
Zaildari system, 29
Zaildars, 20, 22, 27-9, 30
Zails (circles), 19, 20, 28-9
Zamindari, 6-7, 11-2; abolition of, 197-8
Zamindars, 3, 6, 13, 19, 23; two types of (Mughal Punjab), 11-3
Zedong, Mao, 168
Zhukov, 46
Zia, General, 165
Zimis, 124
Ziring, Lawrence, 57, 61, 120